JEREMIAH

JEREMIAH

Chronologically arranged,
translated, and interpreted

Elmer A. Leslie

ABINGDON PRESS
New York   •   Nashville

JEREMIAH

Copyright MCMLIV by Pierce & Washabaugh

Library of Congress Catalog Card Number: 54-7030

SET UP, PRINTED, AND BOUND BY THE
PARTHENON PRESS, AT NASHVILLE,
TENNESSEE, UNITED STATES OF AMERICA

PREFACE

THE AIM OF THIS VOLUME IS TO MAKE THE READING OF THE ENTIRE BOOK OF JEREMIAH AN INTELLIGIBLE, INTERESTING, AND INSPIRING EXPERIENCE. Its appeal is to ministers, teachers and students in colleges, theological seminaries, and church schools, and thoughtful laymen, who are aware that Jeremiah is a great prophet and earnestly desire to know his personality, message, and abiding value.

More is known about Jeremiah's life, ministry, and teachings than about any other Old Testament prophet. He lived under the reign of five Judean kings in one of the most strategic and important periods in world history as well as in the history of the Hebrew people. He stands at the peak of Old Testament prophecy both in his teaching and in his person.

Acknowledgment of indebtedness to particular interpreters of the book of Jeremiah is due, and I record it here gratefully. Most of all I am indebted to Wilhelm Rudolph, the editor of the Hebrew text of the book of Jeremiah in Rudolf Kittel's *Biblia Hebraica* and the author of the commentary *Jeremia* in the series *Handbuch zum Alten Testament,* the general editor of which is Otto Eissfeldt. Rudolph's work rests upon that of the great commentators on Jeremiah who preceded him, such as Bernhard Duhm (1901) and C. H. Cornill (1905). It is enriched by his sensitivity to literary types in the Old Testament, an area in which Hermann Gunkel was the pioneer, but in which, so far as Jeremiah is concerned, Sigmund Mowinckel has done the most stimulating work in his brief but original and brilliant study, *The Composition of the Book of Jeremiah* (1914). Next to that of Rudolph, I am indebted to the commentary on Jeremiah by Paul Volz in the series *Kommentar zum Alten Testament,* under the general editorship of Ernst Sellin. His contribution is rich in insights as regards Jeremiah as a man of religion, and no interpreter has seen more clearly than he how the thoughts of Jeremiah later became the basis of sermons and lectures in the exilic and postexilic synagogues. His sense of the profound

7

way in which Jeremiah's thoughts influenced the religious development of exilic and postexilic religion in the Diaspora sets Ch. IX of this volume in a most constructive light and gives positive and abiding worth to large sections of the book of Jeremiah, parts which had before been minimized by scholars who merely dubbed them unauthentic and largely ignored them.

Three things characterize this volume. First, I have made my own translation of the entire book of Jeremiah, utilizing the latest edition of Kittel's *Biblia Hebraica*. I have given careful and judicious attention to the critical notes in which are concentrated the scholarly insights of generations of skilled Hebraists, and have availed myself of their suggestions. Students of the Hebrew text will recognize this in the translation, although my eager desire to make the fruits of such study available to the nontechnical reader has necessitated the reduction of explanatory footnotes to the minimum. Jeremiah was a poet of unique power as well as a prophet, and in the poetic passages the attempt has been made to retain in the translation the rhythmical stresses characteristic of the lines of Hebrew poetry as they came from his soul.

Second, I have attempted the arrangement of the contents of the book on a chronological principle. Every careful student of this book is perplexed by the seeming lack of concern for chronological order on the part of the final editor by whose hand the book ultimately took shape. Yet of the period covered by the prophet's life we are unusually well informed, and the character and reign of each of the five monarchs who ruled over Judah during his prophetic career is known in considerable detail. No prophet in Israel or Judah was so much a part of his times as was Jeremiah. By speech, by pen, or by both, he was active during the reign of each king. The nature of the evidence is such that certainty as to chronology of his prophetic messages cannot be achieved. But in so far as it is possible to sense in each case the approximate period and likely setting from which his individual utterances come, his message teems with timeliness and vital pertinency. At this point I have at times found the insight of Volz particularly judicious and helpful. Immediately following the table of contents is an index which will guide the reader quickly to the page in which each particular section of the book of Jeremiah is translated and discussed.

Third, the various portions of the words or the experiences of Jeremiah and their interpretation have been so interwoven that the living experience of the man unfolds before the reader's eyes. The reader is prepared for the clear understanding of each portion of the book of Jeremiah in turn, then is led through it so that, portion by portion, he knows what he is reading, understands its allusions, and senses the relation it bears to the total experience of the man. Thus he is kept face to face with the personality of Jeremiah, as well as with the persons who clashed with him or those who protected and assisted him.

Into this volume have gone many hundreds of hours of earnest and conscientious toil. I have lived with this man and have often felt very close to his spirit. It is my hope that this book may interpret this prophet, martyr, and saint of ancient Israel truthfully and inspiringly to every reader.

I am grateful to Boston University Press for permission to use materials from my Boston University lecture, *The Intimate Papers of Jeremiah,* delivered December 11, 1952, and published by Boston University Press, 1953.

To my loyal wife I am deeply grateful for her unfailing co-operation, encouragement, and keen interest in all phases of the book's development. It could not have been written without her help.

ELMER A. LESLIE

CONTENTS

11

CONTENTS

INDEX TO JEREMIAH

CHAPTER ONE

The Call and Early Ministry of Jeremiah

626-624—REIGN OF JOSIAH

THE PROPHET JEREMIAH STANDS AT THE CLIMAX OF THE PROPHETIC MOVE-MENT IN ISRAEL. A. B. DAVIDSON STATES CLEARLY AND PROFOUNDLY HIS unique place in that movement when he writes that the book of Jeremiah "does not so much teach religious truths as present a religious personality. Prophecy had already taught its truths, its last effort was to reveal itself in a life." [1]

As were Saul, Israel's first king, and Saul of Tarsus, Christianity's greatest apostle, so Jeremiah likewise was a Benjamite, and was always proud that he belonged to the Rachel tribes of Israel. But the northern kingdom of Israel, with its capital at Samaria, had fallen to the Assyrians in 721. Judah was all that was left, the inheritor of the memories and mission of all Israel, and, indeed, is often called "Israel" by Jeremiah. The prophet was born in Anathoth, today called Anata, described by George Adam Smith as "a little village not four miles north-northeast of Jerusalem, upon the first of the rocky shelves by which the central range of Palestine declines through desert to the valley of the Jordan." [2] It lies across Mount Scopus and is exposed to the east and the desert. From his home the land falls away in broken, barren hills to the north end of the Dead Sea. "Anathoth, although included in the land of Judah, was actually situated in the terri-tory of Benjamin, the last-born of the Rachel tribes (Ephraim, Manasseh, Benjamin), for which the prophet retained tender, undying affection." [3]

[1] James Hastings, *A Dictionary of the Bible*, II, 576.
[2] *Jeremiah*, p. 67.
[3] John Skinner, *Prophecy and Religion*, p. 19.

17

Jeremiah's prophetic ministry lasted for more than forty years. During his lifetime Judah was first under the domination of Assyria, then of Egypt, and finally of the Chaldeans. He was the prophet of Judah's dying agony, and lived through the decline and beyond the fall of the Judean state.

TYPES OF PROPHETIC WRITING IN THE BOOK OF JEREMIAH

The book is rich in types of prophetic writing. First are the prophetic messages as preached by Jeremiah, most of them in poetry but some in prose. As a poet he is unsurpassed among the writers of the Old Testament. With sensitive seeing eyes he looked out upon the world and noted in the physical universe such analogies to the spiritual as made his words pertinent, startling, and gripping. His prose is simple and direct. His literary skill is ever but an instrument of his prophetic calling. Second is the prose record of the sufferings of Jeremiah, which comes from the hand of the prophet's faithful scribe and admiring loyal friend, Baruch son of Neriah.[4] It is not strictly a biography, but it concentrates upon those episodes in the prophet's career where he comes in such clash with the authorities that there issues personal suffering. A third type of prophetic writing is that which Sigmund Mowinckel's keen eye, sensitive to literary types in the Old Testament, was the first clearly to isolate and explain.[5] It is the prose speeches of Jeremiah in their recasting by an editor or editors imbued with the teaching, spirit, and philosophy of history which characterize the book of Deuteronomy. The style of these speeches is monotonous and unvarying. The same theme is treated over and over. Wilhelm Rudolph, who has greatly advanced the correct understanding of this third type of prophetic writing in Jeremiah, summarizes its characteristic attitude as follows: "Judah and Jerusalem . . . or the king . . . have fallen to destruction because they have not obeyed the words of the Lord; occasionally also the form of exhortation is chosen: 'obey the words of the Lord, otherwise it is all up with you,' but at the same moment it is emphasized that the nation has refused to heed this exhortation." [6]

---

[4] The view of H. G. May, "Towards an Objective Approach to the Book of Jeremiah: The Biographer," *Journal of Biblical Literature*, LXI (1942), 140, 145-46, is that Baruch is not Jeremiah's biographer but his amanuensis. The "biographer" lived "at least a century after Jeremiah." His supreme interest is in "the restoration of the Davidic monarchy" and "the return of both Judah and Israel from exile." This view ignores the significance of the reputation of Baruch in Jer. 43:3, and does not deal adequately with the complexity and diversity of the types of prophetic writing in the book.

[5] In *Zur Komposition des Buches Jeremia*, pp. 31 ff.

[6] Rudolph, *Jeremia*, pp. xv-xvi.

In 1946 Mowinckel modified his views somewhat and now maintains that these prose speeches are not to be viewed as a separate literary "source," but represent exactly "a circle of tradition of their own, within which certain of the sayings by Jeremiah have been transmitted and transformed according to the ideas and style which prevailed in the circle, exactly the deuteronomistic ideas and forms of style and interests. . . . They represent an independent parallel transmission of memories about Jeremiah's sayings." [7]

However, in this type of prophetic writing we do not have the free, independent creations of the editor himself, but in each case authentic utterances of Jeremiah, and several times original words of the prophet are embodied literally in them. Autobiographical accounts lie at the foundation of them. In this type of writing "everything serves the purpose of making clear that the destruction of the Judean state and the exile are a well-deserved divine punishment"; it comes from the Exile, and "just as the historical documents of Israel received their final form at the hand of the exilic Deuteronomists, so we here have an example of how they made the prophetic preaching serve the purpose of preserving the religious quality of the congregations of Judean exiles"; thus these sections are rightly viewed as "examples of discourses in the exilic synagogue," and parallels to them are often found in other sources in Jeremiah, "but in the main at the foundation of them there lie words or autobiographical accounts of Jeremiah which are not elsewhere repeated." [8]

A fourth type of prophetic writing in the book is composed of portions written in the first person, autobiographical or confessional in nature, wherein is most intimately disclosed the character and spirit of the prophet himself.

THE PRIESTLY ROOTAGE OF JEREMIAH

Jeremiah of Anathoth belonged to a priestly family. His father Hilkiah, "one of the priests who were at Anathoth," was of a less pretentious priestly family than that of the high priest who bore the same name under King Josiah. According to the priestly code, a body of priestly history and regulations dating from the fifth century, Anathoth was one of the four Levitical cities, "the cities of the descendants of Aaron, the priests," in the old tribal area of Benjamin—Gibeon, Geba, Anathoth, and Almon (Josh. 21:17-19).

[7] *Prophecy and Tradition,* pp. 62-63.
[8] Rudolph, *loc. cit.*

The roots of Anathoth as a priestly community go back to the family of Eli, who was the priest of the temple of the Lord in Shiloh, where the ark of God was (I Sam. 3:3). This was in the days of Samuel, before the establishment of the Israelite monarchy had taken place. The last of Eli's line to serve as priest of the ark (I Kings 2:26) was Abiathar. Upon being deprived of his priestly office by King Solomon because he had thrown in his lot with King David's son Adonijah in his attempt to seize the throne, he was expelled from his position as priest at the royal court. But since he had borne the ark of the Lord before King David and had "shared in his affliction," Solomon did not put him to death but banished him to Abiathar's own ancestral estate in Anathoth (I Kings 2:26-27). Bernhard Duhm,[9] calling attention to the fact that matters which concern property and inheritance were very stable in ancient Israel, thinks it reasonable to suppose that Jeremiah of Anathoth was a descendant of the priest Abiathar, and so of the old priestly family of Eli. He has further suggested the possibility that when David was king of Judah at Hebron, Abiathar had composed the ancient poem called "The Blessing of Jacob" (Gen. 49), and the probability that the brilliant historical source (II Sam. 9-20; I Kings 1-2) had its roots in the intimate traditions of the family of Abiathar. If such is the case, Jeremiah had somewhat of author's blood in his veins.

No prophet of Israel was so deeply rooted in the historical knowledge of his nation's past as Jeremiah. Since one of the chief functions of the priesthood was "to preserve knowledge" (Mal. 2:7), Jeremiah's detailed information of his nation's history and his spiritual insight into its meaning were due in no small part to this priestly inheritance.

THE AUTOBIOGRAPHICAL ACCOUNT OF HIS CALL

Jeremiah's call to be a prophet came in the year 626,[10] and his prophetic ministry was carried on during the reigns of the last five Judean kings and continued for some time beyond the fall of the Judean state in 587. The five kings are Josiah son of Amon (639-609); Jehoahaz (throne name for Shallum), fourth son of Josiah (609 [three months]); Jehoiakim (throne

---

[9] *Jeremia*, pp. 2-3.

[10] J. Philip Hyatt, *Journal of Biblical Literature*, LIX (1940), 512, argues that Jeremiah did not begin his public career until *ca.* 614-612, nearly a decade after King Josiah's reforms of 621. Without sufficient reason he rejects as "redactional" the precise historial data of Jer. 1:2 for the year 626 as that beginning. If accepted, his view would shorten by from twelve to fourteen years the prophet's career. H. H. Rowley, *Studies in Old Testament Prophecy*, p. 158, rejecting his view, judiciously maintains that "the date of Jeremiah may be assumed without argument to be, broadly speaking, the last forty years before the fall of Jerusalem."

name for Eliakim), second son of Josiah (609-598); Jehoiachin, first son of Jehoiakim (598 [three months]) and Zedekiah (throne name for Mattaniah), third son of Josiah (598-587), who was the last monarch of Judah.

The editor of the book of Jeremiah in his opening paragraph sets the prophet chronologically in his times, from the thirteenth year of Josiah, 626, to the final phase of the exile of the Judeans to Babylon in 587. He omits any mention of the three-month reigns of Jehoahaz and Jehoiachin respectively, and takes no account of that phase of Jeremiah's prophetic career which succeeded the fall of the Judean state. The editor's summary follows:

> 1:1 **The words of Jeremiah, son of Hilkiah, from the priesthood which was in Anathoth in the land of Benjamin, 2 to whom the word of the Lord came in the days of Josiah, son of Amon, king of Judah, in the thirteenth year of his reign, 3 and continued to come in the days of Jehoiakim, son of Josiah, king of Judah, until the end of the eleventh year of Zedekiah, son of Josiah, king of Judah, until Jerusalem was carried into exile in the fifth month.**

The first of "the words of Jeremiah," a narrative that in the nature of the case could be only autobiographical, ushers us into that sacred hour when God's will that he should be a prophet was revealed to him. Jeremiah's consciousness of his prophetic mission came to him as a vision experience. It was not a vision of the divine majesty that mediated his call, as was the case with Isaiah. It was rather an experience of great simplicity, directness, and intimacy. Indeed, it represented the ripening of spiritual influences in his home life and upbringing in the Levitical town of Anathoth.

His call as he reports it was both a vision and an audition. There came to him when he was not more than nineteen years of age a vivid awareness of an audition—God was speaking to him:

> 1:4 **Now the word of the Lord came to me, saying,**
> 5 **"Before I formed you in the womb, I knew you,**
> **And before you came forth from the womb, I**
> **set you apart;**
> **I have appointed you a prophet to the**
> **nations."**

The great world powers, the Assyrians, Egyptians, and Chaldeans, were to be included within the range of Jeremiah's counsels. Likewise the smaller nations with which Judah was more intimately linked—the eastern

Mediterranean city-states of Tyre and Sidon, as well as the Trans-Jordan bloc of Edom, Moab, and the nomadic Ammonites—were destined to come within the area of his prophetic counsels. That he was to be "a prophet to the nations" represents no exaggeration but sober fact. For Jeremiah lived and worked in the age of greatest international clash, realignment and transition in the Middle and Near East previous to the era of Alexander the Great.

Timidity and hesitation, such as Isaiah experienced at the moment of his call, are evident in Jeremiah's initial response to the Lord's appointment. He pleads his youth and his inexperience as a speaker. The term *na°ar*, which he uses to describe his youth (1:6), indicates that he was under twenty when this call came to him.[11] To God's appointment Jeremiah responds:

> 1:6 Then I said, "Alas, Lord God, lo,
> I know not how to speak, for I am but a boy."

Then there came to him from God words of summons and command, but also of encouragement and promise:

> 1:7 But the Lord said to me,
> "Say not, 'I am but a boy;'
> For to all to whom I shall send you, you shall go,
> And all that I command you, you shall speak.
> 8 Do not be afraid in their presence;
> For I am with you, to rescue you," said the Lord.

Thus far the experience was that of audition and response, features which are to continue. But now the vision phase of his call becomes part of the experience. He sees a hand reaching out toward him—the hand of the Lord—and as it touches his mouth, he again hears God's voice disclosing more clearly to him, timid youth that he is, the international nature of his prophetic task. His mission is to nations and kingdoms and it is to be both destructive and constructive. The destructive phase seems to receive the more heightened emphasis, as the four verbs which describe it imply. But at the climax of his commission the constructive aspect which his ministry is to have is stressed. The prophet thus continues the account of his vision and audition.

---

[11] So Skinner, *Prophecy and Religion*, p. 24, n. 1, who also stresses the fact that Jeremiah had renounced marriage as a consequence of his vocation, and that early marriages are a rule among Orientals.

1:9 Then the Lord put out his hand
And touched my mouth; and the Lord said to me,
"Lo, I have put my words in your mouth.
10   See, I have appointed you today
Over nations and over kingdoms,
To uproot and to demolish,
To destroy and to tear down,
To build and to plant."

It was while Jeremiah was living in the glow of spiritual exaltation and in heart-searching meditation occasioned by the experience of his call that two supplementary psychological experiences came to him. They represent ordinary sights which, in the circumstances, teemed with extraordinary spiritual significance. First, he sees a blooming sprig of an almond tree, a beautiful and thrilling sight, for an almond tree in blossom is an indication that spring has come, since the almond is the first Palestinian tree to awake from its winter sleep. Indeed, its name is *shāqēdh*, "the awake tree." As the spiritually sensitized youth gazed upon its glorious spring beauty, he experienced another audition, wherein the Lord spoke encouraging words to his timid young prophet, pledging that his prophetic proclamation would be accompanied by divine power. Thus Jeremiah reports the revelation:

1:11 Now the word of the Lord came to me, saying,
"What do you see, Jeremiah?"
And I said, "A sprig of an almond tree [*shāqēdh*] *I see*,"
12 Then the Lord said to me, "You have seen well,
For I am awake [*shōqēdh*] over my word to accomplish it." [12]

A second supplementary psychological experience was associated with another familiar sight. Jeremiah saw a boiling pot with steam issuing from its mouth; it seemed to be blown as by a strong wind from the north. The wind that was blowing upon the fire appeared to be cooking the contents of the pot and sending forth the column of steam through the orifice with unprecedented vigor. As the youth gazed upon it fascinated, another audition from the Lord suggested its unique import. Trouble was brewing in the north. The national powers that were to set the "pot" of Judah into

---

[12] The view of Pearl Stone Wood, "Jeremiah's Figure of the Almond Rod," *Journal of Biblical Literature*, LXI (1942), 99-103, that the almond rod symbolizes the judgment of God, and that "watch" (here rendered "awake") is used in the sense of foreboding evil, as of a leopard watching against their cities, misses the reality of the divine empowerment of the prophet for his prophetic ministry, which is the center of attention here.

terrible commotion, that were to break upon the walls and gates of Jerusalem and the fortified cities of Judah with destructive violence, were
vaguely designated as "kingdoms of the north." They were to be the
Lord's instrument of judgment upon Judah because the Judeans had forsaken him by their sinful conduct and their worship of gods other than
the Lord, with images which they themselves had made.

> 1:13 Now the word of the Lord came to me a second time, saying,
>   "What do you see?" And I said,
>   "I see a pot blown upon [i.e., heated and so boiling]
>   And turned away from the north." [13]
>
> 14 Then the Lord said to me:
>   "Out of the north shall evil be blown
>   Upon all the inhabitants of the land [Judah].
> 15 For see, I am sending to call
>   All the kingdoms of the north,"
>   Says the Lord,
>   "And they shall come and each shall set its throne
>   At the entrance of the gates of Jerusalem,
>   Against all its surrounding walls,
>   And all the fortified cities of Judah.
> 16 And I will pronounce my judgments against them,
>   Because of all their evil by which they have forsaken me;
>   They have sacrificed to other gods,
>   And have worshiped what their own hands have made."

The youthful Jeremiah stands before his Lord, called and commissioned
by the active God who is "awake" over his word even in the onsweep of
ruthless northern powers. Now comes the call to fearless action. The
girding up of the loins is a metaphor used to suggest immediate preparation
"for energetic action or strenuous conflict." [14] But with that summons to
act comes also the assurance of the Lord's strengthening, heartening, and
rescuing presence. The challenging "As for you" to Jeremiah (vs. 17)
is balanced by the assuring "As for me" of the Lord (vs. 18). How often
during the next forty years he would recall this assurance!

[13] Reading with G. R. Driver, úphānúy instead of úphānau; cf. "Linguistic and Textual
Problems: Jeremiah," *Jewish Quarterly Review*, xxviii (1937-38) , 97: "The figure is that of
a cauldron tilted to one side and so threatening to spill its contents that way, in this case
towards the south."

[14] Cf. Gehazi on a strategic errand, II Kings 4:29; Elijah racing from Mount Carmel to
Jezreel, I Kings 18:46; Job in preparation for conflict with God, Job 38:3; cf. A. W.
Streane, *Jeremiah*, p. 7. Note also Jesus' use of the same summons in his counsel to his
disciples, Luke 12:35: "Let your loins be girded and your lamps burning."

1:17 "As for you, gird up your loins,
    And stand up and speak to them
    All that I command you.
    Be not dismayed at them lest I dismay you before them.
18 As for me, I have made you
    Today a fortified city,
    An iron pillar and a bronze wall,
    Against all the land,
    Against the kings of Judah and its princes,
    Its priests and the people of the land.
19 They will fight against you but will not prevail over you,
    For I am with you to rescue you,"
    Says the Lord.

THE INFLUENCE OF THE PROPHET HOSEA

Jeremiah obeyed the summons of the Lord, made ready for action and stood up to speak. His earliest preaching clearly shows that he had imbibed deeply from the prophetic message of Hosea, the prophet who had preached a century earlier in Israel, when the repeated blows of Assyria, under kings Tiglath-pileser III and Shalmaneser V, were bringing the northern kingdom of Israel to an end. In the Lord's first word to Judah through Jeremiah, the prophet goes back to Israel's normative days to the era of Moses, before the Israelite tribes entered from the wilderness into the "sown" land of Canaan. As Hosea had taught (Hos. 2:14, 19), that was the betrothal time of Israel, when through the "howling waste of the wilderness" (Deut. 32:10) she "followed" the Lord, her divine husband and protector. Then Israel was exclusively his. She was alone with her Lord, his holy property. No foreign entanglements had as yet marred that primal devotion of her heart. She followed him in loyalty (ḥeṣedh) and love ('ahabhath). God speaks through his prophet:

    And he said:[15]
2:2a "I remember about you,[16] the loyalty of your youth,
    The love at your betrothal time,
2b How you followed me in the wilderness,
    In a land not sown."

The prophet suddenly changes his figure of speech. In that idyllic time Israel was "something holy" unto the Lord, reserved for him like first fruits are

---

[15] With Septuagint and Vulgate delete entire first verse and second verse to lē'mōr: vs. 1. Now the word of the Lord came to me saying: vs. 2. "Go and proclaim in the ears of Jerusalem," but read with LXX, "And he said," instead of "saying."

[16] Cf. Davidson, Syntax, 101 R1 (b).

dedicated—something to be put to no profane use and to be touched by no unclean hands.

> 2:3a "Something holy was Israel [then] to the Lord,
> The first fruits of his harvest."

How promising had Israel been in the era of Moses! These sacred "first fruits" of the budding nation were but the foretaste and pledge of national welfare for Israel and a notable "harvest" was to follow. Jeremiah did not view Israel's political advance with its early trend toward tribal unity (Joshua) and its desire for nationality (Samuel) as implying a moral decline, although he well knew its limitations. He realized with gratitude and awe that the youthful nation in its early formative days had wondrously prevailed againt opponents far mightier than itself. With a strong sense of God's concern for his people he had his own interpretation as to why Israel was able to survive the onslaughts of the fierce Amalekite Bedouins, the fortified Canaanites, and the aggressive Philistines—introducers of iron into Palestine and destined to impress their very name (Palestine-Philistine) upon the land. It was due on the one hand to the Lord's protection of his people, and on the other to his punishment of their enemies. Such dealing did not express favoritism shown them by the Lord, but was in consequence of the fact that in this period Israel was in the main true to him and so under his protection. Every would-be destroyer of primitive Israel in those days of the nation's brilliant promise would itself be destroyed by the Lord.[17]

> 2:3b "All who would destroy him [i.e., Israel] would be held guilty,
> Punishment would come to them,"
> Says the Lord.

But unfortunately this primal love of Israel for his Lord did not last. Why was it that "the fathers," the ancestors of those to whom the prophet was speaking, instead of "going after" the Lord began to pursue what the prophet dubs mere "nothings," nonentities? This is a theme of central importance in Jeremiah's teaching, and he introduces it impressively by appealing to the entire nation for close attention.

The prophet cries:

> 4 Hear the word of the Lord, house of Jacob,
> And all the clans of the house of Israel.

[17] See the discerning words by Paul Volz, *Jeremia*, p. 17.

What unjust dealing at the Lord's hand did the Israelites experience in Canaan that brought about their separation from him and made them morally worthless? No longer did they invoke him with the familiar cultic words which were wont to bring him near.[18] They ceased to think in grateful awe of the marvel of their exodus from Egypt—in prophetic thought the Lord's basic act of salvation—and forgot that their wondrous preservation in the arid, barren desert was due to his watchful care. Instead of recalling in grateful recognition and responsive gratitude that it was the Lord's hand which brought them into the fruitful land of Canaan (cf. Deut. 8:7-10), they invaded it with no appreciation of God's mighty work on their behalf, but only to defile it by sensual attachment to the immoral Baal cult which they encountered there. Even the spiritual leaders, the priests, supposedly expert in the requirements of the Lord, and the prophets, presumably under the burden of bearing his word, did not really share in God's counsel. Indeed, the contemporary prophets were exponents of the ecstatic frenzy of Baal rather than of the moral word of the Lord. So the result was that the people generally, following such leadership, worshiped the powerless idols.

Accordingly, Jeremiah delivers this characteristic lament and accusation:

> 2:5　Thus says the Lord:
> What deception did your fathers find in me,
> That they went far away from me,
> And pursued after what is worthless,
> And became worthless [themselves]?
> 6 They did not say, "Where is the Lord
> Who brought us up out of the land of Egypt,
> Who led us in the wilderness,
> Through a land of arid desert and pits,
> In a territory dry and barren,
> In a region which no one passed through
> And where no human being dwelt?"
> 7 I it was who brought you to a garden land
> To eat its fruit and its produce.
> However, you went in and defiled my land,
> And made my property something detestable.
> 8 The priests did not say,
> "Where is the Lord?"
> Those skilled in the law knew me not.
> The rulers transgressed against me;

---

[18] Volz, *op. cit.*, p. 18, suggests that "Where is the Lord?" is such a form of invocation.

The prophets prophesied, inspired by Baal,
So they [i.e., the people] walked after that
which brought them no benefit.

Thus far the Lord's indictment as Jeremiah conceives it has to do with
"the fathers," by whom he means those generations that lay between
Moses and the present. But now (vs. 9) he turns to the present generation
of Judeans and maintains that the Lord's accusation of the fathers continues against their lives also, for they too are guilty. They have shown
themselves to be worse than the pagan peoples to the west and east of
them. The prophet had concretely in mind, as representing the West, the
inhabitants of the Phoenician colony of Kition on the island of Cyprus,
then all Cyprus, then Greece and the West generally. Likewise Kedar,
originally meaning the Bedouins of the Syrian-Arabian desert, here stands
for the whole nomadic East.[19]

Have such pagans ever exchanged their own gods for others? In reality—
the prophet presents God as speaking in an aside—what deities these
pagans have are no gods at all, yet nonentities though they are, they
never exchange them.

Jeremiah here tacitly ignores the well-known syncretism in the religions
of pagan nations wherein local deities from one country are absorbed into
the pantheon of another. Still he was basically right, for when such nations
exchanged their national gods for others, or worshiped the latter alongside the former, it was no real exchange, because they were kindred nature
deities, and accordingly, from Jeremiah's viewpoint, unprofitable, powerless
nonentities.[20]

But how inconceivably stupid is the exchange which Israel has made!
The prophet rhetorically pictures all creation, heaven and earth, as
shocked and horrified by it (vs. 12). It is the exchange of a moral God of
glorious majesty for idols—impotent nonentities! On two counts Israel is
guilty. What a paradox! They have abandoned the fountain with its per-
petually fresh flow of water (the worship of the Lord), and in its place have
hewn out leaky cisterns (the worship of idols), wherein the water stored
becomes stagnant and putrid. "The folly of Israel," as B. W. Anderson
has sensitively said, "is that she has rejected the true Fountain upon which
her life depended and in proud self-sufficiency was seeking to contain the
meaning of her life within cisterns of her own making." [21] Thus the Lord

[19] Cf. Rudolph, *Jeremia*, p. 13.
[20] *Ibid.*
[21] *Rediscovering the Bible*, p. 99.

utters through the prophet his accusation (vs. 9-13) spoken to the present
generation of Judeans:

2:9 **Therefore yet more must I indict you,**
Says the Lord,
And take issue with the sons of your fathers.
10 **For cross over to the coastlands of Cyprus and see,**
Or send to Kedar and consider diligently:
And see if ever it has happened like this.
11 **Do nations ever[22] exchange their gods**
For what are not-gods?
But my people have exchanged their glory
For what is of no benefit.
12 **Be appalled, O heavens, because of this,**
Aye, bristle up with horror, O earth,
Says the Lord.
13 **For two evils my people have done.**
They have forsaken me,
The fountain of living water,
And have hewn out for themselves cisterns,
Broken cisterns
Which cannot hold any water.

Once Israel was something holy to the Lord, and indeed, inviolable, but
one never would know it now. Can it be that this once free and notable
people has fallen into slavery, or yet worse, become a houseborn serf, to
whom the status of a freeman would forever be denied? Why is it that
such a great people as Israel has sunk to the level of mere booty for greedy
foreign monarchs? Jeremiah uses a vivid metaphor to describe the imperial
plunderers of Israel and Judah, the kingdoms of Assyria and Egypt. They
are "young lions" roaring over their prey (vs. 15). He has in mind the
blows dealt Israel by Tiglath-pileser III of Assyria in 733,[23] and by Shalmaneser III and Sargon II in 722-721,[24] which brought the northern kingdom of Israel to its end. He also no doubt has in mind the severe devastation of Judah in 701 by the Assyrian Sennacherib.

In vs. 16 the vivid metaphor which portrays Memphis, famed capital
of lower Egypt, and Daphnae (Tel-Tahpanhes), situated east of the Pelusium
arm of the Nile, the strongly fortified Egyptian border bulwark toward
the east against the Arabs and Syrians, as "shearing Judah's scalp," sets

[22] Cf. Driver, *Hebrew Tenses*, p. 9.
[23] Cf. J. B. Pritchard, *Ancient Near Eastern Texts*, pp. 284-85; cf. also II Kings 15:29,
[24] Cf. II Kings 17:6.

that plundering of Judah by Egypt still in the future. It did not take place in the reign of Josiah, but such action did begin in the reign of King Jehoiakim of Judah, who as the vassal of Egypt naturally looked for help from that quarter. The verse was probably inserted at this point by Jeremiah in 604, when he summarized and dictated his teaching to Baruch.

Such servile Judean dependence for national security upon the great powers, whether Assyria as in the eighth century, or Egypt in the late seventh, has resulted in Judah's desertion of the Lord. Jeremiah was convinced, as were Isaiah and Hosea before him, that for the nation to seek political backing from Egypt or Assyria was to court spiritual disaster. Neither "the waters of Shihor" (pond of Horus), eastern canal of the Nile, standing here for the Nile itself, a symbol for Egypt, nor "the waters of the River" (Euphrates), a symbol for Assyria, could slake Judah's thirst for national security. As a consequence, by its own abandonment of its Lord and lack of submission to him, Judah is bringing disaster upon itself. Israel is here used as the more inclusive designation of what is now Judah.

Asks the prophet:

2:14 Is Israel a slave or a houseborn serf? [25]
Why has he become plunder?
15 Young lions roar against him.
They utter their voice,
And they put his land to waste:
His cities are desolated so that there is no inhabitant.
16 Also the sons of Noph [Memphis] and Tahpanhes
Have sheared bald your hairy crown.
17 Has not this brought about for you
Your abandonment of the Lord your God?
18 And now, what ails you that you go on the way to Egypt,
To drink the waters of Shihor?
And what do you want, that you go on the way to Assyria,
To drink the waters of the River [Euphrates]?
19 Your own evil punishes you,
And your desertion censures you.
So know and see that vicious and injurious
Is your abandonment of the Lord your God.
And you have not turned in awe to me,
Says the Lord of hosts.

Jeremiah now describes in some detail how the idolatrous worship on the part of his fellow countrymen was carried out. Beginning a long time

[25] So G. A. Smith, *Jeremiah*, p. 362, renders y*lidh bayith.

ago, even at the entrance of the Israelites into Canaan, they have broken the ties that bound them to their Lord. Instead of serving God, they absorbed and participated in the sensual and obscene rites which were carried on at the high places. Just as these rites, characteristic of the popular national religion, had been viewed by the prophet Hosea as unadulterated paganism, so Jeremiah sees in them the real root of Israel's degeneracy and misfortune.

In the beginning Israel was of good racial stock, and was not indigenous to Canaan. It was comparable to a superior species of vine, but that vine has now become decayed and foul, utterly alien to what it was at first. The nation's degeneracy has proceeded apace. The root sin has become ineradicable. Yet Judah thinks he can rapidly stop his course and turn back to the Lord, realizing not at all how ingrained his sin has become. No washing, however thorough, can remove from the Lord's sight the bloodstains of the nation's guilt. Through the prophet the Lord thus laments over Judah:

> 2:20 For a long time ago you broke your yoke,
>   You snapped your fetters.
> And you said, "I will not serve thee."
>   But upon every high hill,
> And under every green tree,
>   You bow down and commit fornication.
> 21 Yet on my part I planted you as a choice vine,
>   All of it good stock.[26]
> But ah, how you have changed
>   Into a rotten vine, an alien!
> 22 Although you should wash yourself with lye,
>   And use much soap,
> Your iniquity would still be bloodstained in my sight,
>   Says the Lord.

How superficial and spiritually dull was Judah not to realize the enormity of his guilt. The prophet calls direct attention to Judah's immoral practices in the valley of the Ben Hinnom, which surrounds Jerusalem to the west and southwest, and to which the valley gate (Neh. 2:15) led out.[27] There cultic prostitution may have been practiced,[28] and there child sacrifice was certainly performed. Such immoral rites in the name of religion appealed to the natural physical instincts of the people generally,

[26] So Moffatt.

[27] C. H. Cornill, *Jeremia*, p. 24.

[28] Cf. Fritz Wilke, *Kinderopfer und Kultische Preisgabe im Heiligkeitsgesetz*, pp. 150-51.

and had in them nothing of the stern ethical summons with which the
pure worship of Israel's God had confronted the nation.

The Judean adherents of such sensual rites were like a swift young
camel snuffing up the wind in the heat of her sexual desire, with no restraint strong enough to withhold her from its satisfaction. No male need
take the initiative in seeking her. Indeed, to change the figure, Judah in her
sensualism has become like a paramour who has worn out her shoes shamelessly seeking her illicit lover. Her throat has become dry in calling to
him, yet any warning to her is admittedly futile because of the overpower-
ing strength of her desire.

Complains the prophet to Judah:

2:23 How can you say, "I have not defiled myself,
       Nor have I gone after the Baals"?
     Look at your practices in the valley:
       Consider what you have done.
     [You are] a swift young camel galloping this way and that, [29]
  24   Breaking away to the wilderness;
       In the lust of her craving she snuffs up the wind.
     As for her desire—who can restrain it?
     No male seeking her need become exhausted.
     They shall come upon her in her mating time.

  25 Keep your feet from becoming shoeless [i.e., with much walking]
       And your throat from becoming parched [i.e., with much calling].
     But you repeatedly said, "Hopeless [is your warning]. No!
       For I love strange [gods],
         And after them I will go!"

Shame comparable to that of a thief caught in the act is in store for
the Israelite political and religious leaders. Having abandoned the Lord,
they are worshiping just like pagans, the paternal and maternal spirits
supposedly resident in trees and stones. Their gods, all viewed by them
as in some way connected with the Lord, are actually as numerous as there
are Judean towns, and there are as many manifestations of their Baal as
there are Jerusalem streets. Let such nonentities help these Judeans in crisis
hour—if they can! This situation reveals how urgently pressing was the
need in Judah for such a religious reform as would lift into central emphasis the oneness of God.[30]

[29] Lit., "twisting her ways."
[30] Cf. Rudolph, *Jeremia*, p. 17.

2:26 Just as a thief is ashamed when he is caught,
 So will the Israelites be ashamed,
 They, their kings, their officials,
  Their priests, and their prophets.
 27 They who are wont to say to a tree, "Thou art my father,"
 And to a stone, "Thou didst bear me,"
 But to me they turn the back,
  And not the face.
 Yet in their time of distress they say,
  "Arise and deliver us!"
 28 Where now are your gods which you made for yourself?
 Let them rise up [i.e., for action] if they can save you in the time of your distress.
 For as [many as] the number of your cities
  Are your gods, O Judah.
 And in as many places as there are streets of Jerusalem,
  They sacrifice to Baal.[31]

The Judeans have no real basis for complaint against the Lord or for rebellion against him. Through God's punishment meted out to their fathers, their lives should have received needed correction, but even as was done under King Manasseh,[32] they put to the sword the very prophets through whom that correction was brought.

 Cries the Lord:

 2:29 Why do you make complaint against me,
  [Why do] all of you transgress against me?
  30 To no effect have I punished your fathers,
  Correction they would not receive;
  The sword devoured your prophets,
  Like a ravaging lion.

Although the Lord is Israel's "fountain of living waters," his people shun him as though he were a desert. Although it is contrary to nature for a bride to forget her wedding gown and adornments, Israel, the Lord's bride, has done yet worse. Now for many a day she has forgotten her Lord. She makes herself sensually alluring, flirtatiously attractive to lovers—the implicit reference is to the immoralities practiced in the Canaanized Israelite worship—and she has gone so far as to teach others her immoral techniques of corruption. The Lord laments over Israel:

[31] So add these last two lines to vs. 28 with Septuagint and Vulgate.
[32] Cf. II Kings 21:16; Ascension of Isaiah 2:1-3:12; Justin *Contra Tryphon* v. 1b-14; Heb. 11:37-38.

2:31 Have I been a desert to Israel [33]
Or a thirsty land to her?
Why have my people said, "We have rebelled,
We will not come any more to thee?"
32 Can a virgin forget her ornaments,
A bride her sashes?
Yet my people have forgotten me
Days without number.
33 How you do make your actions alluring
So as to seek for love!
As a consequence, you have even wickedly
Taught your ways.

The prophet with the sensitive eye of spiritual imagination saw upon the garments of many Judean leaders drops of innocent blood, the blood of those slain not because they had been caught in any crime such as burglary, but slain "in the valley" by the horrible rites of child sacrifice. And because these responsible leaders viewed such holocaust as an effective means of pacifying the anger of the Lord,[34] they claimed that they were innocent of any sin. Thus in the Lord's name Jeremiah indicts them:

2:34 Moreover, upon your skirts is found
The blood of innocent persons.
Not with burglars [35] did I find it,
But with all these [notorious offenders].
35 Yet [36] you say,[37] "I am innocent,
Surely his anger has turned away from me."
Lo, I am about to enter into controversy with you,
Because you say, "I have not sinned." [38]

The underlying theme in 3:1-5 is the defilement of Israel by disloyalty to her true "husband," the Lord. Jeremiah is in the earliest phase of his ministry, and he is interpreting and applying the characteristic thoughts of Hosea, his great mentor, who interpreted the Lord as the husband of Israel, his unfaithful wife. The prophet starts from matrimonial procedure in Israel as outlined in Deut. 24:1-4, a law which is but the literary

[33] Delete with *Biblia Hebraica*, as a later addition, the first line "O generation, behold the word of the Lord!"

[34] The sincere question of Mic. 6:7b is a case in point.

[35] The abstract noun *mahtereth*, "burglary," used with concrete meaning "burglars"; cf. such a use of *hetheph* for robber in Prov. 23:28; cf. Duhm, *Jeremia*, p. 31.

[36] Duhm's understanding of this difficult passage gives the most likely meaning.

[37] The following *ki*, as Duhm (p. 32) remarks, merely introduces the clause.

[38] For vss. 36-37 see p. 188.

formulation of much earlier practice. A twice-divorced wife cannot remarry her first husband.

On the background of this familiar legal stipulation the prophet deals with the Lord's relation to his corrupt "wife," Israel, who has been disloyal to her husband, the Lord. In the Israelite worship in which the Lord's people have indulged at the high places, where, as Hosea says,

> They sacrifice on the tops of the mountains,
> and make offerings upon the hills (Hos. 4:13a),

they have entered into cultic acts and practices that are utterly foreign to the true worship of the Lord. They pursue rituals wherein, as Hosea vividly describes them (Hos. 4:13b-14), harlotry and cultic prostitution are practiced in the name of religion, both by men and women. Vividly Jeremiah sees how the worship of the Lord, Israel's true God, cannot possibly be combined with such immorality. At those local sanctuaries on the high places the basic relation of Israel to the Lord is corrupted and even destroyed. As Hosea had led Jeremiah to see it,

> For a spirit of harlotry has led them astray,
> and they have left their God to play the harlot (Hos. 4:12b).

The worship of the Baals at the high places has corrupted Israel, the people of the Lord: it is common adultery in the name of religion. To show up this "harlotry" Jeremiah daringly paints the picture of Israelite worshipers as harlots waiting beside the road to entice their paramours, and again as predatory Arab robbers lying in ambush to rush upon caravans. In his own day and in his own way Jeremiah is trying to get his hearers to think, to see the moral implications of what they were doing in the name of religion.

Thus the prophet begins:

3:1 **Now the word of the Lord came to me saying,**[39]
> **In case a man divorces his wife,**
> > **Or she goes away from him**
> **And becomes [the wife] of another man,**
> > **May she indeed return to him?**
> **Would not that woman**
> > **Be utterly polluted?**
> **Now you have played the harlot with many lovers;**

---

[39] Rudolph, *Jeremia*, p. 20, is probably right in the suggestion that the introductory *lēmōr* ["saying"] here is the remnant of the introductory formula given above.

And do you think [40] to return again to me, says the Lord.
2 Lift your eyes to the treeless heights and see—
   Where have you not been ravished?
   Beside the roads you have sat [waiting] for them [i.e., your lovers]
   Like Arabs in the desert.
   And you have polluted the land by your harlotry,
   And by your evils.

The drought referred to in vs. 3 occurred very early in Jeremiah's ministry and is vividly described in chap. 14. Here in a manner very similar to that of the prophet Amos (4:7-8), Jeremiah interprets it as the judgment of the Lord. The climax of the Israelites' impudent presumption is that in spite of such goings on at sanctuaries on the treeless heights, they put on a shamelessly bold front, and as though they were deeply in earnest, call to the Lord in expressions of tender love and loyalty. But their conduct belies their words (vss. 3-5). Continues the prophet:

3:3 So plentiful showers were withheld,
     And there was no spring rain;
     Yet you have a brazen forehead,
     You refused to be ashamed.
   4 Have you not just now called to me, "My Father,
     Loved one of my youth, art thou.
   5 Will he keep his anger forever;
     Will he retain his wrath perpetually?"
     These things you have said, but you have done
     Evils, and have had your way.

In vss. 19-20 "the house of Israel" means Judah. These verses are a continuation of vss. 1-5. It had been the Lord's aim to make of Judah a people of dignity and honor among the nations, and although she was but a daughter, to give her a son's portion, so that his people would acknowledge him as their "Father," and live in loyalty to him. But Israel has played false with her Lord, just like a wife who, for sake of her paramour, has played false with her husband.

3:19 But as for me—I said,
      How gladly I would set you among the sons,
      And give you a desirable land,
      The most glorious inheritance among the nations!

[40] The infinitive absolute used for the imperfect in indignant questions; cf. Gesenius-Kautzsch; *Hebrew Grammar*, sec. 113 *ee*.

And I said, You will call me, my Father,
You will not turn from following me.
20 But like the faithlessness of a wife because of her paramour,
So has the house of Israel been faithless with me, says the Lord.

Suddenly there is a surprising turn in the prophet's thought, and as Rudolph sensitively notes: "Here Jeremiah's psychological penetration is revealed in its full greatness: behind the outer behaviour of men he is able to fathom their true condition and their inner longing." [41] Jeremiah describes what is not yet a present situation in his people but which he is confident is sure to be heard, the lamenting voice of now faithless Judah in sincere repentance and earnest supplication. And that voice will proceed from those same treeless heights where Judah's immoralities have been perpetrated in the name of religion. And it will come from the lips of those who know all too well that their present corruption roots in their disloyalty to their true Lord. The prophet in anticipation hears the voiceless weeping, the silent entreaties of the Judeans. The prophet's inner ear senses in this wordless admission a longing for something better than the worship at the high places—fellowship with the true God.

3:21 Hark! A voice is heard upon the heights,
Weeping, supplications of the sons of Israel.
For they have perverted their conduct,
They have forgotten the Lord their God.

To their remorse the Lord responds with a clear call to repentance and a promise of help and healing. We are conscious again of echoes from Hosea (14:4) in Jeremiah's heart as he cries in the Lord's name,

3:22a Turn back, faithless children!
I will heal your disloyalty.

How different is the Lord's relation to Judah from that of a husband's relation to a disloyal wife as defined in the civil law! That which the law does not permit, God's grace makes possible. For although a husband could not legally take back a disloyal wife who had married another, the Lord can and will take back to himself his unfaithful people, provided they sincerely repent. But Judah is not repentant. Stubbornly they now say, "We will not come any more to thee" (2:31). But God's patient ear waits for the first sound of Judah's penitent voice. That the Lord will hear

[41] *Jeremia*, p. 25.

that voice is a certainty to the prophet. Disillusioned by the emptiness of the Baalized "noisy throng"—adherents of the cults at the high places—and conscious of the futility of their costly sacrificial gifts, the fruits of their toil in fields and gardens, the Judeans will at length prostrate themselves before the Lord in humble confession of their past failure to hear and heed his voice. Then they will say:

> 3:22b Lo, we come to thee,
>   For thou art the Lord, our God.
> 23   Surely the hills make for disappointment,
>   As does the noisy tumult of the mountains.
>   Only upon the Lord our God
>   Rests the salvation of Israel.
> 24   But the Baal has consumed
>   What our fathers have toiled for from our youth.
> 25   We would lay ourselves prostrate in our shame,
>   And let our disgrace cover us,
>   For against the Lord our God have we sinned,
>   We and our fathers from our youth up,
>   And even to this very day,
>   And we have not listened to the voice
>   Of the Lord our God.

The fate of the northern kingdom of Israel, its people now having been in exile for nearly one hundred years (cf. II Kings 17:6), lay heavy upon the heart of Jeremiah, for he never forgot that although his home community was right on the border of Judah, he himself was a northerner, a Benjamite.

He describes the idolatrous and immoral rites which the Israelites (the Northern Kingdom) performed. The Lord had thought that Israel might at length return to him, but she would not, so the Lord had divorced her, his faithless "wife." We again feel the influence of Hosea in such thoughts. By the Lord's "divorce" of Israel the prophet intends reference to the solemnizing event of 721 B.C., when Samaria, capital of the Northern Kingdom, fell at the hands of Shalmaneser V and Sargon II of Assyria. This should have startled and warned Judah, but it did not at all influence her conduct. Indeed, her harlotry became frivolous and despicable as she continued to worship the stone pillars (*maççēbôth*) and wooden poles (*'ashtārôth*). In Judah, to be sure, there had been many reformer kings, chiefly such as Jehoshaphat and Hezekiah, and Josiah's reform was yet to come. Under King Hezekiah the greatest religious reform movement yet had been launched, wherein he "broke down the sacred pillars, and cut down the sacred poles" (II Kings 18:4) of the high places, but this represented only a superficial return to the Lord, as Jeremiah says, not a return into which Judah had put her very heart—merely a false pretense at regeneration. In comparison with that of Judah, Israel's sin is the lesser. So the Lord made it clear to Jeremiah that Israel, the Northern Kingdom, however guilty of having forsaken the true faith, is yet more worthy than treacherous Judah.

Vss. 6-11 are in prose. Jeremiah reports a kind of spiritual meditation, his colloquy with God, through which he is instructed by him. As Volz says, "it affords an illuminating illustration of a transaction in the prophet's soul which eventuates in a prophetic utterance." [42] Jeremiah reports:

3:6 In the days of Josiah the king, the Lord said to me, Have you seen what faithless Israel did? She frequented every high hill and went under every green tree, and played the harlot there. 7 Now I said, "After she has done all these things she will return to me," but she did not return; and although her treacherous sister Judah saw 8 that because of all the adultery [i.e., idolatrous worship] which faithless Israel had committed, I had divorced her and had given her the deed of her divorce, yet treacherous Judah, her sister, was not afraid, but she went and played the harlot also. 9 And it came about that due to the despicableness of her harlotry she polluted the land and committed adultery with the stones and trees. 10 Still even in the face of all this, her treacherous sister Judah did not return to me with all her heart, but in fraud, says the Lord.

11 Then the Lord said to me, Backsliding Israel has shown herself more righteous than treacherous Judah.

Accordingly, it is the relatively finer spiritual attitude of Israel as compared with that of Judah that forms the ground for the Lord's tender invitation to Israel, Jeremiah's beloved Ephraim, to return to her Palestinian home. Implicit in this call home is the underlying conviction that the guilt of Israel has been atoned for by her exile. The call homeward springs from the gracious disposition of God. Still it is strongly emphasized that Israel must acknowledge her sin of the worship of other gods and her failure to heed the voice of her Lord. Moreover, Israel must accept the fact that the punishment she has experienced at God's hand was deserved. So Jeremiah becomes aware of the Lord's directions that come to him in his Anathoth home, to turn toward the north, toward the Assyrian diaspora of Israel, and call upon his fellow Israelites to return. Thus the Lord commissioned him:

[42] *Jeremia*, p. 44.

3:12 Go and proclaim these words toward the north, saying:
Return, faithless Israel, says the Lord,
I am not conscious of my anger against you,
For kind am I, says the Lord;
I will not maintain my anger forever.
13 Only acknowledge your iniquity,
That against the Lord, your God, you have transgressed;
And have strewn your love among foreign [gods],
And have not listened to my voice.

It is certain that Jeremiah believed that there would also be a return of Judeans to Jerusalem and to Judah. Such confidence he based upon his great faith in the lordship of God over them in the very face of their faithlessness toward him. He had no expectancy of a general return of exiled Judeans, but maintained that they would be brought out from the nations among whom they would then be living, by ones and by twos, and would return to Judah, there to come under the domination of faithful and responsible Judean kings, such rule as they had not experienced since the days of Josiah. Jeremiah expected that they would increase in population and in general welfare. The spiritual presence of the Lord enthroned in Jerusalem in their midst will then be such a reality to them that the people will get over the loss of the ark of the Lord—that ancient and tangible symbol of his presence—not missing it or needing it, indeed, not even remembering it. So to the "faithless" Judeans Jeremiah speaks in the Lord's name:

3:14 Return, faithless sons, says the Lord, for I am Lord over you and I will take you, one from a city, and two from a clan, and will bring you to Zion, 15 and I will give you shepherds after my own heart, and they will shepherd you with knowledge and insight. 16 And when you increase and become fruitful in the land, in these days, says the Lord, they will no longer say, "The Ark of the covenant of the Lord," nor will they remember it, or miss [it], nor will it be made again; 17aa at that time they will call Jerusalem the throne of the Lord.[48]

OH, THAT YOU WOULD RETURN!

How welcome to the Lord is this voice of repentance! "Would you return to me?" the Lord had asked (3:1). Indeed, he desires nothing more eagerly than this. But it must be a true return—a turning away in determined steadfastness from the hideous idols they had cherished. And when they take an oath upon their lips in the Lord's name, it must no

[48] For vs. 17a (beginning "And they shall assemble") through vs. 18 see p. 323.

longer be the mere utterance of a magical formula to bring about what they desire, but rather a confession of their sincerity and an invocation of the presence in their lives of God's righteousness and power. If Israel will thus deal in sincerity with the Lord, the nations round about her, whenever they would call down a blessing on anyone will say, "May it go with you as with Israel," and whenever they would praise themselves, they will say, "It goes well with us as with Israel."

In a voice of unutterable longing the Lord cries:

> 4:1 Oh, that you would return, Israel, says the Lord,
>   Would return to me!
>   Oh, that you would put away your hideous idols,
>   And not flutter aimlessly before me;
> 2 And that you would swear, "As the Lord lives," in sincerity,
>   In justice and in righteousness.
>   Then the nations would invoke blessings upon themselves by you,
>   And would congratulate themselves on the ground of you.

Thus far the Lord's summons has been concerned largely with the abandonment of certain cultic customs and rites. But now Jeremiah goes deeper. True repentance, he maintains, plows deeply into the soul. It consists of a radical change of mind, a transformation of spirit, an alteration of conduct. To explain this, Jeremiah—whose thought at this point is under the influence of Hosea (10:12)—utilizes two illustrations. One is from agriculture. A farmer does not sow his seed upon untilled ground, but first breaks it up by plowing and harrowing it for sowing. He clears out the thorns and weeds so that they will not choke the growth, then he sows his seed. So from the soil of Israel's soul the thorns and weeds of false worship and impure practices must be removed.

Accordingly, Jeremiah gives God's challenging answer to Israel's confession (3:22b-25):

> 4:3 For thus says the Lord to the men of Judah and to the inhabitants of Jerusalem:
>   Plow up for yourselves the unplowed ground,
>   And do not sow among thorns.

REMOVE THE FORESKIN OF YOUR HEART

Jeremiah's second illustration is taken from the universally practiced Jewish custom of circumcision, a purification rite which qualified the one upon whom it had been performed to participate in the Lord's congregation. Jeremiah was well aware that many a person bore that external physical mark of Judaism—the removal of the foreskin—who did not at all qualify in character and in spirit as a true member of the Lord's people. Such an outer indication is not enough, for in itself it gives no access to God. What is needed for this is not an outer cutting of the flesh but an inner, spiritual "cutting" such as penetrates to the innermost heart of man. Man must "circumcise himself" inwardly, that is, he must cut away everything from his heart that is base and unclean, and so mark himself as a true spiritual participant in the worship of the Lord.

In the Lord's name Jeremiah calls to his people:

> 4:4 **Circumcise yourselves to me,**
> **And remove the foreskins of your heart,**
> **Men of Judah and inhabitants of Jerusalem;**
> **Lest my wrath go forth like fire,**
> **And it consume with no one putting it out,**
> **Because of your evil-doing.**

It should be noted that in both of the above illustrations Jeremiah speaks as though this inner heart change could be brought about by man himself (vss. 3-4). In one passage Ezekiel, influenced by his older contemporary, Jeremiah, places the initiative for this inner transformation in man. Says Ezekiel: "Get yourselves a new heart and a new spirit" (18:31). But Rudolph rightly calls attention to Ezekiel's own correction, or supplement, of this very word in Ezek. 36:26, which represents God as saying to Israel: "I will give you a new heart, and will put my spirit within you."

Says Rudolph: "Jeremiah also knows that the new creature depends not on the effort of man but upon the grace of God. Jeremiah has expressed as a basic conviction that it is God alone who can heal (vs. 3:22a). Here we have eternal words, the Gospel in the Old Testament." [44] Both the divine and the human initiative are given rightful place.

The sober threat (vs. 4b) that God might consume the nation because of its evil if Judah did not sincerely repent, indicates how great was Jeremiah's earnestness in warning his people against their destruction as a nation. It reveals how clear to his mind was the chasm that yawned between Judah's expressed longings for a better relationship to God and her actual turning in utter sincerity to him.

THE GREAT DROUGHT

It is likely that chs. 14:1–15:3 come from the earliest years of Jeremiah's ministry. His attitude to Judah and his attitude to the Lord is

---

[44] *Jeremia*, p. 27.

at the beginning of its development. He has not yet become critical of the contemporary prophets, but by the very experience described in this chapter he is to receive from the Lord an indication of their true nature.

The presentiment of war which breathes in these verses has close contact with Jeremiah's opening prophetic message regarding trouble brewing in the north, and with his first utterances regarding the coming war.[45] This section does not form a public address but is presented as a dialogue of the prophet and of the Judean nation with God. Originally the sole heading of the section was "Concerning the Great Drought," the first line (in the Septuagint), "Now the word of the Lord came to Jeremiah," being an editorial insertion.

Vss. 2-6 describe a drought as a catastrophe that fell upon the land of Judah. The Judean towns are all stricken, but especially Jerusalem, the capital. The well-to-do nobles send their slaves to their private cisterns for water, but all in vain. The poor peasants, dependent upon the yield of the soil for their sustenance, cover their heads in lamentation and make gestures of frustration and dismay.

The animals share with human beings in suffering, as two illustrations show. The hind, the animal traditionally viewed as the most devoted to her young, abandons her newborn, for she can find no grass. And even the tough wild ass, greatest in endurance of all beasts, pathetically surrenders to an herbageless and waterless land.

14:1 **Concerning the drought:**

2 **On account of the great dearth Judah mourns,**
   And its towns languish;
   They lie squalid upon the ground,
   And the distress cry of Jerusalem ascends.
3 **Her nobles send their menials for water,**
   They come to the cisterns,
   But they do not find water;
   They return with their vessels empty.
4 **And tillers of the soil are dismayed,**
   For there has been no rain.
   The peasants are ashamed and humiliated,
   And cover their heads.
5 **Yes, even the hind in the field gives birth, but forsakes [her young],**
   For there is no grass.
6 **And wild asses stand on the bare heights,**
   They snuff up wind like jackals;

[45] So Volz, *Jeremia,* p. 162; cf. Jer. 4:5 ff.

Their eyes languish,
For there is no grass.

Because of the calamity, as was the habit in Judah, a solemn fast was called.[46] The inhabitants of the land, adults, children, even nursing infants and bridegrooms and their brides, made a pilgrimage to the temple to lament before God in a holy convocation. Vss. 7-9 form the choir lament which was rendered before the Lord. It opens with an acknowledgment of guilt before God on the part of Judah. Many were the times when the Judeans have deserted their Lord (vs. 7). Then comes the appeal to God's mercy. They dare not beseech him to intervene on their behalf because they know that they deserve what they are experiencing. But let God's help to them root in his own name, his own merciful, forgiving nature. For he alone is Israel's Saviour, as has been proved again and again in times of national crisis.

After this appeal comes the characteristic question of a lamentation—Why? This word of distress and of reproach is twice uttered. Why does God act as though he were but a transient traveler through a land that is verily his own? Why is the mighty and resourceful God struck dumb by his people's crucial need, seemingly powerless to help them? The choir lament closes in a calmer mood but with the earnest petition, "Abandon me not!" a petition based on the unalterable conviction that the Lord is yet present in his land and that he still claims Judah as his people (vss. 7-9). Thus the congregation laments:

> 14:7 Although our iniquities testify against us,
>   Act, Lord, for the sake of thy name;
>   For our desertions have become many,
>   Against thee we have sinned.
> 8 O Hope of Israel,
>   Its Saviour in time of trouble,
>   Why art thou like a guest in the land,
>   Or like a traveler who but turns aside to lodge?
> 9 Why art thou like a man dumbfounded,
>   Like a valiant man, but unable to help?
>   Yet thou art in our midst, O Lord,
>   And we are called by thy name,
>   Abandon us not!

Will such a fast avail? There follows a colloquy between the Lord and the prophet, which is reported in prose. It is the Lord's answer to Judah's

[46] This is best shown in Joel 1:13-14; 2:15-17.

cry of lamentation. God is displeased with Judah's vacillation and loss of moral control. Such repentance as the Judean people express is not sincere penitence, but emergency repentance, arising in their hearts only when outer distress is very great. Accordingly, the Lord must punish his people by their displeasure because of their sins.

To Jeremiah, whose heart is like a spontaneous fountain of loving intercession for Judah, God now reveals that the prophet must no longer pray for his people. For to all their fasts and their entreating cries for help God will turn a deaf ear. Their offerings and sacrifices move him not in the least. Indeed, the time of his patience has run out.

Jeremiah then experienced the solemn foreboding that the drought is but an earnest of imminent war, with all its inevitable attendant evils of famine and pestilence. At vs. 10 Jeremiah quotes verbatim Hosea's words regarding Israel (Hos. 8:13), that God's punishment of Judah is near. Thus the Lord speaks in criticism of Judah:

14:10 Thus says the Lord concerning this people: Their feet love to vacillate and they do not hold them in check, so the Lord is not pleased with them. Now he will remember their iniquity and punish their sins. 11 And the Lord said to me, Do not intercede in behalf of this people for their welfare. 12 When they fast, I will not listen at all to their cry of entreaty, and when they offer burnt offerings and meal offerings, I will not be pleased with them, but I am about to consume them by the sword, by famine, and by pestilence.

Jeremiah now deals with a problem with which he was destined to wrestle throughout his ministry. His own certainty of imminent war clashed head on with what the contemporary prophets of Judah were teaching— men to whom the youthful Jeremiah looked up as men of God. They kept assuring the nation that the Lord would withhold war from Judah, his people, along with its attendant calamity of famine, and would bless them with prosperity.

But now the Lord revealed to Jeremiah that the prophets who held out hope that Judah would not experience war and famine were preaching false visions, worthless divinations, and mental delusions. They had not been sent by God. In solemn words the Lord indicts these would-be seers. For not only will sword and famine consume the people of the land, but the very prophets as well, who had assured to the Judeans the protection of God.

14:13 Then I said, "Alas, Lord God, see, the prophets keep saying to them, 'You shall not experience the sword and you shall not have famine, but I will give you peace and stability in this place.' " 14 But the Lord said to me, "The prophets are preaching falsehood in my name; I have not sent or commanded them, nor have I spoken to them. They are preaching to you false visions, and worthless divinations, and mental delusions." 15 Therefore, thus says the Lord concerning the prophets who are preaching in my name, although I have not sent them, and who are saying, "There shall not be sword or famine in this land," "By the sword and famine shall those prophets themselves be consumed. 16 And the people to whom they are preaching will be thrown into the streets of Jerusalem by reason of the famine and the sword, with no one burying them; they, their wives, and their sons and their daughters, and I will pour upon them their misery."

It is little wonder that such disillusionment of the young prophet as regards the message of the contemporary prophets disturbed him deeply. Moreover, from God's clear revelation to him he now knows that destruction is imminent for his beloved people. Behind contemporary Judah there stalks before him in prophetic certainty a specter of his people slain by military siege with its attendant famine. And in anticipation of the horrible straits to which Judeans will be reduced, he sees in prophetic vision even prophets and priests to whom his countrymen were accustomed to turn for counsel, now roaming about the land, out of their minds. The sensitive, sympathetic young prophet is moved to tears over the impending break up of his nation.

Thus the Lord directs him to speak:

14:17 And you shall say to them this word;
    "Let my eyes flow with tears
      Night and day, never ceasing.
    Because by a fracture the daughter of my people is crushed,
      By a very severe blow.
    18 If I go out to the field,
      See, the slain by the sword.
    If I enter the city,
      See, diseases from famine.
    Yes, even prophets and priests
      Roam about the land and are out of their minds."

AN INTENSE APPEAL OF THE CONGREGATION TO THE LIVING GOD

In vss. 19-22 there bursts forth a new lamentation of the nation. It is more respectful in mood as one compares its content with the sharp complaint of vs. 9a, but it has great passion. It appeals to God out of the intensity of Judah's hope for a cure for its malady, for the healing of its hurt (vs. 19). The congregation acknowledges the depravity of earlier

generations, the sins of the fathers, but also confesses its own sin (vs. 20).
It appeals to God as king. Let him who sits on his glorious throne, who
deals with his people in accordance with his "name," his innermost nature,
as a God who took the initiative in making a covenant with his people,
not break that covenant (vs. 21). And finally, the congregation appeals to
the living God, in contrast with the powerless idols worshiped by the nations, the God who alone as creator can send from the heavens the rain
so desperately needed. In utter helplessness and in dumb silence because
of the crisis of long-continued drought, but with intense eagerness and
humility before the mighty Doer, whose power is unique and unshared, the
congregation cries:

14:19 **Hast thou utterly rejected Judah?**
   Dost thy soul loathe Zion?
   Why hast thou struck us, since there is for us no cure?
   While we look eagerly for prosperity but nothing good comes,
      And for a time of healing, but lo, dismay!
20 **We acknowledge, O Lord, our depravity;**
   The iniquity of our fathers, that we have sinned against thee,
21 **Spurn us not, for the sake of thy name;**
   Treat not with contempt thy glorious throne.
   Remember, break not thy covenant with us.
22 **Is there among the idols of the nations those who can cause rain?**
   Or can the heavens send down copious showers?
   Is it not thou alone? We wait in eagerness before thee;
   For thou it is who doest all these things.

Just as he had done in vss. 10-12, the Lord now answers Judah's new
lament (vss. 19-22) in a message to Jeremiah which must often have steadied
him in his persistent and excruciatingly painful proclamation of doom
upon his people. The answer comes to him as a personal revelation from
God. It responds to the lamenting, despairing question of vs. 19, "Hast thou
utterly rejected Judah?" with an irrevocable "Yes." The Lord's intention toward his people is clear and inexorable. As far as Judah is concerned, intercession upon the nation's behalf is useless: prayers for Judah
will have no effect upon him.

The greatest intercessors the Israelite people had known were Moses and
Samuel. Moses had thus prayed for his people after they had greatly sinned:
"Alas, this people have sinned a great sin: they have made for themselves
gods of gold. But now, if thou wilt forgive their sin—and if not, blot me,

I pray thee, out of thy book which thou hast written" (Exod. 32:31-32).[47]
And Samuel, whose nobility of soul was comparable only to that of Moses,
was likewise the acknowledged intercessor for Israel at the critical period
when the Israelite monarchy was coming into being. To the request of the
Israelites, "Pray for your servants to the Lord your God, that we may not
die" (I Sam. 12:19), Samuel answered: "As for me, far be it from me
that I should sin against the Lord by ceasing to pray for you" (I Sam.
12:23).

If God would heed the prayers of any person in Israel, he surely would
be moved by the intercession of these two spiritual giants. But Jeremiah
is now made aware that even if these noble worthies were alive, and using
their great influence in intercession with God on Judah's behalf, God's
sentence of national destruction would not be changed.

Jeremiah is therefore now shut up to the proclamation of national destruction for Judah. When the Judean people come to him as the Lord's
prophet and ask, "Where shall we go?" he is to hold before them in all
solemnity the fate that awaits Judah—invasion by an enemy power, war
and its attendant calamities. The only alternatives open to them are the
ways whereby destruction will come to them—pestilence, sword, famine,
or captivity. Thus Jeremiah gives the Lord's answer to the inevitable question of Judah, "Where shall we go?" as God revealed it to him to give.

15:1 And the Lord said to me: "Even if Moses or Samuel should stand before
me, my soul would not be favorably disposed toward this people. Send them from
my presence and let them go! 2 And when they ask you, 'Where shall we go?'
say to them:

> Thus says the Lord,
> "Those destined for death, to death;
>   And those doomed to the sword, to the sword;
> Those marked for famine, to famine
>   And those decreed for captivity, to captivity."

3 "And I will punish them with four kinds of doom, says the Lord—the sword
that slays, the dogs that drag off [i.e., dead bodies], the birds of the heavens, and
the wild beasts of the earth that devour and ravage."[48]

JEREMIAH'S EARLIEST ANALYSIS OF HIS PROPHETIC CONTEMPORARIES

In the whole section 23:9-32 Jeremiah deals critically with the prophets of
his time and gives us unique opportunity to see profoundly into the authen-

[47] Cf. also Num. 14:13-19; Exod. 17:11-13.
[48] Vs. 4 comes from the Deuteronomic editor (see p. 315).

tic consciousness of a true prophet of God. The redactor of the book has here gathered together, under the heading "Concerning the prophets," utterances which come from various stages of the prophet's ministry, for Jeremiah came in contact with false prophets very early in his career, and he had to deal with them up to the very end. It is likely that this collection of his oracles was made during the reign of King Zedekiah.[49] They directly follow the section in which, as we have just seen, his oracles concerning the kings of Judah are presented (21:11–23:8). As Friedrich Nötscher has noted, the reason for this arrangement is probably "because the prophets also belong to the responsible spiritual leaders of the nation." [50] We deal here only with the earliest portion of this section, vss. 9-12.

In vss. 9-12 of this section, we have one of the earliest utterances of Jeremiah which comes from the very beginnings of his prophetic ministry. The sensitive young prophet, who had been taught to revere the priests and the prophets as the spiritual guides of Judah, for the first time becomes vividly aware of the general moral collapse in Judah in which the prophets themselves are deeply implicated. The keen insight into the general moral corruption which the Lord's presence and revelation had given him left the youthful prophet shaken and dazed, in a mental state comparable to the stupefaction and bewilderment of a drunken man. All about him he saw adultery and disloyalty and men exercising great power but with no sense of moral responsibility.

The thing that most cut him to the quick was that the prophets and priests, those who dealt with holy things, were actually profane and godless men, who even in their activities pursued in the temple revealed their moral corruption. It was clear to Jeremiah that their immoral conduct could bring on but one result, the punishment of God, when the Lord's plans for it were ripe. Thus he describes the prophets as in moral collapse:

> 23:9 Concerning the prophets:
> My heart is broken within me,
>   All my bones have grown soft;
> I am like a drunken man,
>   Like a man overcome with wine,
> Before the presence of the Lord,
>   In the presence of his holy words.

[49] So G. A. Smith, Jeremiah, p. 254.
[50] Die Heilige Schrift des Alten Testaments VII, 2.

10 For the land is full of adulterers; [51]
   And all of them act faithlessly,
   Yes, their course of life is evil,
   And their might is what is not right.
11 For both prophets and priests are profane;
   Even in my house I detect their evil,
12 Therefore their life course will be to them slippery.
   They shall be thrust down into darkness,
      And shall fall in it;
   For I will bring evil upon them,
   The year of their punishment.

---

[51] Thus Duhm, *Jeremia,* p. 183, fills out the line and accepts vs. 10 as recalling Jeremiah's poem in 9:2 ff. In vs. 10 delete with *Biblia Hebraica,* "Because of them the earth mourns; the pastures of the wilderness are dried up."

CHAPTER TWO

Prophetic Pioneering

624-621—REIGN OF JOSIAH

THE FOURTH CHAPTER OF JEREMIAH IS ALIVE WITH FIRSTHAND PROPHETIC EXPERIENCES. THE YOUNG PROPHET BECOMES VIVIDLY AWARE OF THE EXtreme difficulties of his task. He takes us with him into the human laboratory of the streets of Jerusalem as he studies the lives of the people to whom he is to bring the prophetic word. And here we get for the first time some inkling of the calamity "out of the north," which was first mentioned in the report of his second vision experience that accompanied his call.

As noted in this second vision experience, "the north" was vaguely revealed as the source of trouble which was to come upon Judah (1:13-15). Assyria was still the greatest national power to the north. Who could have told at that time that in fourteen years powerful Nineveh would have utterly fallen, or that in three years more the Assyrian remnant, which was to rally its forces at Harran, would have collapsed? It probably is true that at the beginning of his ministry Jeremiah himself did not know who "the northerner" was. He gives to the conception "the north" no concrete explanation until the Battle of Carchemish in 605 made clear to him and to the whole Middle East that the northerner was the Chaldean nation. Volz is probably nearest the truth when he says: "Jeremiah does not purpose to depict any definite, exactly conceivable enemy. He received from the Lord the information that a military force from the north was forcibly to break in from the north. More he did not know nor did he wish to know more." [1]

[1] *Jeremia*, p. 58.

A Lion Has Gone Up from His Thicket

Jeremiah gives his first graphic and imaginative description of the foe "from the north" (vs. 6) in a unified poem of great dramatic power. It begins (vs. 5) with the news that the foe is on the way, and it ends (vs. 31) with the picture of Zion groaning in death agonies. Here and there we get the clear prophetic insight that the northerner is the instrument of the Lord's judgment upon Judah (vs. 12b). It is because of Jerusalem's evil heart that the Lord is sending this agent of judgment (vs. 14). It is Judah's lack of moral understanding, her out-and-out evil-doing that causes the Lord to bring upon her this awful scourge (vs. 22).

The prophet calls Judah to heed the trumpet of alarm which summons the Judeans to flee to the fortified cities from before the approaching force from the north, which like a rapacious lion is bent upon ravaging the nations. Let Judah lament before the Lord.

4:5 Declare in Judah,
    And publish in Jerusalem,
    Blow the trumpet through the land,
    Proclaim with loud voice,
    Make haste, assemble, and let us go in
    To the fortified cities!
6 Lift up a standard toward Zion,
    Bring to safety, stand not still:
    For evil I am about to bring from the north,
    And great shattering.
7 A lion has gone up from his thicket,
    Yes, a destroyer of nations has set out,
    He has gone out of his place,
    To put your land to destruction.
    Your cities shall fall in ruins,
    Without a single inhabitant.
8 Because of this, gird on sackcloth,
    Lament and wail;
    For the fierceness of the Lord's anger
    Has not turned away from us.

When the enemy comes, the king and princes, the priests and prophets will lament in helplessness and accuse the Lord because his prophets have duped the people with their superficial optimism.

4:9 In that day, says the Lord,
    The courage of the king will vanish,
    And the courage of the princes,

And the priests will be dismayed,
And the prophets will be astounded.
10 And they will say, "Alas, Lord God,
Surely thou hast deluded us,
Saying, 'You shall have peace,'
Whereas the sword has reached to the heart."

When that invasion comes, it will be comparable to a tornado blown across the glaring sun-baked heights, like a wind sweeping up from the sand-baked desert; not a gentle winnowing wind that separates the chaff from the grain, but a fiery sirocco laden with the judgment of God (vss. 11-12). The invading hordes are in his mind as he writes.

4:11 In that day it shall be said
About this people, and about Jerusalem,
"A hot wind from the glaring bare heights
Is sweeping in from the desert to the daughter of my people—
Not for winnowing and not for cleansing,
12 A tornado will come in for me.
Now I, even I, will speak
Judgment against them."

A WARNING FROM DAN

The invaders riding furiously on horseback, the wagons whirling at terrific speed, drawn by swift horses, appear on Judah's horizon like an awful storm—the prophet has seen them or has heard them described. They are the foe from the north. How can Jerusalem escape such a terror? Only by turning from evil, only by cleansing the heart and the imagination. The threat they bring is God's call to repentance.

It is Dan, the northernmost tribe, closest to the source from which the invading hordes will come, which sounds the earliest warning. From farther south, the mountains of Ephraim, the heart of the Northern Kingdom, the people take up the word, passing it on in turn to Benjamin and Jerusalem.

4:13 See! Like clouds he gathers,
And like a hurricane are his chariots;
Swifter than vultures are his horses—
Woe to us! for we are devastated!
14 Wash your heart of evil, O Jerusalem!
In order that you may be saved!
How long will remain in your mind
Your wicked imaginations?

15 For hark! One keeps declaring from Dan,
   Keeps proclaiming trouble from Mount Ephraim!
16a Announce, give warning to Benjamin!
   Make a proclamation in Jerusalem.

It is Judah's rebellious habits and acts that have brought invading enemies against her cities from a. faraway land, for her outer deeds have made
her rebellious toward God in her innermost soul.

4:16b Foes are coming from a distant land,
   And will utter their voice against the cities of Judah;
17 Like keepers of a field, they are upon her from every side,
   For against me you are rebellious, says the Lord.
18 As for your ways and your deeds—
   They have done
   This evil to you—[that] your rebellion
   Has reached to your heart.

THE PROPHET'S ANGUISH FOR JUDAH

As Jeremiah contemplates the suffering that is imminent for Judah, his
heart cries out in anguish. His vivid imagination hears in anticipation the
trumpet alarm of war, and the blows of the destruction which will be
wrought by the invading hordes. He keeps seeing his people in precipitate
flight. He keeps hearing the repeatedly sounded trumpet of alarm. The
prophet's heart goes out to the foolish people who, as he is clearly and sadly
aware, do not really know God. They are skilled in evil but ignorant of
the good life. Yet fools though they be, they are God's people. They belong
to him and he to them.

4:19 My heart! my heart! I writhe in anguish!
   The walls of my heart!
   My soul is in commotion,
   I must not keep silent!
   For the blast of the trumpet I hear,
   The alarm of war.
20 Crash upon crash is experienced,
   For all the land is about to be devastated.
   Suddenly my tents are ruined,
   My tent curtains, in the twinkling of an eye.
21 How long must I see fugitives,
   Must I hear the blast of the trumpet?
22 For silly are my people,
   Me they do not know;

> Foolish children are they,
>   And they have no understanding;
> Learned are they in doing evil,
>   But to do what is good, they know not how!

With vivid imaginative power and with awesome suggestiveness the poet-prophet now paints an unforgettable impressionistic picture of utter chaos which the Lord in his righteous wrath is about to bring upon Judah. This word came to him in a vision at a time when his inner spirit was in distress as he contemplated the near-at-hand descent of the pagan destroyers from the north. Every line has an awe-inspiring picture; the empty earth, the heaven in darkness, quaking mountains and trembling hills, the fruitful plain of Carmel a desert, towns destroyed, no human inhabitant left, no sound to be heard—not even the voice of a bird. God has planned an utter annihilation and his plan shall be carried out.

> 4:23 I looked at the earth, and lo! emptiness;
>   Toward the heavens, but they gave no light.
>   24 I looked at the mountains, and lo! they were in earthquake;
>   And all the hills were atremble.
>   25 I looked, and lo! no man,
>   And every bird of the heavens had flown away.
>   26 I looked, and lo! the garden land was desert,
>   And all its towns were burned,
>   Before the presence of the Lord,
>   Obliterated by the heat of his anger.
>   27 For thus says the Lord:
>   All the land shall become a devastation,
>   Yes, an annihilation will I make of it.
> 28b [2] For I have spoken and will not regret it,
>   I have planned and will not turn aside from it.

The climax of the chapter imaginatively pictures all the inhabitants of the Judean cities and towns in precipitate flight at the terrified cry that the invaders are at hand. In caves, in dense thickets, high up in rocky regions, the refugees are hiding.

The progress of the invaders is imaginatively inferred. Having first mastered the town and country districts as was ever the wont of all invaders of Palestine—Sennacherib, Nebuchadrezzar, Vespasian, Titus[3]—the

---

[2] Omit vs. 28a: "For this shall the earth mourn, and the heavens above be black." It is a marginal comment and cannot be original in the midst of an utterance of the Lord; so Volz, *Jeremia*, p. 51, n. 1.

[3] So Rudolph, *Jeremia*, p. 29.

climax is Jerusalem, lovingly called by Jeremiah "the daughter of my people" (vs. 11). He pictures the capital city as a brazen prostitute adorning herself with ivory and gold and beautifying her person with paint and powder (cf. Jezebel in II Kings 9:30) in the bold hope that she could charm the ruthless invaders as she does her paramours, and so dissuade them from their murderous intent. But instead, there bursts from the tense lips of the daughter of Zion a disillusioned and despairing cry of anguish, like that of a woman in childbirth. Groaning, gasping for breath, she faints before her ruthless slaughterers.

> 4:29 At the cry "Horsemen and bowmen!"
>   All the land flees;
>   They go into the caves, and hide themselves in the thickets;
>   And they climb up into the rocks.
>   Every city is forsaken,
>   And there is no one dwelling in them.
>   30 And you [i.e., Jerusalem]—what will you do when you put on ivory,
>   Decorating yourself with gold ornaments,
>   Making your eyes large with antimony,
>   Beautifying yourself in vain?
>   31 For I have heard a voice as of one writhing in anguish,
>   Groaning like one bearing her first child.
>   Hark! The daughter of Zion, gasping for breath,
>   Spreading out her hands,
>   "Woe to me for my soul faints
>   Before slaughterers!"

JEREMIAH'S EARLIEST REPORT OF PROPHETIC EXPERIENCE

Ch. 4 ended with the vivid, imaginative picture of Jerusalem in the pangs of death at the ruthless hands of the northerners. Ch. 5 is intimately related to this, for it tells us why Jerusalem's ingenuity and cunning cannot save her from destruction. It dates probably from 624-621 B.C., before the great reform that took place in King Josiah's eighteenth year. Chs. 5–6 give us illuminating narratives of Jeremiah's early firsthand experiences in dealing as a prophet with the Judean people. He is not yet sure of himself. He is feeling his way into his task. Although he moves among his people as a prophet, he is not so much teaching as being taught, not so much preaching as learning what the people of Judah are thinking, saying, and doing. All three chapters date within the earliest period of his prophetic career, from 626-621 B.C.

The first of these is 5:1-5, which tells us how Jeremiah learned at firsthand why the Lord's judgment must fall on Judah. That such judgment was coming had been from the beginning the burden of his preaching. There came a time, however, when the reason for God's judgment had to be made more clear to him. Volz is right in interpreting 5:1-5 not as a public address but as describing a private prophetic project whereby Jeremiah is to be taught the moral necessity of the divine judgment which he has been proclaiming.

The assumed background of these verses is Gen. 18, the debate of Abraham with the Lord over the threatened destruction of Sodom. There it is explained that in case ten good men are found in Sodom, the threatened destruction would be withheld. In this present experience the Lord seems to be letting Jeremiah see with his own eyes the actual moral situation in Judah. A divine impulse directs him to go up and down Jerusalem's streets, into the bazaars, stores, and workshops to see if he can find even one person who is living his life with the aim of doing what is just. Thus the young prophet interprets this direction from God.

> 5:1 Go to and fro in the streets of Jerusalem.
> See, I entreat you, and know!
> ' And look in its broad open places
> To see whether you can find one
> Who does justly,
> Who practices faithfulness,
> Says the Lord.

Often had he roamed through those Jerusalem streets, for Anathoth was close to an hour's walk from the capital. But never before had he done this as a prophet. In imagination we follow him as he goes up and down the main streets and the narrow lanes of beloved Jerusalem, looking into the faces of the people, watching what they are doing, listening to what they are saying, his keen eye missing nothing, his sensitive spirit touched with a warm feeling of comradeship with the rank and file of his nation.

Something of prime significance is here taking place. Up until now, since its origin in the days of Moses, the institution of Hebrew prophecy had focused upon the nation as a whole; the prophetic "Thus says the Lord" was addressed to Israel or Judah, that is, to the nation conceived as a social entity. But with Jeremiah Hebrew prophecy begins to take particular notice of the individual as a unit of religious value. And now as the prophet moves out and in among the people living in the capital, he is pioneering far beyond his own realization at the moment.

It was an illuminating experience. His eyes, by his prophetic call now made sensitive to observe the motives of human conduct, note one supreme lack in the people's lives, the quality of faithfulness (*ĕmûnāh). To him unfaithfulness was his people's root sin, more deep-seated even than injustice, one which poisoned the relationships between man and man and between men and God. The prophet was particularly struck by the mockery of the oath. Now the taking of an oath was a common feature of Judean life. The true implication of such a legal rite in the Orient, as Johannes Pedersen points out, is that when a person swears by the familiar formula, "As the Lord lives," he puts "the whole of the substance and strength of his soul into the words he speaks: he concentrates himself entirely on his cause and strains himself to the utmost." [4] But Jeremiah saw that person after person would take a solemn oath upon his lips, yet would ignore any responsibility whatever to be truthful. He would perjure himself without the least sense of contrition. Thus Jeremiah reports to God:

> 5:3a **Do not thine eyes, O Lord, look for faithfulness?**
> 2   **But whenever they say, "As the Lord lives!"**
>   **Actually they swear in perjury.**
> 3b **Thou hast punished them but they show no contrition;**
>   **All of them refuse to receive correction.**
>   **They have made their faces harder than rock;**
>   **They refuse to turn.**

In carrying out this prophetic project to which he felt that God had directed him, the young prophet followed an impulse which centuries later was to characterize distinctly the ministry of Jesus of Nazareth. For Jeremiah instinctively concerned himself first with the poor, the uneducated, the common people who were the rank and file of Judeans. As he now studied their lives, he saw how foolish was their conduct and how ignorant they were of any binding divine requirement whatsoever. But the more he observed them the thought came to him, what could one expect of these small tradesmen, donkey drivers, burden carriers, and the like?

> 5:4 **But as for me, I said, "Surely these are poor;**
>   **Therefore they act foolishly;**
>   **For they do not know the way of the Lord,**
>   **The requirement of their God."**

So Jeremiah decided to turn from the common people to those of distinguished rank, "the great" who (of course!) are familiar with the divine

[4] *Israel, Its Life and Culture,* I-II, 407.

requirement! He decides to observe them closely, to engage them in conversation in order to see whether these important leaders gave evidence of that eagerly sought quality of faithfulness to some divine requirement.

We see how through these impulses to action God is teaching Jeremiah by the findings of his own eyes and ears that "the great" are not necessarily the ethically sensitive. Wealth, education, and position do not bring with them the sense of moral obligation. Jeremiah shares with us his disillusionment as he reports the continuing failure of his search. The lives of the great, no less than the lives of the poor, seem quite unaware that there is a "way" in which they should walk, an ordinance expressing the divine will which they are obligated to obey. Yet the prophet believes that they do know what they should do but have snapped the bonds of moral restraint and are living in open rebellion to God. Thus the prophet describes his frustration:

> 5:5 I will get me to the great
> And I will speak with them.
> For they know the way of the Lord,
> The ordinance of their God.
> But in fact, all alike have broken the yoke,
> Have snapped the [restraining] bonds.

At vs. 6 Jeremiah speaks as a prophet. Among rich and poor alike, among the cultured and learned, as well as among the unlearned masses of common folk, he discerned with his own eyes rebellion against God. It is this moral lack which makes forgiveness impossible and brings God's judgment upon them, for not one man did Jeremiah find who does justly, who practices faithfulness. The "lion of the forest," "the evening wolf," and the keen-eyed "leopard" ready to leap upon anyone who attempts to leave the city, are imaginative descriptions of the enemy of the north through which that judgment is to come.

> 5:6a On account of this, a lion of the forest will strike them,
> An evening wolf will devastate them.
> A leopard is watching over their cities;
> Anyone who goes out from them will be torn.

The Lord cannot forgive his people because of their transgression and repeated prevarications. To his abundant blessings they have responded by forsaking him and turning to other gods. Indeed, even some of their prophets have committed adultery. There followed a wave of immorality. Jeremiah compares these apostate Judeans to stallions in heat, each "neighing to his neighbor's wife." Upon "such a people"—in the prophet's lips a derogatory expression—the Lord can but bring punishment.

> 5:6b For their transgressions have become many,
>   Their apostasies have become numerous.
> 7 Upon what ground can I forgive them, says the Lord,
>   For they have forsaken me, and swear by that which is no God.
>   When I surfeited them they committed adultery,
>   Yes, they went in throngs to a harlot's house.
> 8 They have become [like] stallions in sexual passion;
>   They neigh, each to the wife of his neighbor.
> 9 Must I not punish them because of these things?
>   Says the Lord;
>   And upon such a nation
>   Must not my soul avenge itself?

The Lord has commanded a far-off and ancient nation (vss. 10, 15) to destroy utterly the neatly terraced "vineyard," the Judean nation. For its citizens, who give no evidence by their lives that they belong to the Lord, have denied his efficacy. In superficial and frivolous self-security they have dubbed the serious warnings of the prophets as just so much "wind," thus denying the validity and power of their message. But the Lord will cause those prophetic "words," which the Judeans now treat with utter contempt, to burn like fire. This burning word of God's judgment upon Judah will be expressed by that ancient people from the north, whose throat, as though it were an open sepulcher, will swallow up the self-sufficient Judeans. Four times the prophet uses the word, "and they shall eat up," as expressing the voracious character of the coming foe. They will consume Judah's grain harvest, her vintage harvest, her human population, and will capture the Judean fortresses. Cries the prophet:

> 5:10 Go up upon its vine terraces and destroy them,
>   Yes, make a complete annihilation.
>   Cut away its tendrils,
>   For they do not belong to the Lord.
> 11 For in utter treachery have the house of Israel [i.e., the whole nation of the
>   present]
>   Dealt with me, says the Lord.
> 12 They deny the Lord
>   And say: "He can do nothing to us.
> 13a And as for the prophets—they are mere wind,
>   And the word of the Lord is not in them."
> 14a Therefore, thus says the Lord
>   God of Hosts,

Because they said this word,

13*b* Thus shall be done to them!

14*b* Lo, I am about to make my words
Like fire in your mouth,
And this people as firewood,
And I will consume them.

15 Lo, I am about to bring against you
A nation from afar,
A nation of long duration,
A nation that is ancient,
A nation whose speech you do not know,
Nor can you understand what they say.

16 Whose throat is like an open sepulcher;
All of them are valiant men.

17 And it shall eat up your harvest and your bread,
It shall destroy your sons and your daughters;
It shall devour your sheep and your cattle.
It shall consume your vineyards and your fig trees;
It shall dispossess you of your fortified cities,
On which you are relying.

THEY SET TRAPS, THEY CATCH MEN

The prophet in vss. 26-29 represents the Lord as speaking to him about the people. We sense in these words how the insights which Jeremiah had gained into the acts and motives of the people gave him sensitivity for receiving the revelation that now comes to him.

Among the Judeans there were men of wealth who had acquired their riches by dealing with their fellow men in trickery. Thus in treacherous and deceitful ways they caught men like fowlers caught birds. Go to their homes. See the luxurious things that fill them! See the parade of their prosperity! See their sleek faces and their fat bodies—fat as pigs and, indeed, from eating swine! But do they ever take up the cause of orphans or the rights of the poor? Not they, for they have no conscience, either in the gaining of wealth or in its expenditure, and no sensitiveness whatever to the obligation which possession brings upon the possessor. How can the Lord—moral being that he is—let such a people and nation go unpunished?

5:26 For there are found among my people wicked men
Who acquire the riches of fowlers.[5]

---

[5] Instead of *yāshûr kᵉshakh,* read *yaᵉᵃshîrû 'ōsher,* and transfer *yᵉqûshîm* to the end of the first line, placing the major pause there. The meaning of the second line is "who acquire property of," i.e., in the same manner as "fowlers"; so A. B. Ehrlich, *Randglossen zur Hebräischen Bibel,* IV, (Jesaia, Jeremia) , 254-55.

They set traps;
    They catch men!
27 Like a cage full of birds,
    So are their houses full of treachery.
Therefore they have become great and rich,
    And display prosperity.[6]
28 They have become fat, thy shine [i.e., from fat];
    Yes, they go to excess in things of evil.[7]
They do not make a plea at all [i.e., for the defense of another],
    The cause of the orphan,
Or the right of the poor,
    They do not vindicate.
29 Because of these things should I not punish them,
    Says the Lord;
Or upon a nation such as this,
    Should I not avenge myself?

JEREMIAH'S EARLY CRITICISM OF PROPHETS AND PRIESTS

There were plenty of prophets and priests in Judah, but when the spiritual leadership of a nation is corrupt, something "astounding" and "horrible" has taken place. To spiritual-minded Jeremiah the prophets (cf. 2:8) were not inspired by the stern and solemn word of the Lord, but by the far more pleasant and spectacular "revelations" of Baal, more in line with the natural physical appetites and drives of man than is the direct ethical summons to conduct in line with God's holy will. The priests now in Judah are ignorant of the knowledge of the Lord, which indeed is their rightful province, and in which they should have been fully informed (Mal. 2:6-7); therefore they cannot instruct the people as to the will of God, but the source of their instruction is their own ignorance and their own unillumined authority. If they instructed the people truly in the Lord's will, they would drive away their own followers.

But worst of all, the rank and file of Judeans like it just that way and seek no higher guidance for their life. The outcome—so his solemn and studied words imply—is national destruction, and when and if that comes, what will Judah do?

---

[6] Following Ehrlich (*ibid.*) in transferring *wᵉyaçlîhû* from next to last line of vs. 28 to this point, reading *wayyaçlîhû.*

[7] Following Ehrlich (*ibid.*) in understanding "things of evil" in the second line as referring to "the loathsome things," "the swine," in which these materialists, uninhibited by Jewish rites, have been indulging themselves; cf. Aug. Wünsche: *Der Babylonische Talmud in seinem Haggadischen Bestandtheilen Wortgetreu übersetzt und durch Noten erläutert,* I, 167-68 (Sabbath), and II, 39-40 (Kidduschin).

5:30 An astounding and horrible thing
Has occurred in the land:
31 The prophets prophesy falsely,
And the priests instruct according to their own authority,
And my people love [it] so,
So what will you do at the outcome of it?

THE CERTAINTY OF JERUSALEM'S FALL

In 4:5 Jeremiah had warned his people of the impending disaster and had summoned them to flee to the fortified cities of Judah. He then had imaginatively pictured the progress of the invaders until, after the town and country districts had been mastered, they were at the point of besieging Jerusalem (4:31).

The standpoint at which ch. 6 opens is the certainty of Jerusalem's fall. The prophet calls upon his fellow Benjamites to flee from Jerusalem. They were neither better nor worse than the rest of Jerusalem, but they made up a large section of the capital's population (Josh. 18:28; Judg. 1:21). He thinks of them first, for they were Jeremiah's fellow tribesmen, but his words apply to all the population of Jerusalem. The appeal is particularly moving as he urges his own fellow countrymen, for whom he ever manifested a deep and tender affection, to leave the capital before it was encircled by the foe.

They are to flee to the gorges and caves of the Judean highlands. At Tekoa, home of the prophet Amos, 849 meters high on the border of the desert, let the trumpet be blown. And from the heights of Beth-hac-cherem ("place of vineyards"), a district (Neh. 3:14), probably on the ras esh-Sherafe,[8] 994 meters high, which commands a view of both Dead Sea and Mediterranean, let the beacon light direct the fugitives the shortest way to the wilderness. As we read the prophet's summons to his people we are keenly aware of the atmosphere of overhanging calamity which it exudes.

The invading hordes are now pictured through the figure of nomads taking over the pasture land of Jerusalem and its environs,[9] which Jeremiah calls by the prophet Isaiah's name for it, "the daughter of Zion," and eating it bare. He imagines the pagan hordes first planning an attack upon the city at noon, launching it with sacred war ritual, only to change their plans and escape the burning noontide heat by attacking at night, when they will force an entrance and sack Jerusalem's palaces.

[8] Albrecht Alt, in *Palästina Jahrbuch*, 21, p. 18; 24, pp. 19-21; 28, p. 11, n. 3.

[9] So in 1948 I saw a large group of Iranian Bedouins with their camels descend upon the great plain, fertile for grazing, just outside Shiraz.

As they chop down the trees in brazen unconcern as to the military regulations by which the Judeans were governed (Deut. 20:19-20), and use them for casting up a mound against the wall, also for breaking the wall down, the Lord will not hinder them. For the attacker is the Lord's agent of judgment upon the false city, full as it is of oppression and evil. Indeed, Jerusalem is like a poisonous fountain pouring forth impure water. For it is suffering from the wickedness and violence of its people. From within it we hear the cries of the victims who have been ruthlessly dealt with (vs. 7). We sense the silent suffering of the victims of powerful men who are living in rebellion toward God. It is the same Jerusalem which, on an errand of sharp-eyed investigation undertaken at the Lord's command, Jeremiah had explored at firsthand for many days. There in many lives he had seen the open wounds from the ruthless injustice dealt its citizens; he had heard with his own ears the distress cries of those wronged. To this city that he loves, Jeremiah calls, somewhat as One greater than he was later to cry, "O Jerusalem, let yourself be corrected."

6:1 Bring yourselves into safety, sons of Benjamin,
From the midst of Jerusalem!
And blow the trumpet in Tekoa;
And lift up a signal upon Beth-hac-cherem
For calamity overhangs from the north,
Yes, a vast shattering.
2 Are you not like a delightful meadow,
Daughter of Zion?
3 To her will come shepherds,
Together with their flocks;
They will pitch their tents around her,
They will strip, each one his portion.
4 "Consecrate war against her;
Let us start to go up at noon!
Alas for us! The day has [already] turned,
For the shades of evening are beginning to lengthen.
5 Let us start to go up in the night
And ruin her palaces!"
6 For thus says the Lord of hosts:
"Cut down her trees, and cast up
A mound against Jerusalem!
Alas—the false city!
As for all of it—oppression is in its midst.
7 As a spring causes its waters to flow,
So it [Jerusalem] makes its evil to flow.

> Wickedness and violence are heard in it,
>   Continuously in defiance of me, wounds and blows.
> 8 Let yourself be corrected, O Jerusalem,
>   So that my soul be not alienated from you,
>   So that I do not make you a devastation,
>   A land uninhabited."

In vss. 9-14 we have a second report of Jeremiah's early prophetic experience. He tells us how the Lord led him to intensify his hunt for men of character in Judah.

The prophet's futile search for even one man whose life revealed the quality of moral faithfulness left him pessimistic about Jerusalem. But could he possibly have missed someone who really had this quality? Can Jerusalem really be as corrupt as it seems? While he was meditating over his discouraging results, he tells us of a renewed search that the Lord induced him to undertake. He is to "glean" in Judah, here conceived of in terms of the prophet Isaiah's phrase, as "the vineyard of the Lord" (Isa. 5:7). He is to "glean" for good men, honest and obedient, just as a responsible grape gleaner gleans the vines for good grapes which the gatherers may have overlooked. He reports:

> 6:9 Thus says the Lord of hosts:
>   Glean! Glean! as one gleans a vine,
>   The remnant of Israel.
>   Put back your hand as a grape gatherer does
>   To the vine branches.

Thus back among the vine shoots in the vineyard of Judah the Lord commands him to go. In the account of this new summons we see how the prophet was being taught the patience and persistence of God with men. "Try again," says the Lord to the prophet. Twice comes the verb, "Glean, glean! Put back your hand to the vine. Lift the leaves of the vine branches. Search for any good grapes still left on the vine shoots of Judah. Do not miss even one." And Jeremiah makes us aware of a new element which was thus added to the spiritual equipment of the prophet, and likewise God-given—a strict conscientiousness in the pursuit of his calling. He is to be an indefatigable seeker for persons. He is to search for people of moral worth among the rank and file of men. He is to treasure them, encourage them, nurture and guide them.

We are to infer that Jeremiah accepted this commission to yet more thorough search. But for the time being no optimistic result came from it. He was discouraged and cried out:

> 6:10 To whom shall I speak and warn
>   So they will hear?
>   Lo, they have a film before their ears.[10]
>   And they do not give attention.
>   Lo, the word of the Lord has become to them
>   An object of reproach, they take no pleasure in it.

Regarding Jeremiah's initial discouragement, Rudolph says: "His conscientiousness comes into conflict with his inner weariness, because he speaks the Lord's word but sees no result. In this place we hear for the first time a lament of Jeremiah over the hopelessness of his calling, which later comes more often and is characteristic of him." [11]

He Must Pour Out the Wrath of the Lord

Wrath, such as is not natural to Jeremiah, surges over his soul like angry billows. Although he desperately tries, he cannot hold in; he has to speak.

> 6:11a But I—I am full of the wrath of the Lord;
>   I make myself weary holding it in.

Beginning with the third line of vs. 11, God answers the prophet's lament. This anger that burns in Jeremiah's tender spirit, so the Lord reveals to him, is not his anger but that of God. Through his prophet God would pour it out upon all children, all young men, all the aged, all sexes, wherever he comes upon them. The Lord's retributive wrath will be expressed in their being dispossessed of their houses and lands. The whole population of Judah will experience the punitive action of God. Says the Lord:

> 6:11b I must pour [it] out upon the child on the street,
>   And simultaneously upon the circle of young men;
>   For both men and women shall be caught [i.e., by the judgment of God],
>   The aged along with the young.
> 12 And their houses shall be turned over to others;
>   Their fields to those who eject them.
>   For I will stretch out my hand
>   Against the inhabitants of the land, says the Lord.

[10] Lit., "Lo, uncircumcized [i.e., having foreskin] is their ear."
[11] Cf. Rudolph, *Jeremia*, p. 39.

His renewed search for good men, responsible to God, had failed of its object. The common people and the people of distinction as well—including even prophets and priests—are corrupt in conduct. They are shallow optimists, irresponsible healers, who treat the surface of Judah's wound but leave the cause untouched. They are what Jeremiah's young prophetic contemporary, Ezekiel, called "daubers of whitewash" (Ezek. 13:10; 22:28), and they have lost their ability to blush because of their poor leadership. Thus Jeremiah states his indictment as a conclusion derived from his repeated search:

6:13 For from the least important to the most important of them,
They all make profit wrongfully;
Yes from prophet even to priest,
Every one of them practices fraud.
14 And they have healed the wounds of my people
Superficially, saying, 'It is well,
It is well,' but where is it well?
15 Are they at all ashamed when they act detestably?
Not in the least are they ashamed;
They do not even know how to blush.
Therefore among those falling they shall fall;
At the time of their [i.e., the people generally] punishment, they [i.e., the leaders] shall be overthrown,
Says the Lord.

In every conceivable way Jeremiah attempted to convince his hearers that the immediate future of Judah was fraught with disaster. While he deals much with the disaster itself, and often in vivid, realistic pictures, he was far more concerned as to why, in the purpose of God, it had to come. He takes all pains to show the moral grounds for the imminent catastrophe. He strives with singleness of aim to show that between national guilt and national punishment there is an inner connection. God, moral being that he is, could not deal with his people otherwise. Jeremiah does not use the term "moral law," but his faith is surely in harmony with the concept that the universe is ruled by the moral law of God.

THREE GOD-GIVEN POINTERS TO THE GOOD WAY

It was also clear to the prophet that God had given to Judah every reason to know the paths of thought and action which the Judeans should have taken. In words that are increased in value, because of the fresh context of thought in which Jesus later quoted a clause from them in his universal call to men ("Come to me, . . . and you will find rest for your souls"), Jeremiah called his people to "the ancient paths where the good way is." God had given to his people three pointers to the "good way": history (vs. 16), prophecy (vs. 17), and the law (vs. 19).

The first pointer God has given to "the good way" is Israel's own history. The prophet sweeps through a millennium of time recorded in Israel's own historical records, and covering the period from the Hebrew Fathers to the reign of Josiah.[12] There appears there in the oft-stated belief of the Lord's people that it went well with them only when they were obedient to his will. Moreover, in that history great leaders appear, leaders of thought and of action, such as Moses and Samuel, with both of whom Jeremiah was particularly impressed (15:1). They had blazed the trails for Israel's progress as a people and a nation. The term "ancient paths" means the "paths of the past," "the paths of ancient times."

The second pointer to "the good way" is represented by prophecy. "From time to time" God had raised up "from among their fellow countrymen" (Deut. 18:18) "watchmen." This is the name which Jeremiah gave to the prophets (vs. 17), whose pre-eminent task it was, as Jeremiah's own mission makes sun clear, to warn the people of the peril of their ways. And as Jeremiah well knew, among those watchmen, covering a period of two strategic centuries, the ninth and eighth B.C., God had raised up Elijah in the ninth, and in the eighth century Hosea in Israel, Amos, Isaiah, and Micah in Judah, who as spokesmen for God had warned king and people of wrong policies and had pointed out to their countrymen the paths they should walk, always making clear what is good and what the Lord requires (Mic. 6:8). Only through heeding their warnings, and by following their teaching as the Lord's word came flaming from their lips, could the nation expect to experience health and security. But Judah had refused to walk "in the ancient paths," in "the good way," and to their own inevitable dismay had scoffed at the prophet's warnings.

The third God-given pointer to "the good way" was the law (vs. 19b). In the providence of God Israel had been granted a very remarkable development of laws. The great and beneficent Code of Hammurabi, dating from the middle of the eighteenth century B.C., had largely prevailed in Canaan for centuries before the Israelites entered the land. Likewise influential in Canaan, yet not quite as basically so, were the Assyrian laws, dating from ca. 1350 B.C., and the Hittite Code, dating from the same time.

---

[12] W. F. Albright's date for the Hebrew Fathers is between the twentieth and sixteenth centuries B.C.; cf. The Biblical Period, p. 4.

All of these represent juristic formulation of civil and criminal laws. It is Israel's earliest code of law, the Covenant Code (Exod. 20:22–23:33), through which we become aware how great under the providence of God was Israel's indebtedness to these ancient Oriental codes and more especially to that of Babylonia. Alt has conclusively shown that the origins of Israel's earliest code must be sought outside Israel,[13] among the population which the Israelites found in Canaan, and its original nucleus was the ancient ritual decalogue preserved in Exod. 22:29b-30; 23:12, 15-19. It also included remnants of one or more genuinely Israelitic codes earlier than Deuteronomy (i.e., 621 B.C.) and derived in part from the ancient Bedouin law of the desert which the Israelites brought with them into Canaan.[14] This original and ancient code, as reconstructed by Pfeiffer,[15] had three sections: law of persons, including matters of liability and the family; law of property, including its ownership and possession; and law of procedure as to false witness and the administration of lashes to the offender. The Covenant Code in its original form was adopted by the Israelites after their entrance into Canaan but before the reign of King Saul.[16] An early "summary of the civil, humanitarian and religious legislation dealing with offenses committed in secret and therefore known only to God," is given in the anathemas of Deut. 27:15-16. "These have to do with (a) criminal offenses punishable by death, (b) acts of dishonesty, and (c) misleading the blind." They date from the ninth or eighth centuries B.C.[17]

In their present context all these laws in Israel are definitely linked with Moses. Pedersen says: "We must look upon Moses, as Israel looked upon him, i.e., as the original law-maker to whom all laws are ascribed."[18] We have in Exod. 18 a narrative in which the Yahwist and Elohist sources are inextricably mingled, which presents the picture of Moses settling the disputes of the people, deciding between one man and another, and letting "them know the statutes of God and his decisions" (Exod. 18:16). Here are those primitive precedents of justice which, while oral, lie at the basis of what was distinctly Israelite in spirit. The story tells us how the burden of the administration of justice through these primitive precedents was distributed by Moses among "capable, God-fearing, honest men, with an

[13] Cf. *Ursprünge des Israelitischen Rechts,* pp. 24 ff.; also Robert H. Pfeiffer, *Introduction to the Old Testament,* pp. 33-71.

[14] Pfeiffer, *ibid.,* p. 218; Alt, *ibid.,* pp. 33-71.

[15] *Ibid.,* pp. 214-15.

[16] *Ibid.,* p. 215.

[17] *Ibid.,* pp. 227-28.

[18] *Israel, Its Life and Culture,* I-II, 18.

aversion to improper gain," who were to "act as judges for the people on all ordinary occasions," but the difficult cases were reserved for Moses himself (Exod. 18:21-22, 26). Under the impact of men like Elijah and the prophets the creative and formative spirit of Moses more and more permeated Israelite law with the distinctive spirit of the covenant. As Pedersen says: "Moses becomes the creator of the whole Israelitic type of life." [19]

Such was all the law, so far as we know, that Judah up to 621 B.C. possessed. Quite unknown to Jeremiah, within a very short time after vs. 19b had been spoken by him, a great new lawbook of strategic importance for the political, social, and religious life of Judah was to be discovered and made the law of the land.

But so far as obedience to the great codes that Judah already possessed is concerned, their pointings had been disdained and rejected (vs. 19b).

The calamity that is about to come upon Judah is accordingly "the fruit of their own apostasy" (vs. 19). The punishment of Judah by this calamity represents no whim of a disgruntled deity. Rather is it inwardly based. It is the inevitable outcome of the nation's own conduct. How clear at this point is Jeremiah's glimpsing of a universal moral law that is supranational and suprapersonal. Accordingly, because of its illuminating importance, all the nations of the earth are called upon (vs. 18) by Jeremiah to listen to the Lord's decision of calamity for Judah (vs. 19a).

The Judeans generally seem not to be conscious at all of their moral lack. Do they not bring the burnt offerings to the Lord's temple? Are they not meticulous in the rendering of their sacrifices? Does not the Lord himself find pleasure, as do his temple worshipers, in the aroma of costly incense that comes clear from Sheba (Saba) in South Arabia, and of the calamus cane that is brought from faraway India? [20] Do not these costly gifts and these cultic rites of sacrifice and offering make amends for their sins and win the divine approval? Here is a cultic piety seemingly sincere. Is not this the worship which the Lord requires? Says Volz: "Cultic piety has ever been the most comfortable, most pleasant and most soothing piety; here man may practice his usual way of life without changing his heart; he may have his uplift along with moderately tempered emotions without troubling his will; in things he can see he may enjoy the greatest assurance." [21] But in harmony with Amos (5:21-24), Hosea (6:6), Isaiah (1:10-

---

[19] *Ibid.*

[20] Cf. Assyrian *Kanû tabu;* cf. Zimmern in *Die Keilschriften und das Alte Testament,* p. 600; Duhm, *Jeremia,* p. 72.

[21] *Jeremia,* p. 81.

17), and Micah (6:1-8), Jeremiah here opposes sacrifice and offering as the way for the Judeans to secure the Lord's forgiveness and approval. "To him," says Duhm, "incense and calamus are not the right medicine for the sick nation." [22]

It is a striking fact that it is Jeremiah, son of a priest, and possessing a vivid knowledge of the whole sacrificial system at high place and temple, who is speaking in vs. 20. Indeed, he uses a technical clause that is at home in the terminology of the priestly profession when he represents God as saying in regard to sacrifices, "They are not pleasing to me" [lô lᵉrāçôn]. But it is as prophet uttering the Lord's revelation that he speaks, and all the more weighty are his words which emphasize, in the clear vision of a spiritual-minded, informed observer, the strategic limitation of a cultic ritual that does not change the heart life of the worshiper.

The judgment that is about to come upon Judah is vividly and figuratively pictured in vs. 21 in terms of obstacles placed by the Lord before his people to cause their downfall. Vs. 21 connects in continuity of thought with vss. 18-19. Since they have rejected "the ancient paths where the good way is," upon the way which they have stubbornly chosen they will encounter impediments over which they will trip. It is a vivid picture of the calamity of war which will destroy at one and the same time father and son, neighbor and friend. The picture in vs. 21 of the actual nation as a whole "stumbling" (wᵉkāshᵉlû) forms a sharp contrast to the ideal picture in vs. 16 of the nation in repose (margôaᵉ).

6:16 Thus says the Lord:
I said, "Take your stand at the head of the ways and see,
And ask for the ancient paths,
Where is the good way and walk in it,
And you shall find repose for your soul."
But they said, "We will not go."
17 So I kept raising up over them watchmen [and I cried, understood],
"Give attention to the blast of the trumpet!"
But they said, "We will not give attention."
18 As a consequence, hear, O nations,[23]
And know well what I will inflict upon them;
And hear, O earth,
19 Lo, I am about to bring calamity
Upon this people,
The fruit of their own apostasy.

[22] Ibid.
[23] The term haggôyîm refers to non-Hebraic peoples; cf. Brown-Driver-Briggs, Hebrew Lexicon, p. 156, col. 2, 1, c.

For to my words they have paid no attention;
And as for my law—they disdained it.
20 Why now do you bring incense from Sheba [Saba],
And sweet calumus from a land far away?
Your whole burnt offerings I do not accept,
And as for your sacrifices—they do not please me.
21   Therefore, thus says the Lord:
Lo, I am about to set before this people
Stumbling blocks, and they shall trip over them.
Fathers and sons simultaneously,
Neighbor and friend will perish.

Vss. 22-23 return to the imaginative description of the enemy coming from the north. They give additional features to those already expressed (cf. 4:5 ff; 5:15-18; 6:1-8). Their weapons are bow and javelin. They are horsemen, they are cruel and show no mercy. And when they are on the move, the tumult they make is comparable to the sea's roaring. In his mind's eye the prophet sees them drawn up against Jerusalem in battle array:

6:22 Thus says the Lord:
Lo, a people is coming from the land of the north,
A great nation is roused up from parts remote of the earth.
23 They lay hold on bow and javelin,
They are cruel and show no compassion;
The noise of them is like the roaring sea,
And they mount and ride upon horses,
Arranged in order like men of war,
Against you, O daughter of Zion!

Imaginatively Jeremiah portrays the terror of the people. They are paralyzed with fear, and with anguish comparable to that experienced by a mother in childbirth. They caution one another not to risk being seen outside the walls of fortified Jerusalem, in the fields or on the street, for fear of being struck down by the enemy. Upon every hand the mood of terror is manifest.

Tenderly and sadly the prophet calls to Judah, addressing her in Isaiah's beloved designation, "daughter of my people." [24] His own heart is touched to the quick by the contemplation of the suffering which Jerusalem is about to experience. He summons the whole city to a public lamentation. Jerusalem is to lament with that sharp bitterness such as the death of an only

[24] Cf. Isa. 22:4. From here on the phrase is used often and characteristically by Jeremiah.

son would bring to a mother's heart. For suddenly the destroyer will be upon her.

> 6:24 We have heard report of him,
>   Our hands drop down;
>   Distress has seized us,
>   Anguish like that of a woman giving birth.
> 25 Go not out to the field,
>   And do not walk in the street,
>   Because of the sword of the enemy—
>   Terror on every side.
> 26 O daughter of my people, gird on sackcloth,
>   And sprinkle yourself with ashes:
>   Make you a mourning as for an only son,
>   A bitter mourning.
>   For suddenly will come
>   The destroyer upon you.

We have already seen how the task of the prophet takes on new emphases in the ministry of Jeremiah which both broaden and deepen the nature of prophecy. In vss. 27-30 there are two additional elements which come into prophecy through the living experience of Jeremiah, the prophet as assayer, gold tester, as skilled "tester" of the character of men, and the prophet as "smelter," separator of the dross from the pure metal.

There came to the prophet an impulse from the Lord that led him to think of himself as a gold tester, a hunter for gold in Judean personalities, and one skilled in accurate estimate of the characters of men. This impulse he interpreted as God's summons.

> 6:27 I have made you an assayer among my people, a gold tester,
>   That you may learn to know and test their character.

The closely related view of his mission as the separator of dross from the pure metal of men's lives, he does not so specifically introduce but clearly infers it as a phase of his mission committed to him by the Lord. Vs. 27 is God's word to Jeremiah. Vss. 28-30 are his answer.

These were indeed testing times for Judah, times that try men's souls. The intimation from the Lord gave him a new approach to his task, a new angle of ministry that gave him new feelings about the people to whom he ministered. But it led him to exactly the same conclusion to which the earlier pursued and renewed search for good men had brought him. The result Jeremiah thus reports:

6:28 **All of them are living rebelliously,**
   Going about slandering;
   As for all of them—they are dealing corruptly.

Then he pictures the smelter at the work of refining silver. He hears the snort of the bellows, he sees the fire flame. Lead is consumed. The smelter keeps on smelting, seeking to separate the pure silver, but in vain, for it is all dross. No doubt he had often watched the smelter, even as we shall later see he had watched the potter. He reports the net estimate of the moral worth of Judah as he had seen it with his own spiritual vision.

6:29 **The bellows snort,**
   The lead is consumed by fire:
   In vain he goes on smelting,
   And the dross is not separated.
30 **They [i.e., the people] are called refuse silver,**
   For the Lord has rejected them.

THE PUNISHMENT OF JERUSALEM

Jer. 13:20-22; 25:1–27:22 belong in the context of chs. 4–6, in which the prophet is absorbed by the prospect of the invasion of the foe from the north. The nation of Judah, even from the days of King Ahaz in the middle of the eighth century, had turned away from Isaiah's counsel to trust loyally in God for protection.[25] Just like a disloyal wife turning from her true husband to a paramour, Judah has turned from dependence upon the Lord and has sought political security in alliance with Assyria. What to Judean politicians seemed political necessity was viewed by the prophet as outright disloyalty to God. As Volz puts it: "The city of Jerusalem will suffer punishment like that of a harlot, public disgrace: the punishment consists, as it were, in naked exposure and beating and in public humiliation." [26] So the prophet cries to Jerusalem:

13:20 **Lift up your eyes, Jerusalem, and see**
   Those coming from the north.
   Where is the herd which was given to you,
   Your beautiful flock?
21 **What will you say when they punish**
   You, O Jerusalem? [27]

[25] To Ahaz, who was turning for protection to Assyria, Isaiah had said: "If you will not have faith [in God] surely you cannot have staith" (Isa. 7:9).

[26] *Jeremia*, pp. 156-57.

[27] Following Rudolph, *Jeremia*, p. 80, in reading *y⁰rûsh* instead of *l⁰rōsh*, as an abbreviation for Jerusalem, and transferring it to the end of the previous line.

But you taught them;
   To you they were friends.
Will not anguish seize you,
   Like that of a woman in labor?
22 And when you say in your heart
   "Why has such befallen me?"
Because of the greatness of your iniquity your limbs are exposed,
   Your hinder parts suffer violence.
25 This is your lot, your measured portion
   From me, says the Lord;
Because you forgot me,
   And trusted in deception,
26 So I will even strip off your skirts over your face,
   And your nakedness will be seen.
27 Ah, your adultery and your lewd neighings!
   Ah, the device of your illicit desire!
Upon the hills and in the field
   I have seen your abhorrent acts.
Woe to you, Jerusalem, for you are not clean!
   How long will you delay to return?

In vss. 23-24 we have the climax of Jeremiah's thought in this period of his prophetic pioneering. It is a classic utterance which has become proverbial in the speech of many peoples. Evil has become second nature to Judah. The nation has become so set in evil practices and habits that it has lost the will and the power to do good. To Jeremiah it seems that it is no more possible for corrupt Judah to turn from its evil ways to good, than for an Ethiopian to change the color of his skin or for a leopard to change its spots.

Cries the prophet:

13:23 Can the Ethiopian change his skin,
   Or the leopard his spots?
Only then could you do good
   Who are practiced in doing evil.

Over a century earlier Hosea, the prophet to whom Jeremiah is most akin, had expressed a similar analysis of the Israel of his day:

Israel is defiled.
   Their deeds will not permit them
   To return to their God (Hos. 5:3d-4).

How can Judah overcome such a moral impasse? What is powerful enough to reach with transforming, emancipating power the heart of the nation?

Already Jeremiah has indicated the answer. Only the grace of God is powerful enough to awaken Judah's repentance. Already the note had been struck when Jeremiah earlier cried in the Lord's name:

> 3:12 Return, faithless Israel, says the Lord.
> I am not conscious of my anger against you.
> For kind am I, says the Lord.
> I will not maintain my anger forever.
> 22a Turn back, faithless children;
> I will heal your disloyalties.

But now it is because of Judah's hopeless entanglement in evil that God must discipline his people by the hot wind of exile.

> 13:24 So I will scatter you like chaff swept along
> By a desert wind.

A LISTENING-IN CAMPAIGN

In a third report of his early prophetic experience (8:4-7) Jeremiah describes a listening-in campaign, by which he tries to get at the root lack in his people, and in the process comes upon one of the most profound insights ever received by Old Testament prophets as to the essential nature of religion.

As Jeremiah closely observed the conduct of his fellow Judeans he found in it something inexplicable, for it was contrary to common sense. Ordinarily if one falls down, he quickly gets up again. Or if one discovers that he is on the wrong road, he finds the right road and takes it. But it is not so in Judah. For in the moral conduct of his fellow countrymen Jeremiah observed conscious and persistent alienation from what they knew was right.

He asks:

> 8:4 Do men fall but not get up?
> Or if they miss the way, do they not turn around?
> 5 Why then do these people go the wrong way
> In persistent desertion [of the right]?
> They keep hold on deceitfulness;
> They refuse to turn back.

Again he gave careful attention to what people generally were saying. He noted their conversation when they were off guard and so spoke their minds without inhibition, and he reports his resulting disappointment:

8:6 I gave attention to listening in;
     They speak what is not right.
   No one repents of his evil,
     Saying, "What have I done?"
   Everyone turns to his own course,
     Like a horse rushing headlong in battle.

Jeremiah was a lover of nature and was deeply impressed by what he had observed about the migratory habits of birds. They obey an inward law of their being. Nobody tells them when it is time to fly south or to return north. Yet they "know" their "prescribed times." He sees the storks, the turtledoves, the swifts, and the swallows moving across the heavens in great flocks in response to this deep-seated law implanted in their very being. To this familiar fact in nature his sensitive spirit saw a spiritual analogy. God has so constituted his people, Israel, that the true inner law of their being is the ordinance of the Lord, the will of God. The most characteristic element in Israel is that the Lord is its God, and the one thing above all others that should mark the true Israelite is obedience to his Lord's will. As Albert C. Knudson has finely said: "What instinct is to the birds of passage that religion is to man." [28] Even the birds of the air have something to teach the Lord's dull and unresponsive people.

Thus the Lord speaks:

8:7 Even the stork in the heavens
     Knows its prescribed times;
   And the turtledoves, swifts, and swallows
     Keep the time of their migration;
   But my people do not know
     The ordinance of the Lord.

We are here at one of the deepest insights of religion. Jeremiah teaches us that religious living is not something alien to human nature but a basic part of it. The law, the ordinance of the Lord, is writ deep in the constitution of man. True religion therefore is man's response to this deepest law of his being. The most classic expression of this profoundest truth of religion is the well-known dictum of Augustine: "For thou, O Lord, hast created us for thyself; and our heart is restless until it rest in thee." [29]

[28] *The Beacon Lights of Prophecy,* p. 189.
[29] *Confessions* I. 1.

THE PROPHET INDICTS THE PRIESTS

Jer. 8:8-9 has no relation to vss. 4-7. The final editor of the book of Jeremiah, noting the phrase in vs. 7, "the ordinance [mishpāt] of the Lord," has
connected with it an authentic utterance of the prophet on the law [tōrāh]
of the Lord (vs. 8). By law of the Lord the prophet means the written law of
which the priests were the custodians. As administrators of the law they
were reputedly "wise." As Malachi later said: "The lips of a priest should
safeguard knowledge" (Mal. 2:7). As collectors and chroniclers of the law
they were "scribes."

In vs. 9 "the word of the Lord" represents a contrast to "the law of the
Lord," for it is not as yet Holy Scripture but the living word of the prophet's
preaching. We see in the book of Jeremiah sharp antagonism between the
prophets, who under the inspiration of God spoke with authority as the
bearers of God's word, and the priests, to whom the written law was considered immensely superior to the living word of direct inspiration.

Jeremiah knew from close observation that the law of the priests was an
adulteration of the true law, because they did not put at the center "the
moral demand, the true will of God." Instead of this, their insistence was
upon externals, upon cultic rites and rituals.[30] Accordingly, thus, Jeremiah
indicts the priests:

> 8:8 How can you say, "We are wise
>   And the law of the Lord is with us"?
>   But in fact, see, the false pen of the scribes
>   Has turned it into a lie.
>   9 The "wise" are ashamed;
>   They are shattered and caught in snares.
>   Lo, they have rejected the word of the Lord,
>   And [as for] their wisdom—of what worth is it to them? [31]

The prophet's earnest search among the Judeans for repentant people
who are really concerned over the nation's imminent fate (8:4-7) was in
vain. He was convinced that no moral fruitage would be harvested from
Judah. The people are like a grapevine that bears no grapes. In his words
there is an implicit reference to Isaiah's vineyard song (Isa. 5:1-7), which
likewise stressed the disappointing moral harvest in the nation. The people
are like a diseased, and so barren, fig tree at the gathering season, its withered

---

[30] Cf. Rudolph, Jeremia, pp. 50, 53.

[31] Omit vss. 10-12, which here are repeated from 6:12-15, pp. 66-67, where they are in
their correct context, as they are intended as a threat for the entire people.

leaves falling dead to the ground. We recall the similar thought in Jesus' parable of the fig tree which for three solid years had borne no fruit, and in the consequent directions given by the owner to the gardener, "Cut it down; why should it waste the ground" (Luke 13:6-9), there are overtones from Jeremiah's metaphor. Says the prophet:

> 8:13 Would I gather harvest from them,
>   Says the Lord,
> There are no grapes on the vine,
> And no figs on the fig tree;
> But its leaves wither and fall.

The imminent danger of invasion, of which the Judeans were now themselves aware, was felt by them to be caused by their sins. Consequently nothing but national destruction at the Lord's hand can be their lot. It is hard for them to accept it. But the peril in which it is putting them leads them to flee for protection to the fortified cities, yet condemned as they are by their own conscience, they have little hope of preserving their lives. The prophet is convinced that the Lord will cause Judah to drink "water of gall," as though it were a drink ordeal,[32] intended by the destruction it will surely cause, to prove that the nation is guilty. Although Judah, now in terror, acknowledges that it has sinned against the Lord (vs. 14), Jeremiah is sure that such an admission has come too late to stay the national doom.

Say the Judeans:

> 8:14 Why do we sit [still]?
>   Let us gather ourselves together,
> And go into the fortified cities,
>   And perish there.
> For the Lord our God has caused us to perish,
>   And has made us drink water of gall
> For we have sinned against him.

Already the vivid imagination of the prophet hears the snorting and neighing of the enemy's war horses in the old tribal area of Dan, northernmost section of Israel, and he sees Judah trembling in terror. The picture suddenly changes. The imminent invader is described under the metaphor of venomous serpents which no earthly power can hypnotize into harmlessness or rob their bite of its poison.[33]

[32] Cf. Num. 5:17-28.
[33] Delete vs. 15; it belongs rightly at 14:19b (see p. 47).

8:16 From Dan is heard
    The snorting of their horses;
    At the sound of the neighing of their stallions
    All the land shakes.
    And they shall come and devour the land and its produce,
    The city and those who dwell in it.
17 For lo, I am about to send among you
    Venomous serpents,
    Which cannot be charmed,
    And they will bite you
    Incurably.[34]

Is There No Balm in Gilead?

Jer. 8:18–9:1 is an individual lamentation in which we are given a vivid glimpse into the suffering heart of Jeremiah as he dealt with his sinful, refractory people. He thought not merely in terms of Jerusalem but of the whole area of Judah, and in imagination hears the cry of distress. Surely the Lord, Judah's true king, is in Zion. But the period for repentance is running out; the time of calamity is steadily drawing near: impenitent Judah is doomed. It is sick—morally and spiritually ill—with a fatal disease. It breaks the prophet's heart. We think instinctively as we read of the centuries-later lamentation of Jesus over Jerusalem. The horror of Judah's contemplated fate touches Jeremiah to the quick.

From whence can healing come to his fractured people? Healing makes him think of the fragrant resin from the storax tree, out of which a healing salve was made, a medicine for which near-at-hand Gilead was famous.[35] Is anything comparable to that, available to Judah to heal her open spiritual sores? Could Gilead send a physician to cure the spiritual wounds of Judah? If only Jeremiah could find relief in unending weeping for his people, who even now are as good as slain.

Not once in these words does he speak of the sin of Judah. His heart is all compassion. As Rudolph says at this point: "He is utterly the sympathetic son of his people. So we stand here not in the province of revelation but of human feeling. . . . But this is once again an indication of how very much attached Jeremiah was to his people and how bitter it must have been for him to be preacher of doom to them." [36]

[34] This, the first word in vs. 18, rightly belongs in vs. 17.
[35] Cf. 46:11; Gen. 37:25; 43:11; Ezek. 27:17. Gilead is across the Jordan from Anathoth and a little to the north.
[36] *Jeremia*, p. 57.

8:18   Because there is no healing of the sorrow upon me,
        My heart is faint.
19   Hark, the sound of a cry for help from the daughter of my people,
        From the land that stretches afar.[37]
        Is not the Lord in Zion?
        Is not her King in her?
20   The harvest has passed, the summer is ended,
        But we are not saved.
21   Because of the fracture of the daughter of my people I am broken,
        I mourn, horror has seized me.
22   Is there no balm in Gilead?
        Is there no physician there?
        Why then does there not come
        Healing for the daughter of my people?
9:1 [38] O that my head were waters,
        And my eyes a fountain of tears,
        That I might weep day and night
        Because of the slain of the daughter of my people!

The prophet is bitterly disappointed and disgusted with his people, and saddened to the core of his being by their sinfulness. Some of them were guilty of adultery (vs. 2). But it is the sins of the tongue that have touched him to the quick—lies, slander, deceitfulness, and crafty cunning. They are no congregation of the Lord but a conglomeration of deceivers. Their tongues are like bent bows which send the poison-dipped arrow—a false report, a faithless slander—to its mark. Or their disloyal words are comparable to the arrow sent treacherously against a neighbor with intent to slaughter (vs. 8). Falsehood, not faithfulness, is the law of the land (vs. 3). Ignorant of the Lord as they are, one evil deed follows swiftly on the heels of another (vs. 3). There is no such thing as neighborly confidence, but by cheating and trickery the one takes advantage of the other and every neighbor is a potential slanderer (vss. 4-5). Falsehood has become the rule. Deceit and lying have become habitual. They pervert good into evil and have not the least desire to reform their conduct (vs. 5). One deed of oppression follows hard upon an earlier one, and one fraud has scarcely been put over on the people when another is perpetrated (vs. 5). Truly it is a dark picture that Jeremiah here paints. Life thus portrayed is a hell on earth. And the

[37] So Cornill, as in Isa. 33:17; and delete vs. 19b with Volz, Jeremia, p. 109, "Why then have they provoked me to anger with their idols, with their foreign futilities?" as a later gloss in accordance with Jer. 7:18-19, which puts in the mouth of God an answer to the question of vs. 19b. In this poem of pure lament the Lord does not speak.

[38] Vs. 23 in the Hebrew is 9:1 in the English, and so on through chap. 9.

basic cause of all this corruption of the community, as the prophet makes
perfectly clear, is, in a word, the lack of true religion. The Lord they do not
know (vs. 3) and—a still more solemn judgment—they have utterly rejected him.

What a relief it would be if he could get away from it all, abandon his
corrupt people to their fate, and lodge as a temporary traveler might do in
the wilderness of Judah (9:2-4; 8:5-7). Thus in poignantly human words,
Jeremiah, the man, laments:

9:2　O that I might have in the wilderness
　　　　A traveler's lodging place,
　　　That I might leave my people,
　　　　And go away from them!
　　　For all of them commit adultery,
　　　　[They are] an assembly of deceivers.
3　　They bend their tongue like a bow;
　　　　Falsehood and not faithfulness
　　　　　Prevails in the land;
　　　For from evil to evil they go forth,
　　　　And the Lord they do not know.
4　　Let each be on guard against his neighbor,
　　　　And place not trust in any brother,
　　　For every brother takes insidious advantage,
　　　　And every neighbor walks about as a slanderer.
8 [39]　The arrow of the slaughterer is his tongue,
　　　　Treacherous are the words of his mouth,
　　　He speaks peace with his neighbor,
　　　　But in his heart he plans treachery to him,
5　　And each deceives his neighbor,
　　　　And they do not speak the truth.
　　　They have accustomed their tongues to speak lies,
　　　　They commit iniquity, they desire not to reform.
6　　Oppression follows oppression, deception follows deception;
　　　　They have rejected the Lord.[40]
7　　See, I am about to smelt them and will test them;
　　　　For how can I turn my gaze away from their evil?

PROCLAIM THE TERMS OF THE COVENANT

Jer. 11:1-14 comes to us through the Deuteronomic editor and so in its
present form dates from the exile. But there is unquestionably here a his-

[39] Transfer vs. 8 here with Rudolph.

[40] Omit. vs. 9 (Heb. vs. 8), which appears in 5:9, 29 in its correct context, but is here
intrusive.

torical kernel which comes from Jeremiah. In his able discussion of those speeches of Jeremiah which come to us through the Deuteronomic editor, Rudolph makes it emphatic that "they are not free creations by the editor but rest upon authentic utterances of the prophet. . . . Often original words of Jeremiah are literally taken up into them . . . [and] in half of the cases reports by Jeremiah himself lie at the basis of them." [41] Skinner likewise believes that "a trustworthy tradition lies behind the passage" in ch. 11.[42] In the present section the use of the first person in vs. 5*b* ("and I answered and said") and in vss. 6, 9 ("The Lord spoke to me") are evidence that a biographical account underlies the Deuteronomic editor's narrative.

The passage belongs to the earliest part of Jeremiah's prophetic ministry, from which, as we have seen (5:1-6; 6:9-14; 8:4-7), we have firsthand reports of his prophetic experience, when at the impulse from God he was observing carefully the inner spirit and outer conduct of his fellow countrymen. When Jeremiah preached the message of 11:1-14, he had already formed his own opinion as to the moral and spiritual condition of the Judean people.

He received an impulse from the Lord to pronounce the imprecation of God upon the men of Judah and Jerusalem. To sense the Semitic attitude toward the curse, Pedersen reminds us that in ancient Hebrew thought "curse is to sin as righteousness to blessing." The one cursed is "doomed to failure, . . . the paralysis is in him, whatever he puts his hand to." [43] There is accordingly a deep solemnity in the soul of Jeremiah, spokesman for God, as in obedience to the divine command he utters the Lord's imprecation upon his people.

The prophet goes back to that holy moment in the shaping of Israel when at Mount Sinai the Lord established his covenant with his people (Exod. 24:1-11). Jeremiah thus sweeps through more than six centuries of Israelite history, since under the leadership of Moses, Israel became the people of God and accepted the obligation of the "words" and "ordinances" as mediated to them through him, saying, "All the words which the Lord has spoken we will do" (Exod. 24:3).

In Jeremiah's thought the Judeans to whom he now addressed his message represented the unit of continuity with that mighty past. But did their lives give evidence of it? We feel the importance of this solemn moment when the young prophet felt the summons of God to declare the divine imprecation

---

[41] *Jeremia*, p. xv.
[42] *Prophecy and Religion*, p. 102.
[43] *Israel, Its Life and Culture*, I-II, 437-40.

upon Judah, the people of the covenant, and agreed to do it. Thus the Deuteronomic editor reports the episode:

11:1 The word which came to Jeremiah from the Lord, saying, 2 Speak to the men of Judah and the inhabitants of Jerusalem and 3 say to them, "Thus says the Lord, God of Israel, Cursed be the man who does not listen to the words of this covenant 4 which I commanded your fathers in the day when I brought them out from the land of Egypt, from an iron furnace, saying, Listen to my voice and do in accordance with all that I command you, and you shall be my people and I will be your God, 5 so as to confirm the oath which I took on that day toward your fathers, to give them a land flowing with milk and honey, as at this day." And I answered and said, "So be it, Lord."

The Lord now revealed to him in greater detail how he was to proceed. He was to go to the cities of Judah and to the open places in Jerusalem and proclaim to all Judeans who would listen to him the requirements which that covenant laid upon them. The fathers of present Judah had failed to heed God's voice, even though early and often God, through his spokesmen, had called them to obedience. Everyone had stubbornly held to his own way, heedless of God's will. And consequently the curse of God lay heavy upon them. Thus the prophet tells of his commission:

11:6 Now the Lord said to me, Proclaim all these words in the cities of Judah and in the streets of Jerusalem, saying: "Hear the words of this covenant and do them. 7 For I solemnly admonished your fathers in the day that I brought them out of the land of Egypt up to this day, early and often, saying, Listen to my voice. 8 But they would not listen nor would they bend down their ear, but they went on, each in the stubbornness of his evil heart, so I brought upon them all the words of this covenant which I had commanded them to observe, but which they did not observe."

There is heightened solemnity and deepened earnestness in the prophet's next words as he interprets God's revelation to him as to the enormity of Judah's sin. The nation of Judah has violated the solemn covenant to which it had obligated itself. Its conduct is nothing less than open treason against God. The nation is living in revolt against the God, upon relationship to whom Israel owes its very existence as a people. Judah is bound to God, leagued together with him. But by their crude return to former iniquities in which the Israelites had lived before the Lord became for them the exclusive object of their worship, the Judeans have broken the bond that unites them to their God. Thus Jeremiah reports God's message:

11:9 Now the Lord said to me: Open treason [44] has been detected in the men of Judah and in the inhabitants of Jerusalem. 10 They have turned back to the former iniquities of their fathers who refused to listen to my words, and they have followed other gods to serve them. The house of Israel and the house of Judah have broken my covenant which I made with their fathers.

Because of this open treason against God and his holy will, the Lord is about to bring upon the Judeans inescapable calamity. Their cries to him from the midst of it will be of no avail. For Judah's attitude to the Lord is that of open rebellion and renunciation. In their desperate straits the Judeans will cry for help to the pagan deities, to whom even now they are burning incense, but to no avail. The Lord commands his prophet to cease to intercede with him on behalf of corrupt Judah, for he will turn a deaf ear to his entreaty.

11:11 Therefore, thus says the Lord, See, I am about to bring upon them a calamity from which they shall not be able to escape and they will cry out to me, but I will not listen to them. 12 And the cities of Judah and the inhabitants of Jerusalem will go and cry to the gods to whom they are burning incense and they assuredly cannot save them at the time when they are distressed.[45] 14 So as for you, do not intercede for this people, do not lift up a ringing cry of entreaty or a prayer on their behalf, for I will not be hearing at the time when they call to me in the time of their trouble.

The Parable of the Destroyed Girdle

Early in Jeremiah's ministry, between his call in 626 and the Deuteronomic reform in 621, he received from God a strange impulse which issued in a type of prophetic appeal that was to be frequently employed by him, the acted prophetic parable. Let us listen to his own account of the episode.

13:1 Thus the Lord said to me: "Go and buy yourself a linen girdle and put it on your loins but do not let it go into the water." 2 So I bought the girdle as the Lord had said and put it on my loins. 3 Then the word of the Lord came to me a second time saying, 4 "Take the girdle that you bought, which is on your loins, and arise, go to the Euphrates and hide it there in a cleft of the rock." 5 So I went and hid it in the Euphrates just as the Lord had commanded me.

Many days passed which gave time for Jeremiah to obey this strange command. Then another impulse came to him by divine revelation.

[44] So The Bible, An American Translation, renders the important word qesher.
[45] Delete vs. 13, inserted here from 2:28b, as in the Septuagint, where it is original.

6 Many days had come to an end when the Lord said to me, "Arise, go to the Euphrates and take from there the girdle which I commanded you to hide there." 7 So I went to the Euphrates and I dug up the girdle and took [it] from the place where I had hidden it, and lo, the girdle was ruined and good for nothing.

The reference to the cleft of the rock would indicate that the girdle was hidden not near Babylon but in the upper part of the course of the Euphrates above Carchemish or even above Samosata, where, as Driver informs us, the river still flows between rocky sides.[46]

What is the meaning of this parable? Jeremiah had already sharply criticized the political trend on the part of Judah of seeking help (2:18) from Assyria, picturing the Judeans

> . . . on the way to Assyria
> To drink the waters of the River [i.e., the Euphrates]

In vss. 1-11 the Euphrates represents the religious counterpart of that trend. The Euphrates here stands for the Mesopotamian (Assyrian) influence in Judah, just as the Nile stands for Egyptian influence.

In this acted parable Jeremiah himself represents the Lord, and the lovely new linen girdle, such as priests wore, represents Judah, the Lord's people, deeply loved and prized by him. In Oriental life the girdle is a man's principal ornament, of which he is very proud. And about it there is an intimacy which suggests the person of the owner. For example, when Jonathan, Saul's son, made a covenant with David, because he loved him as his own soul, and gave to him his own robe and his armor, he also gave to him "even his sword and his bow and his girdle" (I Sam. 18:4). Thus the girdle was something prized and intimate, a thing of dignity and beauty.

Three times Jeremiah mentions the fact that the girdle was worn close to his body. As Volz says, "To the prophet it is very important to say how intimate and beautiful the relation was between the Lord and his people when they were close to his heart"[47] before that relationship was corrupted by the Mesopotamian influence that first poured in upon Judah in the days of King Manasseh, who paid tribute to Esarhaddon of Assyria.[48]

When Jeremiah parted with his girdle at the Lord's command and buried it below the surface in the rocky water-drenched river bank for many days, what happened to it symbolized the strong idolatrous influence upon the

46 In A. S. Peake, Jeremiah, II, 193.
47 Jeremia, p. 148.
48 Pritchard, Ancient Near Eastern Texts, p. 291.

religious constitution of the Lord's people, and gradually permeating them, at length made them "good for nothing."

We are in the earliest period of Jeremiah's ministry where, as Cornill says, "the predilection for foreign things over which the prophet Zephaniah laments so bitterly (Zeph. 1:4-6) reigned as yet unbroken in Judah and Jerusalem. The religious syncretism stood essentially under Assyrian influence which demoralized and enervated Judah." [49]

Continues the prophet:

13:8 **Then the word of the Lord came to me saying:** [50] 10 **This evil people— refusing to listen to my words, walking in the stubbornness of their heart, who have gone after other gods to serve and worship them—have become like this girdle which is good for nothing. 11 For just as a girdle clings to a man's loins, so have I made cling to me all the house of Judah, says the Lord, so as to become for me a people, an object of repute, praise, and renown, but they would not hear.**

But that clinging of Judah to the Lord like a prized girdle worn close to a man's body, as in those days when Israel was "something holy" to him, "the first fruits of its yield" (2:3a), has now become but a thing of the past.

The two long journeys to the Euphrates and back that are involved in this prophecy are not imaginary or visionary but real. The entire episode shows us the deep earnestness of the prophet in the delivery of his prophetic message, and demonstrates his ready, obedient yielding of himself to any prophetic impulse, however strange it may have seemed at the time to himself and to others. It must have been impressive to his hearers to have known of his errand and the very distances traveled by the prophet in obedience to the Lord's command must have weighted his words with solemnity and have lifted into searching consideration the destructive influences that had poured in upon Judah from the Euphrates area.

The attempt to identify P'rathah not with the Euphrates but with en fara (so H. Schmidt),[51] only a short distance northeast of Anathoth, while avoiding the difficulties of interpretation involved in two long journeys, misses the

---

[49] Cornill, Jeremia, p. 171; cf. Elmer A. Leslie, The Prophets Tell Their Own Story, pp. 160 ff.

[50] Cornill has conclusively shown that vs. 9, which comes from the supplementer of Jeremiah's work (so Peake) and reads, "Thus says the Lord, Like this shall be destroyed the pride of Judah and the great pride of Jerusalem," misses the essential point of the parable.

[51] Cf. H. Schmidt, Die Grossen Propheten, 2nd ed. pp. 219-20.

essential point of the parable. And the attempt to view the whole experience as a vision (so Rudolph) puts a forced and artificial interpretation upon a plain matter-of-fact narrative.

You Shall Not Take to Yourself a Wife

While Jer. 16:1-9 comes to us heavy laden with turns of speech that are characteristic of the Deuteronomic editor, the passage by its very nature has autobiographical data at its heart, and Rudolph is probably right in his suggestion that the narrative appears at this point because Jeremiah's denying for himself marriage and a family is a striking illustration of vs. 17 in the previous chapter.

> I sat not in the circle of merrymakers.
> .   .   .   .
> Before thy hand I sat alone,
> Because thou didst fill me with indignation.

From the Deuteronomist's point of view Jeremiah's celibacy was a sign for his nation, for Judah is doomed to destruction. Children born to Judean parents will die ingloriously along with their parents as the victims of war and famine.

Moreover, Jeremiah is not to participate in any of the familiar Palestinian lamentation rituals. His words here are informing as to the nature of the rites of lamentation, which are evidently not in themselves objectable to him. They include the shrill wailing of professional mourners, the lamenting cries of the bereaved, self-laceration, the tearing of the hair, the putting on of sackcloth and the singing of dirges.[52] Through his refusal to participate in these mourning rites—just as was the case with Ezekiel when his wife died (Ezek. 24:17)—he is to teach that Judah is suffering under the judgment of God.

Thus Jeremiah reports this revelation that came to him from God.[53]

16:2 **You shall not take to yourself a wife, says the Lord God of Israel, and you shall not have sons and daughters in this place. 3 For thus says the Lord concerning the sons and daughters born in this place, and concerning their mothers who bear them and their fathers who bring them into being in this place, 4 deaths from diseases shall they die. They shall not be mourned for and they shall not be buried. They shall be like dung on the surface of the ground and they shall come**

[52] Cf. also Amos 8:10; Isa. 22:12; Mic. 1:16; Deut. 14:1; Lev. 19:28.
[53] Omit vs. 1 with Septuagint, "Now the Word of the Lord came to me, saying."

to their end by the sword and famine, and their corpses will be carrion for the birds of the heavens and the beasts of the earth.

5 For thus says the Lord: Do not enter a house of wailing, and do not go to lament and do not show grief for them, for I have removed my welfare from this people, says the Lord, along with lovingkindness and compassion. 6 The distinguished and the ordinary shall die in this land. They shall not be buried nor lamented for, and they shall not lacerate themselves and they shall not make themselves bald for them. 7 They shall not break bread of mourning for consolation over their death, and they shall not give one a cup of consolation to drink with respect to one's father or one's mother. 8 Nor shall you enter a household of feasting to sit with them, to eat and drink. 9 For thus says the Lord of hosts, God of Israel, Lo, I am about to put to an end in this place—before your very eyes and in your own lifetime—the voice of exultation, the voice of rejoicing, the voice of the bridegroom and the voice of the bride.

Three Kings, A Prophet, and a Reform

621-605—REIGNS OF JOSIAH, JEHOAHAZ (609) AND JEHOIAKIM (EARLY 608-605)

IN 621, THE EIGHTEENTH YEAR OF THE REIGN OF KING JOSIAH, HILKIAH THE HIGH PRIEST FOUND WHAT HE DESIGNATED AS "THE BOOK OF THE LAW" IN the temple, and delivered it to Shaphan, the secretary of the Judean state, who informed the king of the discovery and read the book to him. The king commanded Hilkiah the high priest, Ahikam the son of Shaphan, Achbor the son of Micaiah, and Shaphan the secretary, to inquire of the Lord as regards the lawbook. This delegation consulted Huldah the prophetess, whose counsel led the king to call an assembly of the elders of Judah and Jerusalem in the temple.

Standing by "the pillar" in the temple, the king read the contents of the lawbook to a great assembly consisting of "all the men of Judah and all the inhabitants of Jerusalem, and the priests and the prophets, all the people, both small and great." He made a covenant before the Lord to obey the laws of the book, in which all the people joined, and on the basis of it he put into action the Deuteronomic reform which is described in detail in II Kings 23:1-24.

While this lawbook was discovered in 621, it probably was written ca. 650, during the reign of King Manasseh, who was the puppet of Assyria, and who officially introduced into Judah many idolatrous cultic rites from Assyria and the whole Mesopotamian area, including the worship of the host of heaven and child sacrifice, even burning his own son as an offering (II Kings 21:5-6). He also rebuilt the high places which King Hezekiah had destroyed (II Kings 18:4) and erected altars for Baal and made an Asherah, the symbol of the female Canaanite deity. The author of the lawbook

90

realized that there was no likelihood whatever that such reforms as the law demanded could be set in motion during King Manasseh's reign. Hence this important document was laid up in the temple in the hope that it would eventually come to official attention and its contemplated reforms be set in motion.

The author of the book of Deuteronomy is not known. But he was a man who was deeply moved by the prophetic teaching of Amos, Hosea, Isaiah, and Micah. A reader familiar with the message of these watchmen of Israel will hear concrete echoes and overtones of their teaching as he reads this first edition of the lawbook. Yet as he reads Deut. 16:1-18, he will also see that while those prophets were sharply critical of the sacrificial cultus of Israel and Judah, and of the pilgrimages to the temple, this lawbook makes pilgrimage and sacrifice obligatory, although to be legitimate it must be centered at the one authoritative place—the Jerusalem temple. The author of the book uses the technique of putting his law into the mouth of Moses, who gave to Israel its original impetus toward law, as though it had been spoken by him from the plains of Moab. He designates the temple at Jerusalem "the sanctuary which the Lord your God chooses out of all your tribes as the seat of his presence" (Deut. 12:5). The law specifically requires that all sanctuaries other than that of Jerusalem shall be utterly and finally destroyed. The law is detailed and specific: "You must be sure to destroy all the sanctuaries . . . on high mountains, on hills, and under every spreading tree; you must tear down their altars, smash their sacred pillars [maccēbhôth], burn up their sacred poles ['ashērîm], and cut down the carved images [p'silîm] of their gods, obliterating the very name of them from that sanctuary" (Deut. 12:2-3).

Thus the reform aimed at purifying the worship of the Lord from all increments of the Canaanite Baal worship as it was still being carried on at the high places which the Israelites had taken over for the worship of their God. This was to be accomplished by utterly destroying these worship centers and uprooting the worship, as there practiced for centuries, from Judean life. It also aimed at exalting the Jerusalem temple as the one legitimate sanctuary for the entire nation, thus making it necessarily a pilgrimate sanctuary for Judah.

The author took the spiritual religion of the prophets along with their penetrating ethical demands, and codified it in concrete laws where justice, mercy, and humility became legal requirements. Festivals in the temple and pilgrimages to the temple were required not as tribute to God but as expressions of gratitude to God.

T. K. Cheyne thus suggestively describes the reform:

> Both in the capital and in the provinces, as far even as Bethel and the cities of Samaria (where a new heathenism had joined itself to the old heretical worship, 2 Kgs. 17: 29-31), a work of purification by destruction was carried out, which is quite unique in the earlier chapters of the ancient history of religion. Where in fact can we find a parallel to the zeal of Josiah in the Semitic East till we come to Mohammed? [1]

The Deuteronomist was a great mediating mind. Robert H. Pfeiffer discerningly says that he was "a man inspired by the prophet's ideals but simultaneously well aware of the current trend and of practical possibilities," and that he "effected a compromise between the two antagonistic religions and thus became the founder of Judaism." [2]

Josiah was twenty-six years old when this new law of the land was promulgated. If Jeremiah were about nineteen years of age when in the thirteenth year of Josiah's reign he felt called to be a prophet, he was not much older than twenty-four years when the Deuteronomic reform was launched. It is important to think of Josiah and Jeremiah as contemporaries in Judah, one of them one of the greatest kings Judah ever had, the other the greatest of the Hebrew prophets. Jeremiah preached, as we have seen, from 626-621. Then we have no message from him that can be dated with confidence until 609, when after the tragic death of King Josiah and the enthronement of King Jehoiakim, his active and public prophetic ministry is resumed.

Jeremiah held King Josiah in high regard. In a sharp and fearless condemnation of the then-reigning King Jehoiakim, he compares the latter's self-seeking, ambitious, voracious, and cruel spirit to that of Josiah, Jehoiakim's father, saying to Jehoiakim:

> 22:15b As for your father—did he not eat and drink?
>   And it went well with him;
>   And he exacted justice and righteousness,
>   16   He pled the cause of the poor and needy,
>   Is not this to know me? says the Lord.

[1] *Jeremiah: His Life and Times*, p. 60.
[2] *Introduction to the Old Testament*, p. 179.

THE SILENCE OF JEREMIAH'S PROPHETIC VOICE

Josiah lived for twelve years after this reform on the basis of Deuteronomy was launched. Jeremiah had accordingly observed the total official career of the monarch who at his tragic death was only thirty-nine. How are we to account for the seeming silence of Jeremiah as a watchman of Judah from 621-609?

Volz is probably right in his maintenance that Jeremiah's preaching in 3:1-5 and 3:19–4:4 prepared the way for the reform under Josiah. Volz says: "It discloses to us that through Jeremiah there took place under Josiah a turn to the true religion. His preaching prepared the way for the reform." [3] No doubt a reform carried out by an act of the state had its limitations, especially as viewed by a man such as Jeremiah, with his profound inwardness of soul. But as Volz further says: "He greeted the proclamation of Josiah joyfully, bringing as it did the fulfillment of many of his wishes, the elimination of the worship of celestial bodies, of the worship at the high places, and of superstitions, and the renewal oath (4:2) of the entire nation to obey the Lord as the one sole God" (cf. II Kings 23:3 ff.).

There can be no doubt that Josiah had Jeremiah on his side as he took advantage of the weakness of Assyria to free his people both from political dependence upon Assyria and from the Assyrian cultic intrusions (II Kings 21:1-9) which had been introduced into the temple worship by King Manasseh, the grandfather of Josiah. He greeted the reform as a welcome ally because of the struggle against everything of heathen nature which it embodied, and the demand for social thinking and action which it expressed he approved from his very soul.[4] Furthermore, we can best interpret Jeremiah's silence during the remainder of the reign of Josiah as implying his concurrence in the aims of the reform.

Moreover, the reign of Josiah represents a remarkable period in Judah both from the angle of religious progress and from that of national brilliancy. Freed from the heavy hand of Assyria, especially after 612, when Nineveh had fallen, Josiah was able to extend his rule over Judah. His sweep of control reached as far north as Bethel, once the seat of a royal palace for the kings of the northern kingdom of Israel and the location of the king's sanctuary (Amos 7:13). That altar and high place were destroyed (II Kings 23:15), and people from cities that had been within the limits of that kingdom—Shechem, Shiloh, and even Samaria—now worshiped at the Jerusalem temple (Jer. 41:5). Ps. 122, with its enthusiastic com-

---

[3] *Jeremia*, p. 42.
[4] Cf. Rudolph, *Jeremia*, p. 69.

mitment to the requirements of pilgrimage to the one legitimate sanctuary of Jerusalem, its sense of Jerusalem as all Israel's unifying bond, and its high respect for the ruling monarch, probably dates from the reign of Josiah.

In all probability Jer. 30–31 were written in this period of Jeremiah's life. These chapters are among the finest both in thought and in feeling which came from his soul. It is reasonable to conclude that the national and religious achievement of King Josiah, with his extension of his kingdom over the area of the former Northern Kingdom, led Jeremiah to brood over the fate of these northern exiles. Jeremiah never forgot that he was a northerner, and such a picture as he gives of Rachel weeping over her children (31:15) interprets the prophet's yearning for these exiles, who along with their descendants, since 734 have been in Assyria or Assyria-dominated areas. To speak to them was impossible, so the prophet resorted to writing and chs. 30–31 are the result.

These chapters date between 621 and 612 and most likely nearer to 612, when Nineveh fell, than to 621. No prophet was better informed than Jeremiah about historical events contemporary with his times. He knew of the rapid decline of Assyria. In his thought the weakening of that dominant power, and the consequent relaxing of its control over the peoples it had so long dominated, opened the way to the possibility of the return of the descendants of those Israelite exiles to their beloved Palestinian home.

SALVATION FOR THE EXILES OF NORTHERN ISRAEL

The opening verse of ch. 30 is editorial and serves to unite chs. 30–31 with the entire book. In chs. 27–29 the prophet dealt specifically with the problem of salvation for the exiles from Judah. The final editor of the book most likely has placed here chs. 30–31 because they deal primarily with the salvation which lay in the Lord's purpose for the exiles from Israel, the Northern Kingdom.[5] It is quite understandable that here and there in this section (30:3-4, 8-9, and in 31:1, 23-30, 38-40) the insertion "of Judah" has been made by the Deuteronomic editor in the aim of claiming for Judah as well the anticipations of salvation and restoration which the Lord awakened in the prophet's soul for the exiles of the Northern Kingdom.

The judgment of Rudolph seems reasonable, that these two chapters, cleared of later accretions, date from the reign of King Josiah, after he had regained Samaria and Galilee for Judah, and so by the reconquest of much territory of the former Northern Kingdom laid the ground work for hope that the Lord would graciously permit the descendants of its former popula-

[5] Cf. G. A. Smith, *Jeremiah*, pp. 293-94, who designates them "Oracles of Hope."

tion to return to the beloved homeland.[6] Otto Procksch likewise interprets Josiah as intentionally and vigorously pursuing his aim to win new territory for the Judean State, pushing forward to Bethel in the north and Ekron in the northwest. And on the newly won perspective of Deuteronomy which viewed Canaan as the inheritance of Israel after Nineveh's fall in 612, he had the opportunity to win back Galilee as well.

Jeremiah is here commanded to write down these two chapters which now follow. He writes because the northern exiles are not where they can hear the prophetic word, and the same impulse led him to write to the northern exiles that led him later to send a letter to the Judean exiles in Babylon. We sense here in unique degree the power and reach of the written prophetic word as the prophet now conceives it. Now he writes at the Lord's command, even as for some fourteen years he has spoken. This written message to the exiles of the Northern Kingdom and their descendants shows that while we have no spoken message from Jeremiah datable between 621 and 609, we do have this written one, but intended for a quite different audience.

30:1 The word which came to Jeremiah saying, 2 Thus says the Lord: You are to write all the words which I have spoken to you in a book. 3 For lo, days are coming, says the Lord, when I will turn the fortunes of my people Israel, says the Lord, and I will bring them back to the land which I gave to their fathers that they might possess it. 4 Now these are the words which the Lord spoke concerning Israel.[7]

We are now suddenly transported in imagination to the exiles taken from the northern kingdom of Israel, who in 734, when Pekah was king, were carrier away from Ijon, Abel-beth-Maacah, Janoah, Kedesh, Hazor, Gilead, and from Galilee and all the land of Naphtali (II Kings 15:29). And our thoughts also turn back to 721, when Samaria, capital of the Northern Kingdom, fell to Shalmaneser V and Sargon, and when the inhabitants of the Northern Kingdom were carried captive to Assyria and settled there as well as in certain other Mesopotamian areas and among the Medes (II Kings 17:6).

These Northern Israelites and their descendants have now been in exile for over a century. They are imaginatively pictured as in great distress. The prophetic writer colors his picture with woes characteristic of the time of the end. But the situation to which such language is here attached is

---

[6] *Op. cit.* pp. 159-60; see also Otto Procksch, *König Josia,* 46-47.

[7] Omit "and Judah" as an addition intended to adapt chs. 30–31 for use in the synagogue; cf. Volz; *Jeremia,* p. 281.

realistic enough—Israelites far away from their homeland. The picture presents them in woe; their voices trembling in terror, strong men in such travail as will usher in a new age, living through a darkness that but precedes the dawn.

> 30:5 A voice atremble I hear,
>   Terror with no peace.
> 6 Ask, now, and see
>   If men ever give birth.
>   Why see I every man
>   With his hands upon his loins like a woman in travail?
>   And all faces are transformed,
>   They have become pale.
> 7 For so great is that day,
>   That none other is like it.
>   Yes, a time of distress it is for Jacob,
>   But out of it he shall be saved.

The yoke of Assyrian dominion is soon to be broken. Assyria is about to fall. The Israelite captives whom the Assyrian has taken in his ruthless campaigns will no longer be subjects of a pagan and foreign power, but they will serve the Lord and a legitimate Judean king of David's line will rule over them.

30:8 And it shall be on that day, says the Lord of hosts, that I will break the yoke from off his neck, and I will snap his bonds, and they will serve foreigners no more. 9 But they will serve the Lord their God and David their king, whom I will raise up for them.

The prophet now represents the Lord as speaking not of Jacob but directly to him, whose name here stands for all northern Israel. The Lord calls him tenderly "my servant Jacob." There is no cause for dismay. Near at hand is rescue for the captive Israelites and their exiled descendants. Disturbances caused by their ruthless captors, terror born of heartless political domination which they have experienced is at an end. Tenderly again comes God's address, "My servant Jacob," his assurance of his presence with the Israelites in exile and his purpose to save and restore them to their homeland. There will take place international revolution in which nations will be destroyed. Yet for Israel this will not bring destruction but tempered punishment such as will chasten the Lord's people.

30:10 So as for you—fear not, my servant Jacob,
  Says the Lord,
   And be not dismayed, Israel;
  For lo, I am about to save you from afar,
  And your descendants from the land where they are captive,
  And Jacob shall return and be undisturbed;
   Yes, he shall rest secure with none to terrify.
 11 As for you, fear not, my servant Jacob,
   For I am with you to help you,
  Though I will make a complete destruction among all the nations,
   Where I have dispersed you,
  Surely in dealing with you I will not make a complete destruction,
   But I will chasten you in just measure,
   Though I will not leave you unpunished.

The Lord knows the desperate plight of long-banished Israel. He has been broken by fracture, seemingly beyond repair (II Kings 15:29; 17:6). He is sore from the harsh treatment of those who had lured the kingdom of Israel into alliance, as when Assyria had inveigled Israel into league with it (II Kings 15:19-20), then abandoned and scattered it. The Lord too seems to have dealt with Israel as though it were his enemy. But God's punishment of his people, cruel as it seems, is intended by him to be disciplinary and corrective (vs. 14b). And the severity of the punishment meted out by the Lord to Israel is not proportionate to the greatness of the nation's guilt (vs. 15).

But God is now at the point of bringing restoration and healing to his "expelled" and "unwanted" people (vs. 17). For Assyria even now is hastening to its doom. The prophet writes these words when the fall of Nineveh is imminent. The great plunderer of the small nations of the Middle East is himself about to become spoil (vs. 16).[8] We sense in vs. 16 the atmosphere of revolution wherein mighty Assyria is at the point of collapse and a new international alignment in the whole Middle East is imminent.

  30:12 For thus says the Lord:
    Incurable is your fracture,
     Sore your blow;
   13 There are no remedies for the wound,
     There is no healing for you.
   14 All your lovers have forgotten you,
     They do not care about your welfare;
    For with a blow [as] of an enemy have I struck you,
     A cruel correction.

[8] Cf. Nah. 3:4-7, 11-13, 18-19.

15 Why do you cry because of your wound,
      That your pain is incurable?
    Because your iniquity is [so] great, your sins [so] many,
      I did these things to you.
17 But as for me—I will bring restoration to you
      And I will heal you of your wounds,
        Says the Lord.
    For "one expelled" they have called you
      For which no one seeks.
16 [9] Therefore all who consume you will be consumed;
      And all your adversaries will go into captivity.
    And those who plunder you will themselves be for booty,
      And all who spoil you I will bestow as spoil.

The Lord is now at the point of restoring the northern section of Israel
to its homeland as it was before 734. The cities will be rebuilt upon their
former sites (tells) which they had occupied before the destructions and
banishments wrought by the Assyrian campaigns of Tiglath-pileser (734),
Shalmaneser V (724-2), and Sargon II (722-1) had taken place. The palaces
will be rebuilt upon their own foundations. Then there shall be heard
again in other restored towns fragments of their sacred songs of thanksgiving
sung by the joyful population, likewise the happy laughter of the people.
The population will grow in numbers and in sense of importance. The
great days of the past, dating back even to the era of the Davidic monarchy,
when Israel and Judah were one, will be restored, including as an established feature the public political assembly of the people (cf. I Kings 12:3),
representative of the entire kingdom. Any people that threatens restored
Israel will become liable to the Lord's punishment, and Israel will be able
to defend itself against outer attack. The ruler of Israel, thus restored, will
not be a foreign monarch but one of themselves (vs. 21), and the Lord will
place him in his position with dignity and endow him with the right of
access to the Lord, and on the king's own part, with a high consciousness of
social responsibility.

30:18 Thus says the Lord:
      Lo, I am about to restore as of yore the tents of Jacob,
        And will have compassion on his dwelling places;
      Cities shall be rebuilt upon their own tells,
        Yes, palaces shall rest upon their own ground plan.
19   Songs of thanks will sound out from them,
        And the voices of those laughing.

[9] Transfer after vs. 17, following Rudolph.

I will increase them and they shall not be diminished.
And I will show them honor and they shall not be insignificant.
20 His [Jacob's] sons will be as of old,
    And his assembly will be established before me;
    I will punish any who oppress him
21   And he will be more powerful than they.
Their ruler will come forth from their own midst;
    And I will present him and let him draw near to me,
For who indeed is this, who dares hazard his life [10]
In drawing near to me, says the Lord.[11]

In 30:23–31:1 the prophet gives a prediction of the Lord's threatening judgment which is about to burst like a tempest upon the wicked within the community. Nor will the storm dissolve until the full purging power of that judgment has been expressed. Then the entire community of Israel, north and south, thus purged, will acknowledge the Lord as their God. Says the prophet:

30:23 Lo, the tempest of the Lord has gone forth,
    A whirling tempest;
    Over the heads of the wicked it whirls.
24   The anger of the Lord will not return,
    Until it has accomplished, until it has carried out,
    The purposes of his heart.
    In the end of the days,
    You will consider it diligently with understanding.

31:1 In that time, says the Lord, I will be God to all the families of Israel.
And they shall be my people.

Again Will You Plant Vineyards on the Mountains of Samaria

In 31:2-6 the prophet, now in awed reminiscence, goes back to the beginnings of the life of Israel as a people. This people, now since 721 but the survivors from the sword of the powerful Assyrian war machine, in the early days had been dealt with graciously by the Lord. Before they had found "rest" from their wilderness wanderings in the land of Canaan, God had promised his people that he would go with them. There in the wilder-

[10] Lit., "who gives his heart in pledge." The prophet emphasizes the solemn responsibility resting upon the ruler and a high sense of social commitment on his part. The construction of the perfect tense here expresses a lively sense of awe; cf. Driver, *Tenses*, 20 (2) ; Davidson, *Syntax*, 4: R2.

[11] Omit with Septuagint vs. 22. It is here premature but rightly belongs in 31:33.

ness—so the ancient epic story of Exod. 33:1-16 tells us—the Lord commanded Moses and his people to go up from that wilderness halt to the
land which God had promised on oath to Abraham, Isaac, and Jacob (Exod.
33:1). The Lord assured Moses of his presence with his people, "My presence
will go with you, and I will give you rest (Exod. 33:14)." There in that
wilderness in the long ago Israel experienced God's grace. Five times in our
prophet's summary of the beloved story, Israel's experience in the wilderness of "finding grace" from the Lord is told. But that was in the distant
pass, and now for over a century the Northern Israelites have been exiles,
their nation destroyed, and they themselves banished to Assyria, northern
Mesopotamia, and Media (II Kings 17:6). They felt disgraced, rejected
of God, and removed from his sight (II Kings 17:18).

But now, far away though they are from Palestine, the Lord again appears to his people, to this same exiled, scattered, and destroyed northern
kingdom of Israel—"survivors of the [Assyrian] sword" (vs. 2). The Lord
tells Israel that he still loves him with an everlasting love (vs. 3). Still, after
these many years he is dealing with his people in lovingkindness (ḥeṣedh).
Indeed, his love for his people had never ceased. Even when he was punishing Israel, chastening him in just measure (30:11b), it was out of his
lovingkindness that he was dealing with his people. Now it is his will to
restore them to their old domain in Palestine. Again will he build his
people. Again the virgin daughter, Israel, will give carefree expression to
joy (vs. 4). Again upon the beloved mountain of Samaria vineyards will
flourish, and those who plant them will themselves begin to use their fruit
(vs. 5). Just as the ancient story, as told in Exod. 33, had five times emphasized God's "grace" in the early epoch of Israel's life, so now three times
appears the word "again" (vss. 4-5), each time marking a new manifestation
of his grace to his exiled people as he opens to them the gates of new life.

In the days of their exile they were deprived of pilgrimage to the great
sanctuaries of Bethel and Dan. But King Josiah had recently swept into
Judean control considerable regions that were in the area of what had
formerly been the northern kingdom of Israel, and already remnants of the
old Israelite population from three of their formerly great cities, Shechem,
Shiloh, and Samaria, now worshiped at the Jerusalem temple (41:5). But,
says the prophet, a day is coming, and indeed is near at hand, when from the
hills of Ephraim the watchmen will again sound out the call to pilgrimage,
not to Bethel or Dan, Gilgal or Shechem, but now to Zion! For it is only
recently that Deuteronomy has been accepted as the law of the land and
Zion—the prophet's beloved name for Jerusalem—has been made the one

pilgrimage goal for all Israel (Deut. 16:2, 11, 15-16). From hill to hill the call to pilgrimage resounds (vs. 6).

31:2 Thus says the Lord:
They found grace as in the wilderness;
A nation [made up] of survivors of the sword,
Israel on the way to its rest.
3 From afar the Lord appeared to him.
With everlasting love have I loved you, (says the Lord),
Therefore I have continued to deal with you in lovingkindness.
4 Again will I build you, and you will be rebuilt,
Virgin daughter of Israel;
Again will you deck yourself with tambourines,
And go forth in the dance of the merry ones.
5 Again will you plant vineyards
On the mountains of Samaria;
Those planting vineyards will begin to use the fruit of them.
6 For a day is [coming] when watchmen will cry
On the highlands of Ephraim,
"Arise and let us go to Zion,
To the Lord, our God."

The Lord now calls upon the people of Palestine to proclaim the glad news that the "remnant of Israel" is returning home (vs. 7). The Lord himself is gathering them from the faraway regions where they are now dwelling—from Media, Assyria, Babylonia, and Syria. The afflicted and those in delicate condition as well as the others are part of the great returning "congregation" (vs. 8). They left Israel as tearful captives bound for exile under the harsh regimen of the Assyrian military officers. But they will return led along by the discerning, consoling, providing, and compassionate God himself. Jeremiah here uses Ephraim, even as had Hosea (11:8) before him, as his tender, and indeed favorite, name for Israel. The Lord, in directing Pharaoh to let Israel go, had said, "Israel is my first-born son" (Exod. 4:22-23). We do not have in vs. 9 any comparison of Israel with Judah. To Northern Israel is here carried over in its entirety that which elsewhere concerns all Israel.[12] The Lord's "first-born" refers to the prophetic idea of God's choice of all Israel,[13] which was not due to any favoritism but rises out of his purpose of mission for his people (vs. 9).

[12] Cf. Rudolph, Jeremia, p. 165.
[13] Cf. Amos 3:2. We are here at one of the roots of Deutero-Isaiah's concept of Israel's mission (Isa. 49:5-6).

31:7 **For thus says the Lord:**
  Raise a ringing cry for Jacob,
    And cry out in joy on the top of the mountains
      Proclaim, praise, and say,
  "The Lord has delivered his people,
    The remnant of Israel."
8 Lo, I am bringing them from the north;
    And will gather them from remote parts of the earth.
  Among them are the blind and lame, the pregnant and she who is about to
      bear;
    As a great congregation they will return.
9 Lo, they went out with weeping,
    But with consolations will I lead them along;
  I will bring them to rivers of water,
    On a level road on which they will not stumble.
  For I am a father to Israel,
    And Ephraim—he is my first-born.

While in vs. 7 the land of Palestine was called upon to praise the Lord
because of the deliverance of Jacob (Ephraim, vs. 9), in vs. 10 the Lord's
word comes to the nations to take up the glad message and declare to the
distant isles of the Mediterranean that scattered Israel is about to be
"gathered," redeemed from foreign domination and restored to Palestine.
There Israel will experience radiant prosperity with abundance of grain,
wine, and oil, and with fecundity in the flock and the herd. Israel will
also experience a comparable recovery of inner spirit. The young and the
old will dance together for joy to the rhythm of the tambourine.

In vs. 13b the Lord himself speaks, and, as he has already intimated, the
sad mourning, which had long become Ephraim's habitual attitude, will
now be turned by him to glad rejoicing. The similarity of situation, the
promise of return from exile, met with also in vss. 8-9, accounts for the
accord of this section with Deutero-Isaiah, but there is no literary dependence.

31:10 Hear the word of the Lord, O nations;
      And declare [it] among the distant isles,
        And say:
      The scatterer of Israel will gather him together,
        And will keep him as a shepherd [keeps] his flock;
  11 For the Lord has ransomed Jacob,
      And will redeem him from the hand of one stronger than he.
  12 And they will come and cry for joy on the mountains,
      And will be radiant over the good things of the Lord,

Over grain and new wine and oil,
    And over the young of flock and herd,
    And their soul will be like a watered garden,
    It will never languish again.
13 Then the virgins will exult in the dance,
    The young and the aged together,
    And I will turn their mourning into rejoicing
    I will comfort them and cheer them out of their sorrow.
14b And my people shall abound in my goodness,
    Says the Lord.[14]

The prophet, himself a Benjamite, was familiar with the grave of Rachel in the vicinity of Ramah just within the old tribal area of Benjamin.[15] Rachel, wife of Jacob, was the mother of Joseph (Gen. 30:24) and Benjamin (Gen. 35:18), and so was viewed as the ancestress of the North Israelites. Jeremiah knew of the popular belief of the continued existence of the dead by their grave, and on the basis of it creates the moving, imaginative picture of Rachel, "mother" of the North Israelites, weeping tears of lamentation over the lot of her "children" who have ceased to exist. We sense the Oriental color as Jeremiah portrays her sobbing, sighing, and weeping bitter tears as she cries, "Alas, they are no more!" But God hears her lamenting words. He rewards her deep motherly concern by assuring her that her "children" will return home (vss. 16-17).

The prophet has already made it clear that the exile of the North Israelites was a punishment. Cruel as it had seemed, it was nonetheless intended by the Lord as a correction (30:14). So now in vss. 18-19, Ephraim (Jeremiah's tender and beloved name for North Israel), still in exile, turns to God in confession and repentance. Ephraim recognizes his banishment as the divine chastisement because of his stubborn, unruly spirit. He longs now to return to Palestine and prays for restoration to his old domain. He cannot, of course, turn back unless the emancipation of God should make it possible (vs. 18). Vividly and with sensitive psychological insight, Jeremiah pictures the North Israelites after having turned away from God, now turning back in repentance. We feel the spiritual process of response to God's call as Ephraim comes through repentance to growing insight, and through deepened insight to a yet profounder mood of repentance, even deep grief such as an Oriental would express by beating upon his thighs.

[14] Delete vs. 14a as representing a priestly addition quite foreign to the thought of Jeremiah: "And I will satisfy the soul of the priests with abundance."

[15] The tradition, dating from the fourth century A.D., that the grave of Rachel was located near Bethlehem rests upon the false scribal insertion, "that is, Bethlehem," in Gen. 35:19; cf. Rudolph, *op. cit.*, p. 167.

Ephraim is deeply ashamed over the sins committed against his Lord in the days of his youth when he was still a nation, and he stands before his Lord humiliated and disgraced, yet accepting in sincerity the moral responsibility for the situation in which he now is (vs. 19).

To the burning tears of Rachel and to the humbled heart agitation of Ephraim, the Lord's "son," God now graciously responds (vs. 20). We are in the mood of Hosea's great word (11:8-9), as Jeremiah now reveals his insight into the heart of God. We are likewise here at one of the deep roots of New Testament teaching as to the fatherhood of God. God's love toward Ephraim is that of a father to a son whom he must chasten with punishment. Yet with every stroke of chastisement upon Ephraim, he holds him in his heart with deepened, not lessened, tenderness. The heart of God "thrills" toward his wayward son, and with detailed recollection yet with individualizing sympathy. For the spring of all God's dealings with Ephraim, his unruly son, is his "own boundless compassion" (vs. 20).

31:15 Thus says the Lord:
    Hark! A lamentation is heard in Ramah,
      A bitter weeping!
    Rachel weeping over her children,
      Refusing to be comforted,
    Over her children—Alas, they are no more.
16   Thus says the Lord:
    Restrain your voice from weeping,
      And your eyes from tears.
    For there is yet reward for your suffering,
      And they [Rachel's children] shall return from the land of the enemy.
17 Yes, there is hope for your future,
      And children will return to their own domain.
18 I have sensitively heard Ephraim's deep agitation:
    "Thou hast chastised me and I let myself be chastened
      Like an unruly calf;
    Restore me that I may return.
      For thou art the Lord my God.
19 For after I had turned away
      I turned back, I repented;
    And after I came to insight
      I smote on my thigh.
    I am ashamed, yes, even humiliated,
      For I feel responsible for the disgrace of my youth."
20 Is not Ephraim a precious son to me?
      Is he not a darling child?
    That the oftener I estrange myself toward him,
      Yet the more do I remember him.

> Therefore my heart thrills toward him;
> I must deal with him in boundless compassion,
> Says the Lord.

In vss. 21-22 Jeremiah, in the Lord's name, summons the Northern Israelites to return to their Palestinian home. He now addresses them as "virgin
Israel" (vs. 21) and "daughter" (vs. 22). On his part God has done all in
his power to prepare the way. Now they must act. But they must organize
their return to their cities. They must send out men to set up clear markings
so that they will keep to the highway. Indeed, it is by the very highway on
which their ancestors went out, when as prisoners they were forcibly taken
away by the Assyrian army, that they are to return. It is evident from vs. 22
that Jeremiah anticipated considerable hesitancy on the part of these northern exiles in responding promptly to God's call. Many of them would
hesitate in grave skepticism, "How do we know that it will not all happen
again, that after our homeland has been resettled we shall not all be carried off into captivity by another conquering nation?"

To this hesitant, delaying, skeptical attitude of the northern exiles the
prophet now gives a mighty assurance. The restoration of North Israel to
its homeland represents not only a natural longing on the part of the exiles
but it is of the essence of God's will. Yes, more—it is a consummation to be
brought about by the creative power of God. Indeed, it is to be a new creation which depends not alone upon the obedience and the return of Israel,
but is made possible in the last analysis by what God himself will there
create for and with his people (vs. 22).

> 31:21 Set up for yourself guideposts,
>   Place for yourself waymarks,
>   Set your mind toward the highway,
>   The way which you went.
>   Turn back, virgin Israel,
>   Turn back to these your cities.
>   22 How long will you dillydally,
>   Thou daughter of disgraceful delay,
>   For I am about to create a new thing
>   In the land of [your] return.

THE NEW COVENANT

It is with this climactic thought (vs. 22) that the new covenant passage in
Jeremiah (31:31-34) was originally connected.[16] The old covenant at Sinai,

---

[16] For 31:23-26 see pp. 326-27; for 31:27-28 see p. 327; for 31:29-30 see p. 322.

was made by the Lord with their Ephraimite forefathers whom the Lord had led out of Egypt. Then the people had agreed to keep the covenant: "All that the Lord has directed we will obediently do" (Exod. 24:4-7).

It was during the reign of Josiah that great new thoughts came to Jeremiah. He had seen the instruction and the teaching which accompanied Josiah's attempt to put into effect the renewed ancient covenant (II Kings 23:1-3). He had seen that great as it was, all this had not sufficed to bring about in Judah the actual doing of the will of God. Judah had not kept its part of the agreement and therefore God is obligated to discipline his negligent people and must reject them (vs. 32).

But why had Israel failed to keep the covenant? In 31:18b the prophet represents North Israel as praying, "Restore me that I may return." The law of the Lord upon which the covenant was based remains unchanged. But as Rudolph has finely said, the new is herein, that now the petition of vs. 18b is fulfilled, that "all without exception will possess the knowledge of the Lord, the right understanding of God," which includes the doing of righteousness. Accordingly, there will be no need of one teaching the other, for each person will have for himself the necessary insight into the divine mind and heart. Accordingly, since there will then be no breaking of the divine law, there will no more be on God's part any punishment.

The old covenant was written on tablets of stone (Exod. 31:18; 34:27-28) or in a book (Exod. 24:4, 7). The Israelites confronted it as something apart from themselves, standing over against them as requirements to which they were obligated to conform. But the new covenant they will carry in the heart; as Rudolph says, "They are inwardly one with it, so that the knowledge of the law and obedience to it coincide." Moreover, as a sure token that the old order is conclusively done away—that is, the disobedience on the part of the nation and the consequent wrath on the part of God—the Lord forgives their sin. This word, the forgiveness of their sins, as Rudolph further says, "stands at the close not as an accidental addition but as the undergirding basis of the whole promise. . . . A new life with God commences." [17]

Jeremiah's emphasis upon the universal knowledge of God—from the least to the greatest—takes on deepened force when we recall how Jeremiah had sought among the poor and the great (5:4-5) for men who know the way of the Lord, yet without success. But when this new life with God begins, the knowledge of God will be possessed by the least and the greatest alike within the nation of Israel.

[17] *Jeremia*, p. 171.

Jeremiah emphasizes that this situation will obtain not "in those days," that is, the days when Ephraim shall have returned and shall have been consolidated in its own beloved territory, but "after those days" (vs. 33). The new covenant thus lies yet in a later stage of development. We stand here in the sphere of eschatology. Man of himself is not able to fulfill the divine commandment. God, as Ezekiel clearly saw, must himself cleanse the heart of man, must forgive his sin, must himself have laid a new foundation before a new life, pleasing to God, can begin (Ezek. 36:22-27). The gracious promise of the new covenant lies in the assurance that God will do just this.

We stand here definitely on the ground of the Old Testament. The fulfillment of the law is still conceived as the necessary requirement of God who has on this basis covenanted with his people. It is not the individual person as such, whoever he may be, to whom this promise comes, but the individual person viewed as a member of the people of the covenant, within the nationally and religiously constituted community of Israel. Yet implicitly in this covenant the limits of the Old Testament are forcibly dissolved. As Rudolph says: "For him whose whole heart is directed in harmony with the will of God the fulfillment of a definitely formulated law or membership in a particular nation is no longer essential." [18]

Says the prophet in the Lord's name:

31:31 Lo, the days are coming, says the Lord, when I will make with the house of Israel a new covenant. 32 Not like the covenant which I made with their fathers on the day that I took [them] by the hand to lead them out of the land of Egypt; I whose covenant they broke, although I was a husband to them, says the Lord; 33 but this is the covenant which I will make with the house of Israel after those days, says the Lord: I will put my law in their innermost being and upon their heart I will write it, and I will be their God and they shall be my people. 34 And they shall not teach any more, each his neighbor and each his brother saying, "Know the Lord," but all of them shall know me from the most insignificant of them to the most important of them, says the Lord, for I will forgive their iniquities, and their sins I will not remember any more.

Vss. 35-37 form a majestic rhetorical climax to Jeremiah's prophecy of salvation for Ephraim. The prophet has been thinking in terms of the nation, his own beloved north. And he has just taken us into the innermost depths of the human heart of the individual Israelite, the center and soul of the new creation. Suddenly from this inner world of the soul he transports us to the majesty of the natural universe, sun, moon, and stars moving

[18] *Ibid.*

according to divine decree. The sea in majestic calm stirred at divine impulse into roaring destruction. It is a universe under divine laws which are the expression of God's presence. As long as those laws of nature exist, so the prophet assures us, will the descendants of restored Israel continue to exist as a national power. Until the limitless heavens can be explored, measured, and charted, until the earth can be investigated, plumbed to its innermost deeps, the descendants of restored Israel will never again because of their evil deeds be banished. How swiftly this poet-prophet passes from the innermost in the human world of the heart to the outermost in the universe of nature. And in all of it is the great thought which in spiritual terms remains ever true—that in salvation there is something inviolable, something of the eternity of God.

31:35 Thus says the Lord,
Who made the sun for a light by day,
Who decreed moon and stars for light by night,
Who stirs up the sea, so its billows roar—
The Lord of hosts is his name.
36 If these laws should be removed
From my presence, says the Lord,
Then also would the population of Israel cease
To be a nation before me for all time.
37 If ever the heavens can be measured upward,
And the foundations of the earth can be explored downward;
Then will I on my part reject all the descendants of Israel
Because of all that they have done, says the Lord.

EYES HAVE THEY BUT THEY SEE NOT

To the original scroll of Jeremiah (36:2) belongs Jer. 5:21-25, and dates from a time after the reform of King Josiah (621). When the scroll was finally prepared in 604 (36:32) there was no reason for the prophet to alter these verses, since the reform had so little changed the hearts of the Judeans.

The prophet is sharply criticizing the Judeans because of their folly and lack of intelligence. They should stand in awe before God and be deeply moved to contrition toward him. He starts from an illustration of God's control in the realm of nature. Turbulent as the sea often is, yet God has made for it a boundary, thus setting the limits to its overflowing turbulence (vs. 22b). But "this people" (vs. 23)—a derogatory aspersion upon the Judeans as a whole—instead of seeing in moral discernment with their God-given eyes, and instead of hearing in ethical discrimination with their God-given ears, are morally blind and deaf. God has provided for their well-being, giving them adequate rainfall, the winter rains and the spring rains (vs. 24a), and he "keeps laws of harvest" for his people (vs. 24b), but Judah has not responded in true piety to such provision. Rather has the nation shown a rebellious and disobedient spirit, and it is because of these sins that rainfall has been withheld and Judah's prosperity thwarted (vs. 25).

5:21 Pray, hear this,
    Foolish people having no mind;
    Eyes have they, but they see not,
    Ears have they, but they hear not.
22 Do you not revere me, says the Lord,
    Or will you not writhe [in contrition] before me,
Who have made the sand the boundary of the sea,
    An eternal law which it does not overstep?
Though it tosses to and fro it cannot overflow,
    And although its waves roar turbulently, they cannot pass beyond it.
23 But this people has
    A rebellious and disobedient heart;
    They have revolted [from me],
    And have had power [i.e., to break God's law].
24 And they do not say in their hearts,
    "Let us fear the Lord our God,
Who gives rain, the early rain,
    And spring rain in its season,
And the prescribed weeks of the harvest
    Reserved for us."
25 Your iniquities have thrust these away,
    And your sins have withheld prosperity from you.

To understand this period in the life of Jeremiah it will be helpful to give a swift review of the history of the Middle East from 626, the year when Ashurbanipal died after a reign of forty-two years, the last vigorous monarch of Assyria, until 609, when King Josiah of Judah met his death at Megiddo. Since 640 the Assyrian Empire, which had been the greatest military power of the ancient world, had become greatly weakened through internal intrigue.

Upon the passing of Ashurbanipal, the Chaldean Nabopolassar, whose family rootage went back to the wiley Merodach-Baladan of Isaiah's time, set up his independent kingdom in Babylon. Ashurbanipal was succeeded on the throne of Assyria, with its capital at Nineveh, by Ashur-etil-ilani (626-621) and he in turn by Sin-shar-ishkun (621-612). By 619 Nabopolassar, the Chaldean, was strong enough to invade the upper Mesopotamian area of Assyria.

Cyril J. Gadd's detailed and excellent historical source, *The Fall of Nineveh*, covers in full detail Nabopolassar's challenge of Assyrian power as he marched up the Euphrates, capturing Qablinu, and then up the Tigris, capturing Madanu. In 614 an alliance was formed between the Medes and the Chaldeans, which issued in 612 in a combined assault by them upon Nineveh, when that famous ancient capital fell before their onslaught. Ashur-uballit then set up the remnant of the Assyrian Empire at Harran, on a branch of the upper Euphrates, which was the residence of the Tartan of the Right, commander in chief of the Assyrian army, who was second only to the king. This was done, as Gadd suggests, because Assyria needed the help of Egypt against the Chaldeans. With Assyria's political center thus moved west to Harran, the remnant of the Assyrian Empire would be near enough to Egypt to receive help from that country, which was then the most powerful ally upon whom the ruined fortunes of Assyria could depend.[19]

By 610 we can clearly see that a realignment of great powers contending for the domination of the Near East has taken place. On the one hand we have the Medes under Cyaxares allied with the Chaldeans under Nabopolassar. On the other hand the Egyptians under Pharaoh Neco are allied with the Assyrian remnant at Harran under Ashur-uballit. Although this Assyrian remnant was very weak, it still could serve Egypt's purposes as a buffer state against the Chaldeans. Harran fell, however, in 610. In 609 Pharaoh Neco hurried an army into Syria to support his weakened ally (II Kings 23:29).

It would seem that under King Josiah Judean sympathies were thrown in with the Chaldeans in the hope that Judean independence might conceivably result from the downfall of crumbling Assyria. It is quite likely that Pharaoh Neco suspected King Josiah of Chaldean sympathies. He appears to have summoned Josiah to him at Megiddo and summarily assassinated him.[20]

A. C. Welch [21] is probably right in his suggestion of an additional reason for Pharaoh Neco's drastic action against Josiah. It was due to the latter's successful effort, as we have seen, to gain control over northern Israel. This made Josiah a dangerous enemy to an Egyptian army, and in doing away with him, "the Egyptian was making sure of his line of retreat before ad-

---

[19] Cf. Gadd, *The Fall of Nineveh*, pp. 476-477; J. P. Hyatt thinks that the *Ummanmanda* of the Babylonian Chronicle are more probably the Medes than the Scythians; cf. "The Peril from the North," *Journal of Biblical Literautre*, LIX (1940), 500, 509.

[20] Cf. *Abingdon Bible Commentary*, p. 799; *ibid.*, p. 69; also *ibid.*, p. 437, which best explains II Kings 23:29.

[21] *Jeremiah, His Time and His Work*, p. 21.

vancing to Carchemish and to the fight for the mastery of Syria, which must take place there."

The Deuteronomic historian, from whom comes the account of the reign of King Josiah, does not inform us as to the aforesaid motive that may have prompted Pharaoh Neco to snuff out his life. He tells us that Josiah's servants brought his dead body by chariot from Megiddo to Jerusalem, where he was buried as befits a king (II Kings 23:30). The historian gives to him such a eulogy as he pronounced over no other monarch in Judah: "Before him there was no king like him, who turned to the Lord with all his heart and with all his soul and with all his might, according to all the law of Moses; nor did any like him arise after him" (II Kings 23:25). The later Judean historian, the Chronicler, informs us that he "was buried in the tomb of his fathers," and that "all Judah and Jerusalem mourned for Josiah" (II Chr. 35:24).

By right of succession, twenty-five-year-old Eliakim, the Judean crown prince, should have been crowned king of Judah upon the death of King Josiah in 609. But the people of the land were opposed to him because he had favored a policy toward Egypt that was directly opposite to that of his father. Accordingly, by act of the people of Judah, twenty-three-year-old Shallum was crowned king and took the throne name Jehoahaz. His enthronement at the popular will represented a repudiation of the ambitions of Pharaoh Neco, who had just ascended the Egyptian throne and in whom lived anew the age-old Egyptian claim to the control of Palestine. At that time Pharaoh Neco had taken up his position at Riblah, a strategic military post on the Orontes River. It was the center of a great fertile plain at the point where the military road running north and south through Palestine was crossed by the road leading from the Mediterranean Sea through the gap between Lebanon and the lower hills of Bargulus on the north, to the desert.[22] It formed an ideal site for a military base, and, as we shall see, was later similarly used by the Chaldeans. There Pharaoh Neco received the submission and fealty of the Phoenician cities.

The word came to him there that the Judeans, by seizing the initiative and enthroning King Jehoahaz had struck a blow at Pharaoh Neco's scheme of the Egyptian domination of Judah. He had the young king of three months, Jehoahaz, brought to him at Riblah in chains, and in his place Pharaoh Neco enthroned over Judah, Eliakim, who took the throne name of Jehoiakim. To punish Judah because of its flaunting of Egypt, Pharaoh Neco laid an indemnity on the land of one hundred talents of silver and

---

[22] Cf. O. T. Olmstead, *History of Palestine and Syria*, pp. 118, 507.

one talent of gold, which amounted to approximately 47,015 English pounds.[23] He took Jehoahaz with him to Egypt, where the Judean monarch of three months died (II Kings 23:31-35).

HE SHALL NOT AGAIN SEE THE LAND OF HIS BIRTH

At the very moment when he was taken away to Riblah, and while the loss of the lamented King Josiah was still a keen bereavement in Judah, Jeremiah pronounced his prophetic oracle concerning Jehoahaz (22:10-12). The prophet calls his Judean countrymen to cease lamenting for the deceased Josiah, to lament instead for Jehoahaz, who is even now "going" away and is destined never again to see his beloved Judah. He was taken to Egypt, as the prose account in vss. 11-12 states, there to die. Ezekiel (19:4) represents him as a young lion whom "the nations . . . brought . . . with hooks to the land of Egypt." It is remarkable that the prophetic prediction of Jeremiah was carried out to the letter.

Cries the prophet concerning Jehoahaz:

> 22:10 **Weep not for the dead [i.e., Josiah] and lament not for him;**
> **Weep instead for him who is going away,**
> **For he will not return again or see**
> **The land of his birth.**

It is most likely Baruch who adds in prose to this oracle:

> 11 **For thus says the Lord concerning Shallum son of Josiah, who reigned in place of Josiah his father, and who went out from this place: "He shall never return there, 12 but in the place to which they exiled him, there shall he die, but this land he shall never see again."**

King Jehoiakim soon showed himself to be a ruler of sharp contrast to his father, the lamented King Josiah. He was the slave of egotism, ambition, extravagance, and display. He was selfish, cruel, reckless, and unjust. He impressed upon Judah the hated corvée (the forced labor gangs). His reign meant to Jeremiah the beginnings of grave tension between the prophet and the authoritative political and religious leaders of Judah. The prophet emerged from the silence which seems to have characterized his prophetic concern during the period from 621 to 609. We can well realize, however, that these had been for him years of keen sensitivity to what was taking place in Judah and in the whole area of the Near East. This period

---

[23] Cf. A. S. Peake, *Commentary on the Bible,* p. 116.

witnessed the astonishing and rapid decline of Assyria, and in 612 the fall of
Nineveh, its famed capital, to the Chaldeans and Medes. It saw also at
Harran the attempt at revival on the part of the Assyrian remnant only to
suffer final and irrevocable collapse in 609. Consequently the world of the
Near East was in chaos and the immediate future most uncertain when
Jeremiah preached his famous temple sermon.

THE EARLY REIGN OF KING JEHOIAKIM (608-605)

The subject of Jeremiah's "temple sermon" (7:1-15) is "What Gives
Protection?" [24] Two elements in the situation create an atmosphere charged
with tension. One is that with the delivery of this utterance Jeremiah
emerged from a period of silence which began at the launching of the
Deuteronomic reform (621) and ended with the death of King Josiah
(609). Externally this period was for Judah an epoch of territorial advance.
We are told that Josiah's dominion reached from Geba in the old tribal
area of Benjamin in the north to Beer-sheba in the extreme south of Judah
(II Kings 23:8). But the northern frontier of Judah really lay to "the north
of Ophrah," and Josiah's actual area of control, in addition to the strictly
Judean region, embraced cities of the former Northern Kingdom, Shechem,
Shiloh, and Samaria (41:4-5). We thus see that one of the achievements of
Josiah's reign was "a wide increase of his territory." [25]

A second element in the setting in which the temple address was uttered
was the increased prestige which had accrued to the temple under the influence of the Deuteronomic reform. Particularly the great annual pilgrimage festivals had contributed richly to this. Since 621, three times in
the year—spring, summer, and autumn—the pilgrimage festivals of Pass-
over, Weeks, and Tabernacles, respectively, were celebrated, and tens of
thousands of pilgrims had worshiped at the temple in Jerusalem, designated
by Deuteronomy (16:6) as "the place which the Lord your God will choose,
to make his name dwell there."

Accordingly, there had come to the temple and its worship a heightened
prestige, so that on the part of Judah a great confidence arose in its protection of them and its deliverance of the nation from harm.

It was in sharp antagonism to such an air of superficial confidence in
the protection of the temple that Jeremiah speaks his mind in a memorable
utterance. It has come down to us in two forms: 7:1-15; 26:1-24. Jeremiah's
aim is clearly "to utter a strong polemic against the temple and the wor-

---

[24] So Volz, *Jeremia*, p. 89.
[25] Cf. Olmstead, *op. cit.*, p. 506,

ship there." [26] The writer of 7:1-15 presents the scene of its delivery, the gate of the temple through which worshipers from all Judah are entering to pray to the Lord.

> 7:1 The word which came to Jeremiah out of communion with the Lord, say-ing: 2 Stand in the gate of the house of the Lord, and speak there this message and say: "Hear the word of the Lord, all Judah who are entering through these gates to pray to the Lord."

The writer of ch. 26 is Baruch, whose primary interest, as we have seen, is to narrate the sufferings of Jeremiah. His version of the sermon and its reception depicts the earliest clash of Jeremiah, the authoritative spokesman of God's word, with the contemporary prophets whom he criticizes through-out his ministry with piercing penetration. Moreover, Baruch informs us that the sermon was delivered at the beginning of the reign of King Jehoia-kim, which refers, as J. Begrich has established,[27] to the time between his accession to the throne and the beginning of his first regnal year. The scene is that of a great festival in the temple, probably intended as a celebration of the enthronement of Jehoiakim. The date is 608. Baruch describes the setting—people from all the Judean cities entering the house of the Lord, and the prophet standing in the temple court preaching the message given him by God for that particular hour. He also gives us the purpose that motivates Jeremiah as he speaks the word of the Lord, to move his fellow countrymen to repentance for their conduct and to morally transformed lives. So runs Baruch's narrative:

> 26:1 At the beginning of the reign of King Jehoiakim son of Josiah, king of Judah, this word came to Jeremiah [28] out of communion with the Lord. 2 Thus says the Lord: Stand in the court of the house of the Lord, and speak to all the cities of Judah, which are entering the house of the Lord to worship, all the words that I have commanded you to speak to them. Do not hold back a word. 3 Perhaps they will listen and return, each from his evil way [of life], and I will change my mind about the evil which I have thought I would do on account of their evil deeds.

In 7:3-6 the sermon itself begins. It is an appeal to the Judeans for trans-formed and corrected living. This and this alone will bring them real security. No trusted formula, no holy words taken on their lips, can make their lives secure. No magic phrases mouthed with rhythmic unanimity

[26] Cf. A. C. Welch: *Jeremiah, His Time and His Work*, p. 137.

[27] *Die Chronologie der König von Israel und Juda*, pp. 91, 93.

[28] With Volz insert "to Jeremiah," with Syriac and Old Latin, and in accord with 27:1.

will assure the real presence of God. It is morally transformed conduct that
God desires of the Judean people. God cannot abide with his people in his
temple unless they who worship him there do it not by excited, magical,
sentimental mouthings of loving ardor for the temple, but by genuine
concern for the helpless classes in society and by social action to correct
the abuses under which they suffer. Thus his sermon opens:

7:3 Thus says the Lord of hosts, God of Israel: Correct your course of life and
your conduct and I will dwell with you in this place. 4 Do not trust in deceiving
words, saying, "The temple of the Lord, the temple of the Lord, the temple of the
Lord is this place." 5 Nay rather, if you will really amend your course of life and
your conduct, if you will indeed deal justly each [of you] with his neighbor,
6 if you will not oppress resident aliens, orphans, and widows and will not go
after other gods to your own harm, 7 then I will dwell with you in this place in
the land which I gave to your fathers, from antiquity and forever more.

These pious and reiterated ejaculations, "The temple of the Lord, the
temple of the Lord," are self-deceiving. The very people who chant them
are guilty of theft, murder, adultery, and perjury. They participate in cultic
acts of pagan intrusions that have no place in the true worship of the
Lord. The only "deliverance" such cultic rites will bring them is "deliverance" of Judeans into their corrupting influence. Indeed, such worshipers make out of this place that is a thing of beauty and holiness where
is heard outflowing praise to God, instead a haunt of robbers where the
judgment they deserve cannot touch them. What a travesty upon the temple
of the Lord is Judean worship! What disgrace upon the house that bears the
name of the holy and righteous God!

Cries Jeremiah:

7:8 But see,[29] you are putting your trust in deceiving words of no effect whatever. 9 Will you steal, murder, commit adultery, and perjure yourselves, and
burn incense to Baal, and go after other gods whom you do not know, 10 then
come and stand before me in this house, to which my name was given, and
say, "We are delivered!" [Aye, delivered] so you may practice all these abhorrent
rites? 11 Is it a cave of robbers that this house, to which my name was given,
has become in your eyes? I too—lo, I have seen [it]! says the Lord.

The prophet, for a striking and telling historical analogy to inform and
move his people, reaches back into Israelite history (vss. 8-11). The temple
seems so secure and its worship so well established that its eventual de-

---

[29] Reading with Septuagint and Syriac *weḥinnēh* instead of *hinnēh*.

struction is practically unthinkable. Here indeed Jeremiah is treading on dangerous ground. To his fellow Judeans the destruction of the temple, that acme of Israelite architecture, with fame of 350 years of existence, was well nigh unthinkable. "But," says the prophet, "remember what happened to Shiloh!" In the days of Eli the priest and of Samuel the prophet that was the most holy place in all Israel, and in its temple was housed the ark of God (I Sam. 3:3). The temple at Shiloh was likewise a great pilgrimage sanctuary in Samuel's day, even as was Jerusalem in Jeremiah's day, yet Shiloh was destroyed *ca.* 1050. For nearly five and a half centuries it had lain in ruins. The mute desolation called Khirbet Selun, which many of his hearers had seen, was a telling witness to the point he was making.

The Deuteronomic editor takes over at vs. 12, and maintains that the destruction of the temple at Shiloh—to the editor its destroyer was the Lord—was due to the sins of Israel. How then can the Temple of Jerusalem escape a similar but yet more awful destruction? And just as the Ephraimites had been exiled to Assyria and elsewhere, so the Judeans will likewise be taken into exile away from the presence of God.

7:12 **But come now to my holy place which was in Shiloh, where I made my name dwell at first, and see what I did to it because of the evil done by my people Israel.** 13 **So now, since you have done all these deeds—I have spoken to you, though you did not hear, and having called to you, though you did not answer—** 14 **I will do to the house which has been given my name, in which you are trusting, and to the holy place which I have given to you and to your fathers, just as I did to Shiloh.** 15 **And I will send you away from my presence, just as I sent away all your brothers, all the descendants of Ephraim.**

Baruch's parallel account of what Jeremiah said at this point (26:4-6) is very limited, as his interest lay more in the public reception of Jeremiah's address and the reaction which it aroused than in specific words of the sermon itself. According to Baruch, the Lord intimated to Jeremiah that he was thus to hold before the Judean people a solemn warning that the temple, unless the oft-repeated prophetic warnings were heeded, is doomed to just such destruction as the mute ruins of Shiloh display.

26:4 **Now you are to say to them, Thus says the Lord: If you will not listen to me about walking in my law which I have put before you,** 5 **about listening to the words of my servants, the prophets, whom I keep sending to you—early and often—since you have not listened,**[30] 6 **I will make this house like Shiloh and this city I will make the object of a curse for all the nations of the earth.**

[30] With Rudolph, *Jeremia*, p. 142, I view vs. 5 as probably from the hand of the Deuteronomic editor.

A DEATH SENTENCE FOR THIS MAN

It is little wonder that such bold words, prophesying the destruction of the very temple in the court of which the speaker and his hearers were standing, aroused passionate resentment, particularly on the part of the priests and prophets. Jeremiah had touched upon a popularly held dogma, the indestructibility of the temple and of the holy city, a dogma which had grown out of the popular but superficial interpretation of the prophet Isaiah's teaching nearly a century before (Isa. 37:33-35). Now Jeremiah's preaching stirred up a popular riot of perilous proportions. Baruch's vivid account describes the situation as it rapidly developed:

26:7 Now the priests and the prophets and all the people heard Jeremiah speak these words in the house of the Lord. 8 And when Jeremiah had finished speak-ing all that the Lord had commanded him to speak to all the people, the priests and the prophets seized him, saying: "You shall surely die! 9 What is your motive that you preach in the name of the Lord, saying, 'This house shall become like Shiloh, and this city shall be in ruins without inhabitants?' " Thereupon all the people gathered about Jeremiah in the house of the Lord.

It was a tense moment indeed. News of the excitement soon reached the royal court and certain of the nobles went up to the New Gate of the temple.[31] Then the priests and prophets demanded of them a death sentence for Jeremiah. Thus Baruch describes the crucial moment, the first one of his master's prophetic ministry that had put his life in peril.

26:10 When the nobles of Judah heard these words, they went up from the palace of the king to the house of the Lord and took their seat in the entrance of the New Gate of the house of the Lord.

The priests and prophets now proceeded to demand that Jeremiah be sentenced to death. It is evident that the situation is being handled in a thoroughly legal way. The nobles have the right of death sentence. Jeremiah, as he makes his defense, does not protest this right. But with calmness and dignity he defends himself and appeals to whatever sense of fairness they possess, making it clear that it is as God's prophet that he has spoken this threat of the temple's destruction. Baruch's account continues:

[31] This was probably the gate which King Jotham had rebuilt (II Kings 15:35), called "the upper gate," probably the same as Jeremiah's upper Benjamin Gate (Jer. 20:2) and Ezekiel's "gate of the inner court towards the north," so G. A. Smith, *Jerusalem*, II, 125, 257.

26:11 Then the priests and the prophets said to the nobles and to all the people: "A death sentence for this man! For he has preached against this city, just as you have heard with your ears." 12 Then Jeremiah spoke to the nobles and to all the people, saying, "The Lord sent me to prophesy concerning this house and this city all the words that you have heard. 13 So now make your courses of action and your practices right and listen to the voice of the Lord your God, and the Lord will change his mind as regards the harm which he has spoken against you. 14 But as for me, see, I am in your hands. Do to me as seems good and right in your eyes. 15 But know for sure that if you are for putting me to death, you are putting innocent blood upon yourselves and to the account of this city and its inhabitants, for it is true that the Lord has sent me to you to speak in your hearing all these words."

It was indeed a tense moment for Jeremiah. His life lay in the balance. Then a quite unexpected thing happened. There were present certain aged Judeans whose memory reached back to what their fathers had told them about the preaching of a certain prophet from Moresheth-gath, Micah by name, who in a manner similar to that of Jeremiah had proclaimed in the Lord's name a like threat to the temple (Mic. 3:12). In his day the political and spiritual leaders, through shallow confidence in the security of their city and its protection by God, had been saying:

> Is not the Lord in the midst of us?
> No evil shall come upon us (Mic. 3:11),

to which Micah had given a solemn and searching answer:

> Therefore because of you
>   Zion shall be plowed as a field;
> And Jerusalem shall be as heaps of ruins,
>   And the temple mount as a thicket-covered height (Mic. 3:12).

So through recall of the earlier prophet's words these elders oppose a death sentence, which would not be even to their own interests. Rather— such is the implication of their words—Jeremiah's words should influence the present king even as Hezekiah [32] had listened to and heeded Micah's. Thus they speak: [33]

26:17 Then some of the elderly men of the land stood up and spoke to all the assembled company of the people, saying: 18 "Micah of Moresheth prophesied

---

[32] The implication is that Hezekiah's reform (II Kings 18:4-5) was to some extent carried out under the incentive of Micah's preaching.

[33] Vs. 16 has been misplaced and should rightly follow vs. 19.

in the days of Hezekiah king of Judah, and spoke to all the people of Judah saying, 'Thus says the Lord of hosts:

Zion shall be plowed as a field;
And Jerusalem shall be as heaps of ruins
And the temple mount as a thicket-covered height.'

19 Was it to death that Hezekiah king of Judah and all Judah sentenced him? Did he not rather fear the Lord and entreat the favor of the Lord, so the Lord changed his mind with regard to the evil which he had said he would do to them? But as for us, we would be doing a great wrong against our own selves."

Impressed by this recall of past experience which dealt with the courageous prophetic teaching of Micah uttered at peril to his life, and no doubt also moved by the straightforwardness and quiet courage of Jeremiah, the nobles and the people arrived at a decision.

26:16 Then the nobles and all the people said to the priests and the prophets: "There shall not be a sentence of death for this man, for it is in the name of the Lord our God that he has spoken to us."

For a few tense moments Jeremiah's life had lain in the balance. That the threat against him was real, Baruch makes perfectly clear to us by reporting at this point in his narrative what actually happened to a contemporary prophet by the name of Uriah, who came from Kiriath-jearim, a town less than twenty miles southwest of Jerusalem on the border of Judah and Benjamin. He shared Jeremiah's convictions with regard to the fate of Judah and Jerusalem and the reasons for it, and as a consequence had to flee to Egypt before the wrath of King Jehoiakim.

26:20 Now there was a man who had prophesied in the name of the Lord, Uriah son of Shemaiah of Kiriath-jearim. And he had preached against this city and against this land similarly to all the words of Jeremiah. 21 When King Jehoiakim and all the princes heard his words, the king tried to put him to death. So when Uriah heard, he was afraid and fled and went to Egypt. 22 But King Jehoiakim dispatched Elnathan son of Achbor and men with him to Egypt. 23 So they brought Uriah out of Egypt and took him to King Jehoiakim and he slew him with the sword and slung his corpse into the grave of the vulgar rabble.

With such a monarch as Jehoiakim upon the throne it needed more than a popular verdict of nobles and people to safeguard the life of Jeremiah. Fortunate indeed was the prophet in having the protection of Ahikam son of Shaphan, a man of noble character and of great influence. Baruch ends this significant chapter with a reference to this loyal friendship which was a source of great comfort and helpfulness to Jeremiah.

26:24 However, the hand of Ahikam son of Shaphan was with Jeremiah so that he was not given over into the power of the people to put him to death.

What Does the Lord Require of Thee?

Jer. 11:15-16 forms an independent prophetic message of great importance which is in harmony with Jeremiah's view as to the very essence of religion. In content it is related to the great temple sermon of 7:1-15, and probably dates from the time of Jehoiakim. It is concerned with one of the greatest questions of religion; What does the Lord desire from his people when they come to his temple? Is it the rites of sacrifice and offering? Is it with the holy flesh of animals presented to the Lord? Is it the vows and the freewill offerings that accompanied them? Does Judah, the Lord's "loved one," think that through the performance of such rites it may escape the consequences of its sins and be pronounced pure in character by the holy God? Here Jeremiah of Jerusalem joins hands with the prophet Amos at Bethel (Amos 5:21-24) in his penetrating criticism of what goes on in the Lord's sanctuary. Cries the prophet in the name of God:

> 11:15 What design has my loved one in my house?
> She perpetrates loathsome rites.
> Can vows and sacred flesh
> Cause evil to pass away from you?
> Can I treat you as pure on this ground?

Jeremiah loved the thought of the Lord's people as a growing thing comparable to a choice vine, or as here in vs. 16, a graceful olive tree such as grew shapely and beautiful in the temple court (Ps. 52:8). That is the picture of the Judean nation as it was held in the gracious purpose of God. But Jeremiah in the solemnity of prophetic insight sees that beautiful olive tree—the nation of Judah—destroyed as by fire. We hear the crackle of the flames fanned into a roar by the wind. It is a picture of the imminent destruction of the unrepentant Judean nation.[34]

The prose sentence of vs. 17 from the Deuteronomic editor sums it up. The Planter, the Gardener of Israel, has condemned the plant of his delight—the whole nation Israel and Judah—to destruction. For they have

---

[34] For an excellent rendering and interpretation of this meaningful passage see the textual study by J. Philip Hyatt, "The Original Text of Jer. 11:15-16," *Journal of Biblical Literature*, LX (1941), 57-60.

forsaken their ethical Lord, who alone is their God, and have fallen back again under the immoral spell of the cult of the Canaanite Baals (vss. 16-17).

Cries the prophet:

> 11:16 An olive tree graceful in form,
> The Lord called you;
> But he will set fire to its foliage,
> With a great roaring sound.

17 Now the Lord of hosts, who planted you, has spoken evil against you on ac-count of the evil of the house of Israel and the house of Judah, who have made themselves gods so as to provoke me to anger by burning incense to Baal.

I WILL BUILD MYSELF A HOUSE ON A GRAND SCALE

King Jehoiakim was the throne name for Eliakim (II Kings 23:34), the second son of Josiah (Jer. 22:18; I Chr. 3:15). He was twenty-five years old when he became king and only thirty-six when he died. Jeremiah deals with him in unparalleled severity and presents us with a vivid picture of his spirit and activity as king. He succeeded to the throne of Judah not by popular choice but through the powerful influence of Pharaoh Neco of Egypt, who set him on the throne in place of Jehoahaz.

The prophet's oracle concerning him may have been uttered directly to Jehoiakim, as vs. 15 seems to imply, and, as Volz [35] suggests, probably in sight of the palace under construction. The date of this oracle is early in the reign of Jehoiakim, *ca.* 607, when the backing of Egypt was purchased by the heavy indemnity of one hundred talents of silver and one talent of gold, which was demanded by Pharaoh Neco (II Kings 23:33). King Jehoiakim had to put a forced levy on the land to secure what was in those days a large sum. He exacted the silver and gold of the people of the land, "from each according to his evaluation" (II Kings 23:35). Release from Assyria, which had been achieved under King Josiah, was thus followed by burdening bondage to another tyrant, Egypt.

In this period of his reign the king had leisure and political security for his building program. And his unprecedented interest in the building of extravagant public works had by then become abundantly apparent. To Jeremiah, who awaited with certainty the near fall of the Judean state, such luxury and display on the part of the king, such aping of the public works of Egypt, was childish and outrageous. What need had the Judean royal palace of such magnificence and luxury? What place in Judah had such spacious

[35] *Jeremia*, p. 222.

roof chambers, large expensive windows, rich cedar paneling, and the costly
painting in deep vermilion such as to make the whole structure awesome
to the young nobles he would thus impress?

But worst of all, the labor entailed in these ambitious enterprises was
forced labor from his own subjects, yes, from his own fellow citizens. These
he has made his slaves and for their labor he pays them nothing.

Cries the prophet:

> 22:13 Woe to him who builds his house by unrighteous means,
>   And his roof chambers by injustice;
>   Who uses his fellow citizen gratuitously as a slave,
>   And does not give him his wages;
>   14 Who says, "I will build myself a house on a grand scale,
>   With spacious roof chambers."
>   So he makes the window wide for himself, paneling [it] with cedar,
>   And paints it with vermilion.

In vss. 15-17 God speaks through Jeremiah directly to King Jehoiakim:
Is it by such ostentation in building and such feverish efforts to excel, thus
aping an Egyptian Pharaoh, that you show that you are the king? Look at
the example that has been set before you of one who really was a king—
Josiah, your own father. He was no ascetic, but he was successful. He was
not only king in name, but in fact. He saw to it that his subjects were justly
treated. He, the strong man of Judah, made himself champion of the rights
of the poor and the unprotected in his realm. Is not this what knowing God
means?

But Jehoiakim is a ruler of a different stamp. He is not capable of such
motivation as had inspired his father, whose serene aim had been to fulfill
the social responsibilities of his office. For the root of all Jehoiakim's acts
is greed. Nor does he stop at violence, extortion, or even murder, to accomplish his objectives.

Thus speaks the outraged soul of Jeremiah directly to the prophet in the
Lord's name.

> 22:15 Would you show yourself king because you
>   Strive eagerly to excel in cedar?
>   As for your father—did he not eat and drink,
>   And did it not go well with him?
>   16 He wrought justice and righteousness;
>   He pleaded the cause of the poor and needy.
>   Is not this the right knowledge of me?
>   ʼ   Says the Lord.

17 **But your eyes and your heart are set on nothing**
   But your unjust gain,
   And pouring out the blood of the innocent,
   And extortion and doing oppressive acts.

The prophetic rebuke of Jehoiakim is at an end. But now soon to follow is the prophet's threat of punishment. The Judeans were still mourning for the lamented King Josiah when his successor Jehoahaz was taken to Egypt. But no one will lament the death of Jehoiakim. The familiar mourning songs for ordinary commoners in Judah, beginning with the words "Ah my brother!" or "Ah sister!" will not be sung over him. Nor will mourning songs fitting for kings, such as "Ah lord!" or "Ah his majesty!" be sung over him. Indeed, he will be buried as an ass is "buried"—dragged outside the city and flung out uninterred (36:30), so that the holy city should not be defiled by such a corpse.

Cries the prophet:

22:18 **Therefore, thus says the Lord concerning Jehoiakim son of Josiah, king of**
   Judah:
   Woe upon this man!
   They shall not wail for him,
   "Ah my brother!" or "Ah sister!"
   Nor shall they lament for him,
   "Ah lord!" or "Ah his majesty!"
   19 **With the burial given an ass shall he be buried,**
   Dragged off and flung out there,
   Outside the gates of Jerusalem.

The Sin of Judah Is Engraved upon the Tablet of the Heart

Jer. 17:1-4 dates from the reign of Jehoiakim. Volz [36] suggests that this brief word may have been spoken by Jeremiah at the temple on the day of atonement. The prophet is astonished at the rapidity and superficiality with which the nation's conscience seems to be cleared. He senses the utter shallowness of the religion of the nation, and speaks out his criticism in two directions, in both of which central and characteristic teachings of the prophet are expressed.

One (vs. 1) has to do with the basic spiritual attitude of the nation. As Rudolph [37] says, the sin of Judah is not like a light lacquer on the surface of the nation's heart, which when readily removed, would reveal the essentially

[36] *Jeremia,* p. 182.
[37] *Jeremia,* p. 97.

good nation underneath. But far more serious than this, it has become firmly entrenched habit. It is not an inconsequential matter which can be passed over lightly or easily eradicated, but it has cut deeply into the heart of the nation and is clearly visible to every discerning eye. It is the estrangement of their hearts from God. This estrangement, which has now become habitual, has cut an incision upon the "tablet" of Judah's heart, just as an iron stylus with adamant-tipped point in the hands of the engraver cuts into a tablet of stone. Already in 4:4, in Judah's need for "a circumcised heart," Jeremiah has touched upon this problem.

The other direction of his criticism of the public sin of Judah (vss. 2-3) has to do with the organized public worship of the nation and with the central institution of that worship, the altar of sacrifice. It was the generally accepted view in Judah that the ritual of sacrifice unto the Lord atoned for the people's sin and assured the removal of its guilt. But as G. A. Smith [38] has said, Jeremiah "had a profound sense of the ingrained quality of evil, the deep saturation of sin, the enormity of the guilt of those who sinned against the light and love of God." This deep-seated apostasy from God the sacrifices of Judah could not reach. So on those holy altars, and on the horns, the most sacred part where Judah thought to atone for its sins, the prophet's spiritual eye sees deeply engraved the sin of the people, sacrifice unaccompanied by moral repentance (vss. 1-2).

So the price which the Lord will cause the nation to pay because of its sins is that Judah will experience the plundering of its wealth and treasures by the conquering Chaldeans. The Judeans will lose their hold on their own beloved land, and as a judgment of God upon them, will be forced to live in exile under the domination of their conquerors.

The prophet cries out:

> 17:1 The sin of Judah is written
>   With a stylus of iron,
>   With a stylus point of adamant, engraved
>   On the tablet of their heart,
>   And on the horns of their altars,
> 2   As a reminder against them.
> 3 Your wealth and all your treasures
>   I will give over to plunder,
>   As the price of all your sins,
>   In all your borders.

---

[38] *Jeremiah*, p. 346.

4 And you must let your hand drop from your inheritance
  Which I gave to you.
  And I will make you serve your enemies,
  In a land you do not know.
  For a fire has been kindled in my wrath;
  It will burn forever.

Do Not Intercede for This People

In Jer. 7:16-20 the prophet reports an experience of conscious, yet to him quite incomprehensible, frustration of intercessory prayer. To Jeremiah the persistent proclamation of destruction to his people gave no emotional release but only deep inner sorrow. For even his most solemn words seemed empty of any awakening influence upon Judah. But then he could still pray for them, and that he did so is clearly and repeatedly noted. But the time came when even the release of intercessory prayer on their behalf was denied him. He felt divinely thwarted from even praying for Judah. He could only stand before God in dumb agony on their behalf. The heavens seemed as brass. Words fell powerless to the earth. He interpreted it as divine frustration. What had brought Judah to so grave a crisis? Why had God thus sealed up the intercessory prayer for his people that was so native to the prophet's heart?

It was a great wave of backsliding on the part of Judah that had led to vigorous revival of the worship of the Babylonian-Assyrian mother goddess Ishtar, under her distinctly Assyrian phase, as at Nineveh and Arbela, the "queen of heaven." This cult had first been introduced into Judah early in the century by King Manasseh, who, as a tributary of Assyria, had himself worshiped the heavenly host and had built altars in both the outer and inner courts for "all the host of heaven" (II Kings 21:3-5).

The religious reform under King Josiah had ruthlessly eradicated this worship from Judean life (II Kings 23:11-12). The priests of this foreign cult, who had been under royal appointment and patronage, had at that time been put down (II Kings 23:5) and the cult itself destroyed.

But following upon the death of Josiah, the worship of the queen of heaven surged back into Judean life with a popularity comparable only to the cult of the Virgin Mary in contemporary Roman Catholicism. It had tremendous appeal to the Judeans. As compared with the relatively limited place of women in the legitimate Judean worship of the Lord, this cult of the mother goddess gave great place to women, who baked the star-shaped cakes to portray the goddess (44:19). Indeed, there were specific features of the cult to be performed respectively by the men, the women, and the children of the Judean households. This cult also included libations of wine as drink offerings to the goddess. But instead of securing divine help, their passionate and industrious adoration of this goddess was bringing upon her worshipers, to their own disillusionment and disgrace, the very calamity that they were thus seeking so intensively to avoid.

Thus the Lord counseled Jeremiah:

7:16 So now do not intercede for this people and do not lift up for them a cry [in supplication] or a prayer, and do not encounter me with entreaty, for I shall not be hearing you. 17 Do you not see what they are doing in the cities of Judah and in the streets of Jerusalem? 18 The children are gathering wood, and the fathers are kindling the fire, and the women are kneading the dough, to make cakes for the queen of heaven, and are pouring out drink offerings to foreign gods, in order to provoke me. 19 But is it I they are provoking? Is it not rather themselves, shame being on their faces? 20 Therefore, thus says the Lord, My anger and my wrath shall be poured out upon this place, upon man and beast, and upon the trees of the field and the fruit of the ground, and it shall burn, and shall not be quenched.

In ancient times among many peoples sacrifice was viewed as a means of communion with the deity. There is little question that in Israel itself the covenant had been inaugurated by sacrifice (Exod. 24:1-11). In case such communion had been interrupted, it could be restored or renewed by sacrifice. In the actual practice of offering animal sacrifice, while a part of the victim was burned upon the altar the rest of it was partaken of by the worshipers in a sacrificial meal. The whole burnt offering, however, was entirely burned unto the Lord upon the altar. This sacrifice was viewed by the worshipers as particularly efficacious.

But the conviction had dawned upon Jeremiah, as an insight from his own deep and intuitive experience of fellowship with God, that the Lord is an ethical being and never had set before his people detailed prescriptions for their worship. Meticulous concern for the appropriate sacrifice for the particular occasion was far from the requirement of God. To Jeremiah the cult, the organized and official sacrificial system, does not belong at all to the essence of religion. It is something superfluous, and indeed, even harmful, in so far as it diverts attention from that which is inward and absolutely essential in the worship of God—moral obedience. To Jeremiah whole burnt offering was no more efficacious than was the offering which provided the sacrificial meal. They might as well add the one to the other—eat the whole burnt offering as well as the peace offering. The only value it had was physical—it gave them enough to eat. It represents no requirement of God.

What the Lord required, as taught by Moses in the era of the Exodus from Egypt, so Jeremiah maintains, had nothing whatever to do with whole burnt offerings and sacrifices. Rather was it that Israel must listen attentively to, and be obedient to, God's voice; thus, and thus alone, acknowledging themselves to be his people. Then all would go well with them. But from that very time, the days of the Exodus, even until now—the prophet thus sweeps through nearly seven centuries of Israel's life—the Israelites had stubbornly given no heed to the Lord's voice. And although from time to time in that long period, with great solicitude for his people and with a sense of their timely need, God had sent them prophets to point the way they should live, by declaring the Lord's word of teaching and revelation to his people, they ignored this divine illumination and outdid their ancestors in the stubborn willfullness of their spirits.

So the prophet speaks:

7:21 Thus says the Lord of hosts, God of Israel: Your whole burnt offerings add to your sacrifices and eat [the] flesh [of them]! 22 For I did not speak with your fathers or command them in the day when I brought them out of the land of Egypt, concerning matters of offering and sacrifice. 23 But this thing I commanded them, saying, "Listen to my voice and I will be your God, and you will be my people; and you are to walk in all the ways that I command you so that it may go well with you." 24 But they did not listen and did not incline their ear, but walked in the stubbornness of their evil heart and so went backward and not forward. 25 It was from the day when your fathers went out from the land of Egypt until this day that I sent to them all my servants the prophets, sending them early and often. 26 But they [the people] did not listen to me and did not turn their ear, but were obstinate and acted more wickedly than their fathers.

God revealed to Jeremiah that regardless of their seeming insulation to his word as uttered in the prophets' messages to Judah, he is to continue to speak to them, preaching to them, however unresponsive they may be. Then—in itself a prophetic oracle—he is to characterize his people in such a direct and penetrating condemnation as may still awaken Judah to hear and heed:

7:27 Now you are to speak to them all these words, but they will not listen to you, and you are to call to them, but they will not answer you. 28 Then you shall say to them: "This is the nation which does not listen to the voice of the Lord its God, and has not received correction. Fidelity has failed from your mouth."

THE DESECRATION OF THE TEMPLE

Again the prophet turns to abhorrent features of the illegitimate worship which have surged back into Judah. Personifying his nation as a woman, he calls upon her to enter upon a lamentation. Let her cut off her long hair, and in characteristic wailing cries let her lament, because God has repudiated and cast off his people. What is it that calls for such rites of lamentation?

For one thing, Judeans have desecrated the Lord's holy temple. In the temple, sacred to the Lord, a place to which the Lord's name had been given, they have set up certain idols—"detested things" the prophet calls them—and have thus polluted it. As to what had been introduced, Ezekiel's testimony of approximately sixteen years later supplements Jeremiah's report. He tells us that at the north gate of the temple there stood a detestable idol, "the image causing [divine] resentment." And in the temple there were idolaters participating in disgusting cultic acts which, as Ezekiel says, were "forcing the Lord away from his sanctuary" (Ezek. 8:1-6).

From the door of the north gateway of the temple, which leads into the inner court, by digging through a hole in the wall, Ezekiel came upon a secret door leading into a room, the walls of which were carved in relief with representations of reptiles and beasts and idols. Coming upon the scene from the rear, he saw seventy prominent men, including Jaazaniah son of Shaphan,[39] standing in the dark before these sculptured figures, with censers of burning incense in their hands. Their Lord, so they think, has left them, and they are seeking help elsewhere from foreign deities and in pagan rites.

Again at the north gateway of the temple Ezekiel is brought outside the door into the inner court where "the image causing [divine] resentment" stood. There, right within the very precinct of the house of the Lord, "sat women weeping for Tammuz" (Ezek. 8:14). This was an already ancient religious rite, Babylonian in its origin, which remotes to 3000 B.C. Tammuz—the name in Summerian is Dumu-zi, meaning "faithful son"—was "the youthful husband or son or lover of Ishtar," "the god of vegetation and of beneficent floods." Every year he vanished into the underworld to "return" the following spring. Public dirges, performed by women, celebrated his departure and sought for his return in life and power.[40] It was a very popular and

[39] Not Shaphan the scribe, Josiah's chancellor, for the latter's sons are Ahikam (26:24), Elasah (29:3), and Gemariah (36:10).

[40] Cf. G. A. Cooke, *Ezekiel*, I, 96-97.

tenacious item in the Babylonian cult, and it likewise was a rite carried out by the women.

Once again in the inner court of the temple, between the vestibule or porch at the eastern end of the temple (I Kings 6:3) and the altar of burnt offering (I Kings 8:64), at the place where in the legitimate cult of the Lord the priests offered prayer (Joel 2:17), Ezekiel saw about twenty-five men facing not the temple, as was the practice of the priests in the legitimate worship of the Lord, but with their backs to the temple and their faces toward the east, worshiping the sun (Ezek. 8:16). This was the worship of Shamash, the Assyrian sun-god, which had been introduced into Judah by Ahaz and Manasseh (Jer. 8:2; II Kings 23:5, 11), and although rooted out by King Josiah's reform, was now again present in power. Such rites give concrete content to "the detested things in my house."

CHILD SACRIFICE

A still more abhorrent feature of worship, once rooted out of Judah by the Deuteronomic reform (II Kings 23:10), now mirroring the desperation of the times, had swept back into Judean religion—the horrible rite of child sacrifice. In the valley of The Son of Hinnom, situated in the south and southwestern area of Jerusalem, today called Wadi er-rababa, they rebuilt the high place of Topheth [41] ("place of fire"), and sacrificed thereon their sons and daughters. This was a pagan intrusion, Canaanite in origin (19:5), and had no part whatever in the Lord's requirements of his people (2:23). What will be the Lord's punishment of Judah for this grievous and horrible perversion of his will?

That same valley is destined to be filled with the corpses of Judean dead, slain by the invading Chaldeans, here again conceived as the agents to express the Lord's judgment upon Judah. In spite of the fact that to these backsliding Judeans Topheth is viewed as a holy place to be defiled by no common burial, since there will be left no other place in Jerusalem for burial, it will be filled with the corpses of Judean dead who shall have met their fate at the hands of the ruthless Chaldean invaders. The very name of the valley will be changed from the valley of the Son of Hinnom to the valley of Slaughter. When there is no longer any more room there for burial, the dead bodies will simply be exposed as carrion for vultures and wild beasts.

The normal sounds of community life, the gleeful banter of bride and

---

[41] The pointing of *tāpheth* as *tōpheth* represents the vowels of the word *bōsheth* ("shame"), suggesting that tōpheth is "the shameful thing."

groom gloriously happy in fellowship with each other, will cease to be heard in Judah, for the whole land will become a desolation. The conquering Chaldean soldiers, thirsty for plunder, will violate the Judean graves and disinter the bodies of the decently buried Jews, the distinguished leaders and the common people alike. And—horrible thought to the Judeans—they will then leave their dead bones uncovered, exposed to the view of the very gods—sun, moon, and heavenly host—before which the Judeans had so passionately and so often prostrated themselves in their illegitimate worship. And any Judeans who perchance escaping death may be banished in exile, will prefer death itself to the life they must then live.

Thus Jeremiah summons all Judah to lamentation:

> 7:29 Shear your hair and throw it away;
> And lift upon your lips a lamentation,
> For the Lord has rejected and forsaken
> The generation that is doing this.

30 For the Judeans have done what is evil in my sight, says the Lord. They have put their detested things in the house to which my name was given, so as to pollute it. 31 And they have built the high place of Topheth, which is in the valley of Ben-Hinnon, to burn their sons and their daughters in the fire— that which I did not command, nor did it [ever] come into my mind. 32 Therefore, lo, days are coming, says the Lord, when they shall not be called any more the Topheth and the valley of Ben-Hinnon, but the valley of Slaughter, and they shall bury in Topheth until there is no [more] room. 33 And the corpses of this people will be carrion for the birds of the heaven and the beasts of the earth and none shall frighten [them, i.e., birds and animals] away. 34 And I will cause to cease from the cities of Judah and from the streets of Jerusalem the voice of joy and the voice of gladness, the voice of the bridegroom and the voice of the bride; for the land shall become a desolation.

8:1 At that time, says the Lord, they shall bring out from their graves the bones of the kings of Judah, and of his princes, and the bones of the priests and the prophets and the inhabitants of Jerusalem 2 and spread them out to the sun and the moon and to all the heavenly host, which they loved and whom they served, and whom they followed, and whom they sought after and whom they worshiped. They shall not be gathered up or buried. They shall be as dung upon the surface of the ground. 3 And death shall be chosen rather than life by all the remnant of this evil people, those who are left in all the places to which I will have thrust them out, says the Lord of hosts.

O HOUSE OF DAVID, EXECUTE JUSTICE

In Jer. 21:11-14 the prophet utters an oracle against King Jehoiakim. Some instance of the king's proud presumption likely led to its deliverance directly to him at a time when at Egyptian initiative he was toying with the policy of revolt against Nebuchadrezzar, which eventually led to the latter's deportation of Judeans to Babylon in 598.

Jeremiah summons Jehoiakim, at the threat of the Lord's consuming wrath, to protect his pillaged subjects by the daily exercise of justice and redress. The royal palace and the other buildings of the palace area were built on Ophel, the northern height of the "city of David." They were constructed of cedars cut from the majestic forests. There the ostentatious king and his court feel all too secure. But these proud dwellings will be but fuel for the fires of the Lord's wrath which will be kindled by the Chaldeans.

21:11 Concerning the palace of the king of Judah: Hear the word of the Lord,
12   O house of David! Thus says the Lord,
    Execute justice every morning,
    And deliver the one who has been robbed from the power of his extortioner,
    Lest my wrath go forth like fire,
    And burn, with no one to quench it.
13   Lo, I am against you, inhabitants of Ophel,[42]
    Thou rock on secure height, says the Lord,
    Who say, "Who could come down against us,
    Aye, who could come into our dwellings?"
14   So I will kindle a fire in their forest,
    So as to consume all its thicket.

Unjust Acquisition of Wealth

The book of Jeremiah is rich in types of literary forms which the prophet employed in his prophetic utterances. A type which we are somewhat surprised to find in a prophetic book is the gnomic or wisdom utterance, such as is met with particularly in the book of Proverbs. The final editor of the book of Jeremiah has grouped together in 17:5-11 three such authentic wisdom utterances from Jeremiah, vss. 5-8, vss. 9-10, and vs. 11. (For vss. 5-8 see pp. 256-57; for vss. 9-10 see p. 147.)

It is possible, as Rudolph [43] suggests, that the figure of King Jehoiakim, whose ill-gotten gain was the subject of the prophet's later rebuke of him (22:13-14) was in Jeremiah's mind as he coined the proverbian utterance of 17:11. It gives an illustration from the realm of nature, where Jeremiah is wonderfully at home, and from bird life, which as we have already seen (8:7), both interested and taught him. It deals with a familiar subject of Hebrew wisdom, ill-gotten gain. A partridge takes possession of another

[42] Reading hāʿōphel instead of hāʿemeq.
[43] Jeremia, p. 99.

partridge's nest and hatches the eggs which are found in it. Woods [44] maintains with evidence that thus far the statement is true to life, but that the implication of the last part of the verse—that the alien brood desert their foster parent—is in all probability "a more popular belief." The application of the metaphor is that riches gained unlawfully by a person slip out of his hands before the half of his life has been lived, and when his end comes, he will have degenerated into a man of folly, lacking both moral and spiritual sensibility.

> 17:11 Like a partridge that hatches out eggs, though not begetting [them],
> Is he who acquires riches, but not by just means.
> Before his days are half over they will leave him;
> And at his end he will be a fool.

Go Down to the Palace and Speak This Word

Jer. 22:1-5 comes from the Deuteronomic editor. It forms a parallel to 21:11-14, and as Rudolph points out, its characteristic wording is placed directly behind those authentic words of Jeremiah. Vs. 3*b* supplements 21:12 and adds concreteness to the prophet's condemnation. While 21:14 describes in anticipation only the destruction of Zion, vss. 4-5 present the two alternatives open to Judah, just as the Deuteronomist did in 17:24-27—on the one hand, the permanence and security of the Davidic throne (22:4); and on the other hand, the royal palace area reduced to ruins (22:5). Jeremiah is now in the temple, from which he is commanded by the Lord to "go down" to the royal palace, there to speak the Lord's words against the king, his servants, and subjects. The expected introduction of the Deuteronomic editor, characteristic of each section of his work, "The word that came to Jeremiah from the Lord, saying" (cf. 7:1; 11:1), does not appear at this point because 22:1-5 originally formed the continuation of the whole section 7:1–8:3, at the beginning of which that characteristic introduction is given. The episode it reports dates from the beginning of the reign of Jehoiakim. Says the prophet:

> 22:1 Thus says the Lord: Go down to the palace of the king of Judah and speak there this word. 2 And say: Hear the word of the Lord, O King of Judah, who sits on the throne of David. You and your servants and your people who are entering through these gates. 3 Thus says the Lord: Accomplish justice and righteousness and recover that which has been robbed from the hands of the one who wronged him. And do not oppress and do not deal harshly with the resident alien, the orphan and the widow: do not shed innocent blood in this place. 4 For

---

[44] Woods and Powell, *The Hebrew Prophets*, II, 104-105, as cited by A. S. Peake.

if you surely perform this word, then there shall enter through the gates of this palace kings who will be seated on the throne of David, riding in chariots and with horses, they and their servants and their people. 5 But if you do not obey these words, I swear by myself, says the Lord, that this palace shall become a ruins.

In vss. 6-7 we have authentic words of Jeremiah. The prophet takes up again his picture (21:14) of the lofty palace area of Jerusalem, destined for fire at Chaldean hands. He pictures the royal palace as something high and lofty, precious to God. It is comparable to Gilead, the high area across the Jordan, which was famous for its rich pasturage and its forests. Changing the metaphor, he pictures the palace as the summit of famed Lebanon, renowned for the majestic cedars such as had made Israel's palace area glorious since Davidic and Solomonic days—but soon all such palatial splendor is to be reduced to a desolate wilderness, a ruins where no human being lives. The unnamed agents of the Lord's retributive purpose toward Jerusalem are the Chaldean "destroyers."

22:6 For thus says the Lord, concerning the palace of the king of Judah:

> A Gilead are you to me,
> The summit of Lebanon.
> [But] I swear I will make of you a wilderness,
> An uninhabited city.
> 7 I will consecrate destroyers against you,
> Men and their weapons;
> And they shall cut down your choice cedars,
> And throw them upon the fire.

SPIRITUAL INSIGHT THE MEASURE OF GREATNESS

Jeremiah deals with a question of universal significance and of supreme importance in 9:23-24. In what dare a man glory? What is honest renown? What is true fame? How can a man who is truly wise lay claim to repute?

There are three great areas of experience in which men of all ages have laid claim to honor—wisdom, physical strength, wealth. Men whom the world elevates to fame are the scholar, the warrior, and the man of material means. Are these the men whom the Lord would put in his hall of fame?

The very words "fame," "renown," "glory," seem inappropriate in the vocabulary of true religion. The truly great are those who have spiritual insight, who in deep inner experience know the Lord, and know him as a spiritual being who is eternally active in promoting in all the relationships of men through the whole earth, kindness, justice, and righteousness. Such persons do not exult in themselves, but in their God, and in their lives God is well pleased.

9:23 Thus says the Lord:
Let not the wise man make his boast on account of his wisdom;
And let not the warrior make his boast because of his strength.
Let not the rich man make his boast on account of his riches;
24   But upon this ground let him who would, make his boast;
That he has insight and knows me,
That I am the Lord who does kindness,
Justice, and righteousness in the earth,
For in these things I take delight, says the Lord.

A POLITICAL BATTLE CRY

Jer. 9:25-26 reflect the political situation of the period 608-604, when apparently under the leadership of Egypt, whose name leads the list, certain smaller peoples combined against the Chaldeans. We know that Nebuchadrezzar had to fight against the desert Arabs (49:28), here designated "the clipped at the temples," which points to their practice of having the corners of their hair clipped in honor of a pagan deity (Lev. 19:27; Herodotus *History* III. 8). As to such a coalition against the Chaldeans, we have no other information, but there is not adequate data available as regards the swiftly changing political alignments in the Near East at the time of the last three Judean kings. These peoples who were thus combined against the Chaldeans all practiced circumcision.[45] The priestly law of Judaism, which views the rite of circumcision as the peculiar prerogative of "the holy people," had not yet arisen. We rightly understand the line-up of the circumcised peoples against the uncircumcised Chaldeans as political propaganda. But even in pre-exilic Judah the rite of circumcision was held in high esteem, and here it has the effect almost of a popular battle cry—"The circumcised against the uncircumcised!" God is with the former and opposed to the latter!

But against such dependence upon physical externals for the protection of the Lord stood Jeremiah with the full weight of his conviction. Earlier he had declared (4:4) that the outward physical mark of circumcision was utterly worthless. It was no indication of spiritual repentance nor did it lead to amended lives. So he now declares that neither Judah nor her allies, how-

---

[45] Egypt, cf. Ezek. 31:18; 32:19, 32; Arabs (Ishmael their ancestor), cf. Gen. 17:23 ff.; Edom, cf. Ezek. 32:29. For the other neighbors of Israel it is only the Philistines that are ridiculed as "uncircumcised" (I Sam. 17:26).

ever faithfully they observe the rite of circumcision, may qualify for the protection of the Lord.

9:25 Lo, the days are coming, says the Lord, when I will punish every person circumcised as to foreskin: 26 Egypt, Judah, Edom, and the sons of Ammon and Moab, and all those clipped at the temples who live in the desert. For all these nations and all the house of Israel are uncircumcised in heart.

THE LORD A FOUNTAIN OF LIFE

In Jer. 18:13-17 the prophet calls attention to the disgusting thing which the Lord's people have done. It is the Lord himself who is represented as speaking to Israel, his "daughter." There is in his people a stubbornness, an incorrigible quality which the prophet's words seem unable to penetrate. There is that in their conduct which is contrary to nature. There comes to the prophet the memory of Mount Hermon—Sirion, as the Phoenicians called it—with its glorious summit ever capped with pure white snow, which, melting, formed the mountain streams that brought fertility to the valleys below. Never does that lofty fountain of life fail. Such the Lord would be to his people—the dependable source of their spiritual life and growth, constantly pouring down his enriching fullness upon his people. But instead of being refreshed by that mighty fountain of moral and spiritual vitality, they are forgetful of the true God and offer sacrifices to idols. Choosing thus to walk not in the old paths, "where the good way is" (6:16), the Lord will cause them to walk in perilous bypaths, for they are calling down upon themselves, as the inevitable fruit of their conduct, the desolation of Judah. It will be an appalling destruction in which their fair land will be so reduced as to become the butt of derisive gibes from all who pass through it, and as the judgment of God, its people will be scattered by their conquerors. Cries the prophet in the name of God:

> 18:13 Therefore, thus says the Lord,
> Ask now among the nations,
>   Who has heard of the like of this?
> A very disgusting thing
>   Has the virgin Israel done.
> 14 Doth e'er depart from the crag of Sirion
>   The pure white snow?
> Or do mountain waters e'er dry up
>   Their cool flowing streams?
> 15 But my people have forgotten me;
>   To nonentities they offer sacrifice.

So I overthrew them in their ways—
   Paths trod from of old—
To walk in bypaths,
   Where the road is not built up,
16 So as to make their land a desolation,
   A butt of derision forever.
Everyone who crosses over it is appalled,
   And wags his head.
17 Like an east wind I will disperse them
   Before their enemies;
I will show them my back, not my face,
   In the day of their calamity.

CHAPTER FOUR

The Intimate Papers of Jeremiah

608-605—Early Reign of Jehoiakim

UNIQUE IN PROPHETIC LITERATURE ARE THE "CONFESSIONS" OF JEREMIAH WHICH MAY QUITE ACCURATELY BE DESIGNATED AS HIS "INTIMATE papers." [1] They were not written for the public. They are genuine outpourings of his soul and were not intended for a group of auditors. They are intimate spiritual autobiography, quite unique in Old Testament prophecy, and contain the most profound and enduring elements of the prophet's teaching. Jeremiah, who was a poet as well as a prophet, sought in these confessions both spiritual relief and intellectual clarity. In the realm of religious literature they represent the transition from prophecy to psalmody, for they are individual laments of high order, alive with the note of authentic religious experience, just such as we meet with very frequently in the psalms. They have vitally enriched the language of prayer, and have been influential in stimulating on the part of other struggling souls similar spiritual autobiography, the most significant of which are *Augustine's Confessions*. It is most fortunate that these intimate passages have been preserved and included in the book that bears the prophet's name. For in no other portion of his work is Jeremiah's innermost soul so clearly revealed, nor is any material that has come from his pen more permanently valuable than this section of his intimate papers.[2]

All these papers date from the reign of King Jehoiakim (608-598), Judah's frivolous, superficial, and despotic king, who was brutal and unscrupulous

---

[1] Pfeiffer, *Introduction to the Old Testament*, p. 497, dates Jeremiah's confessions in the years 605-598, a period of solitary retreat, from which he emerged as truly "an iron pillar and a wall of brass." It is my judgment that they began very early in King Jehoiakim's reign.

[2] Cf. Elmer A. Leslie, *The Intimate Papers of Jeremiah*.

137

to those who crossed him. When Jeremiah's scroll of his prophetic condemnations, which at an impulse from God he had dictated to Baruch, came into Jehoiakim's hands, the king in hot anger had thrown it to the fire and had tried to lay hands on the prophet. From then on his life was in danger. Pashhur, superintendent of the temple, because of the prophet's utterance prophesying the destruction of Judah, after forcing Jeremiah to spend a night in the stocks, forbade him further entrance to the temple. Thus for a time his public ministry ceased. But this was probably a blessing in disguise. For in this forced retreat period, when he could not publicly preach, he was thrown upon himself in deep, honest heart-searching, in earnest, wrestling, grappling prayer. The nearest we come to anything like it in religious literature is the report of the Gethsemane struggle of Jesus. These passages are the most intimate portions of the book, and it is most fortunate that these intimate papers abide as the prophet's most significant heritage to mankind.

LET US CUT HIM OFF FROM THE LAND OF THE LIVING

As we have seen (26:11-19), priests and prophets in Jerusalem had openly attempted, but without success, to secure a death sentence for Jeremiah. But now his death is plotted in a secret and malicious manner. The priestly circles in Jerusalem, through co-operation with Jeremiah's priestly relatives in Anathoth, sought to accomplish the same end.

That violent plans were stirred up against him, 11:19 makes clear. Perhaps we can best understand this enmity on the part of his own brothers by noting the early attitude centuries later of the relatives of Jesus of Nazareth toward him at the beginning of his ministry. When after his strategic wilderness sojourn he taught in the synagogue in Nazareth, "where he had been brought up," and affirmed out of painful experience the truth of the proverb that "no prophet is welcome in his own country," his hearers there, "all in the synagogue were filled with wrath. And they rose up and put him out of the city, and led him to the brow of the hill on which their city was built, that they might throw him down headlong" (Luke 4:28-29). And when after having launched his ministry and chosen the twelve he went home, the crowd gathered around him then in such numbers that "when his friends heard it, they went out to seize him, for they said, 'He is beside himself'" (Mark 3:21). There is little doubt that Jeremiah's own priestly relatives in similar manner had been greatly embarrassed by the young prophet's sharp condemnation of the ancient and time-honored priestly rites such as sacrifice. Even those of his own blood evidently felt themselves justified in lending assistance to an attempt, instigated by the Jerusalem priesthood, upon Jeremiah's life.

At first, due probably to the prophet's spiritual preoccupation, he was quite unaware of how deep-seated was the antagonism which his prophetic ministry had aroused among his own relatives. He was as innocent about it as a lamb that is being led along to be slaughtered, quite unaware of the fate awaiting it. But this youth, who lived habitually very close to God, became so vividly conscious of this plot against his life that he interpreted the sudden intimation of it that came to him as a divine revelation (11:18). As Volz remarks: "It is an example of how the prophet felt himself led by the Lord in everything: the entire life of the religious man is a guiding of God and in particular moments, that comes clearly to light." [3]

Thus Jeremiah tells us of the delicate situation in which he has now discovered himself to be. God's revelation had suddenly stabbed him alert to the mortal peril in which he stood. His foes were those of his own household. Did Jesus of Nazareth have this incident in mind when centuries later he warned his disciples that such would be their experience? (Matt. 10:36.) Those plotting Jeremiah's death were well enough acquainted with his spirit to know that he whom they would destroy was now in the full vigor of great powers. The sooner such a man were put to silence the better! So Jeremiah reports:

11:18 The Lord informed me and I knew it;
Then thou, Lord, didst let me see their evil deeds.
12:6 "Even your brothers, yes, your father's house,
Even they deal treacherously with you;
Even they conspire together behind your back, all of them.
Do not trust them,
When they speak friendly words to you."
11:19 But I—I was like a docile lamb led to slaughter,
And did not know that they had hatched up plots against me:
"Let us destroy the tree in its vigor;
Let us cut him off from the land of the living,
So his name will no more be remembered."

We can readily imagine the shock which the uncovering of this plot brought to Jeremiah's soul. It threw him back upon himself in heart-searching self-scrutiny. But more, it threw him back upon God, "the Lord of hosts," as the prophet Isaiah had first taught the Judeans to think of him. He became aware that the righteous God was judging him, examining his inner

[3] *Jeremia*, p. 139.

being, the seat of his affections and emotions,[4] scrutinizing his mind and his heart, testing the quality of his spirit. God's searchlight penetrated to the most secret depths of his being. The words of his prayer, in which he acknowledges God's perfect comprehension of him, are classic words which reveal the intimacy of his consciousness of the Presence:

> 11:20a But, O Lord of hosts, who judgest righteously,
> Who dost examine motives and heart,
> 12:3a Thou knowest me, thou seest me;
> And dost examine how my heart is with thee.

The vindictive spirit clearly held by the prophet toward those who are plotting to take his life seems in sharp emotional contrast to his vivid awareness of the divine presence. In fairness to Jeremiah it should be noted that he does not pray that he may be avenged upon those seeking his life, but that God's vengeance may fall upon them. They are not in the first instance his enemies but God's. As for those who were leading him, an innocent lamb, to slaughter, let them be marked for slaughter—such is his prayer! Let God wreak his vengeance upon them—the God to whom Jeremiah has committed himself.

> 12:3b Let them be taken like sheep to be slaughtered,
> Consign them for a day of slaughter.
> 11:20b Let me see thy vengeance upon them,
> For to thee I have committed my cause.

Rudolph sensitively notes how far short these words of Jeremiah fall of the pure selflessness of Jesus' prayer, "Father, forgive them; for they know not what they do" (Luke 23:34). And they show us that Jeremiah did not qualify for sainthood in the Christian sense of the term.

Jeremiah does not seem to be aware of any inconsistency between his prayer for vengeance and his faith in God. However, the Lord does not condemn him but makes it clear to him that the divine retribution will overtake his enemies. They had longed that his name be stamped out, but it is their name which will be utterly rooted out, for their sons will die in war and their daughters in famine. Thus Jeremiah reports God's confirming revelation to him:

11:21 Therefore, thus the Lord said concerning the men of Anathoth who are seeking my life, saying, "Do not prophesy in the name of the Lord, else you shall

---

[4] The term $k^e l\bar{a}y\acute{o}th$, lit., "kidneys," means "dominant affections," and is best rendered here by "motives."

die at our hands." 22 See, I am about to punish them. Their sons shall die by the sword and their daughters shall die by famine. 23 So there shall not any remnant of them survive. For I will bring calamity to the men of Anathoth in the year of their punishment.

THE DARK ENIGMA OF PERSONAL SUFFERING

Such undeserved enmity as this, which Jeremiah encountered both in Anathoth and Jerusalem, played a great part in focusing the prophet's mind upon the dark enigma of personal suffering. Up to this time in the development of Old Testament thought, while we often meet with personal religious experience, it is yet true to say that the essential content of religion, as the prophets taught it, had to do with the relation of the Israelite nation to the Lord, and the Lord to Israel as a whole. As Cornill says: "Jeremiah took the enormous step that shifted the seat of religion to the heart and made the individual the bearer of it: religion became a personal relation of the heart to God!" [5] The following passage, which comes from the same period of Jeremiah's career as the preceding, is one in which the prophet gives pioneering expression to the problem of pain, such as antedated that of the author of the book of Job by perhaps two centuries.

The prophet is reverent and thoughtful. Yet he is poignantly aware of the unjust treatment which God permits him to endure at the hands of wicked men. It is not the problem of pain in general that moves him to utterance, but his own acute mental distress caused by the acts against him of deceitful enemies.

These men who are persecuting him are manifestly secure, planted firmly, and their lives are blessed with offspring. They seem to be in the favor of God and they take his name upon their lips quite familiarly as though God were their intimate friend. Yet it is in frankly secular terms that they speak of him, not to acknowledge his power or to praise him, but rather to deny his knowledge of their conduct, saying as though they were uttering an oracle, "God does not see what we do." The prophet as he faces his problem humbly acknowledges God to be "in the right," yet he ventures to voice his complaint that God is not dealing justly with such men when he permits them to prosper, free from care.

Thus laments the prophet before the Lord:

> 12:1 Thou art in the right, O Lord,
>   If I would complain against thee;
>   Nonetheless of a matter of justice
>   I would dispute with thee.

[5] *Jeremia*, p. 154.

> Why does the wicked man's manner of life prosper?
> Why are all who deal deceitfully free from care?
> 2 Thou dost plant them, aye, they take root;
> They reproduce, aye, they bear fruit.
> Intimate art thou in their speech,
> But far from their controlling affections.[6]
> 4bβ For they say, "God [7] does not see our ways."

Through this energetic encounter with his God, Jeremiah receives no light bearing directly upon his problem. The prophet's "Why?" is left unanswered, but he receives from God something better than a direct answer—a call to courage of soul. Perhaps this is the most practical answer that can come to a questioning human being in mental and spiritual pain. It is a call to personal fortitude as he faces a future which is to be characterized by awful spiritual conflict and grave personal peril.

Jeremiah becomes aware of the divine Presence giving him not comfort but challenge. Unquestionably these words were to ring through his soul many a time in the tense days ahead. Up to now Jeremiah's career as a prophet, in relation to the men of Judah, has been—to speak in pictures—a race with foot soldiers, but before long he will be racing, as it were, against mounted cavalrymen. The Lord paints what lies ahead in another picture, saying to him in effect: "The situation in which you will find yourself in the future will compare with your present perils as the lion-ridden Jordan jungle compares with the peaceful Judean plain."

Thus Jeremiah reports God as saying:

> 12:5 If you have run with men on foot, and they tire you out,
> How then can you compete with horses?
> And if in a safe region you have no confidence,
> How then will you fare in the wild thicket of the Jordan?

Driver,[8] maintaining the Hebrew text exactly as it is, renders this passage:

> And if thou fallest flat on thy belly in a land of peace
> How then wilt thou fare in the rising surge of the stream?

"The verse then asks," Driver explains, "how a man who cannot stand upright in a country undisturbed by storms and tumults will be able to resist a torrential flood, and the application of the question is evident."

---

[6] Vs. 3, which follows, rightly belongs after 11:20a (see p. 140), and vs. 4a,b rightly precedes vs. 13 (see p. 187; see also Rudolph).

[7] Inserting *ᵉlōhîm* with Septuagint, and reading with Septuagint and Vulgate, *ᵓorhōthēnû* instead of *ᵓaḥᵉrîthēnû*.

[8] In H. H. Rowley, ed., *Studies in Old Testament Prophecy*, p. 59.

A WOE OF SOUL NEVER CEASING

In 15:10-21, another of the prophet's intimate confessional utterances, he removes from his inner life the veil of privacy and grants us a glimpse into his soul. Fortunate indeed it is for us that he wrote out in accurately descriptive, honest words this account of his spiritual struggles. When at length it was published for eyes other than his own to read, it was in the truest sense "a *confessio*," as Rudolph has put it, "an acknowledgment in which he made known to all the world both his weakness and his reproof" at God's hand.

He begins in deep melancholy and speaks as though communing with his mother who had brought him into the world. He rues his birth because he feels himself continually at outs with all Judah. Although debtor to none, he has become the butt of well-nigh universal reviling. Had he dealt out evil to those who now rail at him, such enmity would be understandable. But these very enemies—and when their need was greatest—had been the persistent burden of his intercession before God. When they were experiencing distress and affliction, he had mobilized all conceivable agencies to help them. He had stormed, as it were, impregnable gates of iron and bronze in their behalf (vs. 12).

Thus he laments:

> 15:10 Alas, for me, my mother, that you gave me birth,
>   A man of strife and contention with all the land!
>   I have not lent and they have not lent to me,
>   But all of them curse me.
> 11 So let it be, Lord, if I had not served thee with good intention,
>   If I had not made entreaty to thee for the enemy
>   In the time of his distress, yes, in the time of his affliction.
> 12   I have broken iron and bronze, thou knowest.[9]

At vs. 15 his prayer turns to petition for God to remember him and give heed to him, and for God to pour out unrestrainedly his vengeance upon those who are persecuting him. He reminds the Lord that the insulting language and disgraceful treatment in general that he has endured comes entirely from men who reject with disdain the words of God—those very words which he himself as the Lord's prophet has spoken. How sharp in contrast to their scornful rejection of God's revelation is the prophet's own attitude to that same word of God as God had imparted it to him! How

---

[9] Cf. Volz, *Jeremia*, p. 171. Vss. 13-14 do not belong here. Vs. 13 belongs at 17:3 (see p. 124), vs. 14 belongs at 17:4aβb (see p. 125).

he had exulted in "finding" the revelation of God! It was food to his soul just to be aware that he was called by God's name, that he was God's prophet, even as the temple was God's house. For just as the temple belongs to the Lord, he too was the Lord's property. God had taken up his abode in his heart. How deep and intimate is this phase of his prophetic experience as he thus describes it!

> 15:15 O Lord, remember me and pay gracious attention to me,
>   And avenge thyself in my behalf on those who are persecuting me.
>   Not in thy self-restraint!
>   Know that on thy behalf have I borne abuse.
> 16 Thy words were found and I devoured them,
>   Yes, thy word was to me [a source of] exultation,
>   For thy name hath been given me,
>   Lord God of hosts.

Jeremiah was not by nature a detached, secretive person who shunned association with others. His was a deep and tender spirit, exceedingly sensitive and of great warmth toward his fellow men. But his prophetic calling created a great barrier between himself and those who made merry among the people. Jeremiah knew all too well the loneliness which great men experience.

Yet at the same time there was in his soul a deep exultation—that of the vivid consciousness that his life was truly in God's very presence. This awareness of God's immediate nearness was the source of unspeakable gladness, even when he felt most sharply his isolation from "the merrymakers" because of the moral indignation with which God had filled his soul. Thus he reports to God:

> 15:17 I sat not in the circle of merrymakers,
>   But I exulted in the gladness of my heart.
>   Before thy hand I sat alone,
>   Because thou didst fill me with indignation.

In vs. 18 the prophet unveils his inner being in his awful depression—a woe of soul never ceasing, comparable to the persistent, hopeless physical pain of an internal, incurable wound. God had promised, "I will be with you to rescue you," but where is that saving help now? Jeremiah had declared to his people that God was "the fountain of living waters," but in his present utter disillusionment God rather seems to him as a deceitful brook, like a wadi containing water only after rain, but at other times deceiving the hope of wanderers. Thus he laments, questioning God with his persistent "Why?"

> 15:18 Why is my pain persistent,
> And my wound incurable?
> Whence shall I be healed?
> Alas, thou art to me
> Like deceptive waters,
> Which are not reliable.

Jeremiah reached here the lowest level of despair in his entire religious experience so far as he has revealed it to us. His feeling of utter isolation from the God who had promised to be with him to help him is never again so straightforwardly and uncompromisingly expressed as here.

Then when he was at his lowest depth of depression and of spiritual loneliness there came to him a message from God. And it is decidedly not a message of comfort. Nowhere in Jeremiah's experience more than here do we sense the virility of his religion. God makes Jeremiah sharply aware that he has fallen backward in his allegiance. He has let the excruciating difficulty of his task sever him from his loyalty to God, from his faith in God's constant though unfelt presence. In this crisis hour God's word to him is not comfort but challenge. If Jeremiah is to be God's prophet, one who stands before him as a servant before his lord, one who both receives and speaks with responsibility God's word to the people of Judah, there are two things which he must now do. First, he must return to God. His present attitude is that of rebellion, not of dependence and trust. Of his own volition he must come back to God, from faultfinding to confidence, for his prophetic ministry is not to be God-compelled, but God-led and God-inspired.

Second, the prophet must accept the experiences of life which come to him, sifting them so as to retain the precious elements in them—all that is of value—and so as to reject all that is worthless. Then the prophetic words that he utters will be the precious truth of God, unmarred by his own human weakness and unalloyed with the bitterness of self-pity.

> 15:19a Whereupon the Lord thus spoke:
> If you will return, I will let you again
> Stand before me.
> And if you bring forth what is precious, without that which is worthless,
> You shall be as my mouth.

If Jeremiah will honestly meet these conditions, four results will manifest themselves in his prophetic ministry. First, he will then be as God's mouth, speaking clearly and understandingly to his fellow men the pure truth of God's word which God would have them know. Here is a remarkable intimation of the New Testament doctrine of the Incarnation, the word become flesh. Then God's truth in all its fullness and reality, unmarred by the limitations of Jeremiah's own spirit, will be uttered by him. Jeremiah will be to his fellow Judeans as God's mouth. Here is suggested to the prophet the cost of being a spokesman for God—in terms of inner heart-searching, ruthless self-criticism, and determined self-pruning. These are all disciplines to which he must submit himself who would be in potent reality God's prophet.

A second result which will obtain if Jeremiah thus returns to God is that he will never trim God's prophetic word to the pattern of the Judean people's wishes, thus becoming merely one of them and no different from them. Rather he will persist as the honest spokesman of God's word however hard it may be for them to receive it. Then eventually they will turn to him in the desperate realization that God's true word does reside in him. However harsh that word may be to which to listen, and however loath they may be to receive it in its naked truthfulness, they will at length turn to him for it.

A third result is that he will become "on behalf of" the Judean people just what God at the time of his call to be a prophet had promised to make him (1:18), a fortified bronze wall against them. Even when sincerely considering him their enemy the Judeans fight against him, they will not be able to overcome him.

A fourth result is that when the courageous pursuit of his prophetic ministry brings his life into danger at the hands of evil men—some of them most formidable enemies—God will protect him and forcibly deliver him from their evil intent.

The prophet continues:

15:19b **They will turn back to you,**
      But you will not turn back to them.
  20 **And I will make you, before this people,**
      Into a fortified bronze wall;
    And though they fight with you,
      They shall not prevail over you.
    For I am with you,
      To save you and to rescue you,
        Says the Lord.
  21 **And I will deliver you from the hand of evil men,**
      And will ransom you from the power of formidable foes.

Who Can Know the Heart of Man?

The second (17:9-10) of the three unique wisdom utterances (17:5-11) which we find in Jeremiah reports an insight which the prophet gained in dealing with his own innermost spirit. It thrills with his experience of a God who knew him and his worth far more profoundly than did Jeremiah himself. It belongs with his "confessions" and probably dates from the reign of King Jehoiakim.

Palestine was a land of heights and depths, and Jeremiah knew them both. But deeper to him than any gully or ravine were the incomprehensible, abysmal depths of his own personality. And here, as we have already noted in ch. 15, he stands before his own inner life like one taken off his guard, shocked, chagrined, and dismayed. Already he knew, as the wise in Israel had taught, that out of the heart "are the issues of life" (Prov. 4:23). Centuries later, One to whom he was uniquely akin in spirit was to teach more specifically that "from within, out of the heart of man, come evil thoughts" and deeds (Mark 7:21). He knew in experience what Carlyle called "the abysmal depths of the human spirit," and was skilled in diagnosing that incurable sickness of man's inner being which defied all human insight. But while no human person could penetrate to the depths of this man, God could. Long before the psalmist wrote, "O Lord, thou searchest me and knowest me" (139:1), this man had felt the presence of the omniscient God searching him to the roots of his being, testing his affections, and by the power of his moral law, the spiritual expression of God's own nature, bringing his conduct to its ultimate spiritual fruitage.

Cries the prophet almost in despair:

> 17:9 Deeper is the heart than anything,
> Yes, incurable is it:
> Who can know it?

Came the answer from God:

> 10 I the Lord keep searching the heart,
> And keep testing the affections,
> So as to reward a man according to his ways,
> And in accord with the fruit of his conduct.

Where Is the Word of the Lord?

Perhaps the hardest response for a prophet to take from his hearers is ridicule. Convinced as Jeremiah was of the truthfulness of his warnings, such taunts from his hearers lacerated his soul. They considered him a willing doom-bearer, one who not only preached the destruction of their nation but apparently wanted it to come. This interpretation of his attitude cut him to the quick.

In self-defense against this accusation he appeals to God, whose knowledge of his every word and of his innermost feelings is absolute. He lifts his lacerated spirit into the presence of him who alone is his hope and who in the encounters just dealt with had assured him of his help (15:20). Thus he prays:

> 17:14 Heal me, O Lord, and I shall be healed;
> Help me and I shall be helped;
> For thou art my hope.
> 15 Lo, they keep saying to me,
> "Where is the word of the Lord? Pray, let it come!"
> 16 But as for me, I have not pressed after thee for the evil day.
> Nor have I longed for the day of woe.
> Thou knowest the utterance of my lips:
> It is before thy face.

The prophet is clear in his own mind that certain terror—sudden and unprepared for—awaits his now-bored hearers. They will experience dismay and shame when at length the evil day of national destruction overtakes Judah. But when it comes, so the prophet prays, may those who have turned a cold shoulder to the Lord's intense warnings, and have even persecuted the prophet who uttered them, experience the shame and dismay which should justly be their lot—yes, and in double portion. But when that day comes, may the Lord who brings it be to his prophet who has proclaimed it, not a source of terror, but rather of refuge and assurance. Thus Jeremiah's prayer continues:

> 17:17 Be not as a terror to me:
> My refuge art thou in the evil day.
> 18 Let my persecutors be ashamed, but let not me be ashamed;
> Let them be dismayed, but let not me be dismayed;
> Bring upon them the evil day,
> And with a double crushing shatter them.

We become aware in such words of an attitude on the part of Jeremiah toward his persecutors which we can understand and even charitably excuse, but which once again we sense is far removed from the normative attitude of Stephen, who prayed, "Lord, do not hold this sin against them"

(Acts 7:60), or of Jesus, who in his dying hour cried out, "Father, forgive them; for they know not what they do" (Luke 23:34).

THE PLOT AGAINST JEREMIAH'S LIFE

It was the official religious leadership of Judah—the priests, prophets, and wise men—which at length combined forces against Jeremiah. He had criticized these classes individually and collectively in considerable detail. When the calamity should come which these leaders did not at all foresee, Jeremiah knew that the priests would be dismayed and the prophets would be astonished. For they had assured "peace," "good fortune," "welfare," to the nation, while the authentic "word" of the Lord had revealed to Jeremiah that the sword was about to strike at "their very life" (4:9-10). He had ridiculed the wise men whose reputed "wisdom" had proved itself worthless in the contemporary national crisis now facing Judah (8:9). Nor was Jeremiah entirely alone in this view, for Ezekiel, his younger contemporary, was likewise doing his utmost to awaken the deluded Judean leaders to the fact of grave national crisis. Ezekiel characterized the prophets as having no authentic "vision," the priests as inadequate in "instruction," and the aged wise men as bereft of dependable "counsel" (7:26-27). Sharply these three classes of leaders maintained that they needed no interloper like Jeremiah to guide them, that God spoke through them, and that their words remained authoritative. It is little wonder that these classes, jealous though they often were of one another, combined against Jeremiah with the vowed intention of doing away with him.

Their method was to trap him into subversive speech, to catch him up in some dangerous utterance, so they watched him in cold animosity and listened with sinister intent to his every word. These three groups of Judean leaders were a unit only in one thing—their intense and determined animosity to Jeremiah.

18:18 And they said: "Come, let us concoct an accusation against Jeremiah. For instruction [tôrāh] shall not fail from the priest, nor counsel ['ēçāh] from the wise, nor revelation [dābhār] from the prophet. Come, let us strike him because of his speech, and let us give attention to everything that he says."

The delicacy of his situation and the grave peril in which he consciously stood drove the prophet to a lamenting prayer, filled with a quite understandable mood of bitterness. These three groups had set themselves to "give attention" to all Jeremiah's words. Using the same term, the prophet pours out his petition (haqshíbhāh) for the "attention" of God (vs. 19). He protests that he is innocent of their trumped-up accusations. Then he pleads for God's fairness to one who had stood before him as an intercessor for these very enemies. The prophet's feeling of outraged righteousness leads him to implore the Lord to take severe measures against these conscienceless designers who are plotting to kill him. With Jeremiah's vindictive spirit in prayer regarding his enemies we have already become familiar: "Let me see thy vengeance upon them" (11:20) ; "Let them be taken like sheep to be slaughtered" (12:3) ; "Avenge thyself in my behalf on those who are persecuting me" (15:15) ; "Bring upon them the evil day and with a double crushing shatter them" (17:18). But now his prayer of vengeance almost makes us shudder. Let those plotting his death die in battle and their sons in famine. Let the reproach of sterility and widowhood fall upon their wives. Because of their plot against his life may their homes be plundered by enemy invaders. His vindictive prayer rises to its peak of passion in his appeal that the Lord who knows their plot upon his life may not gloss over their iniquity and so pardon their sin, but may view it in all its offensiveness and penalize them while his anger is ablaze.

Thus he prays:

> 18:19 Give attention to me, O Lord,
>   And listen to the voice of my plea.
>   20 Should one be rewarded with evil instead of good?
>   Remember how I stood before thee
>   To speak for their benefit,
>   To turn back thy wrath from them.
>   21 Accordingly, give over their sons to famine;
>   And deliver them up to the power of the sword;
>   Yea, let their wives be
>   Robbed of offspring and become widows;
>   And let their men be killed,
>   Their young men smitten by the sword in battle.
>   22 Let a distress cry be heard from their houses,
>   When a band of plunderers has come suddenly upon them.
>   For they have dug a pit to ensnare me;
>   Yes, traps they have hid for my feet.
>   23 But thou, O Lord, dost know
>   All their design to put me to death.
>   Forgive not their iniquity,
>   And as for their sin, let it not be wiped out from thy sight.
>   Let their offense be before thee;
>   Deal with them while thou art angry.

As we hear the prophet in real peril of his life pray such a prayer, we are stabbed into awareness of how far the noblest piety of the Old Testament still is from the heights reached in the New Testament. Particularly are we conscious of the vast gulf that exists between this prayer and the spirit toward the enemy that breathes in Jesus' words: "Love your enemies and pray for those who persecute you, so that you may be sons of your Father who is in heaven" (Matt. 5:44-45). And likewise how far are we here from the spirit of Jesus' prayer from the cross: "Father, forgive them; for they know not what they do" (Luke 23:34). Yet we must remember the utter loneliness of this lamenting soul, and must be grateful for the honesty that draws aside the curtain that for a moment others may see in stark realism the wrestle of his soul with the living God.

A Burning Fire Shut Up in My Bones

In 20:7-18 we have the last of Jeremiah's unique confessional sections, wherein he gives us a glimpse into his inmost soul. The veil of privacy over his inner spirit is here drawn aside momentarily, and we are permitted to see the struggle of his mind and heart with God. Jeremiah had continuously inveighed against King Jehoiakim and his court, and against the political and spiritual leaders of Judah. To him the doom of Judah was certain and near at hand.

But the years flowed along and still the doom proclaimed did not materialize. It is not surprising that the time came when Jeremiah's earnest warnings met with scornful laughter and his solemn charges awakened only mocking derision. Jeers and gibes were hurled at him. For a sensitive nature like his, such response to his solemn words of teaching and preaching was well-nigh unbearable.

It is remarkable that in spite of the irresponsiveness of those to whom he spoke, never once did he doubt that God had commissioned him to speak as his prophet. But under the smarting of his hearers' derisive scorn he felt as though God had deluded him, enticed, overpersuaded—yes, even seduced him. God had put him under superhuman power. On the one hand, the prophet knew the awful pressure of God's hand impelling him to speak. On the other hand, to be the constant butt of ridicule, to be made sport of through each long day, and day after day, was more than he could endure.

Whenever he spoke as God's prophet there was only one message to be delivered, the Lord's solemn condemnation of his people's wickedness, and his censure upon their evil conduct because of the wreck of national and personal life which it was causing. Moreover, as Jeremiah knew his own soul, he was sure that when he uttered such sharp and pointed condemnation, it was God's word, not his own, that he was speaking. In deep depression he pours out his spirit in lament to God:

> 20:7 Thou hast allured me, O Lord, and I was enticed.
> Thou didst overpower me and didst get the upper hand.
> I have become a laughingstock all day long;
> All of them ridicule me.
> 8 For as often as I speak, I must cry out,
> "Deed of violence, act of oppression," I cry,
> Because the word of the Lord to me has become
> A cause of scorn and derision all day long.

Time and again the prophet reasoned with himself: "I shall not speak out the Lord's message. I shall cease appearing before them with 'Thus says the Lord.' I shall keep it to myself." But whenever he yielded to the temptation to keep silent, the divine message that God had given him to declare burned in his inner being like fire. It must out. It overpowered him. He simply had to speak. Volz has truly said that "no words in the classical prophetic literature show so clearly as these [vs. 9] that the prophets in their bearing and in their utterances stand under the divine compulsion." [10] So Jeremiah confesses:

> 20:9 Yet as often as I say, "I will not mention him,
> And I will not speak any more in his name,"
> Then there is, as it were, a burning fire
> Shut up in my bones,
> And I weary myself holding in
> And I cannot.

Jeremiah became aware that a malicious whispering campaign was being carried on against him in Jerusalem. He was constantly under suspicion. He gradually came to the painful consciousness that those who were watching him with malice aforethought were people whom he had counted as his friends. And these very persons were encouraging others to report information as to any utterance on his part that could be used as treasonous against him. They hoped to catch him unawares and get him in their power. How sweet then would be their revenge for all his stern proclamations and scathing criticisms! The prophet had made conspicuous enough the Judean leaders whom he had condemned in the Lord's name. How they

---

[10] *Jeremia*, p. 207.

longed now to make him conspicuous by humiliating and disgracing him
before those against whom he, as the proclaimer of the Lord's judgment,
had taken his stand.

Thus he reports:

> 20:10 For I hear the whispering of many,
>   Terror on every side!
>   "Inform us, and we shall report him."
> All men who are my friends,
>   Watching to see me stumble.
> "Perhaps he will be deceived so we can prevail over him.
> And we can take vengeance on him."

Yet the prophet was not afraid of them. For however strong were these
forces arrayed against him on every side, still stronger was his consciousness of the presence of the Lord in his soul, like a powerful, terror-striking
warrior, protecting him. Before such a protector his enemies could not prevail. Moreover, the certain failure of his enemies to control and silence him
will fill them with undying humiliation. So in his dark hour, when from every
quarter his life is in mortal peril, he turned to his sole defender, to whom
the prophet's problems and inner struggles were as an open book, with a
mighty confidence in his protection. He has the certainty, not of demonstrated fact but of courageous faith. He believes that God is with him and
that God will vindicate him before his enemies by the defeat of their evil
designs and by their own consequent humiliation and disgrace. He is so
sure that the Lord will vindicate him, one of God's "needy" ones, through
rescuing him from his present peril, that before his vindication has been
accomplished, he sings a song of personal thanksgiving, testifying to the
Lord's rescuing presence in this hour of grave crisis.

> 20:11 But the Lord is with me as a terror-striking warrior;
>   Therefore those pursuing me will stumble and not prevail.
> They will be very much ashamed that they did not succeed,
>   Their eternal humiliation will never be forgotten.[11]
> 13 Sing to the Lord,
>   Praise the Lord!
> For he has rescued the life of the needy
> From the power of evil men.

In a manner often quite characteristic of human experience generally,
a mood of deep depression follows hard upon that of spiritual exaltation.

---

[11] Vs. 12 is an addition; it is original in 11:20.

It was so with Jeremiah. Already once before he struck this minor keynote (15:10), but then his mood was but momentary. Here we see him in what seems to be the deepest depression into which he ever sank. His words give expression to a self-inflicted curse. He laments that he was ever born, and curses both the day of his birth and the man who had brought the news of it to his father—such tidings as could never fail to stir the heart of a male parent with joy—the birth of a son. Indeed, Jeremiah had been informed as to how his father had then rejoiced when a messenger brought him that news. But in view of the tragic career of that child, now grown to manhood, in oratorical exaggeration he calls down a curse on that poor unwitting messenger. Because of his own life marked with suffering, in rhetorical overstatement he expresses the wish that his birthday might be the annual bearer of a curse, and that it be celebrated in the morning by cries of human misery and at noontide by the shout of invading forces. But how much better it would be, had he never seen the light of day!

> 20:14 Cursed be the day
> On which I was born!
> The day on which my mother gave me birth—
> Let [it] not be blessed!
> 15 Cursed be the man who with good tidings
> Gladdened my father saying,
> "A male child has been born to you."
> He did rejoice him greatly.
> 16 Let that day be as the cities
> Which the Lord overturned without repenting.
> Let it hear a distress cry in the morning
> And a war cry at noontime.
> 17 Because thou didst not put me to death in the womb,
> And so let my mother be my grave,
> And her womb forever pregnant.
> 18 Why then, came I forth from the womb,
> To experience trouble and sorrow,
> And to end my days in shame?

CHAPTER FIVE

A Book Is Born in International Crisis

605-602—Middle Reign of Jehoiakim

J ER. 25:1-14 COMES TO US THROUGH THE DEUTERONOMIC EDITOR OF THE BOOK. ACCORDINGLY, ALTHOUGH WE DO NOT HAVE HERE THE PROPHET'S exact words, we do have the essential content of what he said. The passage dates from 605, the year when Nebuchadrezzar, the Chaldean, having defeated Pharaoh Neco of Egypt at the decisive Battle of Carchemish, hurried back to Babylon to take the Chaldean throne which had just been vacated by the death of his father Nabopolassar. The Battle of Carchemish was one of the most decisive battles of ancient history, as it inaugurated the period of Chaldean supremacy in the Middle East, a period which was destined to last until 538, when Cyrus the Persian mastered Babylon and wrested the determination of the course of history in that area of the world from Semitic hands.

The decisive triumph of the Chaldean Empire over the Egyptian Empire at Carchemish made it absolutely clear to the prophet, to whom God was the sovereign of history, that "the foe from the north" was the Chaldean Empire.

JEREMIAH SUMMARIZES HIS TWENTY-THREE YEARS OF PREACHING

At this significant turning point in world history Jeremiah was conscious of an impulse from God to summarize the Lord's message which for these twenty-three years he had been preaching. Thus the Deuteronomic editor introduces his account of it (vss. 1-2).

25:1 **The word which came to Jeremiah concerning all the people of Judah in the fourth year of Jehoiakim, son of Josiah king of Judah—this was the first year**

155

of Nebuchadrezzar king of Babylon— 2 which he spoke concerning the people of Judah and concerning the inhabitants of Jerusalem.

The summary begins at vs. 3. In God's name he called the Judeans to turn away (*shûbhû*) from their evil practices, for if they do, only then will they dwell securely (*sh'bhû*) in their Judean territory. We note here a poetic wordplay upon two Hebrew words similar in sound but diverse in meaning, which was a device for arresting attention often employed by Jeremiah.

At first the reform put in operation by King Josiah seemed to be evidence that Judah was truly turning to the Lord. But then came Josiah's death (609), and under King Jehoiakim the nation would not listen to his words. The prophet had called upon them to cease the worship of other deities— the Canaanite Baals, the Assyrian-Babylonian queen of heaven, and Molech, to whom children were sacrificed, but his call had fallen upon deaf ears. Consequently the Lord is about to send the Chaldeans (a nation from the north) against the Judeans. They will exterminate Judah as a nation. Once a people of dignity, beloved of God and honored by other nations, the Judeans will become a butt of scorn (vss. 3, 5-9).

25:3 From the thirteenth year of Josiah son of Amon, king of Judah, until this day—twenty-three years—I have spoken to you, speaking early and often,[1] 5 saying, Return, I entreat you, each from his evil way and from the evil of your practices and so dwell upon the land which I gave to you and your fathers forever and ever. 6 And do not walk after other gods, serving and worshiping them, and do not, by the work of your hands provoke the Lord to evil toward you. 7 But you would not listen to me.

8 Therefore, thus says the Lord of hosts, Because you would not believe my words, 9 lo, I shall surely take a people [2] from the north and will bring them against this land and its inhabitants.

Those will be solemn days indeed for Judah, yes, tragic even to contemplate. In vs. 10 we are aware of the prophet's love of life as he saw it and lived it, the normal daily life of Palestine—the peals of mirth, the carefree laughter of voices bubbling over with "the wild joy of living," the proud dominant voice of him who is taking to himself a wife, the gentler responsive voice of his bride, the universally familiar and loved and ever-present sound of the grinding of millstones, heard in the homes of the

---

[1] Vs. 4 is an addition from 7:25-26; it is omitted here.
[2] Cf. Brown-Driver-Briggs, *Hebrew Lexicon*, p. 1047, 1st col. f., and read with Septuagint *mishpāḥāh miççāphôn*.

wealthy as well as in the homes of the humblest peasants, and the welcome light of the Palestinian lamps, such as excavators of tells in that land today find everywhere. All that loved and familiar life in Judah will be no more. For two generations beloved Palestine will be an uninhabited, desolate waste. All that the prophet has predicted for Judah will become somber reality.

Says the prophet:

25:10 And I will cause to cease from their midst the sound of mirth and the cry of joy, the voice of the bridegroom and the voice of the bride, the sound of the millstones and the light of the lamp. 11 And all the land will become an occasion of dismay and they shall be subject to the king of Babylon seventy years.[3] 13 So I will bring upon this land all the words which I have uttered against it, all that has been written in this book.[4]

Vss. 1-13 serve as a terminating retrospect [5] on chs. 1–24, which in the main deal with the times of Josiah and Jehoiakim.

THE CUP OF THE LORD FOR THE NATIONS

In 25:15-28 we have a collection of the authentic words of Jeremiah, which are entirely independent of vss. 1-14, which, as we have seen, while giving the essential content of what Jeremiah said, come from the redactor. Vss. 15-28 give the content of a vision experience as Jeremiah told it. There was no need for him to stress the visionary quality of the prophecy, for in the very nature of the case the act involved could not actually be carried out. The prophet is commanded to take from the Lord's hand a cup that symbolizes the fate which the Lord, as the determiner of the destiny and fortune of all peoples, is to deal out to particular nations through Jeremiah, his cup-bearer. As A. P. Kelso says: "He is to take the cup of the wine of wrath from God's hand and in a dreadful sacrament give it to all the nations to whom he is sent." [6] The content of the cup, when drunk by the particular nation, will in each case have an effect comparable to intoxication from wine. It will cause the nation to reel in political downfall. And just

---

[3] Omit vs. 12 as an addition (cf. 29:10) ; vs. 12b is derived from 5:26, 62. Jer. 25:12 reads: "And when seventy years shall have been consummated, I will punish that nation and make it a perpetual desolation."

[4] Omit vs. 14 with Septuagint: "For they shall make slaves of them, even they, great nations and great kings. And I will recompense them in accordance with their acts and the deeds of their hands."

[5] So Rudolph, *Jeremia*, p. 139.

[6] "The Religious Consciousness of Jeremiah,"—*American Journal of Semitic Languages and Literature*, xli (1925) , 239.

as a drunken man in his stupor is an object of derision, so each nation to whom the Lord of all history directs the prophet to give the cup of national destruction, will become the butt of derision and an object of disgrace.

Jeremiah is pioneering here in imaginative prophecy. For 25:15-28 and Hab. 2:15-16 represent the earliest references in the Old Testament to "the cup of the Lord." And in both cases it has the background of the Chaldean political domination of the ancient Near East. Jeremiah sensed it vaguely from the moment of his call when the "pot blown upon" by the blower "in the north" gave a hint of the direction from which calamity upon Judah would come. But since 605, the strategic date of the Chaldean victory at Carchemish over the Egyptian Pharaoh Neco—a world-shaking event in that eastern world—the prophet was clear that the northern foe which was to bring national calamity to Judah was the Chaldeans. Behind the authentic words of Jeremiah in this chapter "stands the conviction that the Lord of the whole world now designates Nebuchadrezzar as the one to carry out His will and has given not Judah merely but all these lands into his hand (Jer. 27:6)." [7]

From the moment of his call Jeremiah understood that he was to be a prophet not merely to Judah but "to the nations" (1:5), and already (9:25-26; 12:14) he has touched upon this phase of his commission. We must now sense the atmosphere of imminence and realism which moved Jeremiah's soul.

We note that not all nations are to drink of the cup. We do not have here any conception of a universal destruction. We feel the tension of the situation as in the original words of Jeremiah, the pertinent nations which are destined to come under the Chaldean sphere of influence are singled out. First heading the list comes Egypt (vss. 19-20a) with the Pharaoh, his servants and officials, and the Egyptian foreign population, that is "the whole mixture of nations," such as Ethiopia, Put, Lud, all the Arabians, the Lybians, and the Cherethites (Ezek. 30:5), and such as are referred to later in relation with the Chaldeans, "all the foreign people [$h\bar{a}^\cdot erebh$] in the midst of her" (50:37). Second comes the Philistine area (vs. 20b), and Ashkelon, Gaza, Ekron, and Ashdod are included. Third comes the area to the southeast and east (vs. 21), Edom, Moab, and Ammon. Fourth comes the Bedouin tribal area (vss. 23-24), the great north Arabian tribes, Dedan, Tema, and Buz, and the lesser tribes of the Arabian desert.

In this manner Jeremiah introduces his vision experience (vss. 15-16),

[7] *Ibid.*, p. 229.

then enumerates the people to whom in the vision he handed the cup (vss. 19-24).

25:15 Thus says the Lord the God of Israel to me: "Take a cup of this wine from my hand and give all the nations to drink of it, to whom I am about to send you. 16 And they will drink and reel to and fro and they will act like madmen." 17 So I took the cup from the hand of the Lord and I gave to drink all the nations to which the Lord sent me.[8] 19 Pharaoh king of Egypt, and his servants and his princes and all his people, 20 and the whole mixture of nations and Ashkelon and Gaza and Ekron and the residue of Ashdod. 21 Edom and Moab and the Ammonites, 23 Dedan and Teman and Buz and all those clipped on the temples, 24 who dwell in the wilderness.[9]

With 25:32, 34-38 Jeremiah is again the speaker. Just as the prophet, the cup-bearer of the Lord, has handed each nation within the present sweep of his concern the cup of national destruction, so the prophet now pictures the consequent fall of nation after nation. There can be no escape. The kings (the shepherds) and the rulers (the rams of the flock) in the case of each nation are to be devastated. Behind the destroying nation, the Chaldeans, stands the Lord, for the destroyer is conceived as but his instrument. The lovely pastures and meadows of Judah, which Jeremiah held so tenderly in his heart, are to experience devastation at the hands of that ruthless enemy power. But the vivid imaginative picture of that devastator on the march is reserved for vs. 38. It is Nebuchadrezzar. Already he has left his lair and his objective is Judah. He is but the instrument of the Lord's judgment upon his people.

Cries the prophet:

> 25:32   Thus says the Lord of hosts:
> Lo, evil goes forth
> From nation to nation,
> And a great storm is stirred up
> From the remote parts of the earth.
> 34 Wail, ye shepherds, and cry out,
> And roll in the dust, you lords of the flock;
> For your time for slaughtering has come,
> And you shall fall like desirable rams.
> 35 There is no flight for the shepherds,
> No escape for the lords of the flock.

[8] For vs. 18, which presupposes the destruction of Jerusalem, as an addition, see p. 322.
[9] I owe much in vss. 15-33 to the penetrating analysis of Rudolph, Jeremia, pp. 138-39. For vss. 18, 20 (in part), 22, 24 (in part), 25, 26, 27-31, and 33 see pp. 322-23.

36 Hark, the outcry of the shepherds,
    And the wailing of the lords of the flock!
    For the Lord is about to devastate their pasturage,
37 And the peaceful meadows will be silenced.
38 The lion has left his lair,
    Yes, their land has become an appalling waste,
    Before the sword of the oppressor,
    Before the heat of the anger of the Lord.

THE FOREIGN ORACLES

The Hebrew text of Jeremiah places the foreign oracles (46:1–51:58) at the end of the book. However the Septuagint, the Greek version of the Old Testament, which places them immediately after 25:13, is probably more nearly correct.

In the nature of the case such oracles invite later additions and insertions on the part of the editors of the Hebrew text, and this has unquestionably happened here. But certainly there is in these oracles a core that is historical and 46:1–49:33, when cleared of secondary intrusions, can with reasonable confidence be attributed to Jeremiah. A key passage which has concrete bearing upon this question is 27:6, an authentic utterance of Jeremiah, in which the Lord is represented as saying:

27:6 And now I have given all these lands [Edom, Moab, Ammon, Tyre, and Sidon] into the power of Nebuchadrezzar king of Babylon, and even the beasts of the field I have given to him to serve him.

Rudolph,[10] who argues skillfully for their essential authenticity, says: "In content these oracles are nothing other than the unfolding of the certainty which Jeremiah expressed in Jer. 27:6. . . . He who considers Jer. 27:6 as authentic cannot declare the idea of God of chs. 46–49 as inconsistent with Jeremiah, . . . and he who discerns Jeremiah's voice in the oracle against Egypt in 43:8 ff., cannot deny it in that of ch. 46." At the moment of his call to the prophetic office Jeremiah became aware that he was to be "a prophet to the nations" (1:5), as well as to Judah.

JEREMIAH'S ORACLE CONCERNING EGYPT

The year 605 was of vast political importance in the Middle East because it marked the time when the Chaldeans as the new world power gained

---

[10] Cf. *Jeremia*, p. 229.

the upper hand over Egypt. This is the reason why Jeremiah at that time dealt with the nations in his prophetic utterances.

The superscription in 46:1, which dates the prophecies in 605, is intended for the entire section 46:3–49:33. The section 46:2-28 contains two oracles concerning Egypt, vss. 3-12 and vss. 13-28. The title "concerning Egypt" in vs. 2 includes both vss. 3-12 and vss. 13-28. The remainder of the title in vs. 2, "Against the army of Pharaoh Neco king of Egypt, which was at the Euphrates River at Carchemish, which Nebuchadrezzar king of Babylon routed in the fourth year of Jehoiakim the son of Josiah, the king of Judah," applies only to the first of these oracles, vss. 3-12, and has to do with the earlier event of 609, when Egypt clashed ignominiously with the Chaldeans at Carchemish.

46:1 What was [issued] as the word of the Lord to Jeremiah the prophet concerning the nations in the fourth year of Jehoiakim the son of Josiah, the king of Judah. 2 Concerning Egypt: Against the army of Pharaoh Neco king of Egypt, which was at the Euphrates River at Carchemish, which Nebuchadrezzar king of Babylon, routed in the fourth year of Jehoiakim the son of Josiah, the king of Judah.

Vss. 3-12 describe the battle at Carchemish between Pharaoh Neco of Egypt and the Chaldeans under Nebuchadrezzar. The passage is highly imaginative. The Egyptian commanders of the light and heavy infantry and of the cavalry are summoned to take their stand, fully armed, equipped and ready (vss. 3-4). The Egyptian troops are next pictured as repulsed, shattered, and set in precipitate and ignominious flight (vss. 5-6). Jeremiah portrays the bombastic aim of the Egyptian Pharaoh Neco as that of aggressive and universal destruction, his troops overflowing the earth just as the tossing and rising waters of the Nile inundate the land. The poet taunts Egypt with its famed horses and chariots (cf. Isa. 31:1), and with its troops hailing from all parts of its empire—Cush in the south, the Lybians in the north, the Lydian bowmen in the west—and calls upon them to go into action (vss. 7-8).

But Egypt has not reckoned with him who is the Ruler of the world, whose judgment of doom will fall upon that proud nation at Carchemish on the Euphrates in the north (vss. 9-10). The famed balsam from Gilead and the reputed medicines of Egypt cannot cure Egypt's plight. The nations of the whole earth have heard Egypt's cry of lamentation as its proud military power collapses (vss. 11-12).

46:3 Put in order buckler and shield,
  And draw near for battle!
4 Harness the horses,
  Mount the steeds!
Take your stand with helmets,
  Draw the spears,
    Put on the breastplates!
5 Why do I see
  That they are shattered,
They are driven back,
  And their warriors are crushed?
They have fled in precipitate flight,
  Without turning back.
Terror is on every side!
  Says the Lord.
6 Let not the swift flee,
  And let not the valiant escape;
In the north beside the Euphrates,
  They have stumbled and fallen.

7 Who is this who rises up like the Nile,
  Like the rivers whose waters toss,[11]
8b And says, I will go up, I will cover the earth;
  I will destroy those who dwell in it?
9 Rise up, O chariot horses,
  And jolt madly the chariots!
Go forth, O warriors,
  Cush and Put,
Bearers of the shield,
  And Lydians, wielders of the bow.
10 Aye, that day belongs to the Lord God,
  A day of retribution, for taking vengeance upon his foes,
And the sword of the Lord shall devour,
  And shall be surfeited and sated with blood.
For the Lord God of host has a sacrifice,
  In the land of the north, at the Euphrates.

11 Go up to Gilead, and take balsam,
  Virgin daughter of Egypt.
In vain do you multiply medicines;
  There is no healing for you.
12 Nations have heard your voice,
  And your outcry has filled the earth.
For warrior has stumbled upon warrior,
  Both of them have fallen together.

[11] Delete as redundant vs. 8a.

In vss. 13-26 is given an oracle which came to Jeremiah with regard to
the fall of Egypt to the Chaldeans in 605. This is in perfect harmony with
Jeremiah's conviction that beginning with the defeat of Egypt by the Chaldeans at Carchemish in 605, the Chaldeans will be for many years the
dominant power in the East. Nebuchadrezzar will accordingly invade and
master Egypt.

The region to the north of Egypt, once under Egypt's control, is now
entirely under Chaldean domination (II Kings 24:7). It is in the purpose
of Nebuchadrezzar to invade Egypt and make it subject to the Chaldeans.
So the prophet warns Egypt.

It was the death of Nabopolassar in 605 that had made Nebuchadrezzar
hasten back to Babylon after defeating Pharaoh Neco at Carchemish. Even
then he had been on his way to invade Egypt. So now, says the prophet,
let the border Egyptian city of Migdol, and the capital city of Memphis,
be warned. All around Egypt the Chaldeans have taken their toll and surely
Egypt will not escape. It is a basic conviction with Jeremiah that it is God's
will for Nebuchadrezzar to be lord of Egypt. The powerful and revered
Apis, the bull-god of Egypt, will be driven out. The fall of this revered
deity of the Egyptian state stands for the actual fall of the entire land. The
foreigners who have settled in Egypt, mostly merchants, decide to return to
their own people, for the Chaldean sword is about to reach them there.
Pharaoh Neco is no protection for them. The Chaldean enemy towers in
strength like Mount Tabor, and like Carmel, which rises in majesty right
out of the Mediterranean Sea. Let the Egyptians get ready for exile, collect-
ing the few articles they can carry along with them, for proud Thebes will
become at Chaldean hands an uninhabited ruins.

46:13 The word which the Lord spoke to Jeremiah the prophet as regards the
coming of Nebuchadrezzar king of Babylon to smite the land of Egypt:

> 14 Declare in Migdol,
>   And proclaim in Memphis.
>   Say ye, "Take a stand, get ready,
>   For the sword has devoured all around you."
> 15 Why is Apis fled?
>   [Why] does thy bull not stand firm?
>   Because the Lord has driven him out,
> 16   Thy foreign people have stumbled, have even fallen.
>   They speak, each to his neighbor,
>   "Arise and let us return to our people.
>   Aye, to the land of our birth.
>   From before the oppressing sword."

17 Call the name of Pharaoh Neco "a crash."
    He has let the set time pass by.

18 As I live, says the King,
    The Lord of hosts is his name,
    Mighty like Tabor among the mountains,
    And like Carmel in the sea, comes the enemy,
19 Take thee articles for exile,
    O population of Egypt!
    For Memphis shall become a desolation,
    And shall be burned so as to have no inhabitant.

In vivid pictures the prophet paints the certain defeat of Egypt. The luscious land of the Nile is as a beautiful heifer, and her protectors are but soft "stall-fed" mercenary soldiers, which, stung by the Chaldean gadfly will be thrown into ignominious flight (vss. 20-21). Egypt will fall prey to the Chaldean serpent. We hear its sharp hiss as it springs upon its prey. The Chaldeans coming against Egypt are as numberless woodsmen with sharp axes about to chop down the trees. Yet once more the figure changes. The Chaldeans are as a locust swarm before whose incomputable numbers Egypt is shorn of its honor and power. Egypt, the mighty world power, has succumbed to "the northerner." The date 605 decided the issue. The Chaldeans are now not merely in prophetic anticipation but in reality the Lord of the East (II Kings 24:7).

46:20 A pretty heifer is Egypt,
      A gadfly from the north has come upon her.
21 Also her mercenaries are in the midst of her,
      Like stall-fed calves;
      And they also have turned back, they have fled together,
      They did not stand.
      For the day of their calamity has come upon them,
      The time of their punishment.

22 A sound like a hissing serpent!
      For they shall go with an army
      And shall come upon her with axes,
      Like cutters of wood.
23 They shall cut down her forest,
      For they cannot be computed;
      For they are more numerous than a swarm of locusts,
      And beyond count.
24 The daughter of Egypt is put to shame,
      She has been given into the power of the northern nation.[12]

[12] For vss. 25-26 see p. 285; for vss. 27-28 see 30:10-11 (p. 97), where they are original,

CHALDEAN MASTERY OF THE COASTAL REGIONS

Right on the line of Nebuchadrezzar's advance against Egypt lay the Philistines, Judah's western neighbor. And to the north on the Phoenician coastline lay the city states of Tyre and Sidon. Against this whole Mediterranean area—so warns the prophet—are soon to pour down like a devastating flood the Chaldean troops, "waters rising out of the north." As this torrent of Nebuchadrezzar's soldiers floods the land, the prophet in imagination hears the frightened and lamenting cries of the inhabitants (47:2-3).

At vs. 3 the figure changes and the description becomes realistic. We hear the stamping hoofs of the Chaldean war horses and the rumble of the swiftly moving chariot wheels. We see the frightened faces of fathers and sons who are impotent and panic-stricken before the invaders. For all this coastal area—both Philistine and Phoenician—must submit to Chaldean lordship. The prophet pictures the inhabitants of the ancient cities of Gaza and Ashkelon and the remnant of the prehistoric Anakim—the pre-Philistine coastal population, now concentrated in Gaza, Gath, and Ashdod. Face to face with the crisis, they feverishly employ their rituals of lamentation, shaving their heads and lacerating their bodies (vss. 4-5).

To the prophet these ruthless Chaldeans are "the sword of the Lord," God's agents of his judgment. And this sword of the Lord reposes not in its scabbard. In obedience to the Lord's command it moves with destruction against Philistine Ashkelon and the whole coastal area (vss. 6-7). This entire passage is in harmony with Jeremiah's conception of the Chaldeans in God's purpose.

47:1 Concerning the Philistines:
2 Thus says the Lord:
  Lo, waters are rising out of the north,
    And shall become an overflowing torrent.
  They shall overflow the land and that which fills it,
    The cities and those who live in them.
  And men shall cry out and wail,
    All the inhabitants of the land.
3 At the sound of the stamping of hoofs of his horses,
    At the rocking of his chariot, the noise of its wheels,
  The fathers have not turned back to their sons,
    Because their hands fall helpless,
4 Because of the day that is coming to destroy
    All Philistines;
  To cut off Tyre and Sidon,
    Every sinew of their strength.

For the Lord is about to destroy
The remnant of the coastal regions.

5 Baldness has come to Gaza;
Ashkelon has been destroyed.
O remnant of the Anakim,
How long will you lacerate yourselves?
6 Ah, sword of the Lord!
How long wilt thou not be pacified?
Withdraw thyself into thy scabbard!
Repose thyself and be still!
7 How canst thou be quiet
When the Lord hath commanded it?
Against Ashkelon and the coast of the sea,
There He assigned it.

RABBAH-AMMON WILL BECOME A TELL

Chronologically 49:1-6 rightly precedes ch. 48. In ch. 49, Heshbon is still
an Ammonite city, while in ch. 48 it has already fallen to the Chaldeans. The
Chaldean army, proceeding from the north against the nations revolting
from Chaldean fealty—Ammon, Moab, and Edom to the east of the Jordan,
and Tyre, Sidon, and Judah to the west—has already invaded Ammon, the
nearest of the revolting nations, and has captured Heshbon.

The prophet's thought reaches back to the days of the Israelite invasion
of Canaan, when the Israelite tribe of Gad occupied the Transjordanian
region from the Jabbok River in the south to the Yarmuk River in the
north. Gad, however, early absorbed the territory of the tribe of Reuben to
the south of it, so that eventually Gad's territory extended from the Yarmuk
River in the north to the Arnon River in the south, a distance of more than
seventy-five miles. This region is also designated as Gilead. It was a richly
productive agricultural area, and accordingly it constantly invited invasion
on the part of the Bedouin Ammonites from the south and east. The center
of Gad is the Jabbok River, and as G. A. Smith says, "from first to last, the
valley of the Jabbok is of great fertility." [13]

The prophet, knowing of Israel's ancient right to this land, raises the
question: Why is it not still in Israelite hands, in control of the rightful
successors of that pioneer tribe of Gad? Also, now it is in the hands of the
Ammonites, a people who worship the deity Milcom. Its famous capital
Rabbah (modern Amman) will experience at Chaldean hands such awful

---

[13] *Historical Geography of the Holy Land*, p. 584.

destruction that it will be reduced to a mere tell, a mound of ruins, and the smaller cities of the Ammonites will be destroyed by fire.

Other Ammonite cities besides the capital are not mentioned by name, with the exception of Heshbon, which, as Rudolph [14] suggests, may well have been a recent Ammonite acquisition. From the viewpoint of the prophet these Ammonite dispossessors of what rightly belonged to Israel are not operating as the Lord's agents, as was the case with the Chaldeans, but rather as infringing robbers.

The prophet, in vs. 4, speaks to the capital Rabbah (Amman), condemning its trust for security in the fertility of the region and the riches which result from it. Ammon now feels so safe, so confident, but the whole Ammonite nation will experience the terrors of Chaldean invasion and the destruction of Ammonite nationality (vs. 5). And the Ammonite priests and the images of their famous deity, Milcom, will be taken into exile, along with the Ammonites, by the Chaldeans.

> 49:1 Concerning the sons of Ammon,
>   Thus says the Lord:
>   Does not Israel have sons?
>   Does he not have a successor?
>   Why does Milcom possess Gad,
>   And his people dwell in his cities?
>   2a But I will cause Rabbah of the Ammonites to hear
>   The alarm of war,
>   And it shall become a desolate mound,
>   And its daughter cities shall be burned in the fire.[15]
>
>   3 Wail Heshbon,
>   For the devastator has come up!
>   Cry out, daughters of Rabbah!
>   Bind on sackcloth, wail!
>   And lacerate yourselves with cuttings!
>   For Milcom shall go into exile,
>   Together with his priests and his officials.
>
>   4 Why do you glory in your valley,
>   You dissolute daughter,
>   Who trusts in her treasures,
>   Saying, "Who will come against me?"

---

[14] *Jeremia*, p. 249.

[15] Omit vs. 2b, "And Israel shall become the heirs of those who dispossessed him," as a wishful dream of Israelite reoccupation, possibly based on Zeph. 2:9, but which has no place here, as Israel is one of the nations to be destroyed by the same Chaldeans; cf. Cornill, *Jeremia*, p. 474.

    5 Lo, I am about to bring terror upon you,
       From all around about you;
       So you will be dispersed, each by himself,
       With no one assembling the fugitives.[16]

THE LORD'S JUDGMENT UPON MOAB

Jer. 48, which deals with the Lord's judgment upon the nation of Moab, rightly follows rather than precedes 49:1-6, since the Chaldeans coming from the north would attack Ammon first, then Moab, followed by Edom. Moreover, 48:7, "you also shall be trapped," implies that Ammon has already fallen to the Chaldean invaders. J. Lewy [17] is right in maintaining that the tremendous political significance of the year 605 best explains Jeremiah's preoccupation with the other nations. The chronological datum in 46:2 gives us the chronology for the entire section 46:1–49:33. Accordingly, the oracle against Moab deals with that nation in the light of Nebuchadrezzar's imminent absorption of it into the Chaldean orbit. Jeremiah uses the Hebrew tense which expresses certainty, and narrates what is to take place as though it had already happened. The Chaldean invasion of the west has advanced a step in that the Chaldeans, now masters of Heshbon, have made it the base of operations against Moab, the next Transjordanian nation in the line of the Chaldean campaign against the west.

In 48:1-10 the prophet pronounces the woe of the Lord upon the nation of Moab. From Jerusalem he could see far across the Jordan the lofty skyline of Moab's landscape extending from Nebo, the town on the southwest slope of Mount Nebo (en-nebā), to Zoar at the southernmost point of the Dead Sea.

That skyline lifts itself over 6,200 feet above the level of the Dead Sea. Already Heshbon, formerly an Ammonite possession and situated on the highway leading to Rabbah-Ammon has fallen to the Chaldeans, and from there as a base the Chaldean conquest of Moab is projected, with the intent to destroy it as a nation (vs. 2a).

Moab's northern line of defense, with its bases in Nebo and Kiriathaim, about fifteen miles south of Nebo, are already in Chaldean hands (vs. 1). Madmen (Dibon is meant), situated on the highway leading north, about five miles north of the Arnon River, is doomed (vs. 2). In the imaginative portrayal of the prophet, cries of distress come from the Abarim Mountains

---

[16] Vs. 6, which is lacking in the Septuagint, is a later addition dating from Hellenistic times, when the capital of Ammon (Philadelphia) experienced a new prosperity: "And afterward I will restore the fortunes of the sons of Ammon," says the Lord.

[17] *Forschungen zur alten Geschichte Vorderasiens*, p. 31.

in northwest Moab above the Arnon River, which rise up from the north-eastern shoreline of the Dead Sea (vs. 3). All along the southern extent of Moab clear down to the city of Zoar, just below the Dead Sea, the prophet hears the warning cry counseling flight into the wilderness (vss. 4, 6).

The fortresses and fastnesses of Moab will not protect the land from the Chaldean invaders, who will even capture and carry off the image of Chemosh, god of the Moabites. And following their god into exile will go the priests of Chemosh and Moab's military leaders (vs. 7). Moab's cities, tablelands, and valleys will suffer a like fate of destruction (vs. 8). In rhetorical summons the prophet calls upon the people of Moab to set up a tombstone to their nation, doomed as it is to destruction. Moab will become an unpopulated waste.

> 48:1 Concerning Moab:
> Thus says the Lord of hosts, God of Israel:
> Alas for Nebo, for it has been devastated!
> Kiriathaim has been captured,
> The secure height is put to shame and dismayed;
> 2 There is no more renown for Moab.
> In Heshbon they have devised evil against her:
> "Come, let us cut her off from being a nation!"
> You also, O Madmen [Dibon], will utterly perish;
> The sword will go after you.
>
> 3 Hark! a cry of distress from the mountains of Abarim,
> Devastation and great shattering!
> 4 Moab is broken!
> Sound aloud a distress cry toward Zoar.[18]
>
> 6 Flee, save your life!
> And set up camp in the wilderness.
>
> 7 For because of your trust in your strongholds, in your fastnesses,
> You also shall be trapped;
> And Chemosh shall go into exile,
> His priests and his captains together.
> 8 And devastation shall come to every city;
> No city shall escape.

[18] Omit vs. 5 as a later insertion from Isa. 15:5b, where it is in the correct place:
Aye, the ascent of Luhith,
They ascend it with weeping.
Aye, on the descent toward Horonaim,
Is heard the outcry over its shattering.

The valley shall be destroyed,
And the tableland devastated,
Says the Lord.

9 Set up a monument for Moab,
For it shall surely be completely ruined,
And its cities shall become a desolation,
With no one dwelling in them.[19]

In vss. 11-17 the prophet refers to Moab as a masculine entity. Using as an illustration of early Moab's peaceful national lot, wine unmolested and maturing undisturbed upon its lees, he explains that such was the good fortune of Moab. It had not suffered the experience of national weakening such as results from war and exile, and consequently Moab did not lose its distinctive national quality. But now the "vessel" of Moab is like a jar so tilted that its contents will be emptied out (vs. 12) and even the jar itself shattered. Just as in the very face of the Israelite worship of the god of Bethel the kingdom of Israel was destroyed, so Chemosh, Moab's god, will be unable to protect his worshipers from destruction, nor will Moab's valiant warriors be able to ward off defeat by the Chaldean army. The Chaldean destroyer will attack Moab and bring calamity upon it. The prophet therefore calls upon Moab's proud people to lament over the imminent destruction of "the strong staff," "the glorious rod," the stricken Moabite nation (vs. 17):

48:11 Moab has been secure from his youth,
Yes, undisturbed has he been upon his lees;
He was not emptied out from vessel to vessel,
And did not go into exile.
Therefore his taste stays in him,
And his aroma has not changed.[20]

12 So I will send to him
Tilters, and they shall tilt him,
And they shall empty his vessels,
And they shall shatter his jars.

13 And Moab will be ashamed of Chemosh,
Just as the house of Israel were ashamed
Before Bethel,[21] in which they trusted.

---

[19] Vs. 10,

Cursed be he who does the word of the Lord with laxity;
And cursed be he who withholds his sword from blood,

is a later addition representing an eruption of hate against Moab; so Rudolph, *Jeremia*, p. 239.

[20] Omit with Cornill, "Therefore, lo, days are coming, says the Lord," because the catastrophe is viewed as imminent.

[21] Bethel is here the name of a deity, as in the Elephantine papyri.

14 How can you say:
  "We are warriors,
    And men of valor in battle"?
15 The destroyer of Moab has gone up against him,
    And the best of his young men have gone down in slaughter.
16 Soon to come is the calamity of Moab,
    His evil hastens rapidly.
17 Lament for him, all around about him,
    And all who know his name.
  Say ye, "How the strong staff has been broken,
    The glorious rod!"

The poet continues his taunt. He calls out to the inhabitants of Dibon, a famous city just north of the Arnon River, once the home of Moab's King Mesha, and the chief city of the tableland between Heshbon and the Arnon. He summons them to experience humiliation at the hand of the conquering Chaldeans (vs. 18). He calls upon the inhabitants of Aroer, a city just three miles south of Dibon and on the same main road running north and south, to inquire of fugitives what has taken place (vs. 19). And the answer comes (vss. 20, 25) telling of Moab's destruction and calling Aroer's population to lamentation. For Moab's power is crushed. Let the Moabites forsake their cities and live the precarious life of fugitives, like wild doves nesting in the very mouth of a rocky gorge (vss. 18-20, 25, 28).[22]

48:18 Descend from glory and sit in filth,
      Inhabitants of Dibon!
    For the shatterer of Moab has gone up against you,
      He has destroyed your fortifications.
   19 Take your stand on the road and watch closely,
      Inhabitants of Aroer.
    Ask a fugitive and one escaping,
      Say, "What has happened?"
   20 Moab is put to shame, yes, dismayed;
      Howl and cry!
    Declare at the Arnon
      That Moab is destroyed.

[22] Vss. 21-24 are in prose and give a list of place names in Moab. Thus the editor particularizes the judgment announced upon the various cities of Moab.
   48:21 And judgment will come upon the tableland, upon Holon, Jahzah, Mephaath, 22 and upon Dibon and Nebo, Beth-diblathaim, 23 and upon Kiryathaim, Beth-gamul, and Beth-meon, 24 and upon Kerioth, and upon Bozrah and upon all the cities of the land of Moab, far and near.

25 The horn of Moab has been cut off,
   And its arm crushed.[23]
28 Forsake the cities and dwell in the crag,
   Inhabitants of Moab;
   Yes, be like a dove that makes its nest
   On the sides of the gorge's mouth.[24]

The prophet now pictures the Moabite cities as captured by the Chaldean army and all its fortresses taken. Because of its proud self-security which led to haughty presumption, even Moab's nationality will be destroyed.

48:40 For thus says the Lord: [25]
   41 The cities shall be captured,
      And the fortresses shall be seized;
   42 And Moab shall be destroyed, so that it is no longer a people,
      For it has swaggered against the Lord.

ESAU's (EDOM's) CALAMITY I WILL BRING UPON HIM

Jer. 49:7-11 contains an authentic prophecy of Jeremiah which is probably based, as is Obad. 5-6, upon an older oracle which both adapt, each in his own way.[26] It deals with the complete annihilation of Edom (vs. 10) and its neighboring tribes by the Chaldeans, although these agents of Edom's destruction are not mentioned by name. Teman, a district in central Edom, a region famous for its wise men, of which Eliphaz the Temanite, the oldest of Job's friends (Job 2:11) was one, will not escape destruction. The Arabs of Dedan, southern neighbors of Edom, who dwell on the northwestern area of the peninsula of Arabia, along the eastern shore of the Gulf of Aqabah, are counseled to flee from the same calamity that Edom will experience (vs. 8). No one of Edomite descent will escape (vs. 10). And there will be no one who will concern himself over the resulting sad plight of the Edomite widows and orphans (vss. 10-11).

Thus the prophet speaks:

[23] Vss. 26-27 are also in prose.
48:26 Make him [Moab] drunk for he has swaggered against the Lord and Moab shall throw up its vomit and shall become—even it—an object of derision. 27 And was not Israel an object of derision to you, and was it not found among thieves, so that as often as you spoke of it you shook your head [i.e., in derision]?
[24] For vss. 29-39 see pp. 287-88.
[25] Delete the remainder of vss. 40-41 as an insertion from 49:22, as follows:
      Lo, as an eagle mounts up and darts swiftly,
         And spreads its wings over Bozrah,
      So the heart of the warriors of Moab [Edom in 49:22] will be
         Like the heart of a woman in travail.
[26] Cf. Driver, Book of Jeremiah, p. 293.

49:7 Concerning Edom.
Thus says the Lord of hosts:
Is there not still wisdom in Teman?
Has counsel vanished from the discerning?
Has their wisdom become corrupt?
8 Flee, turn back, hide,
Inhabitants of Dedan!
For Esau's calamity I will bring upon him,
The time when I shall punish him.[27]

10 But I have stripped Esau bare,
I have uncovered his places of concealment,
So he cannot hide himself.
His children are devastated and he is no more,
And no one says of his neighbors,
11 "Leave your orphans; I will keep them alive;
And as for your widows, trust them to me."[28]

Vs. 22 comes from Jeremiah. The metaphor of the eagle mounting up and darting down toward Bozrah, setting the hearts of Edom's warriors in commotion, is a figurative portrayal of the expected Chaldean Nebuchadrezzar's approach to Edom with the intent to conquer it.

49:22 Lo, as an eagle mounts up and darts swiftly,
And spreads its wings over Bozrah,
So the heart of the warriors of Edom will be
Like the heart of a woman in travail.

We have no historical record of the conquering of Edom by Nebuchadrezzar. We do know however, that Nabonidus of Babylon led his troops through Amor (Palestine) to besiege Adummu in 554-3.[29] If Adummu is identical with Edom, we are here given a glimpse of considerable unrest in the smaller states of the west a generation after the Chaldean destruction of Jerusalem. But no historical records mention a Chaldean conquest of Edom in any sense comparable with the expectation of vs. 22.[30]

In vss. 28-32 Kedar and the kingdoms of Hazor are designations of the seminomadic Arab Bedouins of the Syrian desert east of Palestine. Hazor

---

[27] Vs. 9, which follows, is not from Jeremiah, but is dependent upon Obad. 5.
49:9 If grape gatherers came to you,
Would they not leave gleanings?
If thieves came by night,
Would they not damage but as much as they want?

[28] For vss. 12-21, not from Jeremiah, see pp. 290-91.

[29] *Cambridge Ancient History*, III, 405.

[30] For vss. 23-27 see p. 286.

here, is not as in Judg. 4:2, a Palestinian city, but is a collective name for these seminomadic Arabs in contradistinction to the fully nomadic Bedouins of the wilderness. In 25:23, which parallels this passage (vss. 28-30), Dedan, Teman, and Buz are the designations of north Arabian tribes which include both classes of Arabs. It is clear that it was against the half-settled Arabs that Nebuchadrezzar was directing his forces, against those occupying "the villages that Kedar inhabits" (Isa. 42:11), the tent dwellers of North Arabia.

We must keep clearly in mind that in Jeremiah's thought the Chaldeans were the particular agents chosen of the Lord to administer the Lord's judgment. Thus in the name of the Lord the prophet imaginatively summons Nebuchadrezzar to a campaign of plunder which will despoil the Bedouin villages of the tent dwellers, making booty of their tent curtains, their utensils, cattle, and camels. As they proceed, the Chaldeans are to call out the frightening cry, "Terror on every side!" (vs. 29.)

The prophet imaginatively represents the Lord as calling in irony upon these seminomads to flee before this Chaldean advance (vs. 30). Then he speaks again in the Lord's name to the Chaldeans, calling them to go up against these settled Bedouins, whose villages have no protecting fortifications, plunder their dwellings, scattering these people—so strangely marked by their clipped foreheads—to the four winds of heaven.

49:28 Concerning Kedar and the kingdom of Hazor, which
Nebuchadrezzar king of Babylon struck. Thus says the Lord:
Arise, go up against Kedar!
And devastate the sons of the east!
29 Let their tents and their flocks be captured,
Their tent curtains and all their equipment.
And carry off from them their camels,
And cry over them, "Terror on every side!"
30 Escape, take rapid flight,
Inhabitants of Hazor!
For the king of Babylon
Has counseled against you,
And has devised a plot against you.

31 Arise against a prosperous nation,
Which dwells in security,
Without gates and without bars,
They dwell alone.
32 And their camels will become plunder,
And the great number of their cattle will be for spoil,

And I will scatter to all winds
Those clipped on the temples,
And from all sides
I will bring distress to them,
Says the Lord.[31]

The First Record in the Book of the Prophet's Sufferings

Up until ch. 19 the predominant interest of the book is in Jeremiah's successive addresses or utterances. This is the case both for the original words of the prophet himself and for the portions that come to us through the hand of the Deuteronomic editor.

Beginning with 19:1, however, we meet with an entirely different source in which the predominant interest is less in the words but more in the vicissitudes and fate of Jeremiah. The oracles of the prophet are accordingly presented in brevity and in prose. But the situation in which they originated and the consequences that followed upon them are given with fullness and exactness. In this source Jeremiah is always spoken of in the third person. The original part of ch. 19 comes from this source and gives us the first installment in the present book of Jeremiah of an account of Jeremiah's sufferings and persecutions. The author in all likelihood is Baruch, Jeremiah's great friend. Baruch's style, while verbose, is clearly distinguishable from the monotonous form of expression which is characteristic of the Deuteronomic editor.

The Deuteronomic editor, who is the redactor of the entire book, in the arrangement of his materials does not follow the chronological order of events in the prophet's career at this point, for ch. 26, the next portion of Baruch's narrative, with which we have already dealt, belongs chronologically before 19:1–20:6. The reason that the final editor of the book inserted the latter passage here, immediately following the section on the potter, is that in ch. 18 the potter and his work are a symbol of the divine government; here the fate of the pottery vessel is a symbol of the divine judgment.

The original account as it left the pen of Baruch is composed of 19:1-2a,

---

[31] Vs. 33 is a later addition which mistakenly views Hazor as a city and announces upon it permanent destruction:

And Hazor shall become a haunt of jackals,
A perpetual desolation;
No one shall dwell there,
And no human being shall stay in it.

10-11*a*, 14-15. In it Jeremiah tells us of an impulse from the Lord that led him to perform a symbolic prophetic act at the entrance to the Potsherd Gate. He used a vessel of pottery purchased for the occasion, and uttered at the moment only one sentence of prophetic significance (vs. 11). Then he went at once to the temple (vs. 14), where all the people were assembled in the court on a feast day, and there proclaimed the message of the Lord, a symbolic act which was intended to make impressive and plain the "evil" which God is about to bring upon Jerusalem and its surrounding towns, because of the obstinate and stubborn refusal of the Judean leaders to listen to God's "words" as uttered by his prophet.

Baruch's words tell the story vividly and clearly. It is one of the best instances we have in Jeremiah of a new type of his prophetic appeal, symbolic prophecy.

19:1 **Then the Lord said to Jeremiah, "Go, buy a flask of pottery, and taking with you some of the elders of the people and of the priests, 2*a* go out to the entrance of the Gate of Potsherds. 10 Then you shall break the flask of pottery in the sight of the men who are accompanying you. 11*a* And you shall say to them, 'Thus says the Lord of hosts; Like this will I break this people and this city, as a potter breaks a vessel in pieces so it cannot be repaired.'" 14 Then Jeremiah came from the gate, where the Lord had sent him to prophesy, and stood in the court of the house of the Lord, and said to all the people: 15 "Thus says the Lord of hosts, God of Israel, lo, I am about to bring to this city and upon all its [unwalled] towns all the evil concerning which I spoke, because they stiffened their necks so as not to listen to my words."**

JEREMIAH'S PHYSICAL SUFFERINGS AND HIS MESSAGE TO PASHHUR

These words of Jeremiah (19:15), spoken in the court of the temple, were heard by Pashhur of the priestly family of Immer. He was the chief overseer of the temple, and, as such, had authority to arrest and punish anyone whom he judged to be falsely exercising prophetic functions in the temple. When Jeremiah solemnly prophesied evil to come upon Jerusalem and its environs, Pashhur wasted no time in dealing drastically with him. He beat Jeremiah and threw him into the stocks, just inside the upper Benjamin Gate, which was the north gate of the inner court of the temple, thus painfully and humiliatingly confining him for a day and night. In the morning when Pashhur released him, Jeremiah turned upon the overseer, and at an impulse from the Lord gave him a name of prophetic significance. It signified that just as Pashhur had "terrorized" others, he himself would experience terror in the form of a growing intimation of overwhelming and impending doom, for he and all his circle will meet with the fate of death or captivity, and Pashhur himself would be among those who will be exiled. For the first time Jeremiah specifically indicates Babylon as the place of captivity. The prophet's words forcibly remind us of the sharp, condemnatory message spoken by the prophet Amos at Bethel to Amaziah the high priest (Amos 7:16-17).

20:1 Now Pashhur son of Immer, the priest—he was chief overseer of the temple —heard Jeremiah prophesying these words. 2 Then Pashhur scourged Jeremiah the prophet and put him in the stocks which were in the upper gate of Benjamin which was in the house of the Lord. 3 When on the morrow Pashhur released Jeremiah from the stocks, Jeremiah said to him: "The Lord has not named you Pashhur but Terror. 4 For thus saith the Lord, 'Lo, I am about to give you over to terror, you and all your friends, and they will fall by the sword of their enemies with your own eyes seeing it. And all Judah I will deliver into the power of the king of Babylon or kill them with the sword. 5 And I will give over into the hand of their enemies all the treasure of this city, and all its produce, and all the treasures of the kings of Judah, and they shall plunder them and carry them off and take them to Babylon. 6 And you, Pashhur, and all who live in your house, shall go into exile. And you shall go to Babylon and there shall you die, and there you shall be buried—you and all your friends to whom you have prophesied untruthfully.' "

This is the first instance of Jeremiah's suffering as a martyr because of his faith.

A Book Is Born

Jer. 36:1-4 gives the setting of the events of the chapter. The date is 605. The narrator is Baruch. The nation of Judah has changed masters. At the Battle of Carchemish in 605, where two great powers, Egypt and the Chaldeans, fought for control of the ancient Near East, the Chaldeans won the dominance. Thus far the change in the overlordship of vassal Judah from Neco of Egypt to Nebuchadrezzar of Babylon had made little difference to Judah, and the doom predicted by Jeremiah as coming upon his people had not materialized.

But the prophet was never more clear in his mind than now that Babylon was the foe from the north, and that it lay in the purpose of God that the Chaldeans should be the lord of the whole Near East, and the agent which God will use to destroy the national life of Judah. How could he reach the mind and conscience of the nation before this northern power should crush the Judean kingdom? How could he arouse the frivolous King Jehoiakim to responsible national concern?

There came to Jeremiah by revelation from God the project to write down the content of his more than twenty-one years of preaching in the hope that the cumulative effect of his words might succeed where the individual messages had failed, in gripping the attention and conscience of his people. It is most likely that Jeremiah possessed written records of his earlier oracles and used these as a basis for slow and careful dictation to Baruch of the major content of his preaching from 626 until 605.

36:1 Now it came to pass in the fourth year of Jehoiakim son of Josiah, king of Judah, that this word came to Jeremiah from the Lord: 2 "Take for yourself a roll of a book and write in it all the words which I have· spoken to you concerning Jerusalem and concerning all the nations from the day when I spoke to you, from the days of Josiah even until today. 3 Perhaps the house of Judah will listen to all the evil which I am planning to do to them, so that they will return, each one from his evil way, and I will forgive their iniquity and their sin."

4 So Jeremiah dictated to Baruch, and Baruch wrote from the mouth of Jeremiah all the words of the Lord which he spoke to him upon the roll of a book.

Jeremiah awaited a fitting occasion for the reading of the scroll to Judah. In December, 604,[32] the authorities in Jerusalem proclaimed a fast for the inhabitants of Jerusalem and for the whole nation. In all probability the fast was not politically motivated, as the superficial attitude of King Jehoiakim toward the prophetic scroll seems to rule that out. The month of December points to a fast day for all the congregation because of the lack of rain.[33] Jeremiah himself was not at the time permitted to enter the temple, probably because of his earlier clash with Pashhur, the chief overseer (20: 1-3). Accordingly—for the mood of the hour would make for a receptive hearing—Jeremiah commands Baruch to do an unprecedented thing, to read the words of the scroll publicly in the temple so that all the Judean men who come up out of their towns and cities to Jerusalem may hear the prophet's message.

To read publicly prophetic writing out of a book—words of the Lord which had come flamingly from the soul of a prophet, who for almost a quarter of a century had uttered God's word in Jerusalem—that was something new in Judah. As Volz says, "It is a great day in Baruch's life." [34]

Baruch obeys the command of the prophet and stands in the inner court of the temple at the entrance to the New Gate. He read from the chamber of Gemariah son of Shaphan, by whose whole household Jeremiah was

[32] The reckoning of the fourth year of reign, reckoned from autumn to autumn, is from Oct., 605 to Sept., 604. The reckoning of the months follows the Babylonian system from April, so the ninth month of the fifth year is Dec., 604.

[33] Cf. Talmud, Taanit 1:5; cf. Volz, Jeremia, p. 327.

[34] Jeremia, p. 328.

held in deep regard. The chamber opened on the court, so the reading of the scroll could be heard by the princes and the people. Thus runs Baruch's account:

36:9 [35] Now it happened that in the fifth year of Jehoiakim son of Josiah, king of Judah, in the ninth month, that they summoned to a fast before the Lord in Jerusalem all the people in Jerusalem and the entire Judean nation.
5 Then Jeremiah commanded Baruch, saying: "I am hindered, I cannot enter the house of the Lord, 6 so you go and read aloud in the scroll the words which you wrote at my dictation. You shall read them in the hearing of the congregation of the house of the Lord on the fast day, and also in the hearing of all Judah as they come from their cities. 7 Perhaps their supplication will fall before the Lord and they will each turn from his evil way, for great is the anger and the wrath in which the Lord has spoken to this people." 8 So Baruch son of Neriah acted in accord with all that Jeremiah the prophet commanded him. 10 So Baruch read aloud in the book the words of Jeremiah in the house of the Lord, in the room of Gemariah son of Shaphan the secretary, in the upper court [i.e., inner court] at the entrance to the New Gate of the house of the Lord in the hearing of all the people.

We are told nothing about the effect Baruch's reading of the scroll had upon the rank and file of the people, but its effect upon the princes was pronounced. Micaiah son of Gemariah, from whose room Baruch had read Jeremiah's words, and grandson of Shaphan, who had been secretary of state under Josiah, heard the reading and at once sensed its strategic importance. He hurried down from the temple to the royal palace, to the room of the secretary of state, where all the princes were—Elishama the secretary, Delaiah, Elnathan, and Gemariah. Micaiah summarized briefly for them what he had heard Baruch read. The princes sent a committee of two, Jehudi and Shelemaiah, to Baruch, commanding him to bring the roll and come down to where they were. Upon arrival, they requested him to be seated and to read the entire scroll to them. They were frightened at what they heard, and being responsible men who knew all too well the character of their monarch, agreed together that they should inform King Jehoiakim. But first they wanted to learn from Baruch just how the words came into existence, and he answered their questions with directness and exactness.

Knowing Jehoiakim, as they do, they realize that Baruch and Jeremiah now stand in great danger of their lives. They counsel the prophet and his scribe to secret themselves from everybody. Depositing the scroll carefully in

---

[35] Vs. 9 rightly belongs before vs. 5; cf. ibid., p. 325.

the secretary of state's chamber, where they then were, they went to the palace and informed the king of what had taken place. Thus Baruch gives the record:

36:11 Now Micaiah son of Gemariah, son of Shaphan, heard all the words of the Lord from the scroll, 12 so he went down to the palace of the king, to the room of the secretary, and lo, there were seated all the princes: Elishama the secretary, and Delaiah son of Shemaiah, Elnathan son of Achbor, and Gemariah son of Shaphan, and Zedekiah son of Hananiah, and all the princes. 13 So Micaiah told them all the words which he had heard when Baruch read aloud in the book in the hearing of the people.

14 Then all the princes sent to Baruch, Jehudi son of Nethaniah, and Shelemiah son of Cushi, saying, "The scroll in which you have read—take it in your hand and come." So Baruch took the scroll in his hand and went down to them. 15 Then they said to him, "Please sit down and read it in our hearing," so Baruch read [it] in their hearing. 16 Now when they had heard all the words, they were afraid, and one said to the other, "We must certainly inform the king as to all these words." 17 And they questioned Baruch, saying, "Now tell us how you wrote all these words." 18 So Baruch said to them, "Jeremiah dictated all these words to me with his mouth and I kept writing them in ink upon the scroll."

19 Then the princes said to Baruch, "Go, hide yourselves, you and Jeremiah, and do not let any one know where you are."

The princes then sought and were granted private audience with King Jehoiakim, who sent Jehudi for the scroll, and as he read it to the king, column by column, the king would cut up every few columns with his pen-knife and fling them into the fire until the whole scroll had been burned. Baruch's narrative reveals his mingled awe and terror as he tells the story and thinks of this manuscript—to him priceless—thus going up in smoke, apparently with no one present lamenting either the shocking irreverence of the king or the tragic destruction of what was to Baruch pure spiritual treasure (vss. 20-24). Moreover, the king gave no heed to the earnest entreaty of three of the princes who braved their monarch's irreverent secularism and sought to keep the scroll from the flames, but he ordered three men to arrest the prophet and his scribe. But in those perilous hours the prophet and his scribe experienced the wonderful protection of God.

Thus Baruch tells the story:

36:20 Then they went in to the king, into his [private] chamber—now they had deposited the scroll in the room of Elishama the scribe—and they told in the hearing of the king all these words.

21 So the king sent Jehudi to bring the scroll. So he took it from the chamber of Elishama the scribe, and Jehudi read it in the hearing of the king and in the

hearing of all the princes who were standing beside the king. 22 Now the king was sitting in the autumn palace in the ninth month and a fire was burning before him. 23 So it happened that whenever Jehudi had read three or four columns, that he would cut them with a penknife and fling them into the fire which was in the brazier, until all the scroll was consumed by the fire which was in the brazier. 24 And they were not afraid and they did not rend their garments—neither the king nor his servants who were hearing all these words. 25 Although Elnathan and Delaiah and Gemariah implored the king not to burn the scroll, he would not listen to them. 26 But the king commanded Jerahmeel son of the king, and Seraiah son of Azriel, and Shelemaiah son of Abdeel, to seize Baruch the scribe and Jeremiah the prophet, but the Lord hid them.

The scroll was destroyed but the Lord's prophet was protected, and there came to him from the Lord another impulse directing him to rewrite the destroyed scroll (vss. 27-32). Vs. 29 shows us that one of many utterances in Jeremiah's scroll that raised the ire of King Jehoiakim was Jeremiah's prophecy of the destruction of Judah by the Chaldean Nebuchadrezzar.

The Lord revealed to Jeremiah that Jehoiakim would have no descendants who would occupy the Judean throne. The prophecy concerning Jehoiakim's unburied carcass (vs. 30) did not materialize, however, for the Deuteronomic historian of Judah tells us that Jehoiakim slept with his fathers (II Kings 24:6), that is, he received the burial appropriate to a monarch in Jerusalem.

Taking another scroll at Jeremiah's dictation, the contents of the first scroll were repeated, the words being written down again by Baruch, and from time to time other and similar words were added to them.[36]

36:27 Then the word of the Lord came to Jeremiah after the king had burned the scroll, all the words which Baruch had written at the dictation of Jeremiah, saying, 28 Take another scroll and write upon it all the words which were in the first scroll that Jehoiakim king of Judah burned. 29 And say, "Thus says the Lord, You have burned this scroll, saying, 'Why did you write upon it saying that the king of Babylon will come and ravish this land and destroy from it man and beast?' "

30 Therefore thus says the Lord concerning Jehoiakim king of Judah: "Not one of his descendants will he have sitting on the throne of David, and his corpse will be thrown out to the parching heat in the daytime and to the frost at night. 31 And I will punish him and his descendants and his servants, and the consequences of their iniquity I will bring upon them, and upon those dwelling in Jerusalem, and upon the land of Judah—all the evil that I spoke of concerning them, though they would not listen."

[36] The passive manner of expression suggests that the additions were not made at one time.

32 So Jeremiah took another scroll and gave it to Baruch the son of Neriah, the scribe, and he wrote upon it at the dictation of Jeremiah all the words of the book which Jehoiakim king of Judah had burned in the fire, and besides there were added to them many words like them.

Something new is taking place in this chapter. The spoken word is still supreme, for the prophet is uniquely a speaker for God. The importance of the written prophetic word, however, had already begun to be evident a century earlier in Judah in the experience of the prophet Isaiah. He had received from the Lord the impulse to write new words for the future when the people would listen, for the word of prophecy was rejected by them (Isa. 30:8). In the case of Habakkuk, a contemporary of Jeremiah, he too received the impulse to write out the vision which eventually was to become reality (Hab. 2:2-3).

But here the writing down is intended to retain and conserve the content of the fleeting, vocal utterance, giving it both longer influence and wider reach. Also, in the fact of the Lord's divine summons to write (vs. 2) we are aware of his new and creative initiative in teaching humanity. As in the earlier temple address (26:3), the Lord "makes a new attempt to save the nation" [37] by a book. As Rudolph says: "It is only a new way for the old task, to utter God's word to the nation and to point out the signs of the time." [38]

Moreover, in this significant chapter we have our clearest Old Testament evidence as to exactly how one of the prophetic books came to be written— a prophet dictating and a scribe writing down his words in a scroll created the core of the present book of Jeremiah.

Incidentally, the chapter shows us that by this time in Palestine papyrus is used as writing material, thus succeeding stone and clay.[39] The material used for writing is ink made of a black liquid composed of soot, water, and lime. The writing instrument is a reed cut fine with a penknife. D. Winton Thomas maintains that from the ostraca discovered at Lachish, contemporary with the time of Jeremiah, we learn the exact nature of the cursive Hebrew script which would be used by Baruch. We further learn that the language used in the ostraca is the same as the classical Hebrew

---

[37] Volz, *Jeremia*, p. 327.

[38] *Jeremia*, p. 196.

[39] Cf. Pfeiffer, *Introduction to the Old Testament*, p. 72. The Septuagint uses *chartis* or *chartion* throughout the chapter to render the Hebrew *mᵉgillāh* (scroll). D. Winton Thomas, "The Age of Jeremiah in the Light of Recent Archaeological Discovery," *Palestine Exploration Quarterly for 1950*, pp. 1-15 maintains "around 600 B.C. papyrus was being commonly used as writing material."

as we know it in the Old Testament. Thomas further maintains that if the language used in the ostraca "aligns itself more especially with any Biblical book, it is the Book of Jeremiah." "Our Biblical Hebrew," he maintains, "bears upon it the stamp of the dialect of Judah current about the 6th century B.C." [40]

The Lord's Promise to Baruch

The experience of Baruch in ch. 45 took place in 604, probably just after he had finished writing down at Jeremiah's dictation the very heart of the prophet's message as he had delivered it through twenty-three years of ministry. Not until Baruch had lived through that experience of hearing at the mouth of his master the total message of the divine judgment upon Judah did he grasp the sternness of that judgment. Day after day as they worked together and as he wrote down the prophet's words, God's massive indictment of Judah touched to the quick his sensitive soul. He knew Jeremiah probably better than any other person in Judah knew him, and was certain that those solemn words of moral indictment came straight from the prophet's illumined prophetic insight.

Contrary to the dullness of Judean hearts to these solemn messages, Baruch himself was deeply moved even as he received them in dictation, and he cried out as though suffering pain, "Woe to me!" For the prophet's condemnation of Judah had broken upon him in all its concentrated terribleness. The words, even as Baruch wrote them down, hurled him into such despair that he uttered an impassioned cry of grief: "Woe to me! Woe to me! For the Lord has added sorrow to my pain. I am weary of my sighing and I find no relief" (45:2).

Jeremiah then delivered to Baruch the message from the Lord which he greatly needed, such a message as must often have steadied him in the dark days immediately ahead for Jeremiah and himself. It is the mighty Creator who is speaking through his prophet, he who had "built" and "planted" his people with such love as only a builder can expend upon his creation, or a gardener upon the plant of his delight. Now the Lord must tear down the nation upon which he had poured out such potent and gracious concern. He is about to uproot the plant upon which, as divine Gardener, he had expended solicitous care.

But Baruch cannot bear to think of Judah's destruction. He longs that Judah may somehow be immune from it. Jeremiah must have known the struggle that was going on in Baruch's soul even while he was writing. And

[40] *Thomas*, ibid., p. 2.

God gave the prophet words to guide the thoughts of his loyal comrade and scribe—words to temper his nationalism and to check his personal ambitions.

In Jeremiah's utterance of the Lord's oracle to Baruch it is implied that in the intensity of the scribe's own national and personal sorrow at Judah's imminent destruction as a nation, he must accomodate himself to the still greater grief in the heart of God, as the Lord permits the judgment of national destruction to come upon his stubbornly unrepentant people. The Lord, who has found it necessary for Judah's good to destroy his own beloved creation, seeks from Baruch's loyal heart intelligent resignation in that morally necessary destruction. Baruch's ambitions for Judah and, indeed, for himself, must be purged in the fires of the divine resignation.

All that Baruch himself can count on in the days ahead is his bare life, and that, as it were, booty from battle, like a warrior's prize taken against great odds, for hard days are ahead. Behind these gentle counsels to human resignation we seem to see looming the mighty, loving presence of the moral God, who, though surrendering his people to their fate, has not washed his hands of them.

45:1 **The word which Jeremiah the prophet spoke to Baruch son of Neriah, when he had written these words upon a scroll at the dictation of Jeremiah, in the fourth year of Jehoiakim son of Josiah, king of Judah. 2 "Thus says the Lord, God of Israel, concerning you, Baruch: 3 Since you have said 'Woe to me! Woe to me! for the Lord has added sorrow to my pain. I am weary from my sighing and find no relief,' 4 Thus says the Lord: Lo, what I have built I am about to throw down; and what I have planted I am about to uproot. 5 But you—are you seeking great things for yourself? Seek them not. For lo, I am about to bring evil upon all flesh, says the Lord, but to you I will give your life as booty, in all the places where you will go."**

CHAPTER SIX

Twilight in Judah

602-598—LATE REIGN OF JEHOIAKIM (602-598) AND BRIEF REIGN OF JEHOIACHIN (598)

JUDAH REMAINED UNDER EGYPTIAN DOMINATION FROM 609 UNTIL 605, WHEN THE DECISIVE VICTORY OF THE CHALDEANS UNDER NEBUCHADREZZAR OVER the Egyptians under Pharaoh Neco at Carchemish made clear to all discerning eyes that the immediate future of the ancient Near East was politically speaking in Chaldean hands.

Nebuchadrezzar hurried back to Babylon to mount the Chaldean throne, which had just then been vacated by the death of his father Nabopolassar. Nebuchadrezzar was destined to reign over the Chaldeans until his death in 561. He thus introduced the Chaldean period in biblical and world history.

In the year 605 (II Kings 24:1) Nebuchadrezzar "came up" into Judah, and Jehoiakim acknowledged his sovereignty and for three years paid him tribute. Then in 602 he rebelled against Nebuchadrezzar, most likely because of the pledges made to him by Pharaoh Neco of Egypt, to whom he owed his throne.

Cornill is right in viewing Jer. 12:7-12 not as a picture of an anticipated future but as reflecting what was then taking place. Evidently King Nebuchadrezzar was not ready to punish Judah by invading its territory in force, but he gave the nod to marauding nomadic bands, friendly to the Chaldeans, who were near neighbors of Judah. These nomadic hordes, made up of Chaldeans, Syrians, Moabites, and Ammonites, are viewed by the historian of Judah as having been sent by the Lord to punish Jehoiakim (II Kings 24:2). According to Jeremiah, their incursion was the result of Judah's open antagonism to the Lord as shown by the nation's rejection of the prophet, his spokesman. As Jeremiah interprets it, in punishment of his

185

people the Lord has abandoned his "house," his "heritage," "the loved one" of his soul, to destruction.

The mixed nomadic hordes which are invading Palestine, the Lord's "possession," are leaving it destroyed, his prized "property" desolate, his lovely "meadow" a waste. The Lord is represented as calling the nation "the loved one of my soul." But God has become ill-disposed toward Judah. His people must be severely disciplined. Jeremiah vividly compared Judah to a gaudily-colored bird against which, as though it were an intruder, the other birds combine (vs. 9). The Lord laments through his prophet:

> 12:7 I have abandoned my house;
> I have forsaken my possession.
> I have given over the loved one of my soul
> Into the power of her enemies.
> 8 My property has become to me
> Like a lion in the forest,
> Which has uttered against me its roar.
> Therefore I hate it.
> 9 Has my property become a many-colored bird of prey
> That the birds of prey round about are against her?
> Come, gather together, all animals of the field;
> Come to devour!

Jeremiah vividly portrays these ravagers as trampling the Lord's precious land of Judah, His "property," His "desirable possession" into a wilderness waste. And no one in Judah seems concerned. The unprotected land mourns against Him who gave it to His people. These Bedouin destroyers are doing a thorough job, for their devastation has reached all Judah and has thrown all the inhabitants into panic.

> 12:10 Many shepherds have destroyed my vineyard,
> They have trampled my property.
> They have made my desirable possession
> Into a desolate wilderness.
> 11 They have made of it a waste: it mourns
> Against me, devastated.
> All the land has been desolated,
> And no one lays it to heart.
> 12 Upon all the bare heights, in the wilderness
> Have come devastators.[1]
> From one end of the land to the other;
> There is no peace for mankind.

[1] Delete with W. Rudolph the second clause of this verse, "For the sword of the Lord is eating," as an eschatological expansion, p. 74.

In vs. 4abα, along with vs. 13, the prophet seems to view these devastating ravagers as making impossible on the part of the Judeans the cultivating and harvesting of their crops. Thus their toil came to no profit, and the small returns from their labor, along with the devastation of their land, Jeremiah views as the effects of God's judgment. Even wild birds absent themselves from Judean territory and the beasts of the field perish.

> 12:4a **How long will the whole land mourn,**
> **And the herbage of the field wither?**
> 4bα **Because of the evil of those who dwell in it, beasts and birds [even]**
> **Have been snatched away.**
> 13 **They have sown wheat, but reaped thorns;**
> **They have strained themselves, but to no profit;**
> **So they will be ashamed of their returns,**
> **Before the fierceness of the Lord's anger.**

Jeremiah has something to say about these evil neighbors in vss 14-17. It is a fresh new word of great spiritual breadth and international tolerance. As Bedouin allies of the Chaldeans, and quite unaware of performing any spiritual mission or of serving any divine purpose, these nomadic marauding bands—Syrians, Moabites, and Ammonites—did their destructive work upon Judah. Jeremiah is perfectly sure that these very peoples along with Judah itself will suffer exile at the hands of the Chaldeans, the foe from the north (25:8-9). The Lord is about to "pluck them up." But when this shall have been done, the Lord's immeasurable compassion upon them will return them—each nomadic group—to its own area. Strikingly original with Jeremiah is the thought which the Lord reveals to him that these pagan nomadic hordes are "my evil neighbors." They belong to the Lord and he has even for them a redemptive purpose. And there in exile, if they learn "the ways of the Lord's people," learn to base their words and actions upon the Lord, even as—in sharp contrast—Israel had been taught by Canaanites, Amorites, and Phoenicians to base their words and actions upon Baal, then these foreign peoples will be built up. But their permanence as peoples depends upon their responsiveness to such teaching.

This passage gives us a foregleam of Jeremiah's thought regarding the relation of the nations other than Israel to the Lord. As Cornill notes, the content of this passage is "highly original," and "an authentic kernel of Jeremiah's thought lies at its heart." [2] It finds its completest statement in Jeremiah, as we shall see, in 16:19-20.

---

[2] *Jeremia*, pp. 165, 167.

12:14 Thus says the Lord, as regards all my evil neighbors who are harming the
territory which I gave my people Israel as a possession. Lo, I am about to pluck
them up from their land.[3] 15 But after I shall have plucked them up, I will in turn
have compassion on them, and will bring them back, each to his own heritage and
each to his own land. 16 And if they really learn my people's manner of life, to
swear by my name, "As the Lord lives," even as my people were taught to swear
by Baal, they shall be built up in the midst of my people. 17 But if they will not
listen, I will pluck up that nation, rooting it out and destroying it, says the
Lord.

These three or more years (602-598) which preceded the first invasion
of Judah by the forces of Nebuchadrezzar of Babylon were very unsettled
in Judah. King Jehoiakim's rebellion in 602 against Nebuchadrezzar, and
his transfer of his loyalty to Egypt, were viewed by Jeremiah as being fully as
disastrous as Judah's earlier alliance with Assyria had proved to be. He
maintains that the Judean envoys seeking help from Pharaoh Neco's court
will be unsuccessful. And he imaginatively pictures them returning hopeless
from Egypt, and making a typical Oriental gesture of lamentation—the hand
to the head. Lamenting in the Lord's name Jehoiakim's policy, Jeremiah
predicts its utter failure. Says the Lord:

> 2:36 Why do you make very light of me
>   By changing your political course?
> You will be disappointed likewise by Egypt,
>   Just as you were disappointed by Assyria.
> 37 Moreover, because of this you will come out
>   With your hands upon your head;
>   For the Lord rejects [the very basis of] your confidence,
>   And you will not have success with them.

In this troubled time many Judean nomads were forced to flee to the
security of Jerusalem (4:5-8; 8:14-15). Among them was a clan of "Rechabites," a branch of the Kenites (I Chr. 2:55), a nomadic tribe which had
associations with Israel since the days of Moses (Judg. 1:16). They had
settled in the southernmost section of Judah and were now in Jerusalem
where they retained their own manner of life and lived as a community
apart. They represent in essence a protest against the Canaanite elements
that had infiltrated into Judean religion. Their revered ancestor was
Jehonadab the son of Rechab, who in the days of Elisha had joined forces
with King Jehu in his purge of the Canaanite-Phoenician influence in

---

[3] Delete with Giesebrecht and Cornill as an intrusive gloss the clause "and the house
of Judah will I pluck up from the midst of them."

Israelite politics and religion (II Kings 10:15). Their presence in Jerusalem and their maintenance there of their own characteristic practices awakened much Judean interest and curiosity about them.

The practices which represented the tenets of the Rechabites were three: (a) they drank no wine; (b) they were opposed to building or living in houses and the planting of vineyards, and (c) they lived in tents.

Jeremiah received a prophetic impulse from the Lord which led him to invite this community of the Rechabites to a prominent room in the temple, the chamber of the sons of Hanan son of Igdaliah. Jeremiah tells of bringing them there, setting before them bowls of wine with cups for drinking.

We can sense the public curiosity aroused as people saw Jeremiah guiding these Rechabites to the chamber where the tables were set. It was evidently the prophet's own first contact with the group. Upon being invited to drink, they respectfully refused, and cited as their reason their loyalty to the command of their revered ancestor or father (*'abh*), Jonadab. Thus Jeremiah gives his account of this episode.

35:1 The word which came to Jeremiah from the Lord in the days of Jehoiakim son of Josiah, king of Judah, saying, 2 Go to the community of the Rechabites, and speak with them, and bring them to the house of the Lord to one of the rooms and give them wine to drink. 3 So I took Jaazaniah the son of Jeremiah the son of Habazziniah, and his brothers, and all his sons, and all the community of the Rechabites. 4 And I brought them to the house of the Lord, to the chamber of the sons of Hanan the son of Igdaliah, the man of God, which was contiguous to the chamber of the princes, above the chamber of Masseiah son of Shallum, guardian of the threshold. 5 And I set before the members of the community of Rechabites bowls full of wine and cups, and said to them, "Drink wine." 6 But they said, "We do not drink wine, for Jonadab son of Rechab, our ancestor, has laid the command upon us, saying, 'You must never drink wine—neither you nor your sons. 7 And you must not build houses or sow seed or plant vineyards; but you shall dwell only in tents all your days, so that you may live many days on the face of the ground where you are staying.' 8 So we shall listen to the voice of Jonadab the son of Rechab, our father, in all that he has commanded us about not drinking wine, as long as we live—we, our wives, our sons, and our daughters. 9 And to build houses for our dwellings, and vineyards and sown fields shall not be for us. 10 But we shall dwell in tents, and we shall do in accordance with everything that Jonadab our father commanded us. 11 Now it happened that when Nebuchadrezzar king of Babylon went up against the land, we said, 'Come, let us go in to Jerusalem before the army of the Chaldeans and before the army of the Arameans,' so we dwell in Jerusalem."

On the ground of this experience with the Rechabite community there came to Jeremiah from the Lord a message of "correction" to Judah, based

upon the commandment of Rechab their "father." The Rechabites have
faithfully observed the commands of their "father" and teacher. How utterly in contrast with this has been the attitude of the Judeans to the commands of their Lord to return from their unrighteous ways and from the
polytheism of their Baal worship. They would not listen to the Lord's
word nor would they answer his call. The result can be only what the Lord
has accordingly willed, the destruction of the national life of Judah.

35:12 Then the word of the Lord came to me, saying: 13 Thus says the Lord
of hosts, God of Israel, Go and say to the men of Judah and to the inhabitants
of Jerusalem, Should you not receive correction by listening to my words? says
the Lord. 14 Let the words of Jonadab son of Rechab be obeyed, who has commanded his sons not to drink wine, and they have not drunk [it] until this day,
for they listened to the commandments of their father, but I—I have spoken to
you, speaking early and often—but you did not listen to me. 15 And I sent to you
all my servants the prophets untiringly, saying, "Pray, return each from his evil
way and amend your doings and do not walk after other gods in order to serve
them, and so dwell in the land which I have given to you and to your fathers."
But you did not incline your ears and you did not listen to me. 16 Now the sons
of Jonadab son of Rechab have carried out the command of their ancestor which
he commanded them but this people have not listened to me.

17 Therefore thus says the Lord, God of hosts, God of Israel, Lo, I am about to
bring to Judah and to all the inhabitants of Jerusalem all the evil which I spoke
concerning them, because I spoke to them but they would not listen, and I called
to them but they would not answer.

The Lord also revealed to Jeremiah a message which he delivered to the
Rechabite community (vss. 18-19). It assured the stability of their community and the continuity of its leadership. Already it had lasted two
hundred and fifty years. It would endure indefinitely into the future. As Volz
remarks, "The words of Jeremiah show what he prized in the Rechabites
. . . was the moral quality of loyalty." [4] We have here no inculcation on the
part of Jeremiah of the Bedouin ideal but a call for firm and persistent
obedience to the commands of God, and loyalty to the standards set by their
fathers, the willing, practical, and intense devotion of people to a cause.

35:18 And to the community of the Rechabites Jeremiah said, Thus says the
Lord of hosts, God of Israel, Because you have listened to the commandment of
Jonadab your father, and have kept his commandments, and have done in ac-
cordance with all he commanded you, 19 therefore thus says the Lord of hosts,
God of Israel: There shall never fail Jonadab the son of Rechab a man to stand
before me.

[4] *Jeremia*, p. 323.

Arise and Go Down to the Potter's House

Judah's godless and egotistical monarch, Jehoiakim, was still on the throne. Jeremiah could see only doom in store for his people at the hand of the powerful and ruthless Chaldeans. The king and the political leaders, the prophets and priests, were against him. And the people generally were spiritually dull and indifferent. One day there came to him an experience of great moment, of which he informs us in a pure bit of autobiography (18:2-4), now embedded in a narrative from the Deuteronomic editor of the book (18:1-11). The account comes from the narrator's pen. After opening with a characteristic formula used by this source (vs. 1), the autobiographical nucleus follows.

18:1 **The word which came to Jeremiah from the Lord, saying: 2 "Arise, and go down to the potter's house, and there I will cause you to hear my words." 3 So I went down to the potter's house, and lo, he was making a vessel on the wheels.**

What he saw that day he had time and again seen before—a potter fashioning clay into vessels of various sizes and shapes. But under the illumination of God that familiar sight opened a new quality in his prophetic message and a new epoch in his ministry.

By way of illustration, Cornill cites the comparable experience of Newton's discovery of the law of gravitation: "Newton had seen thousands of apples fall from the tree to the earth before he saw the falling apple by which he perceived the law of gravitation." [5]

A visit which I made to a potter's shop in Jerusalem, where the same technique was followed as is now described, makes Jeremiah's experience that day very vivid to me. There sat the potter at the potter's wheels, which were made by two horizontal circular stone disks bound together, the lower one attached to a simple mechanism by which the disk was rotated from underneath by the potter's feet, the upper wheel on the same perpendicular axle supporting a large round lump of prepared clay. The potter set the wheels in revolution. Working from the top of the lump, he sent his left hand down into the clay mass to shape the inside of the vessel he was forming, while with his right hand he skillfully fashioned the outside. He kept the wheel whirling—now swiftly, now slowly, for he knew how to "bend the strength of the clay" [6] with his feet, and to fashion it with his hands. Nearby stood a little vessel of water, in which from time to time he wet his fingers

---

[5] *Jeremia,* p. 221.

[6] Cf. the ancient description of the potter as given by Ben Sirach in Ecclus. 38:29-30.

so as to smooth the clay as it whirled on the wheel. Vessel after vessel he made, cutting each off from the lump and setting it aside for later finishing. Just such a scene fascinated the impressionable poet-prophet as he watched intently every movement of the potter's strong, skilled, sensitive fingers. How perfectly at home was he amidst his prepared clay and whirling wheels!

Then something happened. The potter's project miscarried. The vessel he was shaping was marred in his hand. Jeremiah saw the potter, undismayed, mash the marred vessel into a lump again, then setting the wheels turning, he worked it into another vessel which met with his approval. Thus Jeremiah reports it:

18:4 **Now when the vessel which he was making out of the clay was spoiled in his hands, he made it over into another vessel, just as was pleasing in his sight to do.**

It was at that moment that the insight which God desired to reveal to his prophet dawned upon his mind. It was the realization that Judah, although it was "a spoiled vessel," was still in the hands of God, a God of infinite resourcefulness, and of abiding, enduring love. The purpose of God with his people had been frustrated—yes, but not defeated. The divine potter still loved his clay. Jeremiah now looked at corrupt Judah with illumined eyes. As Skinner sensitively says, putting his thought into a question: "If it was the Lord's pleasure to make of the same clay 'another vessel,' must He not have in His heart some grand design which had been thwarted once but could not be defeated finally?" [7] From this time forward, while not ceasing to proclaim the destructive judgment of God, Jeremiah began to preach as well that beyond certain judgment for Judah, there lay a future of hope (cf. 29:11). From this episode began his ministry "to build and to plant."

This parable in action did not teach God's absolute domination of Judah, but it led Jeremiah to a new confidence in the power of God's enduring love for his people. And it helped him to see that such a righteous, merciful, and persistent love would at length awaken response in the nation, so that it could be fashioned into another vessel, approved of God. Jeremiah sensed all the more clearly that judgment must come to the rebellious nation, but perhaps even by the catastrophe itself Judah's responsiveness would be awakened. From this time forward the expectation of a future of hope for Judah, beyond national calamity, became a most important note of his preaching.

Thus one phase of the "word" that God caused him to hear that day was

---

[7] *Prophecy and Religion*, p. 162.

the sovereignty of God. Skinner [8] remarks that the classical illustration of the divine sovereignty—the image of the potter and the clay—seems to have originated with Jeremiah. God is fashioning his people as the potter fashions clay. So the prophet utters God's word of appeal to his people, which now lay, as spoiled clay, in his hands.

18:5 **Then the word of the Lord came to me saying,** 6 **"Cannot I do to you as this potter, O house of Israel? Lo, as the clay in the hand of the potter, so are you in my hand, O house of Israel."**

But, as G. A. Smith has emphasized, the sovereignty of God "is not fettered by its own previous decrees; . . . It is free to recall and alter these, should the human characters and wills with which it works in history themselves change. There is a Divine as well as a human Free Will. 'God's dealing with man is moral: He treats them as their moral conduct permits Him to do.' " [9]

A second phase of the "word" which the Lord was causing Jeremiah to hear was focused at the point of just how the potter treats a spoiled vessel. He does not throw away the vessel he has spoiled in the making. He knows his clay, realizes its value, knows what he can do with it, and is proud of the finished product. Is God less of an artist than the potter? Does he love the Judah he is shaping less than the potter loves his clay? Is the Lord's power over Judah to be manifested solely in Judah's destruction? Or may not that destruction be but an incident in the potter's creation? As Skinner says: "If it was the Lord's pleasure to make of the same clay 'another vessel,' must He not have in His heart some grand design which had been thwarted once but could not be defeated finally?" [10]

There is that in human nature that frustrates the purpose of God. But God is not in a hurry, and his will for the perfection of what he has created is matched by his unspeakable patience. When the prophet realized that Judah lay in God's hands like a spoiled vessel in the hands of the potter, that day there was born in his soul a mighty conviction that after the marring of the clay, i.e., the destruction of Judah, had taken place, the nation was to be effectively reconciled to him and made over into a new people of God.

In spite of Skinner's view that vss. 7-10 are "the well-meant homily of an over-zealous commentator," [11] I believe that these verses embody the authen-

[8] *Ibid.*, p. 163.
[9] *Jeremiah*, p. 186.
[10] *Op. cit.*, p. 163.
[11] *Ibid.*

tic view of Jeremiah that God's dealings with Judah are upon exactly the same basis as his moral dealings with every nation. There is here an implicit reference to the earlier narrative of the prophet's call, wherein it was to be Jeremiah's mission "to uproot and demolish, to destroy and to tear down, to build and to plant." G. A. Smith sees in this passage the truth of the divine patience, and rightly believes this to be implicit in the acted parable of the potter. If such were intended by the prophet, which seems eminently reasonable, it is "proof that in spite of his people's obstinacy under the hand of God, he cherished, though he dared not yet utter, the hope that God would have some fresh purpose for their service beyond the wreck they were making of His former designs for them and the ruin they were thereby bringing on themselves—that He would grant them still another chance of rising to His will." [12]

Thus the prophet interprets the divine patience of God with every nation. When he says, "I would repent," he means, "I would alter my treatment," for among men change of conduct implies change of purpose.[13] Arthur P. Stanley calls attention at this point to the pioneering quality of Jeremiah's thought: "First of the prophets Jeremiah proclaims distinctly . . . . that predictions were subject to no overruling necessity, but depended for their fulfilment on the moral state of those to whom they were addressed; that the most confident assurance of blessing could be frustrated by sin; that the most awful warnings of calamity could be averted by repentance." [14]

Explains the prophet:

18:7 [If] at one moment I should speak regarding a nation or kingdom purposing to uproot and destroy [it], 8 and that nation should turn from its evil, then I would repent [15] as to the evil which I had thought I would do to it. 9 If at another moment I should speak regarding a nation and concerning a kingdom, to build and plant [it], 10 but it should do what is evil in my sight, in that it would not listen to my voice, then I would change my mind as to the good wherewith I had said I would deal well with it.

In vs. 11 this general principle of God's responsive dealing with a nation is now concretely applied to Judah. The Lord commands Jeremiah to call the men of Judah and Jerusalem to repentance. Let every individual turn from his evil conduct to such as will be in harmony with God's will. But

[12] *Op. cit.*, p. 187.
[13] A. W. Streane, *Jeremiah*, p. 155.
[14] *Jewish Church*, II, 445.
[15] So rightly Driver, *Hebrew Tenses*, sec. 148.

unfortunately their conduct has become habitually evil, and already the Lord is "shaping" or "molding" destruction for Judah.

Just as Hosea more than a century earlier had found to be the case in Israel, so now in Judah,

> Their deeds do not permit them
> to return to their God (Hos. 5:4).

Thus the Judeans reject God's call to alter their lives, even though their decision is prefaced by a despairing cry. In the prophet's accusation (vs. 12) he puts into their mouths his own conclusion, as though they themselves were giving purposive expression to it.

18:11 So now speak, I beseech you, to the men of Judah and the inhabitants of Jerusalem, saying: "Thus says the Lord: Lo, I am about to shape evil against you and to plan a device against you. Turn, pray, each from his evil way and amend your ways and your doings." 12 "But," said they, "No hope! But we will walk following our own schemes, and we will act each in the stubbornness of his own evil heart."

THE FIRST CHALDEAN INVASION OF JUDAH

It was the unfortunate boy-monarch, eighteen-year-old King Jehoiachin son of Jehoiakim, who was to reap the harvest of his father's irresponsible, vacillating, and corrupt rule. Very shortly after Nebuchadrezzar had let loose upon Judah the nomadic Moabites, Ammonites, and Aramaeans, along with some of his own marauding Chaldeans, Jehoiakim died and the youthful Jehoiachin became king, his queen mother Nehushta, because of his youth, also holding a prominent place in the court. He had been king but three months when, in 598, Nebuchadrezzar found himself free to march against the unhappy land of Judah, and the long-proclaimed invasion of the Chaldeans and the siege of Jerusalem took place.

The historical situation implied in 15:5-9 is that of *ca.* 598, before Jerusalem was itself besieged, but when the forces of Nebuchadrezzar the Chaldean had overrun Judah, clashed with the Judean troops, and shut up the cities of the south (13:19), a situation likewise mirrored in Lamentations, wherein Judah laments:

> The Lord in my midst
> Has set at nought all my warriors,
> He has called an assembly against me,
> To crush my young men.

$$\bullet \quad \bullet \quad \bullet \quad \bullet \quad \bullet \quad \bullet \quad \bullet \quad \bullet \quad \bullet \quad \bullet$$

On the street the sword has caused bereavement,
Even as death in the house (Lam. 1:15, 20c) .

Jerusalem itself is doomed and no one is concerned about it. There is no one to lament over Jerusalem, for the capital city has fallen away from loyalty to the Lord and is therefore condemned to destruction. The cities of Judah—he thinks especially of the country districts of the south—have been scattered like chaff at the threshing, and the Judean fighting forces of these southern cities have been destroyed by surprise assaults of the Chaldean troops, an expression of the divine judgment upon Judah. The loss of man power has been very great. As a consequence the widows of Judah are many. One vivid representative picture of the distress is painted by the prophet. A mother of seven sons, having lost all of them in war, collapsed when the news of their death came, for now she must endure the reproach of childlessness with the glory of her life gone. And what is left of the nation is destined by the Lord to fall by the sword.

Addressing Jerusalem the prophet cries out upon it the Lord's condemnation:

15:5   Who has compassion on you, O Jerusalem?
         Who laments over you,
         Or who will go out of his way
            To ask about your welfare?
6   You have forsaken me,
         Says the Lord,
            You have gone backward;
     So I stretched out my hand and destroyed you,
     I am weary of being moved to pity.
7   So I scattered them [as chaff] with a pitchfork,
         In the towns of the land.
     I have made childless, have destroyed, my people;
     They have not turned from their ways.
8$a(\beta)$ I have brought upon them a people that lays waste,
         A destruction at midday.
$b(a)$ I have caused to fall suddenly upon them,
$b(\beta)$ Surprise attack and dismay.
$a(a)$ Its widows are more numerous to me
         Than the sand of the seas.
9   A mother of seven has collapsed;
         She has breathed out her life.
     Her sun has gone down while it was still day,
     She became ashamed and embarrassed,

And what is left of them [the nation] I will give over to the sword,
Before their enemies, says the Lord.

The prophet calls to the Judeans of the highlands and pasture lands,
imploring them to lift up a lamentation because of the imminent desolation
of Judah. When the destruction has come, no human being will be left,
no birds, no domesticated beasts. Their capital will be reduced to a haunt
of jackals, and their now-populous cities to uninhabited ruins.

9:10 Upon the mountains lift up weeping,
    Yes, a lament upon the pastures of the wilderness,
For they shall be laid desolate without inhabitant,
    And shall not hear the lowing of the cattle.
From birds of the heavens to beasts,
    They have fled, they have gone.
11 And I will make of Jerusalem a heap of ruins,
    A place haunted by jackals.
And as for the cities of Judah, I will make [them] a waste,
    Without inhabitant.[16]

Jeremiah calls upon the Judeans to summon the wailing women, strangely
gifted in sensing the dire purposes of the Lord, and uniquely skilled through
their finely rendered lamentations, to draw forth tears from unrepentant
Judean eyes. In imagination the prophet hears the mourning song sung by
the inhabitants of Zion, shamefully bereft of their capital, and by all Judah,
flung from their homes. Let the voices of the professional mourners be
augmented by the laments of Judean women taught by their elders and by
one another to bewail their imminent destruction. And from Zion itself he
hears the wailing song lifted as he imaginatively describes the reaper, Death,
stalking through the Judean meadows, into palaces, and out into the streets
and squares, leaving in his train, like ungathered sheaves of grain, the dead
bodies of the slain, there to decay unburied upon the land.

9:17 Cry to the wailing women that they may come in,
    And send to the skilled women,
    And let them come.
18 Aye, let them hasten
    And lift a lamentation over us.
Let our eyes flow with tears,
    And our eyelids gush with weeping.
19 For the cry of a mourning song
    Is heard from Zion.

[16] Vss. 12-16 are a later commentary upon vss. 10-11; see p. 312.

How sorely devastated are we!
Our shame is very great;
For we must abandon the land
Yes, he will fling us out from our dwellings.
20 Aye, hear, O women, the word of the Lord;
Let your ear receive the word of his mouth;
Teach your daughters a wailing song;
One woman shall teach the other a lament.
21 Death has come up through our windows,
It has entered into our palaces,
So that children are cut off from the street,
Youths from the broad open places.
22 And human corpses have fallen
Like dung upon the surface of the field,
Like sheaves behind the reaper,
Which no one gathers.

PACK UP YOUR BUNDLE

In 10:17-22 the threat of the first Chaldean captivity is nearer at hand and further advanced. The first exile of the Jerusalem inhabitants is in prospect in the mind of the prophet. Says the prophet: "Tie up in a bundle your precious belongings, all that you can take with you." The Jerusalem community must live in a state of siege. The long predicted disaster is near. So the prophet cries:

10:17 Pack up your bundle [to take it] out of the land,
O thou community which lives in [a state of] siege.
18 For thus says the Lord:
Lo, I am about to hurl out
The inhabitants of the land
At this time;
Yes, I will bring distress upon them,
So that they will melt away.

In response to this solemn prophetic word the nation is represented as lamenting before the Lord. Struck by a "malady" sent by God, Judah knows that it is deserved and must be borne. The once-secure nation is now like a tent with the cords that have held it in place snapped, and with no one trying to make it secure. Its "shepherds," the kings of Judah, are dull of mind and secular in spirit. Consequently their uncared for "flock" is dispersed.

From the north, whence hails the Chaldean menace, the nation hears the

rumor of the moving of troops, the coming of an army against Judah that
will reduce its treasured cities to depopulated ruins haunted by jackals.

10:19 Woe to me because of thy destruction.
    Severe is thy blow!
    But I said, "Yet this
    Is my malady and I can bear it."
  20 Yes, all my tent cords are snapped,
    And my sheep—they are not.
    No one sets up my tent any more,
    Or stretches out my tent curtains.
  21 For the shepherds are dull-hearted,
    And the Lord they do not seek.
    Therefore they have not prospered,
    And all their flock is scattered.
  22 Hark, a rumor! Lo, it comes!
    And a great shaking from the land of the north,
    To turn the cities of Judah
    Into a desolation, a lair of jackals.

Such solemn words, portraying the imminence of Judah's collapse, threw
the prophet upon his knees in intercession for his people. Jeremiah knew
that Judah needed the correction of God. Yet he feels himself one with his
people and he pleads on their behalf with God, that he will remember
man's incapacity in his own strength, to do what is right. Let God punish,
discipline, correct his people—yet not in the wrath they deserve but in
mildness (the prophet uses the term *mishpaṭ*, "justice"), in moderation, in
measure proportionate to what Judah can bear.

  23 Thou knowest, O Lord, that not in man is the way he should take
    Nor is it for man to walk and order his steps aright.
  24 Correct us, O Lord, but in reasonableness,
    Not in thy wrath, lest thou cause us to dwindle.[17]

In 16:16-18 we are again in the mood of the certainty and the complete-
ness of the captivity, and of its agent, the Chaldeans. Jeremiah to make it
vivid uses the metaphors of fishing and hunting. The Judeans will be captured as many fishermen catch fish, or to change the figure, as many hunters
hunt down their prey. None will escape capture, though they should hide
on mountains, hills, and in clefts of the rocks. And none can hide their
iniquity from the Lord. It is their idolatry which has made Palestine unclean.
Says the prophet:

[17] For vs. 25 see p. 324.

16:16 **Lo, I am about to send for many fishermen, says the Lord, and they shall catch them and afterward I will send for many hunters and they shall hunt them from every mountain and from every hill and from the clefts of the rocks.** 17 **For my eyes are upon all their ways; they cannot hide themselves from me, and their iniquity cannot be hidden from my sight.** 18 **So I will doubly repay their guilt and their sin because of their pollution of my land by the disgraceful folly of their detested idols, and because they have filled my property with their abominations.**[18]

The Innocent Suffer for the Guilty

Jer. 22:24-27 is an utterance of the prophet concerning King Jehoiachin, son and successor of Jehoiakim. Vs. 24 is the pronouncement itself in poetry, and vss. 25-27, which are in prose, form a commentary upon it. It dates from a time very shortly before King Jehoiachin and the queen mother were carried in captivity to Babylonia, so toward the end of his brief three-month reign in 598. As over against Jehoiakim, the sharply criticized king whom he succeeded on the Judean throne, the blameless young monarch is compared to a signet ring on God's right hand. The bearer of a king's signet ring would stand at his monarch's right as his highest officer in court. And the stamp of his seal ring upon any document would give it royal authority. Although as monarch of the Lord's people Jehoiachin stood in such a relation as that to the Lord, his royal authority as the Lord's king in Jerusalem is to be taken away from him—his signet ring, as it were, "pulled off." The pronouncement is uttered by Jeremiah, as God's spokesman, in the form of a solemn oath which clearly prophesies the young king's dethronement, and it is interpreted as a purposive deed of God.

> 22:24 **As I live, saith the Lord,**
> **Although Jehoiachin were**
> **A signet ring on my right hand,**
> **I say that I would pull it off from there.**

Vss. 25-27, which continue in prose, predict the fate of the young king, who now is timid and fearful before the advancing Chaldeans, and of his mother Nehushta, whose prominence was enhanced by the youth of the king. Nebuchadrezzar and his Chaldean troops will hurl the youthful ruler, along with his mother, to Babylonia, and although they will long to return to their homeland, they shall die in exile there.

22:25 **And I will give you into the power of those who are seeking your life before whom you are in fear, Nebuchadrezzar king of Babylon, and the Chaldeans,**

---

[18] For vss. 19-21 see pp. 325-26.

26 and you and your mother who bore you I will hurl out to an alien land, where you were not born, and there you will die. 27 But to the land to which their souls keep longing to return they shall not return.

In spite of the repeated warnings, Judah paid no heed and now the first blow has fallen. In 13:18-19 the situation described in II Kings 24:11-12 is implied. (It dates from the time very shortly before the armies of Nebuchadrezzar had reached Jerusalem, but Jeremiah can see clearly what the outcome will be.) Eighteen-year-old King Jehoiachin and Nehushta, the queen mother, destroned by Nebuchadrezzar, are now but commoners. They have lost their crowns. Already, as Alt [19] has shown, the Negeb, the region from the hills south of Hebron to Kadesh, has been severed from Judah and is no more accessible to Jerusalem. The prophet can see before him nothing short of the imminent captivity and exile of all Judah.

Cries the prophet:

> 13:18 Say to the king and the queen mother:
>   Sit down in degradation,
>   For from your heads have come down
>   Your glorious crowns.
>   19 The cities of the south are shut up,
>   And there is no one to open them;
>   Judah will be carried into exile—all of it—
>   In a complete captivity.

Jer. 22:20-23 dates from 598. The upper classes of Jerusalem have just been taken into exile (II Kings 24:14-16) in Babylon. This included eighteen-year-old King Jehoiachin, the queen mother Nehushta, and "all the nobles and all the renowned warriors," and all the craftsmen and the smiths, "the chief men of the land."

It was the habit in Israel for the uttering of lamentations to climb to the heights. The more profound the lament and the deeper the sorrow that occasioned it, the higher did the people climb to lament before the Lord. These verses are imaginative poetry. The population that is still in Jerusalem is summoned to betake itself, not merely as was customary to the roofs or to the top of the city wall, but because the distress is great, to the Lebanon Mountains in the north, the highland country of Bashan in the northeast, with glorious snow-capped Hermon its loftiest point, and to the Abarim Mountains (Num. 27:12) in the south, from the highest summit of which, Mount Nebo, Moses many centuries before had viewed the land of Canaan

[19] Cf. A. Alt in "Judas Gaue," *Palestina Jahrbuch* (1925), 108.

(Deut. 34:2). There on the heights they are to bewail the exile of Jerusalem's nobles—the "lovers" of Jerusalem who are destroyed. Volz suggestively calls attention to Jeremiah's "grandiose picture for an unspeakable sorrow," and says, "Today Jeremiah would be counted among the artists who love strong colors." [20]

In more prosperous days God had spoken to Jerusalem's people through the prophets and through Jeremiah himself, but to the prophetic warnings they had turned a deaf ear (2:31; 6:16). But now the time for hearing and heeding the Lord's warning has run out. The monarchs of Judah, instead of being shepherds of their people, protecting them from the gathering storm, have themselves been "shepherded"—but by the storm wind which has whirled off their leaders into banishment and thrown those left behind, "the poorest people of the land" (II Kings 24:14), into a community of humiliation. And all this because of the evil of Jerusalem.

The city itself still remains and is as yet unharmed. Again Jeremiah thinks of Jerusalem as nesting in its lofty palace of Lebanon's cedars. But there it is heavyhearted. Already the pains, as of a woman giving birth, have begun. The woes of the final siege yet to come are in the prophet's mind in vs. 23. But perhaps there is just the bare suggestion in the figure of travail that the pangs of national suffering may at length bring forth a new people.

Calls the prophet:

> 22:20 Go up to the Lebanon and cry out,
> And in Bashan utter thy voice;
> And cry out from Abarim,
> For all thy lovers are destroyed.
> 21 I spoke to you in your prosperity:
> You said, "I will not hear."
> This has been your way since your youth.
> You did not listen to my voice.
> 22 All your shepherds the wind drives away,
> And your lovers must go into captivity.
> Then you will be ashamed and humiliated
> Because of all your evil.
> 23 You who dwell in the Lebanon,
> Who have your nest in the cedars,
> How you will sigh when pangs come upon you,
> Anguish like that of a woman in travail!

Vss. 28-30 also presuppose that the exile of King Jehoiachin to Babylon has already taken place. In vs. 28 Jeremiah formulates the question which the

[20] *Jeremia,* p. 225.

swift dethronement and exile of their young monarch had inevitably aroused in Judean minds. Is the young king, thus ruthlessly banished from Judah, like a rejected vessel to God, thrown out and useless? Why has Jehoiachin been thus pitilessly unseated from his throne? Is this final, irrevocable? Or will there be a restoration of his rule, or at any rate, of his line?

Jeremiah's mind had been clearly illumined at this point by God. It is prophetic insight, not political finesse, that gave to Judeans the answer. He uses a technique of expression which the prophets loved—a solemn triple adjuration. Once before we have met with it in Jeremiah's thrice-uttered "the temple of the Lord" (7:4). It recalls to us Isaiah's Trisagion, "Holy, Holy, Holy" (6:3). And it brings to mind the anonymous Judean prophet's cry, "O altar, altar" (I Kings 13:2), and Ezekiel's "a sword, a sword" (21:28). No doubt there was some remnant of the magical in Jeremiah's utterance as he calls the whole land of Judah—thrice using the word—to awed attention, so that they might grasp the solemn prophetic import and the irrevocable outcome of Jehoiachin's doom, a prophecy that was clearly vindicated in the light of history. Neither did any of Jehoiachin's sons or their descendants occupy the Judean throne.

22:28 Is Jehoiachin [Coniah] despised?
  Is he a vessel in which I take no delight?
  Why should he be hurled out and sent
  To a land which he does not know?
29 O land, land, land,
  Hear the word of the Lord:
30 Register this man proscribed [21] [i.e., stripped of all rights],
  For no descendant of his shall be successful,
  So as to sit upon the throne of David,
  And rule again over Judah.

ISRAEL HAS NOT COME TO AN END

Jer. 24:1-10 belongs to the original collection of the words of Jeremiah. It is in prose. This section has no relation to the prophecies concerning the kings (21:11–23:8) and the prophets (23:9-40) that immediately precede it.

The vision of 24:1-10 reveals the moral foundations for Jeremiah's hope for the future. As we read the prophet's words it is well to keep in mind how true history proved his insight to be, for the restoration of the Judean people

---

[21] So Driver suggests as the correct meaning for *ʿrîrî*. He maintains that "childless" hardly can be right, as Jeconiah had seven sons (I Chr. 3:17-18). The Septuagint has *ekkerukton* ("excommunicated"), and the Old Latin renders it *abdicatum* ("rejected"), cf. "Linguistic and Textual Problems: Jeremiah," *Jewish Quarterly Review*, XXVIII (1937-38), p. 115.

in Judaism stemmed from the Babylonian exiles as did the great Babylonian Talmud.

The situation is as follows. Since 598 there have been two major groups of Judeans. One was composed of those who had been taken captive to Babylonia by Nebuchadrezzar in 598. This group included, certainly in the intention of their Chaldean captor, the elite of the Judean state, namely, King Jehoiachin, the queen mother, the king's wives, his eunuchs, his nobles and chief men, his renowned warriors and those fit for war, the priests, craftsmen, and smiths (II Kings 24:10-16). We must remember that this naturally included "most of the liberal-minded and experienced statesmen who had shielded Jeremiah from the fury of the mob and from the vindictive enmity of Jehoiakim." [22] The other group was made up of the remnant left in Jerusalem, a lower class of men, largely upstarts who had usurped the positions formerly held by the exiled leaders, and had appropriated their palaces, residences, and fields. Jeremiah also connects with these "those who live in the land of Egypt" (24:8). This would include, no doubt, some who had been taken to Egypt by Pharaoh Neco along with King Jehoahaz (II Kings 23:34) in 608. Some were members of the Jewish colony on the island of Elephantine near Assuan, at the first cataract of the Nile, a colony which had been established there long before 525,[23] and some were those who favored Egypt and had escaped to that country when the Babylonian supremacy over Judah had been established.[24]

The Jewish remnant in Jerusalem felt that they stood under the particular favor of God. The Lord had protected them from exile. In the fires of the Chaldean siege, when Jerusalem was surrounded by danger, they were protected like good flesh in a pot. In real exultation over their escape they said: "This city is the caldron, and we are the flesh" (Ezek. 11:3). Moreover, it seemed to them that God had punished the exiles by taking the land out of their control and giving it into the power of the Judean remnant. Concerning the exiled Judeans, those left in Jerusalem exultingly said: "They have gone far from the Lord; to us this land is given for a possession" (Ezek. 11:15). No doubt many felt that it was a good riddance of ambitious, oppressive, and plundering Judean leaders. Some felt that it was a blessing in disguise.

It was while Jeremiah was brooding over these matters, striving to understand the meaning of his times from the angle of God's will, that he had an

[22] Skinner, *Prophecy and Religion*, p. 251.
[23] Cowley, *Aramaic Papyri of the Fifth Century*, B.C., 2.3, p. xiv.
[24] Cf. A. S. Peake, *Jeremiah*, I, 273.

illuminating spiritual experience through which the Lord mediated to him one of his most creative insights and one of the most needed messages both for the exiles and the Jerusalem remnant.

It was the time of the fig harvest in Judah, which began about the end of June. Everywhere one could see baskets of figs which had been brought into Jerusalem. Some of them were full of delicious figs, others with figs that were inedible, good only as fodder for cattle. As Rudolph[25] suggestively portrays it, from these remembered images there arose in Jeremiah's mind a pure hallucination in which he saw two baskets of figs placed "before the temple," set there as though before God to receive his judgment as to their fate. Questioned by the Lord, Jeremiah tells exactly what he sees. Then the Lord explains that the good figs are an image of the exiles in Babylonia, upon whom the Lord looks with friendly eyes (vs. 5), for upon them rests the responsibility for a future, including restoration to their beloved land and permanence upon it. Moreover, with them rests the responsibility and privilege of being in the future the continuing people of that covenant which God has long ago made with Israel.

The bad figs are an image of King Zedekiah, along with his chieftains and the remnant left in Jerusalem and Egypt. These Jerusalem Judeans embodied the superficial, insolent reliance upon the indestructibility of their city, scornful disdain toward their unfortunate exiled countrymen, and the boasting over their own suddenly acquired property. Moreover, as we learn from Ezekiel, a worship of the most degenerate and corrupt sort was being carried on in the temple by them. The strong words employed by Jeremiah in vss. 9-10 were intended to awaken the conscience of the remnant by the creation of moving images of the awful fate awaiting these Judeans of the homeland who did not repent. For God does not see in these Jerusalem and Egyptian Judeans the kind of persons with whom as a nucleus he can rebuild his people.

Thus the prophet reports his new insight and how it came to his soul:

24:1 Thus the Lord let me see, and lo, there were two baskets of figs set before the temple of the Lord—that was after Nebuchadrezzar king of Babylon had carried captive Jehoiachin son of Jehoiakim king of Judah, and the princes of Judah, and the craftsmen and the metalworkers from Jerusalem and brought them to Babylon. 2 The one basket had very good figs, like the first ripe figs, and the other basket had very bad figs, which could not be eaten, they were so bad. 3 Then the Lord said to me, "What do you see, Jeremiah?" So I said, "Figs—the good

25 Jeremia, p. 135.

figs, very good; and the bad figs, very bad, which cannot be eaten they are so bad."

4 Then the word of the Lord came to me, saying: 5 "Just like these good figs, so will I regard for good the exiles of Judah whom I sent away from this place to the land of the Chaldeans for [their] good. 6 And I will set my eyes upon them for [their] benefit and will restore them to this land, and I will build them and not overthrow them, and I will plant them and not pull them up. 7 And I will give them a heart to know me, that I am the Lord, and they will be my people and I will be their God, for they will turn to me with their whole heart. 8 But as for the bad figs which cannot be eaten, they are so bad, so will I deal with Zedekiah king of Judah and his officials and the remnant of Jerusalem that are left in this land as well as those who are living in the land of Egypt, for evil. 9 And to all the kingdoms of the earth I will make them to be [the recipient of] terror, [the butt of] reproach, [the goal of] taunt, [the object of] derision, and [the bearer of] a curse. 10 And I will send among them the sword, famine, and pestilence, until they are consumed from the land which I gave their fathers."

CHAPTER SEVEN

Zedekiah and the Fall of Jerusalem

598-587—REIGN OF ZEDEKIAH

WHEN THE YOUTHFUL KING JEHOIACHIN AND THE QUEEN MOTHER NEHUSHTA WERE CARRIED TO BABYLON AS EXILES IN 598, NEBUCHADREZZAR placed upon the Judean throne Mattaniah, third son of King Josiah and uncle of Jehoiachin. He changed his name to Zedekiah. The most that we know about King Zedekiah we get from the book of Jeremiah, and he comes often into the record in this period of Judah's decline and fall. He was not, like Jehoiakim, a corrupt monarch, nor did he have anything of the strength of his father Josiah. His was an exceedingly difficult and delicate task. When he mounted the throne, several thousand of the leading citizens —ten thousand is reported by the historian in II Kings (24:14) —had just been carried off among the Babylonian exiles. In A. Malamat's article "Jeremiah and the Last Two Kings of Judah," [1] Zedekiah is seen in a new light. His entire reign was a struggle to keep his kingdom. Although Zedekiah owed his throne to Nebuchadrezzar, Judah was closer to Egypt than to Babylon, and there were leaders in Judah who were strong for seeking the backing of Egypt. Since the best stratum of Judean leadership had been taken into exile, the Judean nation was threatened with what Malamat calls "social economic anarchy." The dearth of capable and nationally-minded leaders opened places of responsibility to political adventurers.

But Malamat calls attention to another most complicating factor in Zedekiah's kingship. King Jehoiachin, although an exiled captive in a Chaldean prison, was still alive. Says Malamat: "This duality in the status of the monarchy made itself strongly felt in Judah itself, dividing the Judeans into opposite camps; one of which continued to see in Jehoiachin the king 'de

[1] *Palestine Exploration Quarterly for 1951*, pp. 81-87.

jure' even after he was exiled; these undoubtedly desired his return."
Malamat also calls attention to the seal imprint on a jar handle found at
Tell Beit Mirsim, "To Eliakim, steward of Yaukin" abridged form of
Jehoiachin. He considers this as evidence "that king Jehoiachin kept
an administration in Judah to take care of his royal property during his stay
in Babylon."

I Will Break the Bow of Elam

Jeremiah's prophecy concerning Elam (49:34-39) dates from 598. The
nation of Elam lay north of the Persian Gulf, to the east of the Tigris River,
and southwest of Media. Its capital was Shushan, and Babylon, to which the
young King Jehoiachin of Judah, the queen mother, and the most important
leaders among the Judeans had just been taken, lay only about fifteen miles
across the Tigris River. The fate of Elam was accordingly of great concern
to the exiles and to the Jews of the homeland with whom the exiles were
in constant correspondence. As Cornill thinks likely, Jeremiah may already
have had "a presentiment that the national power which had laid Elam low
might be the destined conqueror of Babylon, as indeed proved to be the
case." [2]

Superior forces will converge upon this people from all directions, and
they will scatter the Elamites and destroy them. The Lord himself will set
up his throne in Elam to implement his judgment of destruction upon its
king and princes, including the dispersion of the outcasts of Elam to the
four corners of the world (vs. 36). Elam's enemies will defeat and humiliate
its warriors—famous as bowmen (Isa. 22:6) —and destroy Elam's nationality.
But behind such national destruction and consequent dismay, as its creative
cause, is the moral God of Israel. There is little doubt that Jeremiah was here
thinking of the Chaldeans as God's agent in this destruction, a conception
to which he had already given definite expression (20:4).

The editor in vs. 34 introduces the utterance of Jeremiah as having been
given shortly before the month of Nisan (March-April), 597.

49:34 **That which was the word of the Lord to Jeremiah the prophet concerning
Elam, in the beginning of the reign of Zedekiah king of Judah, as follows:**

35 **Thus says the Lord of hosts:**
"Lo, I am about to break the bow of Elam,
The chief part of their might.

[2] So Peake, *Jeremiah*, II, 252; cf. Cornill, *Jeremia*, p. 489.

36 And I will bring upon Elam the four winds
   From the four extremities of the heavens,[3]
37 And I will dismay Elam before their enemies
   And before those who are seeking their life,
   And I will bring trouble upon them,
   My burning anger, says the Lord.[4]
38 And I will set up my throne in Elam
   And I will destroy from there king and princes,
   Says the Lord.[5]

JEREMIAH'S LETTER TO THE EXILES IN BABYLON

It is to Baruch's narrative of Jeremiah's conflicts, sufferings, and tribulations that we owe the account in ch. 29 of Jeremiah's letter to the exiles who had been taken to Babylon along with King Jehoiachin and the queen mother Nehushta in 598, for it brought him again into conflict with the priestly authorities in Jerusalem.

It was written not long after 598, for it is concerned about the attitude which the exiles are to take toward their exile. It is probably somewhat later in date than the vision experience of the two baskets of figs which Jeremiah had in Jerusalem and which we have just interpreted. The prophet has grown in prestige and authority. The vindication of his preaching concerning the destruction which was to stem from the north has given him a greater impressiveness. His letter came to them over his own signature, but also by the permission and tacit approval of King Zedekiah, for it was carried to Babylon and delivered to the exiles there by a delegation of two very important citizens from Jerusalem. The leader of this was Elasah son of Shaphan, who had been King Josiah's secretary of state, nephew of Gedaliah and brother of Gemariah, who had tried to restrain King Jehoiakim from burning Jeremiah's scroll (36:10). The other member was Gemariah son of Hilkiah who had been high priest under King Josiah (II Kings 22:4). These two men were prominent members of the Jerusalem nobility. Their errand might have been simply to bear the annual Judean tribute to the king. It is more likely that its primary purpose was the attestation to Nebuchadrezzar of a pledge of loyalty on the part of his Judean vassal, King Zedekiah. This would be a necessary and important mission if, as is likely, the abandonment

---

[3] The rest of vs. 36 ("And I will scatter . . .") is a later insertion into the text from 9:16.

[4] The rest of vs. 37 ("And I will send the sword . . .") is an addition which sharpens the threat of vs. 36.

[5] Vs. 39 is a later addition to the text; it reflects the change experienced by Elam when it had come under the power of the Persians.

of the plot of the Palestine-Mediterranean bloc to throw off the Chaldean yoke formed its immediate background. Thus Baruch introduces Jeremiah's letter.

29:1 Now these are the words of the letter which Jeremiah the prophet sent from Jerusalem to the elders of the exiles and to the priests and to the prophets and to all the rest [6] of the people whom Nebuchadrezzar had taken into exile from Jerusalem to Babylon.[7] 3 By the hand of Elasah son of Shaphan and Gemariah son of Hilkiah, whom Zedekiah king of Judah sent [on a mission] to Nebuchadrezzar king of Babylon, in Babylon.

Jeremiah's letter opens with very practical counsel which was greatly needed by the exiles. Many of them, inspired by such thoughts as had been spread abroad in Jerusalem by prominent men such as Hananiah, expected a speedy return to Palestine, and they found it hard to plan for anything that looked toward long-term residence in Babylon. This letter shows us that Nebuchadrezzar's treatment of the captives was broadminded and liberal. They were not confined in detention camps but lived in assigned settlements with free movement within the territory allotted them.[8] And there was considerable knowledge on their part as to what was going on in Jerusalem, just as the Jerusalem community knew much about what their exiled fellow countrymen were doing. The exiles for the most part represented the nationally-minded Judeans, and their ties to the homeland were naturally intimate and strong. Many of Jeremiah's own great and powerful friends were exiles. He himself missed them, even as they must have missed him and his counseling, and he was deeply concerned for their welfare. By revelation from the Lord he knew that it would be more than two generations—in round numbers seventy years—before there would be a return to Palestine. Few of that generation would ever return. This conviction was not easy to get accepted in that far-off community of devoted, patriotic Judeans. We can well imagine the intense interest on the part of those who revered Jeremiah in any prophetic insight and counsel that he had to give.

So Jeremiah's letter began by counseling the Judeans to settle down in the land of their exile and to plan for the future as though they expected to stay there many years. Do not live in temporary shacks, said the prophet.

---

[6] Transferring *yether* to immediately before *hā⁶ām*, following Volz, *Jeremia*, p. 266.

[7] Vs. 2, which breaks the connection between vs. 1 and vs. 3, is an addition based on II Kings 24:14-16. It reads, "After Jehoiachin the king and the queen mother and the eunuchs and officials [reading with Vulgate *principles*] of Judah and Jerusalem and the artisans and the smiths had gone out from Jerusalem."

[8] Cf. Rudolph, *Jeremia*, p. 155.

Build yourselves homes. Even in this foreign, heathen land, build homes to live in. Marry Judean wives. See to it that your sons and daughters marry. Bear children, let the Judean community not diminish in number or in character. Indeed, let it increase. In a time of grave uncertainty, when the future was unpredictable, Jeremiah gave them this down-to-earth counsel.

Again he told them that rather than count Babylonia as a hated enemy, they were to make the land of their exile the subject of their prayers. Judah's welfare is tied up with the welfare of Babylon—yes, even with that pagan, heathen land which knows not the Lord. How strange such words must have sounded. Pray for the very nation that has thus exiled you! Pray for this people that has plundered your sacred temple of its holy vessels! Pray for your enemies! As Volz says, this is "the only place in the Old Testament where intercession on behalf of enemies and unbelievers is commended." [9] Only one who had learned to pray for his enemies in Jerusalem could have given such counsel, meaning every word of it (18:20). As Volz suggestively says: "An entirely new judgment of the heathen and those of other faiths was given with this exhortation of Jeremiah to the exiles. . . . The contrast between Jew and heathen recedes, the community of intercession begins to unite the Judean nation with the pagan world; from now on it was possible to think of Mission," [10]—such a concept as was to find pioneering utterance from this very same Chaldean area in Deutero-Isaiah (42:1-8; 49:1-6).

Cries Jeremiah:

29:4 Thus says the Lord of hosts, God of Israel, to all the company of exiles who have been carried captive from Jerusalem to Babylon. 5 Build houses and inhabit [them], and plant gardens and eat fruit from them. 6 Marry wives and bear sons and daughters, and take wives for your sons and give your daughters to husbands, that they may give birth to sons and daughters, so you will increase there and not become few. 7 And seek the welfare of the land to which I have carried you into exile and pray to the Lord on behalf of it, for in its welfare lies your welfare.

The letter goes on to make more explicit the basis for his counsel just given. Almost certainly some who read his letter or heard it read had already learned that the prophet had given utterance in Jerusalem to God's revelation to him as regards the length of the Chaldean domination. Few to whom his letter was read would be alive seventy years hence. Few indeed of them would at the end of that time be "brought back" to Jerusalem. But their

[9] *Jeremia*, p. 269.
[10] *Ibid.*

sons and their daughters would be alive, and, in turn, their sons and daughters as well. It was upon that Judean community of the future that the prophet's eyes were resting in mighty faith. Then God's good and gracious word "Return," would be uttered by the Lord. God is now at work "forming plans," not for the exiles' harm but for their good, to open to the Judean people a new day. We sense the challenge in the prophet's thought. You will not see it, but your descendants will. Exile is not God's goal for you. Rather is that goal a hopeful future and a return for the Judean exiles, and through them a new epoch for the Judean people (vss. 10-11).

THE DEVELOPMENT OF LAY RELIGION

In the meantime, while the Judean community in exile is growing in numbers, building for a future, even though they are in a pagan land, far away from the temple, they are to pray to the Lord, calling upon him, seeking him, even as the prophet Amos had taught (5:4-5). We see here with vivid pertinency the significance of Jeremiah's noninstitutional conception of religion. They need not say, even in longing, "The temple of the Lord!" For neither temple nor sacrifices nor priests are necessary. In Babylon, where there is no Judean temple and no established cult, they can pray to God, and he will listen to them, be found by them, and as was particularly Ezekiel's experience, he will "appear" to them. As Volz says: "Neither temple nor priest nor prophet are indispensable; indeed the good man *as an individual* must himself find the way to God, and indeed he has access to Him." Volz also calls attention to the fact that in these words "the lay element in religion comes to its right. In place of the temple, the synagogue comes forward, alongside the prophet and priest the devout man out of the congregation who explores his Bible and participates in the congregation as speaker and as one who prays." [11]

29:10 **For thus says the Lord, When there shall have been measured out for Babylon seventy years' time, I will deal with you graciously and will carry out in your behalf my good word that I would bring you back to this place. 11 For I know the plans that I am forming, which have to do with you, plans for [your] welfare and not for [your] harm, to give you a future and [a ground for] hope. 12 And you will call upon me and will pray to me, and I will listen to you. 13 And you will seek me and find [me], when you seek with all your heart. 14 And I will appear to you.**

[11] *Ibid.*, pp. 269-270.

The letter next deals (vss. 15, 8-9) with the prophets who are with the exiles in Babylon. We must remember that not all of the prophets who were with the exiles were of the stamp of the nationalistic prophets such as Hananiah in Jerusalem. Ezekiel was also there; as a youth he had unquestionably heard Jeremiah in Jerusalem before 598.[12] And one of the fascinating things to note in this period is how at one Jeremiah and Ezekiel are in combating the predictions of the false prophets. But false prophets were there with their wiles, and Jeremiah knows by name many of them and solemnly warns the exiles against them. They foretell the future by lots, and through dreams of their own minds, uninspired by the Lord, they claim to discern it. They are false, presumptuous imposters whom God did not send.

Writes Jeremiah:

29:15 Since you have said, "The Lord has raised up for us prophets in Babylon." 8 Yet thus says the Lord of hosts, God of Israel: Do not let your prophets who are in your midst or your diviners deceive you, and do not listen to their dreams which they keep dreaming, 9 for they are prophesying to you falsehood in my name. I did not send them, says the Lord.[13]

Two of the false prophets Jeremiah singles out by name for sharp, direct accusation. He speaks in the Lord's name, and we can feel the burning moral passion of his own dedicated prophetic soul that fills his words. They are Ahab son of Kolaiah, and Zedekiah son of Maaseiah. These men were prophets who claimed to be sent by God. But they did not stand in the Lord's counsel, and all that Jeremiah said against the prophets who keep saying, "All is well," applied to them. They had no inkling of the place the Chaldeans occupied in the purpose of God. And the inevitable issue of the political machinations of these prophets against the Chaldeans, as Jeremiah clearly saw, was arrest by the Chaldean state and sentence to death by fire—a rare punitive sentence even in pagan Babylon. Let these men know that although they are far away from the Lord's land, they are still under his eyes, and what they have done and are doing is to him an open book. But the thing that most touches Jeremiah to the quick is that these men who have the presumption to call themselves prophets of the Lord are actually sensual, immoral men who "wrought disgraceful folly in Israel," [14]

---

[12] Probably by ca. 593, however, he had returned to Jerusalem, where he remained until shortly before the fall of Jerusalem, when he returned to Babylonia.

[13] For 29:16-20, which are intrusive, see pp. 321-22.

[14] Cf. Rudolph, Jeremia, p. 157.

for some of them have even committed adultery with the wives of their countrymen. Jeremiah pictures these men as so vile in character that their names will serve as a curse formula in the speech of Judeans when one seeks to bring upon another an ultimate imprecation.

Writes the prophet:

29:21 Thus says the Lord of hosts, God of Israel, concerning Ahab son of Kolaiah and concerning Zedekiah son of Maaseiah, who are prophesying to you in my name: Lo, I am about to deliver them up to the power of Nebuchadrezzar king of Babylon, and he will slay them before your eyes. 22 And a curse formula shall be derived from them by all the company of Judean exiles who are in Babylon, namely: "May the Lord make you like Zedekiah and like Ahab, whom the king of Babylon roasted with fire." 23 Because they wrought disgraceful folly in Israel, and committed adultery with their neighbors' wives, and spoke words in my name which I did not command them [to speak], and I am he who knows, aye, a witness.

THE SEQUEL TO JEREMIAH'S LETTER

From 29:24-32 we learn that Jeremiah's letter to the exiles had an interesting and illuminating sequel. Shemaiah the Nehelamite, having heard Jeremiah's letter read, on his own initiative, without any authority from the elders of the exiles, wrote a letter to Zephaniah the priest in Jerusalem, who at the time was chief overseer in the temple. Now Shemaiah was one of the nationalistic prophets among the exiles who were plotting a speedy return to Jerusalem. He had been nettled by Jeremiah's counsel to the exiles to settle down, build homes, and expect a long residence in Babylonia under Chaldean domination. Evidently he was keenly aware that the import of Jeremiah's letter tended to slacken Judean resistance to the Chaldeans and to undercut all plans for rebellion. So Shemaiah wrote to the chief overseer of the temple, asking why he did not throw that "madman" into "the stocks and collar," instead of letting him spread such ideas abroad.

Zephaniah the priest, upon receipt of the letter, did not take any action against Jeremiah, but as though to say, "We know what you are saying, and we have our eyes on you," he read the letter aloud to him. Upon its conclusion the word of the Lord came to Jeremiah commanding him to send a message to all the exiles definitely warning them of the danger and futility of Shemaiah's viewpoint and of his presumption in claiming to be the Lord's prophet. As the Lord's punishment, not one relative of Shemaiah will experience the return which the Lord will one day make possible to his people. Thus Baruch reports the sequel of Jeremiah's letter:

29:24 Now Shemaiah the Nehelamite 25 sent in his own name letters to Zephaniah, son of Maaseiah the priest, saying: 26 "The Lord has made you priest in place of Jehoiada the priest to be overseer in the house of the Lord, as regards any madman or anyone who makes himself a prophet, and you are to put him in the stocks and in the collar. 27 So now why have you not rebuked Jeremiah of Anathoth, who is representing himself as prophet to you? 28 For he has sent to us in Babylon saying: 'It will be long. Build houses and dwell in them, plant gardens and eat the fruit of them.' "

29 Now Zephaniah the priest read the letter in the hearing of Jeremiah the prophet. 30 Then the word of the Lord came to Jeremiah, saying: 31 Send to the company of exiles, saying, "Thus says the Lord, of Shemaiah of Nehelam: Because Shemaiah prophesied to you, although I did not send him, and led you to trust in a lie, 32 therefore thus says the Lord, Lo, I am about to punish Shemaiah of Nehelam and his posterity. He shall not have one person living in your midst who will experience the good which I will do for my people."

A SYMBOLIC PROPHECY

In 51:59-64 we have an informing illustration of symbolic prophecy on the part of Jeremiah. While the prophetic word came to him as a revelation from the Lord, it was actually to be delivered by Seraiah son of Neriah, the brother of Jeremiah's loyal scribe Baruch. The prophecy has no connection with the long oracle on Babylon now found immediately preceding it (50:1–51:58),[15] but is an entity in itself. It is dated 594, and accordingly, some time after Jeremiah's letter to the exiles of 598, who had been taken to Babylon along with King Jehoiachin. Whether King Zedekiah went to Babylon with Seraiah, as stated in vs. 59, is uncertain, because the Septuagint tells us that Seraiah, as "commissary of the tribute," went from Zedekiah. It may well be that King Zedekiah, having raised in Nebuchadrezzar's mind the suspicion of disloyalty when the nations of the Mediterranean area were plotting revolt at Jerusalem (ch. 27), was commanded to present himself at the Chaldean court. We learn of this episode only from Baruch, and that solely because of the relationship of Jeremiah to it.

The theme of this oracle is the ultimate and complete destruction of Babylon. Jeremiah had proclaimed in his letter to the exiles, sent shortly after 598, that they were to pray for Babylon, and that the welfare of the Judeans was bound up with the welfare of Babylon (29:7). But he had also proclaimed the certainty that Babylon's time of judgment would come in

---

[15] The words of vs. 60b, "all these words written concerning Babylon," which connect vss. 59-64 to the long oracle that proceeds, are, as Karl Budde pointed out as early as 1878, *Jahrbuch für deutsche Theologie*, pp. 551-52, the clamp which binds 51:59-64 with 50:1–51:58, and therefore make it seem that the prophecy of 51:59-64 is the whole preceding oracle.

approximately two generations (29:10), and this oracle is intended to emphasize to the exiles in the time of the supremacy and brilliance of Chaldean dominion the certainty of the eventual fall of that great empire. Moreover, this was to come about not as the result of political machinations but as the working out of the purpose of an ethical God who is Lord of the world.

On a single scroll, at the command of the Lord, Jeremiah wrote out the evil that was to come upon Babylon. Seraiah the quartermaster, an officer essential to an embassy to Babylon, whether or not the king was a member of it, was commissioned by the prophet to carry that scroll with him. He was to hold it in his most careful consideration, and was to read it aloud at some place evidently near the Euphrates River. It is not said that he should read it in the presence of the exiles. Indeed, as Cornill notes, such might have put the exiles in great danger, would perhaps awaken false hopes for the near-at-hand end of the Chaldean lordship, and would rob them of their greatly needed tranquility. The prophet had predicted the triumph of Babylon over the Judeans. But that did not mean in his thought Babylon's permanent supremacy. The all-powerful word of the Lord through the prophetic message would not only pronounce God's judgment upon Babylon but would help to bring it about. For when Seraiah had finished reading the Lord's word as it had been revealed to Jeremiah, he was to roll up the scroll, and so that it would not merely float on the surface, he was to tie a stone to it and then throw it into the Euphrates. There it would sink, and the doom announced by it would spread with the great river's flow to every part of the Chaldean Empire. There is no doubt an element of magic here, for the word of the prophet released such energies as would bring about its realization. But as Peake says: "The conception of prophecy as working out its own fulfillment is not magical; the word of the living God was itself living and active, and could not return to Him void." [16] To Jeremiah's thinking, that which Seraiah was to read, then throw into the Euphrates, was as truly a word of God as though he himself were there proclaiming it.

Thus Baruch narrates the episode:

51:59 **The word which Jeremiah the prophet commanded Seraiah son of Neriah, son of Mahseiah, when he went with Zedekiah king of Judah to Babylon, in the fourth year of his reign. Now Seraiah was the chief quartermaster. 60 And**

[16] *Jeremiah*, p. 279.

Jeremiah had written all the evil which would come to Babylon in one scroll.[17] 61 And Jeremiah said to Seraiah. "When you go into Babylon, see that you read aloud all these words.[18] 63 And it shall be that when you have finished reading this scroll, you shall tie a stone to it and throw it into the midst of the Euphrates. 64 And you shall say, 'Thus will Babylon sink down, not to rise up.'"[19]

YOU HAVE LET MY FLOCK BE SCATTERED

Jer. 23:1-6 reflects the fact that Zedekiah was a ruler of good intentions, as his frequent consultation of Jeremiah shows, but who felt himself helpless among his headstrong government officials, and was under their domination (38:5).

At the present time these royal ministers and officials are allowing the Lord's "flock," the Judean nation, to be "scattered" and "thrust out." They have not been true to their responsibility, so the Lord must punish them for their criminal neglect.

Jeremiah in the Lord's name sharply calls them to task:

23:1 Woe to the shepherds who let the sheep of their flock be destroyed and scattered, says the Lord. 2 Therefore thus says the Lord, God of Israel, concerning the shepherds who are shepherding my people: You have let my flock be scattered, and have thrust them out, and have not attended to them. So I am about to punish you because of your evil deeds.[20] 4 And I will raise up shepherds over them and they shall tend them so they shall not fear any more or be terrified or punished, says the Lord.

Indeed, continues Jeremiah, days are coming when there will be on the throne of Judah a king who will be a direct contrast to the present reigning monarch, Zedekiah. He will be of the house and lineage of David, but of another line, for while Jeremiah was clear that Zedekiah would have no descendant who would occupy the Judean throne, there were other members of the Davidic house of another line.[21] He will be a righteous sprout, and will be recognized by his subjects as being in actuality what Zedekiah, whose name means "The Lord is my righteousness," is solely in name. This future

---

[17] Omit as a later editorial insertion intended to connect this oracle with 50:1–51:58, "all these words which were written concerning Babylon"; cf. footnote 15.

[18] Omit as a later insertion, vs. 62, which has echoes (cf. 50:3; 51:26) of the long and later prophecy of 50:1–51:58.

[19] Omit as a scribal addition "because of the evil which I am bringing upon it."

[20] Omit vs. 3 as an insertion which presupposes the exilic dispersion of the Judeans. Jer. 23:3: And I will assemble the rest of my flock from all the lands to which I have thrust them out, and I will bring them to their pasture, and they shall be fruitful and multiply.

[21] Ishmael, "of the seed royal," was one such person at that time; cf. 41:1.

king will be a "righteous" descendant, not only in the sense of legitimate ruler but also in that he will embody in his person the twofold concept which the name his subjects will call him imply, "The Lord is our righteousness," where "righteousness" (çidh'qēnû) means not only the righteousness of the king's character but also his mediation to the whole nation of justice and salvation. There is striking realism in Jeremiah's expectancy of a future ruler who will contrast so sharply with the present reigning king.

The climax of Jeremiah's oracle is in poetry:

> 23:5 Lo, days are coming, says the Lord,
>   When I will raise up unto David a righteous sprout,
>   When he shall reign as king and shall have success,
>   And accomplish justice and righteousness in the land.
> 6 In his days Judah shall be liberated,
>   And Israel shall dwell in security,
>   And this is his name by which they shall call him,
>   "The Lord is our righteousness."

THE SYMBOLIC PROPHECY OF THE WOODEN YOKE

It was in 594, King Zedekiah's fourth year of reign, that at an impulse from the Lord, Jeremiah performed a very significant prophetic act. The exile of King Jehoiachin and the upper-class Judean leaders to Babylon had then lasted four years. There was naturally great antagonism to the Chaldeans felt by these Jerusalem exiles because of this subjection. At the moment Egypt, the great power to the south of Judah, was stirring up revolt among the small states of the Palestinian and Mediterranean area—Edom, Moab, Ammon, Judah, and the Phoenician city-states of Tyre and Sidon—to join in a conspiracy to throw off the Chaldean yoke. Already, as we have seen, a significant number of Judeans had escaped to Egypt when in 605 the Chaldean supremacy over Judah had been established, and these Egyptian Jews also were fomenting revolt against the Chaldeans.

Jeremiah received a prophetic revelation from God which led him to do a strange and bold thing. The Lord directed him to make a wooden yoke and harness it to his neck with thongs and bars, just as would be done to a plowing or threshing ox. He is commanded by the Lord to go before a group of emissaries, representatives from each nation of the Palestinian-Mediterranean bloc who have come to Jerusalem to plot rebellion against the Chaldeans, wearing the yoke, and is to deliver through them to their respective rulers a message from the Lord to guide them in this crisis.

Although the Lord's message has clear political implications, it is not a political but a religious message, arrived at not by political acumen as to the relative military strength or strategy of peoples, but by the prophet's religious insight into the nature of God, who was to him the creator of the world, the Lord of nations and men. This concept is at the very heart of his message. This Lord of the whole earth it is who has now given world dominion to Nebuchadrezzar, the Chaldean, a dominion, however—such is the prophet's conviction—that is to be limited to approximately two generations (27:7).

From the angle of Jeremiah's thought, the domination of the Palestinian and Mediterranean area by the Chaldeans is not any indication that the God worshiped by the Judeans is impotent, but rather that he is omnipotent, for even when Nebuchadrezzar is lord of the Near East, God is still Lord of him and of the Chaldean people. God's will is being worked out even by the Chaldeans as his unknowing instruments.

So the prophet seeks to turn aside these emissaries of the five kingdoms from following the counsel of their own native leaders, for each of these nations had its own "prophets"—its "diviners" who sought guidance by resort to the subconscious, its "augurers" who foretold the future by signs and omens, and its "sorcerers" who employed magic and witchcraft. If the plotting emissaries depend upon such counselors as these, and as a consequence attempt to resist the domination by the Chaldeans, the extermination of each of their several nations by those very Chaldeans will surely result. But if they submit to the Chaldeans, although it should mean a subservience lasting many years, they will not be carried into exile, as already many Judeans have been, but will be left unmolested upon their own land to till their own soil.

It is indeed a dramatic moment, and probably unprecedented in Judah, when the prophet of the creator and Lord of the whole earth confronts these official political emissaries of five foreign states. Jeremiah is now not younger, and but little older if any, than fifty years of age. Since 598, when Nebuchadrezzar had taken several thousands of Jerusalem's leaders into exile, the prophet had grown in importance in the eyes of his own people, and even King Zedekiah had begun to seek him out from time to time to secure knowledge as to what the Lord was about to do. The prophet now stands before the foreign statesmen with the yoke upon his neck, thus delivering a symbolic message even in his silence. But soon he speaks. Thus he reports his symbolic act and its meaning:

27:1 In the fourth year of Zedekiah son of Josiah, king of Judah, this word came to Jeremiah out of communion with the Lord, saying: 2 Thus the Lord

said to me: Make for yourself bonds and bars of a yoke and put them on your neck. 3 And you shall send to the king of Edom, the king of Moab, the king of the sons of Ammon, the king of Tyre, and the king of Sidon, by the hand of their ambassadors who are coming to Jerusalem, to Zedekiah king of Judah, 4 and you shall send them to their lords saying: "Thus says the Lord of hosts, God of Israel, Thus shall you say to your lords: 5 I made the earth, man and beast which are upon the surface of the earth, by my great strength and by my outstretched arm, and I give it to whomsoever it seems right in my sight. 6 And now I have given all these lands into the power of Nebuchadrezzar king of Babylon, and even the beasts of the field I have given to him to serve him. 7 And all the nations will serve him and his son and his grandson until the time for his land also comes, and it will be subject to mighty nations and great kings. 8 And the nation and kingdom that will not serve him, that is, Nebuchadrezzar king of Babylon, and that will not put its neck under the yoke of the king of Babylon, I will punish that nation with the sword, famine, and pestilence, says the Lord, until I shall have brought them into his power. 9 Now as for you, do not listen to your prophets, or your diviners. or your dreamers, or your predictors [sooth-sayers] or your augurers [diviners by evil spirits]—they who keep saying to you, 'You will not become subject to the king of Babylon.' 10 For they are prophesying to you what is false, so as to remove you from your land, yes, with the result that I must banish you and you will be exterminated. 11 But the nation which brings its neck under the yoke of the king of Babylon and serves him as subjects, I shall let remain on its land, says the Lord, and it may cultivate it and dwell in it."

We have no report as to how Jeremiah's word was received by these representatives of the conspiring states.

Jeremiah then sought an interview with King Zedekiah. Still wearing the yoke, he came into the presence of the king and gave him the same message. Jeremiah, however, emphasizes to King Zedekiah the alternatives—on the one hand, out-and-out war with the Chaldeans, with its attendant loss of life in battle and from the scourges of famine and pestilence which would inevitably follow invasion and siege, or on the other hand, honorable subservience to Babylon. He sharply warns Zedekiah against heeding the nationalistic prophets, who are not sent by God, and whose message counseling resistance has no truth in it whatsoever, for the sure issue of the line of action which they counsel is banishment in exile and possibly national extermination. Jeremiah informs us:

27:12 And to Zedekiah king of Judah I spoke similar words to these, saying: "Bring your necks under the yoke of the king of Babylon, and serve him and his people, and so live.[22] 14 So do not listen to the words of the prophets who keep

[22] With Rudolph, *Jeremia*, p. 148, omit vs. 13 as a later addition. It alludes to vs. 8, which Zedekiah has not heard: Why will you die, you and your people, by the sword, by famine, and by pestilence, just as the Lord said to the nations which would not serve the king of Babylon?

saying concerning you, 'You shall not serve the king of Babylon.' For it is a false-hood that they are prophesying to you. 15 For I have not sent them, says the Lord, but they keep prophesying falsely in my name, with the result that I must banish you, and you must perish, both you and the prophets who continue to prophesy to you."

In the same period Jeremiah uttered in the Lord's name a similar message to the priests and the Judean nation as a whole. The priests had been strongly influenced by the nationalistic prophets who had been predicting that the prized and cherished holy vessels which Nebuchadrezzar had taken from the temple in 598 (II Kings 25:14) are soon to be brought back from Baby-lon. Jeremiah urges the priests and people to pay no attention to such words, for they are spoken not by true prophets of the Lord but by prophets to whom the Lord's word has not been revealed. Rather, let all true prophets who really do stand in the Lord's council implore God that the vessels of the temple and palace which Nebuchadrezzar left undisturbed will not soon suffer the same fate as the others. For the Lord has made it clear to Jeremiah that it is exactly this which is going to happen. Nor will the temple ever see them again until the Chaldean dominance of the Near East shall have been ended by the Lord himself.

Said the prophet:

27:16 And to the priests and to all this people I spoke saying, Thus says the Lord, Do not listen to the words of your prophets who are prophesying to you saying, "Lo, the vessels of the house of the Lord are now quickly to be brought back from Babylon," for they are prophesying to you falsely. I have not sent them.²³ 18 But if prophets they really were, and if the word of the Lord were with them, they would have entreated me that the vessels which are still left in the house of the Lord and in the palace of the king of Judah and in Jerusalem should not go to Babylon. 19 For thus says the Lord of hosts concerning the rest of the vessels that are left in this city, 20 which Nebuchadrezzar king of Babylon did not take from Jerusalem when he carried into exile Jehoiachin son of Jehoiakim, king of Judah. 21 For thus says the Lord of hosts, God of Israel, concerning the vessels left in the house of the Lord and the palace of the king of Judah and in Jerusalem, 22 To Babylon they shall be brought, says the Lord.

BENJAMITE FACES BENJAMITE

Ch. 28 belongs to Baruch's account of Jeremiah's sufferings. His narrative connects closely with ch. 27 and comes from the same period. The foreign emissaries, as we may infer from vs. 14, are still in Jerusalem, and Jeremiah is

²³ Omit vs. 17 with the Septuagint: Do not listen to them. Serve the king of Babylon. Why shall this city become a ruin?

still wearing the wooden yoke upon his neck wherever he goes. This had evidently awakened public comment, and it is in direct answer to Jeremiah's prophecy of Babylonian domination that another prophet of a different stamp from him utters his message.

It was in the fifth month (July-August) of 594. The place was apparently in the temple area, for many priests and many people were present. The prophet, a fellow tribesman of Jeremiah, was from Gibeon,[24] one of the four Levitical cities of the tribe of Benjamin. Baruch thus introduces the episode: Still wearing the yoke upon his neck, Jeremiah the prophet faces Hananiah the prophet; Benjamite faces Benjamite.

28:1 Now it was in that same year, in the fourth year of Zedekiah king of Judah, in the fifth month that Hananiah son of Azzur, the prophet who came from Gibeon, spoke to Jeremiah in the house of the Lord in the presence of the priests and all the people saying, 2 "Thus says the Lord of hosts, God and Israel; I have broken the yoke of the king of Babylon. 3 Within yet two years' time I will be bringing back to this place the utensils of the temple of the Lord, which Nebuchadrezzar king of Babylon took from this place and carried to Babylon. 4 And Jehoiachin and the exiles of Judah in Babylon, for I will break the yoke of the king of Babylon."

We feel the implicit appeal to the priests in his audience as Hananiah stresses the near-at-hand return of the prized holy vessels.

Here are two prophets, both of them sincere, both of them lovers of their nation and eager for its welfare, but with messages that are in direct contradiction to one another, yet both claim to be spokesmen of the Lord.

Jeremiah speaks up in direct answer to his fellow prophet. From his first words we can sense how deep is his sympathy with the patriotic devotion to Judah that is evident in Hananiah's pronouncement. Jeremiah too longs to see the exiles and their loved young monarch back in Jerusalem. How he wishes he could share Hananiah's conviction (vs. 6). But Jeremiah is under prophetic compulsion to deliver a message hard to speak and hard to receive, and which clashes head on with the word that Hananiah had just uttered.

Jeremiah, as we have seen, had faced with conscience-searching earnestness the task of speaking to the nation as a prophet of God; he knew what uniquely distinguished his work. It was the effort, by his prophetic word, to bring God's people back from their evil deeds (23:22). Hananiah's message, however, did not take into any account Judah's moral condition which

[24] The modern El Jib.

patently calls for God's righteous judgment. The note of judgment upon the nation, which has characterized true prophecy in Israel and Judah, is its most authentic note, and any honest consideration of the moral spirit of Judah at the time would reveal how greatly that note was needed right then. It is this that is in Jeremiah's mind when he makes the characterizing mark of the true prophet the threat of war, famine, and pestilence. Moreover, Jeremiah's own inner experience had led him to see how dangerous it was to trust the natural disposition to look at the bright side of things, as being divine in its origin. Accordingly, before a prophecy of welfare could be accepted as divine, as Skinner says, it "needed attestation by the course of providence." [25]

28:5 Then Jeremiah the prophet spoke to Hananiah the prophet in the presence of the priests and in the presence of all the people who were standing in the temple of the Lord. 6 And Jeremiah the prophet said, "Truly! So may the Lord do! May the Lord carry out your word which you have prophesied, in particular, to bring back the vessels of the temple of the Lord and all the exiles from Babylon to this place. 7 Only listen, I entreat you, to the word of the Lord which I am about to speak in your hearing and in the hearing of all the people. 8 The prophets who were before me and before you from of old prophesied concerning many lands and against great kingdoms with reference to war. 9 That prophet who prophesies for peace, it is only when his word comes to pass that he will be known as the prophet whom the Lord has truly sent."

The reaction of Hananiah to Jeremiah's words was immediate and passionate:

28:10 Then Hananiah took the bars from off the neck of Jeremiah the prophet and broke them to pieces. 11a And Hananiah spoke in the sight of all the people saying: "Thus says the Lord: Like this I will break the yoke of the king of Babylon within two years from the neck of all the nations."

It was a tense moment. What would the prophet Jeremiah say? No words at the moment were at his disposal. We are impressed here with the calm self-control and patience of Jeremiah with Hananiah. As G. A. Smith says, Jeremiah "believed in the liberty of prophesying. He had no fear of the issue being threshed out between them. The wheat would be surely cleared from the straw." Baruch simply reports:

28:11b Then Jeremiah the prophet went his way.

25 *Prophecy and Religion*, p. 193.

As Smith adds, such an episode reveals in Jeremiah "marks of an honest, patient and reflective mind which weighs opinions opposite to his own." [26] We can readily imagine that people generally, who had witnessed this clash, spread it abroad with varying reactions, some no doubt saying, "Jeremiah had it coming to him!" Most certainly Jeremiah searched his own mind in the light of the seeming certainty of Hananiah's convictions, and sought from the Lord what next he should do and say. And eventually light came. A prophetic impulse from God sent Jeremiah to face Hananiah again. Baruch describes the second clash between the two prophets as follows:

28:12 Then the word of the Lord came to Jeremiah after Hananiah the prophet had broken the yoke from off his neck, saying: 13 Go and say to Hananiah: "Thus says the Lord: You have broken bars of wood but I will make in place of them bars of iron. 14 For thus says the Lord of hosts, God of Israel, A yoke of iron have I put on the neck of all these nations, that they must serve Nebuchadrezzar king of Babylon." 15 And Jeremiah the prophet said to Hananiah the prophet, "The Lord has not sent you and you have made this people trust in a lie. 16 Therefore thus says the Lord: 'I am about to hurl you from off the face of the earth. This year you will die.' " 17 And Hananiah died that same year in the seventh month.

The swift fulfillment of Jeremiah's prophecy concerning Hananiah was impressive. Unquestionably this entire altercation between the two prophets had its influence upon public sentiment. The contemplated rebellion did not at the moment materialize. It may well have been that Jeremiah's preaching had some determining influence upon Zedekiah and his counselors and upon the Palestinian-Mediterranean bloc.

JEREMIAH'S INDICTMENT OF THE PROPHETS

During the reign of Zedekiah Jeremiah summarized with remarkable clarity and forcefulness the findings of his own experience in dealing with the prophets who were his contemporaries. With one of them, Hananiah, as we have seen, he had clashed, to the latter's humiliation and disgrace.

In 23:13-32 Jeremiah brilliantly records his findings concerning the contemporary prophets in Judah, who were among his greatest opponents. Nowhere in the Old Testament is the true nature of prophecy expounded with greater insight than in this section. Volz's suggestion of the date 597-594, in the time of Zedekiah, seems most likely.

In vss. 13-15b Jeremiah deals with the immorality of the prophets. He starts with the Lord's criticism of the prophets of Samaria, the famous capital

[26] *Jeremiah*, pp. 263-64.

of the old Northern Kingdom, built by Omri and Ahab. There the worship of Baal had early flourished, the prophet Elijah having been its fearless opponent. In Jeremiah's day it was customary for pilgrims to come from Samaria to the temple at Jerusalem (41:5). While the "I have seen" in vs. 13 refers to the Lord, it is most likely that Jeremiah here speaks from his own observation of what still was going on in Samaria in terms of the activities of the prophets. There he had seen in the prophets indecency, moral unseemliness. The old immoral Baal influence still lived on, drawing both the spiritual leaders and those they led into grave error. But even in Jerusalem, where the moral and spiritual voices of the prophets Amos, Isaiah, and Micah had already been heard, conditions were little better. Indeed, the situation there was utterly disgusting. The prophets in Jerusalem were guilty of adultery. They were not men of honor but men of falsehood. They did not face evildoers with a call to repentance, but repeatedly even allied themselves with them. For Judah, Sodom and Gomorrah were the classic symbols of unspeakable wickedness and corruption. But comparable to the immorality of Sodom and Gomorrah is the pollution which has gone out from Jerusalem's spiritual leaders, filling the whole land with secularity and defilement. Says Jeremiah:

> 23:13 **Among the prophets of Samaria**
> **I have seen indecency:**
> **They prophesy by Baal**
> **And they lead my people Israel into error.**
> 14 **Aye, among the prophets of Jerusalem**
> **I have seen what is disgusting:**
> **They commit adultery and go about in falsity,**
> **Repeatedly strengthening the hands of evildoers,**
> **So they do not turn from their wickedness.**
> **All of them have become to me like Sodom;**
> **And its [Jerusalem's] inhabitants like Gomorrah.**[27]
> 15b **For from the very prophets of Jerusalem,**
> **Pollution has gone out to all the land.**

In vss. 16-22 Jeremiah analyzes the false prophets from his abundant experience of firsthand contact with them. He goes beneath their disreputable morals and gives us their characteristics, such as had been revealed to him in the painful clashes he had experienced with them. He makes four counts against them: (a) The visions by which they claim to be informed as to

[27] Omit vs. 15a as an addition.

the Lord's message do not have their origin in the Lord, but the prophets have spun them out of their own minds (vs. 16). Their visions have no divine source. (b) These false prophets are shallow optimists. To men who need above every other thing a call to repent and turn back to God they say, "It will be well with you" (vs. 17). And they promise that no harm will come to men who utterly spurn the true word of the Lord and stubbornly persist in their evil conduct. (c) They never have stood in the intimate circle of those who "see" God and "hear" his word (vs. 18), nor have they been "sent" by him (vs. 21). So what they proclaim is not God's word but their own. Had they truly shared in God's council, then uttered with arresting power what God had revealed to them (vs. 22), the result of their ministry would have been repentance on the part of the people. (d) They were not "sent" by God as his messengers but "ran" to men with their own unillumined words (vs. 21).

Jeremiah utters his pentrating analysis:

23:16 Thus says the Lord of hosts:
   Do not listen to the words of the prophets
      They fill you with vain hopes;
   Visions of their own minds they declare,
      Not from the mouth of the Lord,
17 Saying to those who spurn the word of the Lord,
      "It will be well with you!"
   And to everyone who acts in the stubbornness of his heart,
      "Misfortune will not come to you."
18 But who of them has stood in the council of the Lord and has seen him,
      And heard his word?
   Who has given attention to his word and proclaimed it.[28]
21   I did not send the prophets,
      Yet they ran.
   I did not speak to them,
      But they prophesied.
22 But if they had stood in my council,
      And had caused my people to hear my words,
   They would have brought my people back
      From their evil deeds.

In vss. 23-32 the prophet deals with one of the most important questions concerning prophecy. How does God reveal his word to the prophet? Jeremiah here starts with the concept of the omnipresence of God. God is not

---

[28] Omit vss. 19-20, which appear again in 30:23-24, where they belong. Here they are intrusive.

limited, as are we, in vision, so that he can see only what is near at hand. God's presence fills heaven and earth. He is omnipresent and he is omniscient. How does this all-wise and universally present Deity communicate his will?

Here we see Jeremiah take a significant step forward, away from the irrational and toward the rational. For ancient Israel (Gen. 28:12; Num. 12:6) the dream was an accepted medium of the divine revelation. And still in postexilic Israel dreams were viewed by some of the teachers of the congregation (Joel 2:28; Job 4:12-17) as the way God spoke to men. But Jeremiah stands opposed to this with all his being. And into his view, as here expressed, there went not only the clear practical realization that dependence on the dream brought about lack of dependence upon God, but that the prophet who had the most brilliant dream would likely be viewed as the leader most to be heeded (cf. vs. 32). He also saw all around him the faulty spiritual revelation that led to seeking after dreams and dependence upon them for the revelation of God. To Jeremiah the dream is to the word of the Lord as chaff is to wheat.[29]

When a presumptuous prophet said the thrice-repeated magic words, "I have dreamed! I have dreamed! I have dreamed!" the Lord says to him through Jeremiah, "Is God's name in your heart? Do you put your dreams above his word?" Dependence on dreams for divine guidance is like depending upon the Baal worship which led ancient Israel to forget the presence, the potency, and the concern of the Lord on behalf of his people.

There is a note of realism and sarcasm in Jeremiah's sentence, "The prophet who has a dream, let him recount his dream" (vs. 28). Then let men compare what such a dreamer says with the words of that prophet who is profoundly aware that within his soul is God's word committed to him as the bearer of the Lord's message to his people.

To what then can God's true word be compared? It is like a burning fire (vs. 29). How well Jeremiah knew this in his own soul (20:9). It is like a hammer shattering a rock (vs. 29); something indeed like dynamite.

For one who claimed to be a prophet, but because he is insincere has no word from the Lord, it was a persistent temptation to steal the words of an authentic prophet and thus weaken the authority of God's true interpreter. When a prophet speaks forth what he claims to be a revelation from God, but knows in his soul that no such revelation has been received, he is a fraud, and the Lord is opposed to him. How searching, how penetrating, how unanswerable is this prophetic analysis and contrast!

Thus the prophet represents God as speaking:

[29] Cf. Rudolph, *Jeremia*, p. 133.

23:23 Am I a God near at hand,
Says the Lord,
And not a God afar off?
24 Can a man hide himself in secret places
And I not see him?
Says the Lord.
And do not I fill
Heaven and earth?
Says the Lord.

25 I have heard what the prophets say who preach falsely in my name, saying: "I have dreamed! I have dreamed! I have dreamed!" 26 Is my name in the heart of the prophets who are preaching what is false and who keep preaching the delusions of their own heart? 27 those who scheme to make my people forget my name for their dreams which one tells to one's neighbor, even as their fathers forgot my name for the Baal? 28a The prophet who has a dream, let him recount his dream but [the prophet] who has within him my word, let him speak my word faithfully.

28b What has chaff in common with wheat?
Says the Lord,
29 Does not my word burn like the fire,
Or [is it not] like a hammer that shatters the rock?

30 Therefore I am against the prophets, says the Lord, who keep stealing my words, each from his neighbor. 31 Lo, I am against the prophets, who take their own tongues, and speak [as though it were] a prophetic oracle. 32 Lo, I am against the prophets who prophesy deceptive dreams, and who narrate them and [so] mislead my people, by their deceptions and by their recklessness. But as for me— I did not send them or command them nor do they benefit this people in the least.

A Jest Turned into a Threat

Jer. 13:12-14 dates from a time well along in the reign of Zedekiah. The final editor of the book who has placed this passage here links his thought of ruin to the key word "ruined" in vs. 7, but there is no connection in thought between vss. 1-11 and vss. 12-14. Jeremiah starts from a facetious remark probably uttered jestingly by a winebibber at a time and place where the mood of revelry prevailed and where witticisms of the imbibers flew back and forth. It may have been, as Erbt suggests, at a sacrificial repast where the prophet hears the remark jocosely uttered by a generous imbiber, "Every jar is to be filled with wine!" Suddenly, just as the prophets loved to do, Jeremiah takes up the remark in sober earnest and turns it into a solemn threat that the Lord is about to fill the inhabitants of Judah—kings, priests, prophets, and the masses—with "drunkenness," an oft-used prophetic symbol for the helplessness and stupefaction which the Lord will bring in judgment upon the people; for they will be compelled to drink of the cup of his wrath and so experience ruin at his hand.

The Lord commands Jeremiah:

13:12 So say to this people, "Every jar is to be filled with wine." And if they say to you, "Sure, do we not know that every jar is to be filled with wine?" 13 Say to them, "Thus says the Lord, Lo, I am about to fill with drunkenness all the inhabitants of this land, the kings who sit on the throne of David, the priests, the prophets, and all the inhabitants of Jerusalem. 14 And I will dash them in pieces one against another, fathers and sons together, says the Lord. I will neither spare nor pity them, nor have compassion upon them, so as not to ruin them!"

As Jeremiah utters this solemn warning to his people the realization surges in upon him that time is running out. The light of hope for Judah is rapidly fading. Deep darkness will soon overtake them. We feel in his words the sob of a great soul because haughty Judah ignores God's clear warning:

> 13:15 Give ear and listen; be not haughty,
>   For the Lord has spoken.
> 16 Give honor to the Lord your God,
>   Before he makes it dark.
> Aye, before your feet stumble
>   Upon the mountains in twilight,
> And you wait eagerly for light,
>   But he makes it darkness.
> 17 And if you will not listen to it,
>   In secret places my soul will weep
>   Because of your pride
> And my eyes will flow with tears
>   For the flock of the Lord will be taken captive.

THE FINAL SIEGE OF JERUSALEM

In spite of Jeremiah's repeated warnings, Zedekiah persisted in attempting to shift his allegiance from Nebuchadrezzar to Pharaoh Hophra, even sending Judean ambassadors to Egypt seeking military protection against the Chaldeans. This was the overt move which gave Nebuchadrezzar the incentive and excuse to punish the southern Syrian states, including Judah, and to advance against Egypt.

As headquarters for his military campaigns he chose Riblah on the Orontes River, a point of intersection of the caravan road and military routes from which he could proceed particularly against Phoenicia and Judah. Nebuzar-

radan, Nebuchadrezzar's top military officer, commanded his troops to proceed against Judah.

Jer. 34:1-7 is a part of Baruch's narrative.[30] The forces of Nebuchadrezzar
have come, and we are at the beginning of the final Chaldean invasion of
Judah, shortly after the tenth day of the tenth month of Zedekiah's ninth
year, 589 (II Kings 25:1). A sector of the Chaldean troops is attacking
Jerusalem, but other sectors, as 34:7 informs us, were attacking two other
major fortified cities, Lachish and Azekah, which along with Jerusalem are the only fortresses which have not surrendered. This is the earliest
account we have of the final invasion which followed swiftly upon the rebellion of King Zedekiah against Babylon (II Kings 25:1).

Jeremiah, moved by a prophetic impulse from the Lord, took the initiative
in confronting King Zedekiah, and declared to him the oracle of the Lord
for that hour (34:2-3). Since it is the will of God that Jerusalem shall fall
to the Chaldeans, it will be captured, and Zedekiah will be called to personal
account by Nebuchadrezzar. But if Zedekiah would obey the Lord's word,
let him surrender his capital to Nebuchadrezzar (vs. 4). Jeremiah evidently
believed that such a move would lead Nebuchadrezzar to show the king
clemency so that he might even retain his throne, and after a peaceable death
receive honorable burial with mourning rites of the burning of incense and
of lamentations worthy of a king. Baruch thus gives his account of the
Lord's word to the king:

34:1 The word which came to Jeremiah from the Lord when Nebuchadrezzar
king of Babylon, and all his army and all the kingdoms of the earth ruled by
his hand, and all the nations of the earth, were fighting against Jerusalem and
all its cities. 2 Thus says the Lord, God of Israel, Go, speak to Zedekiah king of
Judah, and say to him, "Thus says the Lord: This city shall certainly be given into
the hand of the king of Babylon, and he shall capture it. 3 And you yourself will
not escape from his hand, but you shall surely be seized and taken prisoner, and
you will see the king of Babylon. 4 But obey the word of the Lord, Zedekiah king
of Judah, then you will not die by the sword. 5 Peaceably in Jerusalem will you
die, and with the burning of spices as was done with your fathers, the kings who
were before you, shall they burn for you, and with 'Ah, Lord!' they shall wail for
you, for it is a revelation that I have spoken, says the Lord."
6 So Jeremiah the prophet spoke to Zedekiah king of Judah all these words.
7 Now the army of the king of Babylon was fighting against Jerusalem and against

---

[30] Vs. 1, as Rudolph, *Jeremia*, p. 187, rightly maintains, is editorial. Its somewhat
bombastic characterization of the Chaldean army (vs. 1a) and its too early setting of the
final concentration of Nebuchadrezzar's total forces against Jerusalem itself stems from
the later redactor of the book.

all the cities of Judah that were left, namely, Lachish and Azekah, for these only were left of the fortified cities of Judah.

The Lord's message to Zedekiah had no influence upon him. In 21:1-7 we are at a point farther on in the siege. Now all other Judean fortresses have capitulated, and the Chaldean army has at length concentrated its attack upon Jerusalem. In this strategic moment King Zedekiah, now himself taking the initiative in seeking Jeremiah's counsel, sends a delegation to the prophet to inquire as to whether the Lord might "in accord with all his wonderful deeds"—that is miraculously—bring about the lifting of the Chaldean siege. The delegation is composed of two prominent men. The leader is Pashhur son of Malchiah, who as we learn from 38:1, 4 was one of the princes, and his colleague was Zephaniah, who was probably, as Driver[31] maintains, the "second priest," that is, the one next in rank to Seraiah the chief priest (52:24). It is a significant moment when, now for the first time, so far as we have any record, Jeremiah the prophet is consulted at the initiative of the king.

21:1 **The word which came to Jeremiah from the Lord when King Zedekiah sent to him Pashhur son of Malchiah, and Zephaniah son of Maaseiah the priest, saying: 2 "Inquire, pray, of the Lord in our behalf, for Nebuchadrezzar king of Babylon has come to blows against us. Perhaps the Lord will deal with us in accord with all his wonderful deeds and cause him to lift the siege from us."**

Jeremiah's answer to the delegation was clean-cut and definite. As yet the Judean resistance within the wall had kept the Chaldean troops outside. But now the Lord is at the point of weakening that resistance, and indeed, of manifesting his mighty power against Jerusalem's inhabitants by bringing about their defeat and their unconditional surrender to the Chaldean king, who will give them no quarter or favor.

Thus the Deuteronomic editor reports Jeremiah's answer in the Lord's name which he gave to the delegation:

21:3 **So Jeremiah said to them, Thus you are to say to Zedekiah 4 "Thus says the Lord, the God of Israel: Lo, I am about to turn back the weapons of war with which you are fighting the Chaldeans, who are besieging you from the outside of the wall right into the midst of this city. 5 And I will fight against you with outstretched hand and strong arm and with anger, rage, and great wrath. 6 And I will strike the inhabitants of this city, man and beast, and they shall die, due to great pestilence. 7 Then afterward, says the Lord, I will give Zedekiah king of Judah, and his servants, and the people who will be left in this city from**

---

[31] *Book of the Prophet Jeremiah*, p. 175, note *b*.

the pestilence, sword, and famine into the hand of Nebuchadrezzar king of Babylon, and into the hand of those seeking their life, and they shall smite them without quarter. I will not look upon them with pity nor will I show them compassion."

The dignity with which Jeremiah is treated in this conference contrasts
sharply with the harsh treatment and mental suffering experienced by him
in 20:7-18. And the Pashhur, chief overseer of the temple, who was his perse-
cutor in 20:1-6, contrasts unfavorably with the Pashhur—one of the two
nobles—who composed this delegation sent by King Zedekiah to consult the
prophet.

The two episodes narrated in 20:7-18 and 21:1-7, respectively, and which
have been placed here side by side by the final editor of the book of Jeremiah, actually occurred nearly seventeen years apart. In 20:7-18 the year
was 605 in the reign of King Jehoiakim, while in 21:1-7 it is the last year
of King Zedekiah's reign. The editor responsible for this arrangement thus
relieves the account of the harsh treatment accorded to Jeremiah in the
earlier narrative by the dignity accorded him here by his monarch.[32]

The siege of the city grew increasingly severe and things looked black for
Judah. The king then took the initiative in a quite remarkable and official
act (34:8). There existed in the Covenant Code (Exod. 21:2) a law which
made it obligatory upon the buyer of a Hebrew slave to set him free after he
had served six years. This law is included in the Deuteronomic Code (Deut.
15:12) with a deepened quality there in terms of humanity—for the slave
is viewed as a fellow "countryman" to his or her owner. This law was accepted under King Josiah as binding upon Judah. But it evidently had not
been observed. With a desire to make a dramatic appeal to God to secure his
help in the grave crisis, Zedekiah made a covenant with the Jerusalem population that all the Hebrew slaves, male and female, were to be freed.

Evidently this emancipation was not limited to those whose time for freedom had come, but included all slaves. It was definitely agreed that they
were not in the future to be forced back into slavery. There may have been
additional motives for the king's action. The emancipation of the slaves
would certainly increase the forces of defense of Jerusalem against the Chaldeans. On the other hand, since the slaves could not work in the fields
during the siege of the city and must remain within the walls, the obligation upon their owners to feed them was a heavy economic drain. The
primary reason for the edict and covenant of emancipation, however, was

---

[32] Rudolph, op. cit., p. 116, offers this reasonable explanation.

religious, the appeal for God's help demonstrated by obedience to a great socially-motivated law, thus accepted as a binding moral obligation. And to make that appeal the more powerful, all the slaves were included regardless of how long they had served their masters.

In telling of this development Baruch describes right out of Hebrew life the ritual through which such a covenant was made (34:18-20). A calf was killed and its body divided into two parts. These portions were laid side by side, but some distance apart, so that all the members to the covenant—the king, the officials, the eunuchs, the priests, and the full citizens—passed between the two halves of the calf. As Peake explains, "the parties to the covenant are united by being taken within the life of the same sacred victim." But there is another side to it here. The parties to such a covenant took on themselves a curse which in case of their violation of the covenant would become effective on them, "Just as the body of the calf lies dead upon the ground, so the violators of the covenant will suffer the same fate as the victim, and their dead bodies will serve as carrion for the birds and wild beasts." [33] Thus runs Baruch's story:

34:8b King Zedekiah had made a covenant with all the people who were in Jerusalem to proclaim liberty to them, 9 each one to set free his male slaves and his female slaves so far as they were Hebrew men or Hebrew women—so that no Jew would compel his brother into slavery. 10 So all the officials and all the people who had entered into the covenant that each would free his male slaves and his female slaves so as not to force them any more into bondage, sent them off.

The desperate situation in Jerusalem which had prompted this unusual covenant of freedom seemed relieved when suddenly the rumor came that the army of Pharaoh had marched out from Egypt on its way to help Judah. The Chaldean troops lifted the siege of Jerusalem (vs. 5) in order to deal summarily with this threat of Egyptian aid. In this same critical hour of uncertainty King Zedekiah again sent an official delegation to consult the prophet Jeremiah. It was composed of Jehucal (Jucal) who later (38:1-6) is one of Jeremiah's enemies, and Zephaniah the priest, second in rank to the chief priest. They bore a message from the king asking Jeremiah, who at the time was free to go or come as he choose, to pray for Judah.

The reply was a revelation from God, which made clear that the lifting of the Chaldean siege of Jerusalem was only temporary, for the Egyptian army would return to Egypt and the Chaldeans would resume their siege and be successful. The prophet is so certain of the Chaldean conquest of

[33] *Jeremiah*, II, 143.

Jerusalem that he tells the delegation that if only the wounded soldiers were left to the Chaldean fighting forces, they would nonetheless light the fires of Jerusalem's destruction.

Thus Baruch tells the story:

37:1 Now Zedekiah son of Josiah ruled in the place of Coniah [Jehoiachin] son of Jehoiakim, whom Nebuchadrezzar king of Babylon made king in the land of Judah. 2 But he did not listen—neither he nor his servants nor the people of the land—to the words of the Lord which he spoke by the agency of Jeremiah the prophet. 3 Now Zedekiah sent Jehucal [Jucal] son of Shelemiah, and Zephaniah son of Maaseiah the priest, to Jeremiah the prophet, saying: "Please intercede for us with the Lord our God." 4 Now Jeremiah was coming and going in the midst of the city and they had not put him in prison. 5 The army of Pharaoh had gone out of Egypt, and when the Chaldeans, who were besieging Jerusalem, heard rumor of them, they took themselves away from Jerusalem.

6 Then the word of the Lord came to Jeremiah the prophet saying: 7 Thus says the Lord, God of Israel: Thus shall you say to the king of Judah who is sending you to me to seek me, Lo, the army of Pharaoh which is coming out for help to you will return to his land of Egypt. 8 And the Chaldeans will come back and will fight against this city and capture it and will burn it in the fire!

9 Thus says the Lord, Do not deceive yourselves saying, "Surely the Chaldeans have gone away from us!" For they have not gone. 10 And if you smite all the army of the Chaldeans who are fighting with you, and there are left among them but wounded men, they shall rise up each in his place and burn this city with fire.

In spite of this solemn warning, those who had freed their slaves forced back into bondage those whom they had emancipated by solemn covenant. This treacherous act of perfidy, as well as of ethical and religious irresponsibility, shows us clearly the utter lack of justice and humanity in the leadership of Judah at this time, from king even to commoner. Thus Baruch reports this heartless injustice:

34:11 But after they had thus sent off the male and female slaves whom they had set free, they brought the male and female slaves back into bondage.

We would not expect Jeremiah to remain silent in the face of such breach of faith. Twice we are told that the Lord's word came to him in blistering condemnation of such treachery:

34:8a The word which came to Jeremiah from the Lord after King Zedekiah had made a covenant. 12 Then the word of the Lord came to Jeremiah saying: 13 Thus says the Lord, God of Israel: I made a covenant with your fathers in the day when I brought them from the land of Egypt, from the house where slaves live, saying: 14 "At the end of six years each [of you] shall set free his brother, the Hebrew who sells himself to you and has served you six years, and you shall set him free from your custody." But your fathers did not listen to me nor did they incline their ear [to me]. 15 But as for you, you turned this day and did what is right in my sight, proclaiming liberty each to his neighbor and negotiated a covenant before me in the house to which my name was given. 16 Then you turned and defiled my name and each man took back his male slave and each his female slave whom you had set free, so that you brought them into bondage to you as male and female slaves. 17 Therefore, thus says the Lord [since] you did not listen to me, to proclaim liberty each man to his brother and each to his neighbor, see, I am about to proclaim to you liberty, says the Lord—unto the sword, the pestilence, and famine, and I will make you an object of terror to all the king-doms of the earth. 18 And I will make the men who are the transgressors of my covenant—who have not carried into effect the words of the covenant which they made before me—like the calf which they cut in two and passed between its parts, 19 the officials of Judah and the officials of Jerusalem, the eunuchs and the priests and all the full citizens who passed between the parts of the calf. 20 And I will give them over to the hand of their enemies and into the power of those seeking to take their life. Their corpses shall become carrion for the birds of the heavens and for the beasts of the earth. 21 And Zedekiah king of Judah, and his officials I will give into the hands of their enemies, and into the hands of those seeking their life, and into the hand of the army of the king of Babylon which has with-drawn from you. 22 Lo, I am about to command, says the Lord, and I will bring them back to this city, and they shall fight against it, and shall capture it, and shall burn it in the fire, and I will make the cities of Judah a waste, without inhabitant.

JEREMIAH ACCUSED OF TREASON

Taking advantage of the temporary lifting of the Chaldean siege of Jeru-salem, Jeremiah attempted to go to Anathoth to conduct some business, the exact nature of which we do not know. Cornill[34] suggests that his purpose was to procure from there, where he had property, the means of livelihood for the uncertain days ahead. The situation in which the prophet found himself was delicate in the extreme. He had counseled his fellow countrymen to go over to the Chaldeans. His counsel was religiously based, for the clearest and most certain conviction of his mind was that it lay in the will of God for the Chaldeans to conquer Jerusalem. And unquestionably some had at length been convinced of the wisdom of his counsel on religious grounds. Probably in other cases from grounds of self-interest, many had already gone over to the Chaldeans. For whatever reason, all of these were viewed by the men in political power in Jerusalem as national rebels and traitors.

The princes who were now in positions of political responsibility in Jerusa-

[34] *Jeremia*, p. 396.

lem were men of a different stamp from those who had been in power in 598, when Nebuchadrezzar had taken them into captivity. They were political nationalists, very antagonistic to anyone who viewed resistance to the Chaldeans, from whatever motive, as futile and unwise, and were ready to deal with any such Judeans as political suspects or captured fugitives. They had turned the house of Jonathan the secretary, a high official, into a prison with underground dungeon cells. Thus they were ready for any disloyalists. Moreover, the military leaders dubbed as traitor anyone whose outspoken attitude tended to weaken resistance to the Chaldeans. Jeremiah's attitude, which had been taken fearlessly and in the open, was known even to the common soldiers who were defending Jerusalem.

Jeremiah tried to go out through the Benjamin Gate, the northern gate which led to the tribal areas of Benjamin and Ephraim. He was stopped by a sentinel, whose name Irijah gets into the record merely because of the importance of this citizen whom he challenged and accused of deserting to the Chaldeans. Despite Jeremiah's indignant denial, the sentinel arrested him and took him to the princes who wrathfully scourged him and imprisoned him in the dungeon cells without even so much as notifying the king. He was destined to be detained there for a long while. Baruch's record follows:

37:11 Now when the army of the Chaldeans had taken itself off from the siege of Jerusalem at the approach of the army of Pharaoh, 12 Jeremiah wanted to go out of Jerusalem to the land of Benjamin to acknowledge in the circle of the family the receipt of a share of an inheritance from there. 13 And it happened as he was in the Benjamin Gate that a sentinel was there whose name was Irijah the son of Shelemiah, son of Hananiah, and he arrested Jeremiah the prophet, saying, "You are deserting to the Chaldeans." 14 But Jeremiah said, "That is false. I am not deserting to the Chaldeans." But he would not listen to him, so Irijah arrested Jeremiah and brought him to the princes. 15 Now the princes were wrathful against Jeremiah, and they scourged him and put him in the prison in the house of Jonathan the scribe, for they had made it into a prison. 16 So Jeremiah came to the prison and to the dungeon cells and Jeremiah lived there many days.

King Zedekiah's Secret Conference with Jeremiah

Zedekiah had not been consulted or informed at the time of the imprisonment of Jeremiah in the dungeon cells of the temporary prison. Weak as that monarch was, he respected Jeremiah as the spokesman of the Lord. In his uncertainty as to what the future held for Judah he sent to the dungeon cells, the temporary prison in the house of Jonathan, where Jeremiah had been confined already for many days, and called the prophet to a secret conference in his palace and inquired as to whether in the national crisis the Lord had revealed to him his word. With startling frankness, definiteness, and objectivity Jeremiah declares the Lord's word to his monarch.

But he adds a very natural appeal to whatever of humanity there was in the king. In effect he says: "Let the king point out to me why I have deserved such treatment at the hands of the king, his officials and his people" (vss. 18-20). In a powerful rhetorical question that evidently must have touched some sense of fairness in the soul of the king, he argued the truthfulness of his own prophetic teaching as compared with that of the nationalistic prophets as it now lay open to every honest mind. His words made such appeal to the king's humanitarian instinct that his status was changed from imprisonment in the dungeon to confinement in the guard court, and he was given assurance of a meager daily ration as long as food lasted in the city. Baruch's narrative is eloquent in its simplicity and directness:

37:17 Then Zedekiah sent and summoned him and inquired of him in his palace secretly, saying, "Is there any word from the Lord?" and Jeremiah said, "There is!" And he said, "You shall be given over into the hand of the king of Babylon." 18 And Jeremiah went on to say to the king, "How have I sinned against you and against your servants and against this people, that you have put me in prison? 19 Where now are your prophets who prophesied to you saying, 'The king of Babylon shall not come against you or against this land?' 20 So now hear, I entreat you, my lord the king, please let my supplication fall before you that you do not send me back to the house of Jonathan the secretary, lest I die there." 21 So the king commanded that they put him in the guard court, and that they give him a loaf of bread daily from the bakers' street until all the bread was consumed. And Jeremiah stayed in the guard court.

The section 38:24-28 rightly follows 37:17-21. King Zedekiah was not in the good graces of his princes, nor they in his. He was much concerned lest the gist of this interview might leak out and the princes should learn what had taken place. Zedekiah swore Jeremiah to secrecy at peril of death. If the princes by threat of death to the prophet try to worm out of him what the king said and what he said, the prophet was simply to say that he had humbly begged the king not to send him back to the dungeon cells in the house of Jonathan. To be sure, it was not all the truth but it was truthful as far as it went, and Jeremiah acceded to the king's insistent request. Baruch thus reports the king's concern:

38:24 Then Zedekiah said to Jeremiah, "Do not let anyone know about these words and you shall not die. 25 And if the princes should hear that I have spoken with you and should come to you and say to you, 'Please tell us what you said to the king and what the king said to you; do not conceal it from us and we will not put you to death,' 26 just say to them, 'I was presenting my supplication that he not send me back to the house of Jonathan to die there.' "

27 Now all the princes did come to Jeremiah and asked him, and he reported in accordance with all these words which the king had commanded him. Then they stopped speaking with him, so the word of the Lord was not reported. 28ª And Jeremiah remained in the guard court until the day when Jerusalem was captured.

The Chaldeans, as we have seen, had temporarily lifted the siege of Jerusalem in order to deal with Pharaoh Hophra of Egypt and his army, which had come out to help Judah (37:5). But just as Jeremiah had predicted with utter certainty, the Egyptian army was defeated and the Chaldeans returned and resumed the final phase of their assault upon Jerusalem. The return of the Chaldeans took place most likely shortly after Jeremiah had been released from the dungeon and confined in the guard court. It was then that he received an impulse from the Lord which led him to speak words both startling and offensive to the Judeans of King Zedekiah's court, who were bent upon the protection of their capital.

To Jeremiah nothing was more clear now than that God had given to Nebuchadrezzar of Babylon the lordship over Judah (27:6). When the prophet now speaks it is not in any sense as a politician but as a prophet of God. Repeatedly he had tried to convince King Zedekiah that military resistance to the Chaldeans was in the last analysis resistance to God. Jeremiah felt keenly that it was not the mission of Judeans to die simply because of the stubborn obstinacy of the king and his court. Many Judeans, convinced of the folly of resistance, had "gone over to the Chaldeans." [35] It is likely that already enough had done this to make King Zedekiah fearful of the indignity he would suffer at the hands of his fellow countrymen who had already gone over to the Chaldeans, in case he should decide to surrender (38:19).

To deliver this message must have been to Jeremiah a painful task, for he had no desire to "save his own skin." Indeed, this man who counseled, "go over to the Chaldeans," did not accept that council for himself, and when accused of doing it, sharply denied it (37:13-14). But he knew how important every individual Judean was for the future of his people, envisioning that future as it lay in the divine intention, and so he stayed at his post to the bitter end. But for the Judeans of Jerusalem he saw that the existing situation, with the Chaldeans bracing themselves for a final assault upon

[35] Cf. Volz, Jeremia, p. 215.

Jerusalem, faced his people with a sharp alternative. Judah was face to face with the way of life and the way of death. Even when he called them to go over to the Chaldeans from the God-purposed doom which overhung Jerusalem, he did not assure them of their safety. When Jeremiah says that the one who follows this counsel will have his life as a spoil of war, he is probably utilizing a proverb which counsels scorn of danger. If he takes the risk, and thus escapes the enemy's destruction, he will at least have his life as "booty." Thus the Lord directs him to speak to the Judeans in their crisis hour:

21:8 Now to this people you shall say: "Thus says the Lord, Lo, I am setting before you the way of life and the way of death. 9 Whoever remains in this city shall die by the sword, by famine, or by pestilence, but whoever goes out and surrenders to the Chaldeans that are besieging you, shall remain alive, although his life shall be but as a spoil of war. 10 For I have set my face against this city for evil and not for good, says the Lord; it shall be taken by the hand of the king of Babylon, and he will burn it in the fire."

JEREMIAH'S PURCHASE OF THE FIELD AT ANATHOTH

The section which forms the heart of ch. 32 is the purchase by the prophet Jeremiah of a field in Anathoth. It was essentially a prophetic act, and was itself a message to the Judeans to give them a basis of confidence in the future welfare of Judah. The chapter owes its present place in the book not to chronological considerations, because the transaction it describes falls in the last year of the Judean state, but to the nature of its content as a prophecy of future salvation. The Deuteronomic editor, who is responsible for the present arrangement of the book, placed it alongside of chs. 27–29, which give Jeremiah's prophecy of salvation for the Judean company of exiles in Babylon, and chs. 30–31, his prophecy of salvation for the exiles from North Israel.

In 32:1-5 the Deuteronomic editor gives the chronological setting for the events, with a parenthetic synchronization of Judean and Chaldean chronology (vs. 1). Then he summarizes in a few words the events which led to Jeremiah's confinement in the guard court of the palace, as narrated fully in 37:3-21. His abbreviated narrative gives no report, however, of the role played by the royal ministers in that restriction of the prophet's freedom. Thus the editor introduces the episode:

32:1 The word which came to Jeremiah from the Lord in the tenth year of Zedekiah king of Judah. (That was in the eighteenth year of Nebuchadrezzar.) 2 Now at that time the army of the king of Babylon was besieging Jerusalem, and

Jeremiah the prophet was confined in the guard court, which was in the palace of the king of Judah. 3 Because Zedekiah king of Judah had confined him, saying, "Why do you prophesy, saying, 'Thus says the Lord, Lo, I am about to give this city into the power of the king of Babylon and he will capture it; 4 and Zedekiah king of Judah will not escape from the hand of the Chaldeans but he shall surely be given into the power of the king of Babylon, and he shall speak with him face to face, and the eyes of the one shall behold the eyes of the other; 5 and he will take Zedekiah away to Babylon, and there will he be until I visit him, says the Lord; although you will fight with the Chaldeans you will not be successful?' "

The transaction is described in vss. 6-15, which rest on an autobiographical account from Jeremiah. As Rudolph says, the words of vs. 6a, "And Jeremiah said," "mark the transition from report to autobiography." [36] Here Jeremiah tells of his purchase of property in Anathoth. The account is an informing illustration of a characteristic legal procedure in ancient Israel. When, because of impoverishment or some other reason, a member of the Judean nation found it necessary to sell some of his property, his nearest blood relative was obligated to come to his rescue and "redeem" the property by purchasing it, so that he would thus keep it intact in the family inheritance.[37]

Hanamel, a cousin of Jeremiah, the son of his father's brother Shallum, possibly due to the exigencies of the Chaldean siege, found it necessary to sell his field in Anathoth. Now before any objective knowledge of this had come to Jeremiah, while the prophet was confined in the guard court, he was aware of a definite intuition that this cousin was on the point of visiting him to ask him to come forward as his next of kin and purchase a particular piece of property in Anathoth. And when Hanamel appeared upon exactly that errand, Jeremiah knew that the Lord's hand was in it (vs. 8), that it was a matter of prophetic significance, and that in the whole affair God was revealing a message of great importance for Judah. Thus the prophet gives his account in vs. 6, so "the word of the Lord" refers back to vs. 1 ("the word which came to Jeremiah").

32:6 So the word of the Lord came to me, saying: 7 Lo, Hanamel the son of Shallum your uncle is about to come to you to say, "Buy for yourself my field which is in Anathoth, for the redemption right to buy is yours." 8 So Hanamel the son of my uncle did come to me in the guard court and said to me, "Buy, pray, my field which is in Anathoth, for yours is the right of inheritance, and you are the elder."

[36] *Jeremia*, p. 175.
[37] Cf. Lev. 25:25, from the Holiness Code, *ca.* 550, but representing at that time ancient practice.

Without a moment's hesitation Jeremiah buys the field. He carries out the transaction of purchase with meticulous care, for the whole thing is to him a prophetic act with meaning in every detail. The money had to be weighed out, the deed of purchase drawn up, signed, sealed and witnessed, and an exact copy of the original deed made. The original and copy were to be put in a place where they would be preserved intact for a long time. Then the Lord revealed to him the prophetic significance of the transaction (vs. 15). Right now Judah was doomed, as Jeremiah was absolutely sure. But beyond the imminent destruction God had plans for his people. Again houses, fields, and vineyards would be bought there. The Lord's people will be coming back. New people would be coming in. There is a future in God's purpose for his people—beyond destruction!

So runs the account in accurate detail as the prophetic act is performed and interpreted.

32:9 So I bought the field from Hanamel, the son of my uncle, and I weighed out for him seventeen shekels of silver. 10 And I inscribed a deed and affixed the seal and took witnesses and weighed out the money in the scales. 11 Then I took the deed of purchase, that which was sealed and that which was open. 12 And I gave the purchase deed to Baruch son of Neriah son of Mahseiah, in the presence of Hanamel, my uncle's son, and in the sight of the witnesses whose names were written into the deed of purchase, and in the presence of all the Judeans who were sitting in the guard court. 13 And I commanded Baruch in their presence, saying, 14 "Take these documents, this deed of purchase, the sealed [one] and this open deed, and put them in a pottery jar so that they may last many days. 15 For thus says the Lord of hosts, God of Israel, 'again houses and fields and vineyards shall be bought in this land.' "

From that unique prophetic revelation of a hopeful future for his people, in which Jeremiah had reveled, he awakes to the stark realism of the dreadful present (vs. 24), not comfortable houses, fertile fields, productive vineyards—far from it! He was sure of impending doom. For years he had preached it and warned his people of it. And now it is here.

But he is keenly conscious of the sharp inconsistency of the doom-bound present with the revelation of that hopeful future. To be sure, he knows that all things are possible to God (vs. 17), but now Jerusalem is besieged. The Judean nation is all but destroyed. "Lord," he cries, "see the great military embankments of the storming Chaldean army in final assault upon Jerusalem" (vs. 24). The bodies of the Judean slain lie unburied. Famine stalks the streets of the capital and there is no bread. Pestilence is breaking out.[38]

[38] For these conditions to which vs. 24 refers cf. 37:21; Lam. 2:21; 4:4; 5:10; Ezek. 5:12 (pestilence).

Yet God had asked him to buy a field in Anathoth! Had he rightly understood God's meaning? It is in this prayer that immediately followed his revelation that his disturbed soul "seeks ultimate clarity" [39] from God.

32:16 And I prayed to the Lord after I had given the deed of purchase to Baruch son of Neriah, saying: 17 "Alas, Lord God,[40] 24 Lo, the siege mounds have come to the city to capture it, and in consequence of the sword, the famine, and the pestilence, the city is given into the power of the Chaldeans who are fighting against it. 25 What thou didst say has come to pass, and lo, thou dost see it, yet now thou sayest to me, Lord God, 'Buy thee the field with the silver and take witnesses,' but the city has been given over into the power of the Chaldeans."

THE LORD'S ANSWER TO JEREMIAH'S PRAYER

The Lord convinced the prophet of his omnipotence (vss. 26-27). Although it is clearly God's purpose that Jerusalem shall succumb to the Chaldean conquerors and that they will destroy the city by fire (vss. 28-29a), it is just as certainly God's purpose that at length he will bring upon his people a blessing comparable in greatness to his present punishment of them (vs. 42). We must keep clearly in mind that security for the future, which Jeremiah's possession of property in Anathoth seemed to imply, had nothing whatever to do with his own individual security. To him the entire transaction was a prophecy for his people. It was a message from God, a message of hope for their future. In that future time—approximately seventy years was in the prophet's mind—which the Lord is even now planning just as surely as that he is planning immediate destruction, Judeans will settle in all parts of the homeland. The climax in the Lord's answer to Jeremiah's prayer is vs. 43, which recalls and stresses the inner prophetic meaning of the purchase of the property in Anathoth, as given in vs. 15.

Considered in terms of political districts, that restored homeland would then include the cities and towns of Judah, Jerusalem, and the land of Benjamin. From the standpoint of the nature of the territory embraced, it would include the low-lying hills of the Shephelah, the high tableland. 2,000-3,000 feet above sea level, the central Judean highlands, and the Negeb, the nomadic steppe area extending about sixty miles south of Hebron, which forms the transition to the uninhabitable desert (vs. 44).[41]

Thus Jeremiah tells the Lord's answer to his prayer:

[39] Rudolph, Jeremia, p. 179.

[40] For vs. 17 (after "Alas, Lord God") to vs. 23, see pp. 293-94.

[41] Cf. Martin Noth, Journal of the Palestine Oriental Society for 1935, p. 103; cf. 17:26; 33:13.

32:26 The word of the Lord came to me saying, 27 Lo, I am the Lord, the God of all flesh. Is anything too difficult for me? 28 Therefore thus says the Lord, This city shall surely be given into the hand of the king of Babylon and he will capture it. 29a And the Chaldeans, those engaging in battle against this city, shall enter and set this city on fire and burn it.[42] 42 For thus says the Lord, Just as I brought to this people all this great evil, so will I bring upon them all the good of which I am speaking. 43 And there shall yet be fields bought in this land of which you are saying, "It is destitute of man or beast, it has been given over into the hands of the Chaldeans." 44 Fields and vineyards shall they buy and they shall inscribe deeds and seal them, and take witnesses in the land of Benjamin, and in the districts of Jerusalem, and in the cities of Judah, and in the cities of the hill country, and in the cities of the Shephelah, and in the cities of the south, for I will restore their fortunes, says the Lord.

JEREMIAH'S CRUCIAL NEED FOR INSIGHT

A little later a second message came to Jeremiah from the Lord. The creator-God invites the prophet, in his need for insight into mysteries that his own knowledge cannot plumb, to call upon him with the assurance of God's response. The prophet stands in one of the most crucial moments of Judean history, and as the interpreter of the Lord to his people, greatly in need of illumination as to that divine meaning of events which can come only from the revelation of God. It would seem likely, as Rudolph [43] suggests, that the Lord's name here is interpreted as meaning "He causes to come into being."

33:1 Now the word of the Lord came to Jeremiah a second time (he was still confined in the court of the guard), saying, 2 Thus says the Lord, maker of the earth and fashioner of it so as to establish it—the Lord is his name, 3 Call to me and I will answer you, and I will declare to you great things and secret things which you do not know.

How great in these hours of Judah's imminent fall was the need of Jeremiah for interpretation, from the angle of the divine vision, of what was taking place. Only through divine revelation could he have access to that profound knowledge preserved in the secret counsels of God. For God's prophet must be able to see beyond houses destroyed by the military genius of the Chaldeans, yes, beyond the corpses of Judean men whose wickedness had made even God ashamed. For this is God's judgment which had often been predicted by the prophet, but is now a bitter reality. Yet beyond awful judgment upon Judah, necessary since God is a righteous being, lies restora-

---

[42] For 32:29b-41, see p. 329.
[43] *Jeremia*, pp. 182-83.

tion (*"*rûkhāh*) and healing (*marpē'*). We note these two gracious words which are characteristic of Jeremiah. And behind the healing which God will bring to his people lie vast stores of that in God's character which will bring to men welfare, health, and peace, and also reliableness, faithfulness, and stability. The great days when Israel was an undivided kingdom will return. In vs. 7 the prophet is referring implicity to Isa. 1:26. God's purging of their sin and his forgiveness, such as Jeremiah had emphasized as a result of the new covenant, will be experienced. And beloved Jerusalem, soon to be in ruins, and seemingly cursed of God and derided by men, but then restored and rebuilt, will stand out before the nations of the earth as "a thing of glory." Nations of the world looking on, as Jerusalem comes to its own in God's purpose, will tremble at the amazing transforming recovering grace of God. There is an extravagance in these verses that can be understood only psychologically, when from the depths of unspeakable dismay, by faith in a God-planned future the soul leaps to heights of hope and joy unspeakable. Says G. A. Smith concerning this passage: "It is not unnatural to believe that his great soul broke out with a vision of the hope beyond for which he had taken so practical a pledge." [44]

33:4 **For thus says the Lord, God of Israel, concerning the houses of this city and concerning the houses of the kings of Judah, which shall be torn down, against which 5 the Chaldeans are advancing, to fight them with mounds and sword and to fill them with corpses of men whom I will strike down in my anger and wrath and from whom I hid my face because of all their evil.**[45] **6 Lo, I am about to bring to them restoration and healing. And I will heal them, and I will reveal to them stores of peace and stability. 7 And I will restore the fortunes of Judah and the fortunes of Jerusalem, and I will rebuild them as at first. 8 And I will purge them of all their iniquity wherein they have sinned against me, and I will forgive all their iniquities wherein they have sinned against me and wherein they have transgressed against me. 9 And Jerusalem shall be a cause of exultation, an object of praise, and a thing of glory to every nation of the earth which hears of all the good that I am about to do, and they shall stand in awe and tremble because of all the good and all the prosperity which I am about to bring to them.**

The prophet loved the familiar sounds of normal life in Palestine, the lilt of merry voices, the proud and happy voice of the bridegroom, the gentle and happy responding voice of the bride. But now Jerusalem has become a ruins. The city has fallen. No longer are those happy sounds of normal life heard. But they will be heard again! And Jeremiah, who loved

---

[44] *Jeremiah*, pp. 290-91.
[45] Following Cornill, *Jeremia*, p. 369.

the temple, even though he had to criticize his people's dependence upon it, recalled an ancient feature of its worship, which ritualistic though it was, yet was of all cultic acts the most free from a warped externalism, the glad cry of praise to God for his goodness, as bearing their thankoffering, God's people entered his courts. Yet again will restored Judah have wondrous reason for gratitude when God will have turned its fortunes.

33:10 Thus says the Lord: Yet again shall be heard in this place, of which you are saying, "It is a waste without man or beast," in the cities of Judah and in the desolated streets of Jerusalem, without man and without inhabitant and without beast, 11 the voice of exultation and the voice of joy, the voice of bridegroom and the voice of bride, the voice of those saying,

"Praise the Lord of hosts, for the Lord is good
For his lovingkindness endures forever,"

of those bringing a thankoffering to the house of the Lord, for I will turn the fortunes of the land to like what it was at the first, says the Lord.

Now Jerusalem is a ruins and all Judah is destroyed—men, cattle, and sheep, all are gone. But one day the shepherds will be back, and in all areas of this shepherd country, in the highlands, the lowlands, and the nomadic areas reaching toward the desert, the land will be dotted with shepherds' homes. And the prophet pictures the shepherd counting his sheep as they go out of the fold and at eventide when they are again enfolded. A picture of homely beauty and simple dignity, in a life of security—such lies ahead for Judah in God's purpose.

33:12 Thus says the Lord of hosts: There shall yet be in this desolate place [now] without men or cattle, and in all its cities, abodes of shepherds who cause their flocks to lie down, 13 in the cities of the hill country [Shephelah] in the cities of the south [Negeb], in the land of Benjamin, in the districts of Jerusalem, and in the cities of Judah. Yet again shall they pass by the hands of him who counts them, says the Lord.

Jeremiah Is Thrown into a Cistern

While Jeremiah was in the guard court he had much freedom to speak his mind and he took advantage of it thus to keep talking with the people, with soldiers in the guard court, and indeed with any who would listen. The Chaldean army, which as we have seen had temporarily lifted the siege of Jerusalem, was now back, and the siege had been resumed, just as Jeremiah had maintained would be the case. Unquestionably the prophet's

views were gaining for him prestige, if not popularity. One day a group of
nobles heard Jeremiah speaking to "all the people" in the guard court.
These nobles were important men at court. Of the first named, Shephatiah,
we know nothing. Gedaliah, the second mentioned, was probably the son of
the Pashhur, who as superintendent of the temple had earlier put Jeremiah
in the stocks (20:1). A third, Jehucal (Jucal), had been one of the delegation of two who had consulted Jeremiah when the Chaldean troops had
withdrawn for a time in order to put a stop to the advance of Egypt to
the help of Judah (27:3), and Pashhur had been one of an earlier delegation of two sent by Zedekiah to seek the prophet's counsel from God when
Nebuchadrezzar first attacked Jerusalem (21:1) in 598.

The prophet kept declaring to all the people in the guard court the Lord's
revelation to him of the certainty of the Chaldean conquest of Jerusalem
(38:3). The princes promptly went to King Zedekiah and complained that
the prophet's influence was cutting the nerve of resistance to the Chaldeans,
that he was thus guilty of treason and should be put to death. Although
King Zedekiah on the whole was himself friendly disposed to Jeremiah, he
was a weakling, and frankly admitting his inability to resist the will of his
princes, he left Jeremiah in their hands to do with as they wished. Seizing
the prophet, with no humanitarian feeling and with no concern whatever
for his dignity, the princes threw him into a stagnant and muddy cistern
which belonged to Malchiah, one of the princes. It was empty of water, but
in the bottom there was soft miry mud, into the cold and desolate dampness
of which Jeremiah sank. As Volz says, "Their base character devised an
especially horrible and torturous manner of death." [46] The prophet must
have been nearly sixty years of age at this critical period of his life. All of
this took place without the direct knowledge, although with the tacit permission, of the king (vs. 5). Baruch thus tells of this indignity suffered by
the prophet:

38:1 Now Shephatiah son of Mattan, along with Gedaliah son of Pashhur, and
Jehucal [Jucal] son of Shelemiah, and Pashhur son of Malchiah, heard the words
which Jeremiah was saying to all the people.[47] 3 Thus says the Lord, This city of a
certainty will be given over to the power of the army of the king of Babylon and
he will capture it. 4 Then these princes said to the king, "Pray let this man be put
to death, for by means of this he is demoralizing the men of war who are left in
this city and weakening the hands of all the people in saying to them words such
as these, for this man is not speaking for the welfare of this people but to their

[46] *Jeremia*, p. 338.
[47] Omit vs. 2 as a marginal gloss from 21:9.

injury." 5 So the king said, "Lo, he is in your hands, for the king is not able to do anything against you." 6 Then they took Jeremiah and flung him into the cistern of Malchiah son of the king, which was in the guard court, and they let Jeremiah down by ropes. Now there was no water in the cistern, but mud, and Jeremiah sank down in the mud.

JEREMIAH IS RESCUED BY AN ETHIOPIAN EUNUCH

How generally known this heartless and brutal treatment of Jeremiah was we cannot say. But now there takes place an episode, the story of which, as George Adam Smith remarks, "is one of the fairest in the Old Testament." [48] An Ethiopian (Cushite) eunuch of the royal palace, Ebed- melech by name, and so far as we know the only person whose concern for Jeremiah drove him to act, had the courage to bring this dastardly treatment of the prophet to the ears of the king.

At the time the king was sitting in the Benjamin Gate, either to give audience to his subjects and settle disputes, or from there to follow the progress of the siege which threatened most severely the north of the city.[49] Ebed-melech went direct to the king himself, told him the cruel injustice that had been done to Jeremiah, and warned him that the prophet was certain to die under the exposure and misery he was suffering. The king was moved by the eunuch's appeal, and ordered him to provide himself with three men and draw Jeremiah up out of the cistern.

Taking the three men, he went to the wardrobe of the storehouse, where he secured from the keeper worn-out clothes and rags to protect the prophet's arms and shoulders. Then they went with these materials and the required ropes to the cistern. Ebed-melech gave directions to Jeremiah as to how to place the rags so that his frail and emaciated body would not be cut by the ropes, and they carefully drew him up to the light of day to remain— but still in confinement—in the guard court.

Here is Baruch's vivid account of the prophet's rescue:

38:7 Ebed-melech the Cushite—he was a eunuch in the palace of the king— heard that they had put Jeremiah into the cistern. Now the king was sitting in the Gate of Benjamin. 8 So Ebed-melech went out from the royal palace to the king and spoke to the king, saying: 9 "My lord the king, these men have wrought injury in all that they have done to Jeremiah the prophet, whom they flung into the cistern; now he will die under it." 10 So the king commanded Ebed-melech the Cushite, saying: "Take with you from here three men and draw up Jeremiah the prophet from the cistern so that he will not die." 11 So Ebed-melech took the men

48 *Jeremiah*, p. 281.
49 Cf. Volz, *op. cit.*, p. 339.

and went to the palace of the king to the wardrobe of the storehouse and took from here rags of worn-out garments and let them down to Jeremiah in the cistern with ropes. 12 Then Ebed-melech the Cushite said to Jeremiah: "Please put the clothes and rags under your armpits over the ropes," and Jeremiah did so. 13 So they drew up Jeremiah with the ropes and brought him out of the cistern, and Jeremiah remained in the guard court.

KING ZEDEKIAH'S LAST INTERVIEW WITH JEREMIAH

In 38:14-23 is given the report of the last interview which King Zedekiah had with the prophet. Sending to the guard court for the prophet, the king had him brought to the third entrance to the temple, probably the entrance on the south which led from the temple to the palace.[50]

With no introductory formalities, the king informs the prophet that he is going to ask him a question to which he wants an unequivocal answer (vs. 14). Exactly what the question was Baruch does not say. But from Jeremiah's answer we can reasonably infer that it concerned whether the king should surrender himself and his capital to the Chaldeans.

In response to the king Jeremiah raises two objections. First, if he answers the king truthfully, he will be put to death. Second, if in the Lord's name he should venture to give the king counsel, Zedekiah would give no heed to it. The prophet is here speaking out of copious experience in dealing with Zedekiah and from penetrating insight into the king's character.

In answer to these objections the king makes a solemn and secret oath that he would under no circumstances put the prophet to death or give him into the hands of those who are out to kill him (vss. 15-16).

Then the prophet speaks out his counsel in the Lord's name. If the king should surrender to the Chaldeans, he would preserve his own life and would save his capital city from destruction. If he should refuse to surrender, the city would surely be captured and destroyed by fire, and the king himself would be captured (vss. 17-18). Thus runs Baruch's account:

38:14 Then King Zedekiah sent and brought Jeremiah the prophet to him in the third entrance to the house of the Lord, and the king said to Jeremiah, "I am asking you something. Do not hide anything from me." 15 And Jeremiah said to Zedekiah, "If I should tell you, would you not surely put me to death? And if I should advise you, you would not listen to me." 16 Then King Zedekiah swore to Jeremiah in secrecy, saying: "As the Lord lives, who has given us this life, I will not put you to death, or give you into the hands of these men who are seeking your life."

17 Thereupon Jeremiah said to Zedekiah: "Thus says the Lord God of hosts,

[50] So Peake, *Jeremiah*, p. 172.

God of Israel, If you actually go over to the captains of the king of Babylon, your soul shall live and this city will not be burned by fire, but you shall live, you and your household. 18 But if you do not go out to the captains of the king of Babylon and give over this city into the hand of the Chaldeans, then they will burn it with fire and you shall not escape out of their hand."

19 Then said King Zedekiah to Jeremiah: "I am afraid of the Judeans who have gone over to the Chaldeans, lest they give me into their hand and deal ruthlessly with me."

We feel the extreme tension of the moment and sense the deep solemnity in Jeremiah's manner and voice as in the Lord's name he answers his monarch and utters this, his final prophetic appeal to the king:

38:20 And Jeremiah said: "They shall not give [you over]. Pray listen to the voice of the Lord, as regards what I am saying to you, and it shall go well with you and you shall remain alive. 21 But if you refuse to surrender, this is the vision which the Lord has shown me. 22 See, all the women who are left in the palace of the king of Judah will be brought out to the captains of the king of Babylon and they will be saying,

> 'They have allured you and have prevailed over you,
>   Your good friends.
> They have sunk your feet in the mire;
>   They have taken to their heels.'

23 And all your wives and your sons shall be brought out to the Chaldeans, and you will not escape from their hand; but you yourself shall be captured by the king of Babylon and this city shall be burned by fire."

In this poetic lament of satire (vs. 22), a pure poem in the rhythm of lamentation—three stresses followed by two stresses—the poetic skill of the prophet is apparent. For into this poem he has woven his own bitter experience of sinking in the mire, and the faithlessness of the king's irresponsible nobles, who have egged him on in disastrous resistance to the prophet's call to Judah and its leaders. Vs. 23 simply puts the teaching of the satirical lament into plain prose. The royal household will be brought out of the palace as prisoners. Zedekiah himself will be seized and Jerusalem destroyed by fire. These are the last words which Jeremiah spoke in the Lord's name to his monarch (vss. 19-23).

JEREMIAH'S MESSAGE TO EBED-MELECH

Jer. 39:15-18 rightly follows ch. 38, which is concerned with the certain and near-at-hand capture of Jerusalem by the Chaldeans. Jeremiah's mind moves out in intercession and appreciation toward the Ethiopian eunuch who in his most desolate hour had so graciously befriended him. In the extremity of the prophet's own physical and mental suffering, when exposure, famine, and human neglect had made very fragile his hold upon life, Ebed-melech had been to him an instrument of divine providence. Well did the prophet know the inevitable fear of retaliation on the part of the infuriated princes in which the eunuch now lived (vs. 17). And as he brooded over it all there came to him a clear certainty from God—an oracle from the Lord. It assured Ebed-melech that when the calamity of Jerusalem's capture would finally come, the providence of which the Ethiopian eunuch had himself been the instrument would likewise protect him from the princes' vindictive desires. Yet it was only his bare life of which he could be assured—his life as a prize of war—but supported by his faith in God.

39:15 Now to Jeremiah came the word of the Lord when he was confined in the guard court saying: 16 Go and speak to Ebed-melech the Cushite saying, "Thus says the Lord of hosts, God of Israel, Lo, I am about to bring to pass my words concerning this city for evil and not for good. 17 But I will save you in that day, says the Lord, and you shall not be given into the hand of the men of whom you are afraid. 18 For I will certainly deliver you, and you shall not fall by the sword, but your life you will have as booty, for you have put your trust in me, says the Lord."

THE PROPHETIC ORACLE

It was probably the new dignity accorded the prophet by King Zedekiah in seeking from his mouth the oracle of the Lord that led Jeremiah to brood over the significance of the prophetic oracle. To the prophet it was a thing of awe and deep solemnity to be within the Lord's counsels in these desperate and strategic hours of Judah's life, just before the final blow was destined to fall. In 23:33-40,[51] a passage which deals with the prophetic oracle, it is only vs. 33 which comes from Jeremiah. Well did he know from repeated experiences how the prophetic word was sought at his lips, listened to, and then utterly ignored. No element in his total prophetic experience had been so hard for the prophet, or so heavy a burden upon his heart, as this.

In vs. 33 Jeremiah, whose interest in words is very keen, and whose use of them as a prophet was truly brilliant, plays upon the double import of the Hebrew word massā'. In the first place, it may mean "oracle," in the sense of a prophetic word or revelation from God. Such is its use, for example, in II Kings 9:25, where it refers to the solemn, condemnatory oracle uttered by the prophet Elijah against King Ahab because of his

[51] For 23:34-40 see p. 321.

crime against Naboth, whom Ahab had ruthlessly dispossessed of his vine-yard. In this same sense of prophetic "oracle" *massā'* appears in the super-scriptions of the prophecies of Nahum (oracle on Nineveh), Zech. 9–11 (an oracle), and Zech. 12–14 (an oracle).

But in the second place, *massā'* may simply mean "burden," in the sense of a load to be borne.

Vs. 33 represents the nation of Judah as asking Jeremiah for an "oracle" from the Lord, now that the final siege of Jerusalem has come. At long last the Judeans consider Jeremiah as an important personage, and his prophetic counsel is in great demand on the part of people and king. By monarch and nation he is now consulted, and guidance from the Lord is sought at his mouth.

But Jeremiah knows all too well that his prophetic word from God is not obeyed. His oracle is heard but ignored. The prophet, who is likewise a poet, knew that by a play on words he could leave upon the people an ineradicable impression. Thus through his appeal to the outer ear the prophet sought to reach the inner ear of the nation's soul. The Lord directs the prophet to answer the people when they now ask him, "What is the oracle [*massā'*] of the Lord?" in an arresting and conscience-searching man-ner. Thus the Lord directs him:

23:33 **When this people ask you, "What is the oracle [*massā'*] of the Lord?" you shall say to them, "You are the burden [*massā'*] of the Lord, and I will abandon you, says the Lord."**

It is a sharp prophetic word full of bitter irony. Stubborn, disobedient Judah has increasingly become an intolerable "burden" to the Lord. It is the Lord's intention to throw off that burden into exile. Jeremiah is not for the moment concerned with the continuity of the divine solicitude for Judah in the coming exile, but only with the people's failure in this critical hour to heed the Lord's word.

Malamat's study, "Jeremiah and the Last Two Kings of Judah," [52] helps us to see the reign of Zedekiah in a new light. He emphasizes the extreme difficulty of the king's task, and that for a whole decade Zedekiah struggled for the existence of his kingdom, since peace and order were continually disturbed. The exile of thousands of its foremost citizens in 598 caused the social economic anarchy which prevailed in Judah and "prepared the ground for the ascent of various political adventurers." He calls attention to the difficulty created for Zedekiah by the fact that King Jehoiachin, although

---

[52] *Palestine Exploration Quarterly for 1951*, pp. 81-87.

in exile, was still alive, and he says: "Evidently this duality in the status of the monarchy made itself strongly felt in Judah itself, dividing the Judeans into opposite camps; one of which continued to see in Jehoiachin the king 'de jure' even after he was exiled; these undoubtedly strongly desired his return."

Zedekiah is never disrespectfully spoken to by Jeremiah. Noting Jeremiah's earnest appeal to the king in 34:4-5, Malamat suggestively says: "These words are of greater importance if we consider that in the prophet's vision of a king's final fate is expressed the essence of his opinion on the king's character."

The seal imprint on the jar handle found at Tell Beit-Mirsim, "To Eliakim, steward of Yaukin" (abridged form of Jehoiachin), is evidence "that King Jehoiachin kept an administration in Judah to take care of his royal property during his stay in Babylon."

It is instructive that from this very period when, as the biblical record reports, only Lachish and Azekah of the fenced Judean cities remained unconquered by the Chaldeans, we learn from the Lachish ostraca[53] that for some reason the fire signals of Azekah could not be seen in Lachish, and that the Chaldean siege of Lachish had not yet taken place, as communication between these cities and Jerusalem was still possible at the time when the ostraca were written.[54]

THE FALL OF JERUSALEM

Jer. 52:1-27 is in large part taken bodily from II Kings 24:18–25:21. It is placed here by the final editor of the book of Jeremiah because of the fullness of its information and its pertinency to the career of the prophet. However, this editor omitted II Kings 25:22-26, which is itself a summary account of what happened to the Palestinian remnant left in the land after the capture of Jerusalem. It traces the history of this remnant as far as their flight to Egypt, the full narrative of which, however, is given by Baruch in Jer. 39:11–43:7, and is discussed below.

Jer. 52:28-30 is an independent source of great importance which is not found elsewhere in the Hebrew Bible or in the Septuagint. It deals with

[53] Eighteen were found by J. L. Starkey in 1935, and three more in 1938. The latest occupation level dates immediately before the beginning of the Chaldean siege in the autumn of 589 or 588; cf. D. Winton Thomas, "The Age of Jeremiah in the Light of Recent Archeological Discovery," *Palestine Exploration Quarterly for 1950*, pp. 1-15.

[54] D. Winton Thomas, "Ostraca III from Tell ed-Duweir," *Palestine Exploration Quarterly for 1948*, pp. 131-36.

specific numbers of Judean captives taken into exile by the Chaldeans at different times, beginning in 598.[55]

This final chapter of the Book of Jeremiah rounds out the career of the prophet and richly supplements the narrative of Baruch. It gives the official Judean record of the rebellion of King Zedekiah against Nebuchadrezzar, his Chaldean overlord. The prophet Ezekiel, who lived through and beyond the period of the fall of Jerusalem, tells us in considerable detail what is only implied in Jeremiah, and in the official record in II Kings, that Zedekiah had actually pledged his fealty to Nebuchadrezzar of Babylon and that he broke that pledge (Ezek. 17:13, 18).

The Hebrew text in Jer. 52 is much better preserved than the parallel account in II Kings. It is our best primary source for the fall of Jerusalem and what happened to the city, its king, and his people. For the career of Jeremiah the fall of Jerusalem was the climactic event toward which his life message had thus far pointed, and from which there was to open "a future of hope." The chapter begins with the work of the Deuteronomic historian who in the characteristic framework of his narrative gives King Zedekiah's age upon accession to the throne, the length of his reign (598-587), the name of his mother, his estimate as to the moral quality of the king's leadership, and the Lord's judgment upon the nation as manifest in the exile of its people from their land.

52:1 Zedekiah was twenty-one years old when he became king, and he ruled eleven years in Jerusalem. The name of his mother was Hamutal daughter of Jeremiah from Libnah. 2 And he did what was evil in the sight of the Lord in accordance with all that Jehoiakim had done. 3 Indeed, the situation in Jerusalem and Judah became such that, due to the anger of the Lord, he hurled them away from his presence. And Zedekiah rebelled against the king of Babylon.

Jer. 39:1-10, which is Baruch's report of the siege and capture of Jerusalem, is based upon 52:4-16, and is simply an abbreviated account of it. It is concerned solely with the capture of Jerusalem and does not deal with the nation as such. Jer. 39:3, for which there is no parallel in ch. 52, adds the concrete detail of the names of the Chaldean officials who, upon the capitulation of Jerusalem, set up administrative headquarters in the central (chief) gate of the wall of Jerusalem. The correct list is given, however, in 39:13, and 39:3 should read in accordance with it. And 52:12, which reports the memorable day just a month and a day after the fall of Jerusalem, when

[55] For vss. 31-34, see p. 294.

Nebuchadrezzar's highest officer, Nebuzaradan the captain of the guards, entered Jerusalem, is not paralleled in ch. 39.

The corresponding portions of these two records are here presented in parallel columns so that the fuller record may be before the reader as he notes the particular portions which are utilized by the narrator in ch. 39. It gives the best information available about the siege and capture of Jerusalem and the final exile of its people.

The siege of Jerusalem as herein reported may be briefly summarized as follows. It began on the tenth day of the tenth month (Tebet, December-January), 589, the ninth year of King Zedekiah, and lasted until the ninth day of the fourth month (Tammuz, June-July), 587. Famine broke out in the fourth month of the final year, and on the ninth of that month the city was taken. The Chaldeans pursued King Zedekiah and his army as they sought to escape to Trans-Jordan. Overtaken at Jericho, the army was scattered and Zedekiah captured. Taken to Riblah on the Orontes River, south of Hamath, the military headquarters of the Chaldean expedition, the king was compelled to witness the slaughter of the princes of his court and of his own sons, then his eyes were put out, and bound in chains, he was exiled to Babylon, where he was imprisoned for the rest of his life.

A month and a day later, in 587, on the tenth day of the fifth month (Ab, July-August), Nebuzaradan the captain of the guards, Nebuchadrezzar's commander in chief, entered Jerusalem, burned the temple, the royal palace, and the residences of the people, tore down the walls, and carried the population into exile—all except some of the poor of the land who were left to till the soil and tend the vineyards.

Jer. 52:4-16	Jer. 39:1-10
4 So it came to pass in the ninth year of his reign, in the tenth month, in the tenth day of the month, Nebuchadrezzar king of Babylon, he and all his army came against Jerusalem, and encamped against it, and built against it all around a siege wall.	1 In the ninth year of Zedekiah king of Judah, in the tenth month Nebuchadrezzar king of Babylon, and all his army came to Jerusalem and besieged it.
5 So the city went into a state of siege until the eleventh year of King Zedekiah.	
6 In the fourth month famine seized the city so that there was no bread for the people of the land. 7 And the city was broken into on the ninth of the	2 In the eleventh year of Zedekiah in the fourth month, in the ninth of the month

the city
was broken into. |

month,

and the king saw and all

the soldiers, and they fled and went out of the city by night, by way of the gate between the two walls which were alongside the king's garden.

Now the Chaldeans were against the city on all sides, so they went toward the Arabah.

8 But the Chaldean army pursued King Zedekiah and overtook him in the steppes of Jericho, and all his army were scattered from attachment to him. 9 Then they captured the king and took him up to the king of Babylon at Riblah in the land of Hamath, and he pronounced sentence against him.

10 The king of Babylon slew the sons of Zedekiah before his eyes, and likewise all the princes of Judah he slaughtered at Riblah.

11 Then he blinded the eyes of Zedekiah, bound him in chains, and took him to Babylon, and put him in prison until the day of his death.

12 In the fifth month, on the tenth day of the month—this was the nineteenth year of King Nebuchadrezzar king of Babylon—Nebuzaradan captain of the guard who stood before the king of Babylon came to Jerusalem.

13 And he burned the house of the Lord and the house of the king and all the houses of Jerusalem.

14 And all the walls around about Jerusalem the Chaldean army which was with the captain of the guards tore down.

3 And all the princes of the king of Babylon came in and took their seat in the Middle Gate: Nergal-Sarezar Sar Simmager, Rab-Mag (chief of the soothsayers) and Nebushazban, Rab-Saris (chief of the eunuchs).

4 And when Zedekiah king of Judah and all his soldiers saw it they fled and went out of the city by night, by way of the king's garden through the gate between the two walls

toward the Arabah.

5 But the Chaldean army pursued them and they overtook Zedekiah in the steppes of Jericho

and they captured him and took him up to Nebuchadrezzar king of Babylon at Riblah in the land of Hamath, and he pronounced sentence against him.

6 The king of Babylon slew the sons of Zedekiah at Riblah before his eyes, and likewise all the nobles of Judah the king of Babylon slaughtered.

7 He blinded the eyes of Zedekiah and bound him in chains to bring him to Babylon.

8 And the Chaldeans burned the house of the king and the houses of the people and they tore down the walls of Jerusalem.

15 And the rest of the people who were left in the city, and the deserters who had fallen away to the king of Babylon, and the rest of the throng, Nebuzaradan chief of the guardsmen carried away captive.
16 But some of the poor of the land
Nebuzaradan captain of the guard left

to tend the vineyards and
to till the soil.

9 And the rest of the people who were left in the city, and the deserters who had fallen away to him,
and the rest of the throng, Nebuzaradan captain of the guard carried away into exile to Babylon.

10 But some of the poor people who had no property
Nebuzaradan captain of the guard left in the land of Judah and he assigned them vineyards
and fields.

A WISDOM UTTERANCE APPLIED TO ZEDEKIAH

The redactor of the book of Jeremiah has placed in 17:5-11 three sayings of the prophet which present religious truths in the form of Hebrew wisdom utterances. The second and the third have already been discussed: for vss. 9-10 see p. 147; for vs. 11 see p. 132. These show conclusively that such forms of utterance as were characteristic of the Hebrew sages were also utilized by Jeremiah, the deepest thinker among the prophets.

The first of these utterances (vss. 5-8), which possibly was in the mind of the psalmist who wrote Ps. 1 as an introduction to the Psalter, is chiefly concerned with the problem of retribution. In Jeremiah's view the man who lives only in the world of men and things, and knows nothing of trust in God, lives under a curse which hampers and destroys his life. He places his confidence in human and material things rather than in God and spiritual reality. For such a person, wherever he may settle down, it is "a parched place in . . . a barren land" (vs. 6).

Thus the comparison:

> 17:5 Cursed is the man who puts his trust in humankind,
>   And considers flesh his strength.
>   6 He shall be like a juniper bush in a [treeless] plain,
>   And he shall not see that good will come;
>   But he shall settle down in a parched place in the steppe,
>   [In] a barren land which cannot be inhabited.

Cornill[56] suggests a good reason why this authentic utterance of the prophet was inserted here by the redactor of the book. To him it applied aptly to King Zedekiah, who by putting his trust in Egypt, had depended

[56] *Jeremia*, p. 212.

upon men rather than God. Bereft of his children and blinded, the last king of Judah had been taken in chains to Babylon. The parable in Ezek. 17:5-10, of which Zedekiah was the subject, was probably also in the redactor's mind. This unfortunate monarch who had trusted in the Egyptians, whose horses are "flesh, and not spirit" (Isa. 31:3), had indeed become "a lonely shrub in a dry wilderness," "like a juniper bush in the plain." Accordingly, vss. 5-6 were inserted immediately after 17:4, which, as we have seen, refers to the Babylonian exile.

In contrast, the man who puts his trust in God and in the realm of spiritual power is comparable to a tree by a stream which retains its freshness and fruitfulness even in times of widespread drought and dearth.

> 17:7 Blessed is the man who trusts in the Lord,
>   And who does not turn aside his heart from the Lord.
>   8 He shall be like a tree planted by water,
>   That sends forth its roots beside a stream;
>   It does not fear when heat comes,
>   But its leaves will be fresh,
>   And it will not be anxious in a year of drought,
>   Nor will it cease to bear fruit.

THE RELEASE OF JEREMIAH FROM THE GUARD COURT

When Jerusalem was captured, the Chaldean princes took up their station in the middle gate for the administration of the defeated city and land. These responsible officers released Jeremiah from the guard court and gave him his freedom. This we learn from Baruch's account (38:28b; 39:3, 14).

38:28b Now it came about that when Jerusalem was captured, 39:3 that all the princes of the king of Babylon came in and took their seat in the middle gate, Nergal Sar'ezer, Sar Simmager, Rab-Māg and Nebûshazbān, Rab Saris,[57] and all the officers [58] of the king of Babylon,[59] 39:14 and they sent and took Jeremiah from the guard court,[60] and gave him permission [61] to go out and come in among the people.

[57] Reading with *Biblia Hebraica*, from v. 13 where the list is correct, *Sar Simmāgēr, Rab-Mag* and *N⁴bûshazbān, Rab Sāris,* instead of *Samgar-n⁴bhû, Sar-S⁴khîm, Rab-Sāris, Nēr-gal sar'eçer, Rab-Māg.*

[58] Delete *sh⁴'erîth,* with *Biblia Hebraica*.

[59] Omit vs. 13 with *Biblia Hebraica*. "So Nebuzaradan, chief of the bodyguard and Nebushazban, the Rab Saris and Nergal Sarezer, the Rab Mag and all the chiefs of the king of Babylon" as an addition to the inserted vss. 4-12.

[60] Delete with *Biblia Hebraica, wayyitt⁴nû 'ôtho 'el-g⁴dhalyāhû ben'⁴hîqam ben-Shāphan.*

[61] Delete *'el g⁴dhalyāhû ben ⁱⁱhîqām ben Shāphan* and read *l⁴hôçî'ô w⁴lah⁴bhî'ô.*

It was not until four weeks later, on the tenth day of the fifth month (Ab) that Nebuzaradan captain of the guards, the highest military officer of King Nebuchadrezzar, entered Jerusalem in person as conqueror. He destroyed the city, tore down its walls, burned the temple, the royal palace, and the citizens' houses. The Jews that he found living under the protection of the Chaldean military forces, those who had gone over to the Chaldeans along with the people "left in the city"—"the implication of the phrase is that the Judean casualties had been very heavy"—[62] he assembled for the long trek to Babylon.

The captain of the guard brought with him orders from Nebuchadrezzar himself to deal graciously with Jeremiah and to honor his wishes. But where does Nebuzaradan find him? Not as a free man in Jerusalem, as vs. 14 would naturally lead us to expect, but as a prisoner in chains among the other captive Judeans at Ramah, the march of captives to Babylon being already on the move. It is likely that in the quite understandable chaos and confusion that then existed in Jerusalem, the officer in charge of rounding up the captives, probably in the face of Jeremiah's protest, violated the prophet's right to the freedom he had earlier been officially granted. He was in manacles when Nebuzaradan came upon him at Ramah, the first organization station for the long, sad journey of the captives to Babylon.

Scholars who doubt the likelihood of this official Chaldean concern for the welfare of Jeremiah fail to estimate the influence the prophet's plea to his countrymen to go over to Babylon and his persistent counsel to Zedekiah to surrender to Babylon had actually exercised. Rudolph at this point blazes a new trail. He maintains that deserters to Babylon and those who for profounder reasons had followed Jeremiah's counsel to "go over to Babylon," had informed the Chaldeans of his role during the siege. Jeremiah viewed Babylon from the standpoint of God's overruling purpose. He saw Babylon's relation to Judah as God's punishing disciplining agent. The Chaldeans, to be sure, may also have learned of Jeremiah's teaching that Babylon's time was coming, when that nation also would be at the receiving end of God's judgment. But seventy years is a long way off, and for the moment Jeremiah was viewed by Nebuchadrezzar not as a Chaldean liability but as a distinct asset.

When at Ramah, Nebuzaradan unexpectedly faced manacled Jeremiah, he treated him with gracious courtesy. Baruch in 40:2-3 represents Nebuzaradan as speaking to Jeremiah about what the Chaldeans had done to Jerusalem almost as though Nebuzaradan were himself a prophet like Jeremiah and

[62] H. Freedman; *Jeremiah* p. 354.

talking in Hebrew! Naturally these fluent words, as Rudolph says, were composed by Baruch. But there is no question as regards the respect which Nebuzaradan showed for Jeremiah at Ramah. He removed his manacles, gave him food and a present, and the yet more priceless gift of absolute and unrestricted freedom as to his next move. No one who has followed the career of this brave man of God in his nearly forty years of ministry will be surprised at the choice the prophet makes between two alternatives—preferment at the court in Babylon, where the most influential leadership of Judeans will soon inevitably be concentrated, or toil amid vast problems, perplexing uncertainties, and grave perils with Gedaliah at Mizpah in desolated Judah. One of the finest sentences in Baruch's whole story of Jeremiah's career and one of the most revealing as to the quality of the prophet's soul is that in which the scribe registers his hero's choice:

40:6 Then Jeremiah came to Gedaliah son of Ahikam, at Mizpah.

As Rudolph says: "That is proof not only of love for his native home and of the absurdity of the charge that he was deserting to the Chaldeans (37:13), but also of his belief in the future (32:15), which is for him bound up with the person of Gedaliah." [63] Baruch too was already there, as the word "came" suggests, and as the succeeding narrative makes clear.[64]

39:11 And Nebuchadrezzar king of Babylon gave Nebuzaradan captain of the guards orders saying, 12 "Take him, look after him and do him no harm, but deal with him as he says to you." 40:2a So the captain of the guard took Jeremiah. 40:1b When he took him—now he was bound in chains in the midst of all the captives of Jerusalem and Judah who were being taken in exile to Babylon— 2b, he said to him: "The Lord your God spoke of this evil for this place. 3 And the Lord brought about and did just as he said. Because you sinned against the Lord and did not listen to his voice, this thing has come to you. 4 See, now, I have released you today from the manacles which are on your hands. If it seems good to you to come with me to Babylon, come and I will be considerate of you. But if it is displeasing to you to come with me to Babylon, do not be troubled about it. Look, all the land lies before you, 5 or if it seems good in your eyes to stay, turn back to Gedaliah son of Ahikam, son of Shaphan, whom the king of Babylon has appointed over the land, and stay with him among the people, or go wherever it seems right in your eyes to go." Then the captain of the guards gave him a ration and a present and set him free. 6a So Jeremiah went to Gedaliah son of Ahikam, at Mizpah [65] 40:1aβ after Nebuzaradan captain of the guards sent him from

[63] Rudolph, *Jeremia*, p. 211.

[64] I follow here the rearrangement of verses as given in *Biblia Hebraica:* 39:11, 12; 40:2a, 1b, 2b, transposing 40:1aβ after 6a and deleting 40:1aα, "The word which came to Jeremiah from the Lord."

[65] Inserting with *Biblia Hebraica* from 40:1aβ.

Ramah. *6b* And he remained with him in the midst of the people who were left in the land.

A Bitter Gleaning of Leaders of the Judean Rebellion

The editor of ch. 52 singles out for particular mention certain important personages who were taken into exile by Nebuzaradan captain of the guards. Already we have been told of the exile of King Zedekiah, himself blinded, after having witnessed the slaying of his sons, and then of his imprisonment in Babylon for life. We have also learned that "all the princes of Judah" were slain. We recall the rage of some of these same princes at Jeremiah at an earlier time when they thought he was deserting to the Chaldeans (37:15). It was they who had fanned the flame of Judean rebellion against the Chaldeans. Consequently, from the angle of Babylon they bore the heaviest guilt and had to suffer the severest penalty. But now the keen eye of Nebuzaradan conducts a search that results in "a bitter gleaning,"[66] a second group destined for the death sentence at Riblah, where the king of Babylon will slaughter them also. These were headed by the high priest Seraiah and the priest second in rank, Zephaniah son of Maaseiah, who only a few months before had been one of a delegation of three sent by King Zedekiah to consult Jeremiah at the critical moment when the Chaldean army had temporarily lifted the siege of Jerusalem (37:3). The next mentioned were three keepers of the threshold, important temple officials who were responsible for money that was brought into the temple and who stood next in rank to the high priest and his deputy.[67] In addition to these taken from among the cultic leaders, he took an important officer in military command, seven men who were known as counselors to the king, the scribe of the recruiting officer of the army, and sixty ordinary citizens. It is likely that some Judeans who had deserted to the Chaldeans helped Nebuzaradan to single out quickly those who had been leaders in the rebellion. These were all taken to Riblah and summarily executed. The last line of vs. 27 is the narrator's way of saying that the nation of Judah was no more.

52:24 And the chief of the guardsmen took Seraiah the high priest and Zephaniah the second priest, and three keepers of the threshold. 25 And from the city he took one eunuch who was in charge of the men of war and seven more of those who were in personal service[68] to the king, who were found in the city, and the[69]

66 This fine designation comes from Rudolph, *Jeremia*, p. 279.
67 Cf. A. W. Streane, *Jeremiah*, p. 218.
68 Lit., "of those who see the face of the king."
69 Prefixing the article as in II Kings 25:19.

scribe of the captain of the army who mustered the people of the land to military service, and sixty of the population of the land, who were lighted upon in the midst of the city. 26 And Nebuzaradan the chief of the guardsmen took them away to the king of Babylon at Riblah. 27 And the king of Babylon scourged them and put them to death in Riblah in the land of Hamath. So Judah went into exile from its land.

SPECIFIC NUMBERS OF EXILES

In vss. 28-30 we have a unique source from an unknown author, but one who was accurately informed. It gives specific numbers of various groups of Jewish exiles taken to Babylon in three different periods. His systems of chronology differs from that of the Deuteronomic historian, for his "eighteenth year" (vs. 29), manifestly 587, is the Deuteronomic historian's "nineteenth year" (vs. 12). The 3,023 people of vs. 28 were those captured from the Judean fortresses other than Jerusalem in 588. The 832 persons of vs. 29 refer to those taken from Jerusalem itself in 587. The 745 people of vs. 30 have to do with a deportation of Jewish captives, probably by a punitive expedition from Babylon five years later (582), to suppress anarchy and rebellion in the now Chaldean province.[70] We have accordingly no record in this source of the number taken from the population of Judah outside of Jerusalem in 587, which must have been very large.

52:28 This is the nation which Nebuchadrezzar took into exile in the seventeenth [year] of his reign [588], three thousand and twenty-three. 29 In the eighteenth year of Nebuchadrezzar [587] from Jerusalem eight hundred thirty-two. 30 In the twenty-third year of Nebuchadrezzar [582] Nebuzaradan chief of the guardsmen took into exile seven hundred forty-five Judeans, all together four thousand and six hundred persons.

THE STRIPPING OF THE TEMPLE

The Deuteronomic editor's interest in the temple and its cultic implements is remarkable. His description of what the Chaldean conqueror Nebuzaradan took from it as he stripped it of its valuables becomes an important source as to what the temple then contained in objects of gold, silver, and bronze (vss. 17-23). His account helps us appreciate how great, from the economic, architectural, and cultural point of view, was the achievement of King Solomon in the erection of so significant a structure as early as the last half of the tenth century. Incidentally, this passage enriches with additional emotional content the thrice-uttered cry of wonder, reverence, and awe, "The temple of the Lord is this place" (7:4).

[70] Cf. Skinner, Prophecy and Religion, p. 284.

52:17 And the pillars of bronze which were in the house of the Lord, and the stands, and the sea of bronze which was in the house of the Lord, the Chaldeans broke in pieces and carried off all bronze of them to Babylon. 18 And they took with them the pots, and the shovels, and the snuffers, and the bowls, and the pans, and all the vessels of bronze with which they ministered. 19 And the basins and the firepans, the bowls and the pots, the lampstands and the vessels, the sacrificial bowls, which were of gold and silver, the chief of the guardsmen took. 20 As regards the two pillars, the one sea, the twelve bronze [oxen] which were under the sea, the stands which King Solomon had made for the house of the Lord—the bronze of these was too much to be weighed. 21 And the pillars, eighteen cubits the height of the one pillar, and twelve cubits its circumference, and its thickness four fingers, hollowed out. 22 There was a capital, upon each, of bronze. The height of each capital was five cubits, and there was network and pomegranates on the capitals round about, all of bronze, and the same for the second pillar and pomegranates. 23 And there were ninety-six horizontal pomegranates, one hundred pomegranates in all upon the plaited work round about.

CHAPTER EIGHT

The Community of the Judean Remnant

THE LAND OF JUDAH WAS NOW BUT A JUDEAN PROVINCE OF THE CHALDEAN EMPIRE. NEBUCHADREZZAR HAS APPOINTED AS ITS GOVERNOR A STRONG JU-dean with his roots in the best soil of the nation, Gedaliah, son of Ahikam and grandson of Shaphan, and the Judean remnant are now to be under him. This Judean community was set up at Mizpah, a town about ten miles from Jerusalem, and probably to be identified with Nebi Samwil.

There were scattered through the territory of Judah groups of armed soldiers, Judean guerilla troops, under commanders who had been dispersed and had scattered at the Chaldean capture of Jerusalem. These officers learned of the establishment of the seat of the Judean remnant at Mizpah, and seven of them were glad to come with their men to consult with Gedaliah, who assured these military leaders that if they live in the land as co-operative subjects of the occupying Chaldean power, all will be well. When the Chaldean officers come to reap the material results of Judean labors in the field, vintage and olive orchards, the Judeans themselves will share generously in the yield. There lies before them also the task of laying hold upon Judean areas outside Mizpah which they can work. In many instances they would naturally continue to live in and work the regions which they had occupied before the fall of Judah. We sense the breadth of view and the statesmanship of Gedaliah, his freedom from any spirit of revenge toward the dominant Chaldean nation, and his expectation of fairness and co-operation both on the part of the Chaldeans and his fellow Judeans.

The response in the beginning was encouraging. When the news of the setup at Mizpah became generally known, Judeans who had sought refuge among the neighboring countries—all of whom, over against the Chaldeans, had been Judean allies—returned, rejoicing that a remnant for Judah had been granted them by Nebuchadrezzar. The yield of vineyards and orchards was already rich and abundant. Thus the account of the new setup is given by Baruch:

40:7 Now all the captains of the armies which had been distributed through the regions—they and their men heard that the king of Babylon had appointed Gedaliah son of Ahikam as governor over the land, and that he had entrusted to him men, women, and children, and some of the poor of the land who were among those who had not been exiled to Babylon. 8 So there came to Gedaliah at Mizpah: Ishmael son of Nethaniah, and Johanan son of Kareth, and Seraiah son of Tanhumeth, and the sons of Ephai, the Netophathite, and Jezaniah son of the Maacathite, they themselves and their men. 9 And Gedaliah son of Ahikam, son of Shaphan, swore to them and to their men saying: "Do not be afraid of being servants of the Chaldeans. Live in the land and serve the king of Babylon, and it will go well with you. 10 As far as I am concerned, lo, I am dwelling in Mizpah on your behalf as a servant of the Chaldeans, who will come to us. And as for you, harvest the wine and summer fruit and oil, then they will put back in your vessels. So continue to dwell in your towns which you have occupied." 11 Likewise all Judeans who were in Moab, and among the Ammonites, and in Edom, and those who were in any land, when they heard that the king of Babylon had given a remnant to Judah, and that he had appointed over them Gedaliah son of Ahikam, son of Shaphan, 12 all the Judeans returned from all the places to which they had been dispersed, and they came to the land of Judah to Gedaliah at Mizpah, and they gathered in wine and fruit in great abundance.

Rumors of the Plot of Ishmael

All seemed to be going well in the "remnant of Judah." The dispersed, defeated, and destroyed people were rallying to Gedaliah, when suddenly a sharp and discordant rumor came to Gedaliah's ears. Its bearers were Johanan and the other army captains; as military men they were perhaps in a position to be more closely in touch with currents of ill-will among neighbors of the reconstructed Jewish community than was Gedaliah. The rumor was that Baalis, chieftain of the Bedouin Ammonites, had concocted a plot wherein Ishmael son of Nethaniah, the first-named of the Judean leaders of the guerillas, would act as his tool in assassinating Gedaliah. The Judean reconstruction evidently did not fit in with the schemes of this tricky Trans-Jordan Bedouin chieftain. However, Baalis well knew that if he openly showed his hand against Gedaliah and his program he would experience the swift wrath of the Chaldeans. The wiley Baalis accordingly chose as his puppet the Judean captain, Ishmael, who had royal blood in his veins, being himself a member of the Davidic line (41:1), but of another strain than Zedekiah, and whose fires of envy and hatred of Gedaliah, already smoldering, could easily be blown into the flame of revolt.

Gedaliah, as Johanan and men like him felt, was indispensable to the Judean recovery, but when Johanan and the other military leaders warned him of Ishmael's plot, he gave it no credence. And when later Johanan appealed to him privately, imploring him, because of Gedaliah's own inexpendability for the Judean recovery, to grant Johanan authority to slay Ishmael before the latter's plot had time to materialize, he rebuked Johanan, maintaining that what he was saying had not an iota of truth in it.

40:13 Now Johanan son of Kareth and all the captains of the armies came to Gedaliah at Mizpah. 14 And said to him: "Do you not indeed know that Baalis king of the Ammonites has sent Ishmael son of Nethaniah to destroy your life?" But Gedaliah did not believe them. 15 Then Johanan son of Kareah spoke to Gedaliah secretly in Mizpah, saying, "Please, let me go and slay Ishmael, and no one will know. Why should he murder you and all Judah that is gathered to you, and the remnant of Judah perish?" 16 But Gedaliah son of Ahikam said to Johanan son of Kareah, "Do not do this thing, for what you are saying concerning Ishmael is a pack of lies [sheqer].

ISHMAEL THE MURDERER

In Duhm's examination of the possible motive of Ishmael he puts forward the likelihood that among the guerilla military leaders of Judah he was one of the most sharply antagonistic. He was

neither a mentally deranged man nor a common brigand, but an embittered Chaldean hater, presumably one of those who would have compelled king Zedekiah to war, and who, together with his partisans, had been brutalized by the war and so decided to become a ruthless guerilla. His patriotism was indeed tigerlike, malicious, but—taking into consideraton the circumstances—comprehensible.[1]

Along with the ambitions of royalty of which no doubt the crafty Baalis was aware, it was probably that element in Ishmael's make-up that fired him into action.

Only two months had elapsed since the fall of Jerusalem to the Chaldeans. The Judean remnant under Gedaliah had barely been organized when the suspicions of the army captains generally, and of Johanan in particular, were shown up to be by no means "a pack of lies" (sheqer), as greathearted Gedaliah had dubbed them, but all too justified. Ruthless and reckless Ishmael, accompanied by ten men, went to Mizpah to Gedaliah, who invited them to dine with him. While they were at meal, in bold violation of the Oriental law of hospitality Ishmael and his men rose up, set upon

[1] *Jeremia*, p. 319.

Gedaliah and his colleagues, including the Chaldean officials, and murdered them all.

41:1 Now it came about in the seventh month that Ishmael son of Nethaniah, son of Elishama of the seed royal, and ten men with him came to Gedaliah son of Ahikam to Mizpah, and they ate bread together at Mizpah. 2 Then Ishmael son of Nethaniah and the ten men who were with him rose up and struck Gedaliah son of Ahikam, son of Shaphan, with the sword and killed him whom the king of Babylon had appointed over the land. 3 And all the Jews who were with him, along with Gedaliah, at the feast, and the Chaldeans who were found there, and the men of war, Ishmael killed.

Evidently Ishmael, who had sized up Gedaliah as the willing tool of the Chaldeans in the Jewish remnant, stayed on at Mizpah to consolidate the issues of his horrible crime. Two days later he is still there when a delegation of religious pilgrims bound for the ruined altar at Jerusalem stop at Mizpah. There are eighty of them, and they hail from three famous sanctuary cities of the former northern kingdom of Israel, all of which, however, as we have seen, had been incorporated by King Josiah within the Judean domain (II Kings 23:15, 19-20). It was the seventh month, and they were bent upon celebrating the great autumnal festival of the New Year. But this year it was to be not a festival of gladness but sadness, and lamentation was their mood. Baruch pictures these pilgrims vividly. We see their shaven beards, their torn garments, their lacerated bodies; we hear their shrill cries of lament and note that they are laden with materials for sacrifice. There is something deeply moving in Baruch's account as he pictures these northern pilgrims coming along wailing as they come. Ishmael saw them approaching and went outside the town limits to meet them, as though he were receiving them on behalf of Gedaliah. But when they had come within the city, Ishmael brutally murdered them—all but ten who saved their lives by disclosing to Ishmael that they had supplies of provisions hidden in the fields. Ishmael flung the slaughtered dead into an ancient cistern. Baruch's interest in Judean history leads him to inform his readers (vss. 9-10) that famed King Asa of Judah, three centuries before, had built that very cistern as one of his defenses at Mizpah against the ruthless and crafty King Baasha of Israel (cf. I Kings 15:22).

His dastardly work done, Ishmael compelled the entire population of Mizpah, including the royal princesses who had been put in Gedaliah's care, and almost certainly including Jeremiah and Baruch, to proceed toward Ammon. It is as eyewitness that Baruch writes, for it is virtually certain that both of them saw with their own eyes the tragic collapse of the Judean remnant at Mizpah.

41:4 Now it happened on the second day after the murder of Gedaliah 5 that men came from Shechem, from Shiloh, and from Samaria, eighty men with beards shaven and with torn garments and lacerating themselves, and with meal offerings and with frankincense in their hands to bring to the house of the Lord. 6 And Ishmael son of Nethaniah went out from Mizpah to meet them. Now they were going along weeping, and when he met them, he said to them, "Come in to Gedaliah son of Ahikam." 7 And when they had entered into the midst of the city, Ishmael son of Nethaniah slaughtered them and flung them into the cistern, he and those who were with him. 8 Now ten men were found there who said to Ishmael, "Do not kill us, for we have hidden provisions in the field—wheat, barley, oil, and honey." So he refrained from killing them along with their companions. 9 Now the cistern into which Ishmael flung all the bodies of the men whom he had smitten—that was the one which king Asa had made for fear of Baasha king of Israel; Ishmael son of Nethaniah filled it with those slain. 10 Then Ishmael took captive all the rest of the people who were at Mizpah and the daughters of the king over whom Nebuzaradan, chief of guardsmen, had appointed Gedaliah son of Ahikam. So Ishmael son of Nethaniah made an early start and went to cross over to the sons of Amon.

Such news travels rapidly. Ishmael must have been known as a military leader of dispatch, for in his first mention of him Baruch puts him at the head of the list of the seven captains of Judah's fighting forces who reported to Gedaliah at Mizpah (40:8). Now when Johanan son of Kareah, and all the captains who were with him, heard the calamitous news of Ishmael's revolt, Johanan struck out with his fighting men to stop him. He knew the route Ishmael would likely take toward Ammon, and he encountered him at the pool of Gibeon, where several centuries before (II Sam. 2:13) the twelve picked soldiers of Abner, Saul's general, had contested against the twelve choice men of the army of Joab, the general of David. The Judean fighting forces, taken as a whole, were first of all Judeans, and thus loyal to the Mizpah program of Judean recovery. Consequently, when the captains and their forces marching under Johanan in pursuit of Ishmael came upon him at Gibeon, the Judeans whom Ishmael had forced to accompany him, in great joy and relief, immediately abandoned him and went over to Johanan. Ishmael himself, however, slipped out of their hands and with eight accomplices barely escaped into the Ammonite country of king Baalis. Thus runs Baruch's vivid account:

41:11 Now Johanan son of Kareah, and all the captains of the armies who were with him, heard of all the evil that Ishmael son of Nethaniah had done. 12 So he took his army and went to fight with Ishmael son of Nethaniah, and they encountered him at the great waters which were in Gibeon. 13 And when all the people who were with Ishmael saw Johanan son of Kareah, and all the captains of the armies which were with him, they rejoiced. 14 And all the people whom Ishmael had taken captive from Mizpah turned about to Johanan son of Kareah. 15 But Ishmael son of Nethaniah escaped, with eight men from before Johanan, and they went to the sons of Amon.

Due to the exigencies of the situation and neither by knowledge of nor appointment by Nebuchadrezzar, Johanan the son of Kareah now becomes leader of the Judean remnant. The predominant mood which then characterized them was fear, fear of the future, fear of what the Chaldean government would do to them. Johanan and the other army captains had a reasonably clear idea of what reprisals upon the Judeans Nebuchadrezzar would inflict as soon as he learned of the debacle at Mizpah. "What shall we do now? Where shall we go? What should be our next move?" Such questions were uppermost in their minds. They were desperately afraid. As Skinner remarks, they might well have "kept their heads and stayed on in the country, trusting to an impartial investigation by Nebuchadrezzar's government." [2] How great was the need of strong, fearless leadership right then in the remnant of Judah! How the greatness of what Gedaliah had been towers over the timidity of the fear-ridden men in whose hands were now left the responsibility of decision!

They did not return to Mizpah. There was strong sentiment in that huddled Judean remnant that the only safe policy was to make for Egypt, the land which since patriarchal times had served as a place of safety for Palestinian refugees. And at the time, as Volz says: "Egypt was the generally accepted mainstay for such as would flee from Babylonian domination." [3]

There was a "shelter of Kimham" not far from Bethlehem. Cornill,[4] in his understanding of the nature of this place, views it as "a place of shelter," a "harboring place," a khan or caravansary, such as would be suitable for a long stay. It may have been founded long ago by the wealthy Kimham, who proved to be so great a friend to King David (cf. II Sam. 19:37-40). Its very location headed the Judean remnant toward Egypt. So Johanan and the five loyal captains who were left took all available elements of the Judean remnant, not only those who had been at Mizpah, to this place.

[2] *Prophecy and Religion,* p. 282.
[3] *Jeremia,* p. 352.
[4] *Jeremia,* p. 418-19.

41:16 Then Johanan son of Kareah, and all the captains of the armies who were with him, took all the rest of the people whom Ishmael son of Nethaniah had taken captive from Mizpah, after he had killed Gedaliah son of Ahikam—warriors, and the women and children, and eunuchs, whom they brought back from Gibeon. **17** And they went and dwelt in Gidhroth[5]-Kimham,[6] which is near Bethlehem, so as to go toward the entrance to Egypt **18** because of fear of the Chaldeans, for they were afraid of them because Ishmael son of Nethaniah had killed Gedaliah son of Ahikam, whom the king of Babylon had set over the land.

In the meantime Jeremiah had won a position of respect among the Judean remnant. Its two most prominent leaders, Johanan and Azariah, were both military men. Evidently at a time when a large group of the people were together, in the name of the two leaders they respectfully ask Jeremiah to seek guidance on their behalf as to what is God's will that they should do. There is no question of their sincerity. They realize that for them it is an hour of most important decision (42:1-3). Jeremiah answers them with respect and in a spirit of genuine co-operation. He tells them that already (vs. 4) he is praying for God's guidance, and when God's word comes to him, he will speak it to them in fullness, without diminishing it or adapting it in the least. We are conscious of the deep sense of responsibility which the prophet here feels toward his people.

Before God as witness, on behalf of the people generally, the two leaders swear that whether the counsel of God is in accord with their desires or contrary to them, they will implicitly follow that counsel (vss. 1-6). Thus Baruch tells of their request and of the way it was met by the prophet:

42:1-6 Then all the captains of the armies and Johanan son of Kareah, and Azariah son of Maaseiah, and all the people, insignificant and great, drew near **2** and said to Jeremiah the prophet: "Please let our supplication fall before you, and intercede with the Lord your God on behalf of all this remnant (for we are left few from many, as your eyes see) **3** that the Lord your God may tell us the way in which we should go and the thing we should do." **4** And Jeremiah the prophet said to them: "I have heard; lo, I am praying to the Lord your God in accordance with your request, and everything which the Lord your God answers, I will declare to you. I will not withhold anything from you." **5** So they said to Jeremiah: "May the Lord be with us as true and faithful witness that in accordance with every word which the Lord your God will send you, so we will do. **6** Whether it is good or bad, we shall be obedient to the voice of the Lord our God to whom we are sending you, so that it may go well with us, for the voice of the Lord our God shall be yielded to."

---

[5] Reading with Hitzig, *Der Prophet Jeremia*, pp. 320-21, b⁺gidhrôth, "folds," after Josephus and Aquila; so also G. A. Smith, *Jeremiah*, p. 308.

[6] Reading with many MSS and Q⁺rê, kimhām, "shelter of Kimham."

It is illuminating as to the nature of prophetic revelation that Jeremiah at the time of their request is not ready to give them the word of God. Ten days elapse. We can be sure that for the prophet they were days of heart-searching in which he brooded and prayed and sought the divine presence and illumination. In this instance the prophet, in the method of discovering God's will, draws very near to the rank and file of Jews and Christians who pray for light upon a problem, then wait in earnest thought, quiet faith, and persistent eagerness until light comes.

At the end of ten days the revelation of God's will has come to the prophet with convincing certainty. Accordingly, he calls Johanan and the captains and all the people together, and he gives to them a clear counsel from God. God has revealed to him that the divine will for the Judean remnant is, in brief, "Stay in this land, and do it calmly, without fear of the king of Babylon." The people are to have confidence that God is with them as their helper, full of compassion and sympathy, and he will "cause them to dwell," that is, let them stay in their own land. But if tired of the struggle against the Chaldeans, and full of awful memories of the recent war—its frightful famine and hunger—they should go to Egypt to live, calamity will overtake them there, the sword, famine, and pestilence. Not a Judean will survive. The wrath of God will find them there just as it has already overtaken Jerusalem. Three times in his message Jeremiah emphasizes "thus has the Lord spoken" (vss. 9, 15, 18). We feel the deep and solemn earnestness of the prophet and are conscious of Baruch's attempt to give his master's very words.

42:7-18 Now it came about at the end of ten days that the word of the Lord came to Jeremiah. 8 So he called for Johanan son of Kareah, and for all the captains of the armies who were with him, and for all the people, young and old, 9 and said to them: Thus saith the Lord God of Israel, to whom you sent me to present your petition before him. 10 If you calmly stay in this land, I will build you and not tear [you] down, and I will plant you and not uproot you, for I have repented as regards the evil which I have done to you. 11 Do not be afraid of the king of Babylon, before whom you are afraid, do not be afraid of him, says the Lord, for I am with you to help you and to deliver you from his hand. 12 And I will bestow compassion upon you and will show you sympathy and will cause you to dwell in your own land. 13 But if you continue to say, "Let us not remain in this land," not listening to the voice of the Lord your God, but saying, "No, let us go to the land of Egypt where we shall not experience war, and where the blast of the trumpet will not be heard and where we shall not be hungry for bread, and there remain"—15 now in this case listen to the word of the Lord, remnant of Judah, thus says the Lord of hosts, God of Israel: If you firmly set your faces to go to Egypt, and go in to remain there, 16 it will happen that the sword of which you are afraid will overtake you in the land of Egypt, and the hunger about which you are concerned will pursue after you there into Egypt, and there shall you die. 17 And it will happen that all the men who have set their faces to go to Egypt to dwell there will die by the sword, famine, and pestilence, and they will not have a savior or a refuge from the evil which I am bringing upon them. 18 For thus says the Lord of hosts, God of Israel: Just as my anger and my wrath were poured out upon the inhabitants of Jerusalem, so shall my wrath be poured out upon you when you go into Egypt, and you will become an object of execration and an occasion of horror, and a cause of a curse, and a butt of reproach, and you shall never see this place again.

But the prophet's earnest words come to people whose minds are no longer open and receptive to the Lord's word. How different is their mood in 43:2 to what it was in 42:5-6! Then they were uncertain but open-minded, eager and teachable. But ten days have made a great change. Azariah seems here to take the initiative just as Johanan had before. Baruch describes the leaders generally as "presumptuous" and "refractory." They challenge the truthfulness of the prophet's message as the Lord's word when he tells them that God is opposed to the Judean remnant's seeking refuge in Egypt. How hard it must then have been for the remnant to sense what Jeremiah so deeply felt, that Judah's hope for the future lay, so far as the present was concerned, in co-operation with the Chaldeans, not in antagonism to them. To go to Egypt is to imperil the "future of hope," which temporary submission to Babylon will protect and assure.

But the people criticize Jeremiah on another count. They accuse him of being unduly influenced in this counsel by Baruch, who, as Babylon's puppet, has aroused the prophet to oppose their trend toward Egypt (43: 1-3). Such a word written in all truthfulness by modest and loyal Baruch himself helps us see that in Judean eyes he was a very influential figure. The modesty of his own story is here given welcome supplement as to Baruch's forcefulness and strength—even though their thought of him was wrong. They say in effect, "You preface what you tell us by 'Thus says the Lord,' but you would be more true to the facts if you would say, 'Thus says Baruch.'"

43:1 Now when Jeremiah had finished speaking to all the people all the words of the Lord with which the Lord had sent him to them—all these words 2 Azariah son of Maaseiah, and Johanan, son of Kareah, and all these presumptuous and refractory men spoke to Jeremiah saying, "What you are saying is false. The Lord has not sent you to us to say, 'You shall not go to Egypt to dwell there.' 3 But Baruch son of Neriah is inciting you against us, so as to give us into the hand of the Chaldeans to kill us and to carry us into exile to Babylon."

Jeremiah met this criticism directly by solemnly emphasizing the divine origin of this word of illumination and guidance. "The Lord it is who has spoken," he says. It is not Baruch, or indeed is it Jeremiah. The people did not ask him for his own judgment, or for that of Baruch. It was to the Lord the people had sent him. And it is from the Lord that he has come, bearing the Lord's word. Jeremiah was never more certain than in this critical moment that he had stood within the counsels of God. He recalls their former pledge of strict obedience to that word whether, when it should come to them, it were pleasing or displeasing. Jeremiah in 42:21 makes the solemn charge that they have not listened to God's voice but to the insistent urgence of their own desires. To go to Egypt is no escape from calamity, for they are going contrary to the divine will and calamity will overtake them there.

42:19 And Jeremiah answered, "The Lord it is who has spoken to you, remnant of Judah. 'You shall not go to Egypt.' You shall surely know that I have admonished you today. 20 For you have erred at the cost of your lives, for you sent me to the Lord your God saying, 'Pray on our behalf to the Lord our God and in accordance with all that the Lord our God says, so tell us and we will do [it].' 21 So I declared to you today, but you have not listened to the voice of the Lord your God as to all for which he sent me to you. 22 So now, know for certain that you shall die by the sword, famine, and pestilence in the place where you are eager to go to dwell."

THE REMNANT LEAVES FOR EGYPT

The die has been cast, the decision has been made. The deeply earnest voice of the prophet, courageous and sure, has been heard by the people and definitely rejected. The Judean remnant leaves for Egypt. This remnant was no inconsiderable number of people. The nucleus of it is what was left of the community at Mizpah, where had been set up a concentration of qualified Judeans, including the royal princesses. Johanan son of Kareah and the other four military officers were leaders of it. Those who had gathered at the caravansary of Kimham near Bethlehem before the decision had been made, formed a considerable part. Perhaps the largest contingent, not available when Johanan took leadership, were the remnant of Judah who had now returned from the surrounding nations, Ammon, Moab, Edom, and Phoenicia, that had been allies with the Judeans against the Chaldeans, and from wherever they had taken refuge during the Chaldean siege (43:6). It must have included, at the least, several thousand people. And among them were Jeremiah and Baruch, for although the remnant had ignored the prophet's counsel and frankly denied it, they nonetheless wanted him and his faithful scribe there. Of the journey to Egypt we know nothing. We know only that they came at length to Egypt's frontier fortress Tahpanhes, where already many Jews lived and from whom they would naturally receive a welcome. Thus Baruch's account continues.

43:4 So Johanan son of Kareah and all the captains of the armies and all the people would not listen to the voice of the Lord, to remain in the land. 5 And Johanan son of Kareah and all the captains of the armies took the entire remnant of Judah, which had returned from all the nations to which they had been driven out, to dwell in the land of Judah, 6 the men, the women and the children, and the daughters of the king, and all the persons whom Nebuzaradan chief of the guardsmen had left behind with Gedaliah son of Ahikam, son of Shaphan, and Jeremiah the prophet and Baruch son of Neriah. 7 And they went into the land of Egypt, for they did not listen to the voice of the Lord. So they went in as far as Tahpanhes.

NEBUCHADREZZAR WILL ALSO PLUNDER EGYPT

We would be glad at this point to know more about the life of this remnant of Judah in Egypt, how they made the journey, how they were received, and what contact they made upon arrival with Jews already there. We know that at that time there were Jews in Migdol and Tahpanhes, Jews who had come in earlier times, refugees from the rod of Assyria. But Baruch's narrative, upon which alone we are dependent, is not concerned with Jewish history in this period but solely with Jeremiah, what he did and what he said.

We have seen the Judean remnant stubborn and headstrong in their conviction that in Egypt they would be safe from the vengeance of the Chaldeans. The accession of Hophra as Pharaoh of Egypt, just one year before Jerusalem fell (588 B.C.), had given new hope in Judah. For while the Judean expectation of help from Egypt, when the final siege of Jerusalem was in progress, had ended in disillusionment, the old Egyptian program to recover Asiatic dominions lived anew in Hophra. Consequently the Judean remnant felt that now in Egypt they were under the protection of a monarch of real power. To the prophet's thought this idea that in Egypt they would be outside the range of the vengeance of the Chaldeans was an illusion.

It was in brooding over this attitude on the part of the Judean leaders as Jeremiah moved among them in Tahpanhes, his mind constantly open to divine light, that the Lord inspired in him again a striking symbolic prophecy. Shortly after they arrived in Tahpanhes a divine impulse came to the prophet which he explicitly obeyed. "In secrecy," which Skinner interprets as implying a night scene, Jeremiah took some large stones and buried them in the quadrangle into which opened the gate of the royal government office building. This act would be viewed only by a few of "the men of Judah," who would of course tell their compatriots all about it. To any passing Egyptians the prophet would be viewed simply as a Hebrew night worker preparing a durable platform for something. To his fellow Judeans it would mean that something of prophetic significance was being enacted by him, and they would watch with eyes concentrated on the prophet's acts, and listen with all their ears to its meaning. Then (43:10) comes the word of the Lord—he is bringing Nebuchadrezzar of Babylon in a plundering campaign against the Pharaoh of Egypt. He will bring the Egyptians under his power, and these buried and now invisible stones will form the foundation for the Chaldean invader's throne over which he will stretch his canopy. The very land in whose protection Judah, fleeing from the Chaldeans, has placed her trust, will itself be smitten by those same Chaldeans. Then the Egyptians will experience the same bitter calamities Judah has experienced—exile, death, and the destruction of the great Egyptian temples by fire, and as one concrete instance, the destruction of the pillars of the temple at Heliopolis (On) to the sun-god.

Jeremiah presents us with a graphic picture. A shepherd sits picking off one by one the lice which he finds upon his garment. The lice are powerless before his ruthless search. So Nebuchadrezzar will plunder one by one the cities of Egypt, for the Egyptians will be helpless in the face of this superior might, and the Chaldean King will withdraw in safety when he has taken off what he wants. The picture here vividly portrayed makes Egypt a laughingstock.

It adds weight to the prophetic import of these words of Jeremiah when we bring alongside of them the prophetic witness of Ezekiel, Jeremiah's younger contemporary, who ca. 570 B.C. also prophesied the plunder of the whole of Egypt at Chaldean hands, from Migdol in the extreme north to Assuan (Syene) in the extreme south (Ezek. 30:1-26).

Jeremiah's prophecy, which did not imply the permanent occupation of Egypt by the Chaldeans but a chastizing expedition of superior strength, was actually fulfilled in the thirty-seventh year of Nebuchadrezzar, 568,[7] some nineteen years after Jeremiah's words were spoken. Thus Baruch reports this symbolic prophecy:

[7] Cf. Langdon: *Die newbabylonischen Königsinschriften*, 1912, 206-7, No. 48.

43:8 And the word of the Lord came to Jeremiah in Tahpanhes saying: Take in your hand great stones and bury them in secrecy in the quadrangle which is in the gate of the palace of Pharaoh in Tahpanhes, in the sight of the men of Judah, 10 and say to them, "Thus says the Lord of hosts, God of Israel: Lo, I am sending and will take Nebuchadrezzar king of Babylon, and will set his throne upon these stones which I have hidden, and he will stretch out his canopy over them. 11 And he will come in and smite the land of Egypt. Those [marked] for death [he shall put] to death and those [doomed] to captivity he shall take into captivity, and those destined for the sword [he shall kill] by the sword. 12 And he shall kindle a fire in the temples of the gods of Egypt, and he shall burn them, and he shall clean out the land of Egypt [8] just as a shepherd picks the lice off of his garment, and he shall go out from there unmolested. 13 And he shall break in pieces the pillars of the temple of the sun, and the temples of the gods of Egypt he will burn in the fire."

THE LAST PROPHECY OF JEREMIAH

In ch. 44 we have the last prophecy of Jeremiah to the people of Judah. An assembly was called for all Judeans who were in Egypt. It included those living in the extreme northern part of the country (Migdol and Tahpanhes and Memphis), and those who were in upper Egypt (Pathros), both Jews who had been settled there a long time and those who were newcomers on the scene. It embraced the entire Diaspora in Egypt (44:8). Certain verses in this chapter—vss. 3-6, 9-14—represent the work of the Deuteronomic editor and are characterized by prolixity and Deuteronomic style. They are later in origin than the rest of the chapter, and form a supplement which expands, extends, and amplifies certain of Jeremiah's thoughts in the form of a homily. In that portion of the chapter we are in the atmosphere of the homiletical discussions in the synagogue.

When those amplifying vss. 3-6, 9-14 [9] are removed from the chapter the remainder (vss. 1-2, 7-8, 15-22) are a unity which forms the concluding portion of Baruch's narrative.

To the Diaspora in Egypt comes the Lord's message through Jeremiah. The truth of that word should now be clear to every Judean, that the desolation of Jerusalem and all Judah represents the Lord's judgment upon his people because of their sin (vss. 1-2). Why then have the Judeans cut themselves off from the midst of Judah so that there is no longer a Judean remnant in the land? For now in Egypt they are not holding themselves true to the Lord but are sacrificing to other gods in the land they have entered.

[8] That is, "Nebuchadrezzar shall clear out the land as a shepherd clears his garment of lice;" cf. G. A. Smith, *Jeremiah*, p. 310, n. 3.

[9] For Jer. 44:3-6, 9-14, see pp. 283-84.

They claimed that they were not surrendering their faith in the Lord. But it was extremely difficult to worship the Lord apart from the cult of the Jerusalem temple, and all the more so because the Deuteronomic law had centered all legitimate public worship at the temple in Jerusalem, which now lay in ruins. They felt, even as the Jews in Babylon had felt, how difficult it really was to "sing the songs of the Lord in a foreign land" (Ps. 137:4). They had not yet attained that level of religion where cultic acts are not necessary to religious faith.

Strangely enough it was evidently not Egyptian deities or rites to which they turned. But in the new foreign environment they found themselves turning back to the worship of the queen of heaven, to which Judah had been introduced under King Manasseh. They worshiped the Lord, yet they clung to other gods. Their peril was one of the most real in religious history, and to it Jeremiah was exceedingly sensitive. As Rudolph rightly sizes up the issue: "So at the end of his life there recurred the religious condition which characterized the beginning of his ministry, and in the face of this religious syncretism he had to set forth the basic demand of the Lord, 'You shall have no other gods before me.' " [10]

We are aware of Jeremiah's deep concern as he thus utters the Lord's message to the great assembly of Jews from the total extent of Egypt.

44:1 The word which came to Jeremiah for all the Judeans who were living in the land of Egypt, those living in Migdol and in Tahpanhes and in Memphis, and in the land of Pathros. 2 Thus says the Lord, God of Israel: You have experienced all the evil which I brought upon Jerusalem and upon all the cities of Judah, and lo, this day they are desolations with no one living in them. 7 So now, thus says the Lord God of hosts, God of Israel, Why are you doing great harm to yourselves in cutting yourselves off, man and wife, child and infant, from the midst of Judah so that there is no remnant left to you, 8 in that way provoking me by what your hands do, as you sacrifice to other gods in the land of Egypt into which you are come to settle, that you may be cut off, and that you may become an object of curse, and a butt of insult for every nation of the earth?

The words in vss. 15-18 are clearly spoken to Jeremiah by "a great company" of men and women, and in vs. 19 it is the women alone of the throng who speak to him. Jeremiah's earnest and solemn warning made no impression upon them. They lend no ear to his words, but rather will be obedient to vows that they have made to the queen of heaven, the deity whose wor-

---

[10] *Jeremia*, p. 225.

ship in their homeland,[11] as we have already seen, was vividly described in 7:17-18.

This cult, which since the Deuteronomic reform of Josiah's day had been largely suppressed, now flared into the open again. Instead of accepting Jeremiah's judgment that the calamity of Judah's national breakup was due to the people's failure to obey the call of God to national and personal repentance, these women maintain that calamity has come because they had ceased to worship the queen of heaven.

Thus Baruch reports their answer to Jeremiah's grave warning:

44:15 Then all the men who knew that their wives were burning incense to other gods, and all the women who were standing [by], a great company, answered Jeremiah saying: "16 As for the word that you have spoken to us in the name of the Lord—we are not listening to you at all. 17 But we will certainly do all that we have vowed to do, namely, to burn incense to the queen of heaven and to pour out drink offerings to her, just as we and our fathers have done, our kings and our princes, in the cities of Judah and in the streets of Jerusalem. Then we had our fill of bread and it went well with us and we did not experience calamity. 18 But since we stopped burning incense to the queen of heaven and pouring out drink offerings to her, we have lacked everything and have been consumed by the sword and famine." 19 And the women said, "So we will keep on burning incense to the queen of heaven and pouring out libations to her. Have we, without the knowledge of our husbands, baked cakes to make images of her and poured out to her drink offerings?"

The prophet for a moment turns from the women and speaks to all the people. Do they not realize, he says, that the Lord has seen their meticulous observance of this pagan and idolatrous cult—such care in the worship of the queen of heaven as they had never given to the worship of the Lord. But God cannot longer tolerate the evil of their lives and the idolatry which has turned the people from what should have been their sole aim—to listen to his voice and to walk in accord with his laws.

44:20 Then Jeremiah spoke to all the people—to the men and to the women, and to all the people who kept answering him—a word saying: 21 "As to the incense which you burned in the cities of Judah and in the streets of Jerusalem— you and your fathers, your kings and your princes, and the people of the land— did not the Lord remember it and did it not come into his mind? 22 And the Lord could not longer bear with the evil of your deeds, with the abomination which you have performed, so your land has become a butt of insult, an occasion of

[11] On an important lot of papyri found at Tûna el-Gebel in Upper Egypt mention is made of the queen of heaven, hitherto known only from this and other allusions (Jer. 7:18) in the book of Jeremiah. Cf. Albright, "Archaeology of the Ancient East," in Rowley, *Old Testament and Modern Study*, p. 47.

horror and an object of course, without inhabitant, as it is today. 23 Before which [abomination] you burned incense, and sinned against the Lord and did not listen to the voice of the Lord or to his laws and his statutes and did not walk by his solemn charges. Therefore this evil has befallen you such as [you are experiencing] this day."

The Women Could Have Turned the Tide

At vss. 24-25 the prophet turns again to the Jewish women who were the willful leaders in the worship of the queen of heaven. We sense in these two verses, packed as they are with intense feeling, how great in that hour of decision was the moral responsibility of womanhood in the Jewish remnant. They could have turned the tide. As Jeremiah saw their fidelity to that pagan cult he could not help realizing the power they might have been had they shown such fidelity in their vows to the Lord their God, whom alone they should serve. It is in irony but in the atmosphere of finality that he says: "You will indeed give effect to your vows." They have made their choice.

44:24 And Jeremiah said to all the women, "Hear the word of the Lord,
25 Thus says the Lord, God of Israel:
Ye women, you have said with your mouth
And have done with your hands,
'We will faithfully perform our vows
Which we have vowed
To burn incense to the queen of heaven,
And to pour to her libations.'
You will indeed give effect to your vows
And will surely carry out your words."

In vss. 26-28 Jeremiah proceeds to charge that because of the wrong choice they have made and which they have stated with such boldness, the true worship of the Lord by the Egyptian Jews shall cease. The worship of the Lord and the worship of the queen of heaven are irreconcilable opposites. They cannot exist together in the life of him who claims the Lord as his God. The Judean wives have chosen. But the Judean men have acquiesced. So in the Lord's name in these verses Jeremiah addresses himself to all Judeans in Egypt.

As at the very beginning of his ministry, Jeremiah became aware that the Lord was "awake over his word to perform it," so at the end of it he is solemnly aware that God is awake over his word to perform it in judgment upon the remnant of Judah. Keenly did he feel how great was the responsibility of this present Judean remnant for the future of Judean religion. The tragic fact was that they had no true faith in the Lord to pass on.

Jeremiah thinks of the familiar and potent formula which Jews always used in taking an oath or in making a solemn declaration, "As the Lord lives." Soon that formula will never be heard in Egypt. For the worship of the Lord on the part of these Egyptian Jews is a dead faith. In all that land soon the time will come when the worship of the Lord will be extinct. And what is now a religion empty of power will soon become apostasy— the conscious and utter forsaking of the Lord by Egyptian Jews. We seem to hear the prophet saying, "I appeal to time. Time will show whether your word or my word is true." These are the last recorded words of Jeremiah:

> 44:26 Therefore hear the word of the Lord, all Judah who have settled in the land of Egypt.
> Lo, I sware by my great name,
> Says the Lord,
> That my name shall no more be called
> By the mouth of any man of Judah,
> Saying, "As the Lord God lives,"
> In all the land of Egypt,
> 27a Lo, I am awake over them for evil
> And not for good.
> 28b And the remnant of Judah shall know
> Whose word shall stand—mine or theirs.[12]

The words of Jeremiah are at an end. And this final message carries the vivid memory of the first moments of his awareness of God's commission to him some forty years before and of the Lord's assurance, "I am awake over my word to accomplish it" (1:12).

---

[12] Vs. 27b and vs. 28a, which prophesy the destruction of all Jews in Egypt, are a prose expansion which misses the point Jeremiah is making, and vs. 28a is inconsistent with vs. 27b. They read:

27b And every Judean who is in the land of Egypt shall be consumed by the sword and by famine until they are annihilated. 28a And those who have escaped the sword shall return from the land of Egypt to the land of Judah few in number.

CHAPTER NINE

Supplements and Adaptations from the Diaspora

587-200

DIASPORA IS A GREEK WORD MEANING "DISPERSION" OR "SCATTERING." IT IS THE TERM WHICH WAS EMPLOYED BY THE HELLENISTIC JEWS LIVING DISpersed among the Gentiles after the captivity. The Diaspora began, however, as early as 734, when Tiglath-pileser III of Assyria carried as captives to Assyria Israelites from the Northern Kingdom (II Kings 15:29). At the end of the Northern Kingdom in 721, when Samaria fell to Sargon II of Assyria, he carried into exile an additional 27,290, settling them in various areas that were under Assyrian rule (II Kings 17:5-6). As we have seen, it was to the descendants of these two groups of Israelites that Jeremiah wrote chs. 30–31.

We have observed that in two movements of the exile of Judeans—one in 598, the other in 587, close to a century and a third later than those of the Israelites, many thousands of Judeans were carried into exile in Babylon by the Chaldeans under Nebuchadrezzar. Famed historian of the ancient world, Eduard Meyer, estimates that the whole population of Israel before the Assyrian and Babylonian captivities numbered 750,000.[1] Six centuries later, as Bevan maintains, the Jews in the Roman Empire are calculated to have numbered something between four and seven millions. "Israel, a scattered and subject people, had become a far more important factor in the world—numerically at any rate—than Israel when composed in two little Palestinian kingdoms under independent kings." [2]

How potent was the influence of that very considerable and widely scattered population of Jews? This question is informingly and authoritatively answered by Bevan, and it sets the Diaspora in a significant light:

[1] Cf. Bevan and Singer, "Hellenistic Judaism," in *The Legacy of Israel*, p. 1.
[2] *Ibid.*, 29.

There was only one tradition in the Mediterranean world which did not go down under the predominance of Greece and Rome, which met with equal power and showed a unique stubbornness of resistance—the tradition of Israel. Judaism might indeed enter into various combinations with Hellenism, in which the Jewish tradition underwent notable modification, but it always gave as well as received, and in the end, Greek intellectual culture and Roman imperial sagacity had to accept the supremacy of a Hebraic religion.[3]

In the transition from Israel in Palestine, with its temple-centered, sacrifice-centered religion, to Israel in the Diaspora with its synagogue-centered religion and its emphasis upon corporate and personal prayer, Jeremiah played a most significant role. The exact origins of the synagogue are not known. Welch is convinced that "Jeremiah was the spiritual founder of the synagogue." Continuing, he maintains that "the conviction which gave vitality to the synagogue—that the Jew could live a loyal Jew without sacrifice, but could not so live without prayer—derived directly from the prophet." [4]

The last authentic utterance we have from Jeremiah, as we have seen, was his great address to a large congregation of Jews of the Diaspora in Egypt ca. 586. That is the last recorded information about him. The profoundest voice among the prophets had ceased. But his personality and influence lived on. His thoughts were brooded upon, seen from time to time in new light, and were applied to concrete situations.

We have seen the influence of Jeremiah's letter (ch. 29) to the exiles. Somewhat comparable to this letter to the exiles would be these messages stimulated by the teaching of Jeremiah and written by the Deuteronomic redactor, often but not always related to some nugget of truth as it had come fresh and creative from Jeremiah's lips or from his pen.

In many of these words the soul force of the master mind is evident. In others we are aware of a far lower level of insight and feeling. These adaptations and supplements range in time from shortly after 587 until, as in one instance, near 200. There are five groups into which these supplements and adaptations may be divided, representing either specific geographical centers of interest or topical areas of concern. The first geographical center is Egypt, where already thousands of Jews were living at the time when Jeremiah vanished from the scene, probably shortly after 586. The second geographical area stands apart as the most unrelated of all to the prophet. It includes Damascus, which is not one of the nations to which the

[3] *Ibid.*
[4] *Jeremiah, His Time and His Work*, p. 248.

cup of the Lord's wrath was handed in Jeremiah's vision (25:15-26). It also includes Moab and Edom but bears no relation to the teaching of Jeremiah. The third geographical area of concern centers in Babylon. It was to this area that Jeremiah looked for a future of hope. A fourth, and topical, area is the Jews of the Dispersion generally, seen under the aspect of the judgment of the Lord. A fifth, and topical, area is the Jews of the Dispersion generally, but seen under the aspect of the saving grace of God. In these five areas now arise adaptations and supplements to the great prophet's thought. These messages read in the synagogues and in little gatherings of Jews would have an effect on the Jews who were present in some measure comparable to the effect Jeremiah's own letter had upon the earliest exiles in Babylon.

The greatest problem which the Jew faced after 587 was the problem of survival. Spiritually speaking, Jeremiah himself had paved the way for this by his teaching that the institutions of religion—temple, ark, law— were not essential, for the seat of religion is in the individual heart. It is not an affair of cult but of the relation of the individual soul to God. And Ezekiel had taught that every Judean was directly related to God, not as member of a race or nation, but purely as an individual person. The soul that sins shall die. The soul that does righteously shall live. We can well realize how the sense of serious responsibility for Jewish survival must have filled the souls of thoughtful Jews wherever even two or three of them met together in whatever section of the world—after 587—they were to be found.

The signficance of this was borne home upon me by an experience in Iraq in 1940. One Sunday evening, through the kindness of a Christian missionary to the Arabs in Iraq, I was permitted to meet with a little group of Jewish laymen at Hilla, the modern city just outside of which lie the ruins of ancient Babylon. They were but one little group of Jews among the many thousands who are in Iraq today, and of which at that time 100,000 were in Baghdad alone. Through the missionary as interpreter I talked with them. I tried to find out whether that group of Jewish men had any awareness of a sense of linkage with their forefathers who had been first exiled to Babylon in 598 and 587.

To my surprise there was no consciousness of that linkage. For them there was but one problem of Jews in Iraq, the problem of Jewish survival, and they were together that very night to do something about it. That evening helped me to understand the encouragement that such a letter as Jeremiah wrote shortly after 598 would bring to group after group of exiles when read to them, wherever they were settled. Similarly, we must think of these later supplements, adaptations, and applications of the great prophet's thoughts as coming to groups of Jewish exiles in places where they were settled, with messages of warning, judgment, encouragement, and hope.

MESSAGES OF JUDGMENT TO JEWS IN EGYPT

1. *Preaching on Idolatry During the Exile* (44:3-6, 9-14).

This section is the work of the Deuteronomic editor. Just as the records of the history of Israel come down to us through the hand of the editors who write under the influence of the Deuteronomic interpretation of that history, so similarly "we have in the Deuteronomic source in the Book of Jeremiah an example of how the prophet's preaching was made serviceable to the preservation of the religous character of the exilic congregation." [5] These congregations of Jews in the exile, wherever they were, needed to be taught that they had brought on themselves the suffering of exile, and that it had its bearing upon how they should act in the future. These passages are largely "samples of lectures in the exilic synagogue." [6] For the most part, at the heart of them are words of Jeremiah of which we would not otherwise know. These sections in the book are very important as they help us see Jeremianic thoughts feeding into the developing thought and soul life of the synagogue.

In vss. 3-6 this Deuteronomic editor starts from Jeremiah's thought of the evils which the Lord had brought upon Jerusalem and Judah. He goes on to speak of the idolatry of the Jews and their worship of other gods. The prophets whom God sent to warn them were given no heed. The destruction of Jerusalem and Judah was the judgment of God upon his people.

44:3 Because of their evil which they did so as to provoke me to anger by walking after, by sacrificing to, and by serving other gods which they did not know. 4 But I sent to you all my servants the prophets early and often saying, "Pray do not practice this abominable thing which I hate." 5 But they would not listen and would not incline their ear so as to turn from their evil, so as not to sacrifice to other gods. 6 So my wrath poured forth and my anger consumed the cities of Judah, and the streets of Jerusalem, and they became a waste, even as [they are] this day.

In vss. 9-14 the Deuteronomic writer calls attention to the evils of the fathers of Judah, of the kings and their wives, and of the present Judeans and their wives. For the Judeans of the present have not learned the lessons

[5] Cf. Rudolph, *Jeremiah*, p. xvi.

[6] *Ibid.*

of the past. So the Lord has determined to destroy those whose hearts are set upon dwelling in Egypt. To that land the judgment of God which they are trying to escape will follow them, mediated by the sword, famine, and pestilence. This deserved judgment will bring upon them disgrace and ignominy. Of those Judeans who entered Egypt there will not be a single survivor or fugitive. However great may be their longing to return, they will not return. Thus the Deuteronomic editor writes:

44:9 Have you forgotten the evils of your fathers, and the evils of the kings of Judah and their wives, and your own evils, and the evils of your wives, which they did in the land of Judah and in the streets of Jerusalem? 10 And they have not restrained themselves unto this day, and they were not afraid and did not walk in my law and in my statutes which I set before you and before your fathers.

11 Therefore thus says the Lord of hosts, God of Israel: Lo, I am setting my face against you for evil, to cut off all Judah. 12 And I will take the remnant of Judah which set their faces to enter the land of Egypt to dwell there, and all who are in the land of Egypt shall be consumed; they shall fall by the sword and they shall be consumed by famine, young and old: they shall die by the sword and by famine, and shall become [the cause of] an execration [an occasion] of horror [an object of] a curse and a [butt of] scorn. 13 And I will punish those living in the land of Egypt just as I have punished Jerusalem, by the sword, by famine, and by pestilence. 14 And there shall not be a fugitive or a survivor of the remnant of Judah entering into the land of Egypt to dwell there, who will be for returning to the land of Judah. They may be desirous of returning so as to dwell there, but they shall not return.

2. Few Jews Will Return from Egypt (44:27b-28a).

The Deuteronomic Editor has little confidence in any significant return to the land of Judah on the part of Jews who were then in Egypt.

44:27b And every Judean who is in this land of Egypt shall be consumed by the sword and by famine until they are annihilated. 28a And those who shall have escaped the sword shall return from the land of Egypt to the land of Judah few in number.

3. Jews in Egypt Will Not Be Safe from Nebuchadrezzar (44:29-30).

This passage in all probability is a "prophecy after the event," representing an interpolation which reflects events which took place in Egypt later than Jeremiah's lifetime. The Jews who are there feel that they are far away from Chaldean destruction. And they are trusting in the protection of Egypt, just as in Jerusalem the Jews had looked with straining eyes toward help from Pharaoh Hophra (called Apries by Herodotus). But Hophra was dethroned in 570 and in 564 was strangled by an Egyptian mob,[7] and Nebuchadrezzar himself, sworn enemy of the Jews, invaded Egypt in 568. Thus runs the interpolater's supplement:

44:29 And this shall be a sign to you, says the Lord, that I will be punishing you in this place, in order that you may know that my words against you for evil will surely be confirmed. 30 Thus says the Lord, Lo, I am about to give Pharaoh Hophra king of Egypt into the hand of his enemies, and into the power of those who are seeking his life, just as I gave Zedekiah king of Judah into the hand of Nebuchadrezzar king of Babylon, his enemy, and the one seeking his life.

4. The Jews Are Not Safe in Upper Egypt (46:25-26).

These verses form a later editorial supplement in prose to vs. 24, which prophesied the Chaldean mastery of Egypt. The writer of this supplement disillusions the Jews who feel that they are safe in Thebes, famed capital of Upper Egypt, whose guardian deity was Amon. For that very capital will succumb to Nebuchadrezzar of Babylon. At the time this editor writes, however, Egypt is again, as of old, experiencing a period of peace.

46:25 Says the Lord of hosts, God of Israel: Lo, I am about to punish Amon of Thebes and Egypt, its gods and its kings and Pharaoh, and those who have confidence in him. 26 And I will give them into the hand of those who are seeking their lives, yes, into the hand of Nebuchadrezzar king of Babylon, and into the hand of his servants. But afterward it will remain undisturbed as in days of old.[8]

MESSAGES OF JUDGMENT TO DAMASCUS, MOAB, AND EDOM

1. Damascus. How Thou Art Deserted, O City of Fame (49:23-27). With the final breakup of the Assyrian Empire in 609, Damascus, which since 732 had been under its sway, was evidently incorporated along with Hamath (II Kings 23:33) into the area of control exercised by Pharaoh Neco of Egypt. Probably its later transfer after 605 to the Chaldean orbit of domination was effected without challenge.

This oracle against Damascus (49:23-27) almost certainly does not come from Jeremiah. Damascus does not appear in Jeremiah's strategically important list of nations (25:17-26) who are to drink of the Lord's cup of punishment. From the standpoint of geography, in its present position it represents an intrusion of a northerly power between the authentic oracles against Edom on the one hand, and that against the Arabian tribes on the other. Moreover, as compared with the authentic oracles, it is extremely

---

[7] Herodotus History II. 161-62, 169.

[8] Vss. 27-28 are here an editorial insertion; see 30:10-11 (p. 97), where they are original.

mild and is entirely lacking in the moral quality which is present in every utterance of Jeremiah where he brings the nations of the area to the bar of the Lord's judgment.

Hamath is an Aramaean city-state on the Orontes River about 110 miles north of Damascus, and Arpad is an Aramaean city-state 95 miles north of Hamath, identified with *tell erfad* 10 miles north of Aleppo.[9] To these cities bad news has come as regards Damascus, which has put them into anxious trepidation. The population of Damascus has been seized by panic and put to flight. This delightful merchant city of great fame, situated in a richly watered oasis right on the edge of the Arabian Desert, has become deserted.

> 49:23 Concerning Damascus.
> Hamath is disconcerted and Arpad,
>   For bad news they have heard;
> Their heart has melted away from anxiety,
>   They cannot show themselves calm.
> 24 Damascus has lost heart, she has turned to flee,
>   For panic has seized her.
> 25 How thou art deserted, O city of fame,
>   City of delight!

Thus far the oracle itself; vss. 26-27 are an addition. Vs. 26 has been editorially inserted from the authentic oracle against Babylon (50:30). And vs. 27 has been added from the authentic oracle of the prophet Amos against Damascus (Amos 1:3; cf. 1:14).

> 49:26 Therefore her young men shall fall in her streets,
>   And all the warriors shall be destroyed.
> 27 And I will kindle a fire in the wall of Damascus,
>   And it will devour the palaces of Ben-hadad.

2. *Two Passages Centering in Moab* (48:29-39, 43-47). Jer. 48:29-39 reveal many parallels to the oracle against Moab as found in Isa. 15–16 which dates from 550-540 and rests upon an earlier Moabite poem.[10] But the selection of material and the order of its presentation shows without a doubt that the original oracle is that in the book of Isaiah. It is not likely that any of this section comes from Jeremiah.

In his taunting wail against Moab the prophetic author of this oracle gives central emphasis to Moab's haughty pride and boastful arrogance, with

---

[9] Cf. S. R. Driver, *Jeremia*, p. 297, noted.
[10] Pfeiffer, *Introduction to the Old Testament*, p. 444.

which is coupled unrighteousness in national conduct (vss. 29-30). He expresses his own sharp antagonism to the metropolis of Moab, Qir-Heres (called in Isa. 15:1, Qir-Moab), which is to be identified with modern el-Kerak, situated on the Wadi Kerak (vs. 31). The famous vineyard area of Moab reaches from Sibmah, identified by Abel [11] with Qurn el-Kibsh, between Heshbon and Nebo, to Jazer, identified by Noth [12] with el-jādūde, to the north of Heshbon. Using prophetic hyperbole, the prophet describes the vines of this great vineyard area as spreading out in luxuriance even to the eastern shores of the Dead Sea (vs. 32). But Moab will be bereft of gladness. For Moab there will be no joyous treading of grapes (vs. 33). The grapes must be abandoned ungathered upon the vines. The prophet, whose spirit is sharply antagonistic toward Moab, gloats over his fate.

48:29 We have heard of the pride of Moab—
          Very proud—
          Of his haughtiness, his conceit, and his majesty,
          Yes, his heart is exalted.
30 As for me, I know his arrogance,
          And his boastings are unfounded.
          Not as they boast do they act.
31 Therefore I utter a wail for Moab,
          Aye, against all Moab I cry,
          Against the men of Qir Heres [Kerak] I cry.
32 More than over Jazer, I weep over you,
          O vine of Sibmah!
          Your tendrils crossed over to the sea,
          Until they reached Jazer.
          Upon your summer fruit and your vintage
          He will devastatingly fall.
33 And gladness and joy are taken away
          From the land of Moab.
          I have caused wine to fail from the wine vats;
          The treader [of grapes] will not tread out with shouting.

Vss. 34-39 are in prose. Cries are imagined going up from Moabite cities, from Elealeh, which is chirbet el'al, a little north of Heshbon,[13] as far as Jahçah, chirbet iskander, on the Wadi el-wale,[14] and from Zoar, south of the Dead Sea, to Horonaim in southern Moab, probably at el-'araq,[15] south of Kerak. Here the watercourse, en-numera—possibly identical with the

---

[11] *Géographie de la Palestine*, II, 458.
[12] *Das Buch Joshua*, p. 52.
[13] Abel, *op. cit.*, p. 312.
[14] *Ibid.*, p. 354.
[15] So A. Musil, *Arabia Petraea*, I (*Moab*), 73, 75.

"waters of Nimrim," arises. This fertile region will be devastated (vs. 34).
The familiar pilgrimages to the high places and the customary sacrifices
will cease in Moab. Before the contemplated destruction, the prophet's heart
laments over Moab and over the people of the Moabite metropolis, Qir
Heres (el-Kerak), in a lament such as is accompanied by the plaintive
music of the flute.

Imaginatively the prophet describes the people of Moab, as with shaven
heads, clipped beards, cuttings on hands, and sackcloth on loins, they perform the cultic rites of lamentation. From the roofs of the houses, and in
open places of the cities and town, he hears the wailing cries. For Moab,
once proud and prized, is soon to become an object of disgrace, a butt
of derision and a terrifying warning to other nations.

48:34 **The cry of Heshbon and Elealeh unto Jahaz; they have uttered their voice
from Zoar to Horonaim and Eglath-Shelishiyyah, for the waters of Nimrim
also will become a devastation.** 35 **And I will cause to cease in Moab, says the
Lord, going up to the high place and sacrificing to his gods.** 36 **Therefore my heart
is toward Moab, it murmurs like the flutes; and my heart is toward the men of
Qir Heres; it murmurs like the flutes. Therefore the abundance which he has gotten
has perished.**

37 **Yes, every head is bald and every beard is clipped. Upon all hands are
lacerations and upon all loins is sackcloth.** 38 **Upon all roofs of Moab and in its
broad open places—all of it is one wailing. For I have broken Moab as though
it were vessels in which no one delights, says the Lord.** 39 **How he is dismayed!
How Moab has shamefully turned his back! So Moab will become a butt of derision and an occasion of terror to all around it.**

Jer. 48:43-47 are not original but are dependent on Isa. 24:17-18a, which
dates from the Greek period of Old Testament history (after 333), and the
thought context of that passage is the inescapable world judgment of the
Lord. Here the prophet is made to apply that judgment solely to Moab.
Terror, the pit, and the snare—one of these three calamities—is to be the
lot of every Moabite. The oracle against Moab comes to its end in a vivid,
imaginative picture. To paint it the poet reaches back into the ancient
poetry of Israel's early triumph over the Amorites at Heshbon, when that
was the capital of Sihon, the Amorite king, who had humiliated the Moabites,
"the people of Chemosh" (Num. 21:27-29). Now again the Moabites are to
be humiliated, but by another foreign power, and again "Heshbon is
viewed as the starting place of the conflagration which is to desroy Moab." [16]

[16] Driver, *Book of the Prophet Jeremiah*, p. 290, note c.

There stand the Moabite fugitives from disaster beside Heshbon. And now once again from that ancient capital starts that inescapable fire of destruction, now at Chaldean hands, in which the people of Chemosh will perish as a nation, and its sons and daughters will be exiled to Babylon. In vs. 47a the one who wrote these words—perhaps impressed by Jeremiah's promise of a future of hope (29:11)—looks forward to a time when God will turn the sad lot of Moab to better days. The last line of the oracle is the editor's comment that the oracle of judgment upon Moab here comes to its end. Thus writes this late author:

> 48:43 Terror and the pit and the snare
> Are upon you, inhabitants of Moab!
> Says the Lord.
> 44 The fugitives from the terror
> Shall fall into the pit;
> And he who escapes from the pit
> Shall be taken by the snare.
> For I will bring these things to Moab,
> The year of their punishment,
> Says the Lord.
> 45 Beside Heshbon they stand—
> Fugitives from the terror.
> For fire has gone forth from Heshbon,
> And a flame from the City of Sihon;
> And it has devoured the temples of Moab,
> And the hairy crown of the warriors.
> 46 Woe to you, Moab!
> You have perished, people of Chemosh!
> For your sons have been taken captive,
> And your daughters into captivity!
> 47 But I will turn the fortunes of Moab in the future.
> As far as here is the judgment upon Moab.

3. *Edom* (49:12-22). *Edom Must Drink the Cup of the Lord's Vengeance.* This section does not come from Jeremiah but dates from a time considerably after the fall of Jerusalem in 587 and the exile of the Judeans. It reflects the Judean antagonism toward Edom which received sharp impetus at the time of the capture of Jerusalem "in the day of his calamity," when, as Obad. 11 informs us, Edom "stood aloof" toward the sad plight of his brother Judah.

Vss. 12-13 are in prose. Judah considered itself to be in a peculiar sense the Lord's people, and so felt that it had the right to expect that it might escape the cup of the Lord's judgment. Yet it was Judah's lot to drink of that bitter cup. If this were the case, surely Edom must suffer. Edom too will be required to drink of the cup of the Lord's severe judgment. For the Lord has bound himself by oath to reduce Bozrah, Edom's capital, to ruins.

49:12 For thus says the Lord, Lo, if those whose rightful due it is not to drink of the cup must certainly drink, are you one who shall be altogether exempt from punishment? You shall not be exempt, but shall certainly drink. 13 Surely I have sworn by myself, says the Lord, that Bozrah shall become a cause of horror, a butt of insult, a desolation, and an object of a curse, and all its cities shall become perpetual ruins.

Vss. 14-16 are in poetry. Imaginatively a message from the Lord is imparted to Edom, revealing that God has sent his envoys among the nations to arouse them to fight against the hated Edomites, who for the time being feel quite secure in their mountain fastnesses. The shudder of fear which other nations have felt when they looked toward Edom's impregnable heights has deceived that nation into a false sense of security, from which God will bring it down in humiliation. Thus God is represented as speaking:

49:14 A report have I heard from the Lord's presence,
　　　That an envoy has been sent among the nations.
　　"Assemble yourselves and come against her,
　　　And arise to the battle!"
　15 For, lo, I will make you small among the nations,
　　　Despised among men.
　16 The shudder at you has deceived you,
　　　The presumption of your heart.
　　You who dwell in the concealed retreats of the rock,
　　　Who hold the height of the hill:
　　Although you make your nest on high like the eagle,
　　　From there I will bring you down,
　　　　Says the Lord.

Vss. 17-18 are in prose. Desolate Edom will then be a butt of scorn to all passers-by and its destruction will be an appallment comparable to that of Sodom and Gomorrah, a ruins bereft of all human occupancy.

49:17 And Edom shall become a desolation: everyone who passes by it shall be appalled and shall hiss [in derision] because of all its blows. 18 As at the destruction of Sodom and Gomorrah and their neighbor cities, says the Lord, no one shall settle there and no human being shall dwell in it.

Vss. 19-22 are in imaginative poetry. In vss. 19-20 a vivid illustration is used to portray the desolation which Edom will experience. A lion is pictured as moving swiftly out of the thicket of the Jordan and making for a watered meadow where it startles and falls upon the well-fed flocks of Edom. The Lord is such a lion. While shepherds could ordinarily frighten a lion away, no one is powerful enough to frighten away the Lord. Before him no human shepherd can stand. And God himself has determined upon the complete destruction of Edom. Not only the great of the people (choicest rams) but the most ordinary as well (poorest of the sheep) will be dragged away (vs. 20). Edom will fall with such a crash that the reverberation of its collapse will be heard at the far-off Sea of Reeds, where in ancient times, Egypt's army in pursuit of fleeing Israel was destroyed (vs. 21). In vs. 22 Nebuchadrezzar is vividly pictured coming against Edom like a majestic griffon-vulture, swooping down with its mighty wings upon its prey and bringing to the warriors of Edom woe such as is comparable to that of a woman in birth pangs. The author of the oracle against Moab (48:40-41) has made use of this same striking picture.

49:19 Lo, as a lion goes up
     Out of the thicket of the Jordan to a watered meadow,
   So will I startle the flock of its [Edom's] pasturage,
     And I will muster the choicest of its rams.
   For who is like me, and who can summon me?
     And who is the shepherd who can stand before me?
20 Therefore listen to the design of the Lord
     Which he has determined against Edom,
   And his plans which he has devised
     As regards the inhabitants of Teman.
   Surely even the most inferior of the sheep shall they drag away;
     Surely their own meadow is appalled at them.
21 At the news of their fall the earth quakes;
     The report of it is heard in the Sea of Reeds.
22 Lo, as an eagle mounts up and darts through the air,
     And spreads its wings over Bozrah,
   So the heart of the warriors of Edom will be on that day
     Like the heart of a woman in travail.

MESSAGES CENTERING IN BABYLON

1. *You Must Be Servants in a Foreign Land* (5:18-20). This forms a supplement which dates from the Exile. The verses interpret the Exile as a time when the Judeans, who had abandoned the Lord, and even while in their own land had served foreign gods, are now as a political conse-

quence serving foreigners in a foreign land. To the Judeans in exile, who, as regards all this, raise the question "Why?" this is the Deuteronomist's answer.

5:18 But even in those days, says the Lord, I will not make a complete end of you. 19 And when they ask, "Why has the Lord our God done all these things to us?" you are to say to them: "Just as you abandoned the Lord and served foreign gods in your own land, so must you be servants in a land that is not yours."

Vs. 20 which in the face of vs. 21 is superfluous, is intended by the editor to make it clear that the following utterance of the prophet (vss. 21-25) is not addressed to the exiles but to the Judeans in Palestine.

> 5:20 Declare this in the house of Jacob,
> And publish it in Judah saying. . . .

2. *Condemnation of the Idolatry of the Judean Exiles* (16:10-13). It was inevitable that when the prophet uttered such words and backed them up by refusing to have any share in the mourning rituals, it would give rise to serious questions on the part of Judeans. The Deuteronomic editor who is responsible for this section states them clearly. Peake is probably right in saying that large numbers of exiles may well have felt that "the destruction of the state had snapped the tie which bound them to the Lord." [17]

16:10 And when you declare to this people all these words, they will say to you: "Why has the Lord threatened us with all this evil, and what is our iniquity and what is our sin which we have perpetrated against the Lord our God?" 11 You shall say to them: "Because your fathers forsook me, says the Lord, and followed other gods and served them and bowed down to them, but me they forsook and my law they did not observe. 12 And [because] you have done more wickedly than your fathers, and lo, you—each living in accordance with the stubbornness of his evil heart, not listening to me—13 I will hurl you out of the land to a land which you do not know, and you and your fathers shall there serve other gods which will not show you favor."

3. *The Beginnings of Ecclesiastical Prayer in the Exile* (32:17-23). In the exilic times during which the Deuteronomic editor did his work, the need was felt at this point (32:16) for a longer prayer, and vs. 17, beginning "Lo, thou hast made the heavens," immediately following Jeremiah's

---

[17] *Jeremiah*, I, 217.

lamenting address to God, "Alas, Lord God," through vs. 23 were inserted.

Volz says of this prayer (vss. 17-23): "The imposing description of the divine attributes and the formal manner of expression are well adapted to a public service of worship and to a congregational prayer, but not to the inner desires of an individual suppliant." [18] We have evidence here, and in the other portions of the Deuteronomic editor's work, of the exilic use of the prophecies of Jeremiah in the synagogue. In such utilization of the prophetic scriptures during the Exile there was a felt need to expand and adapt the personal prayers for use as public prayers, even such prayers as this. Thus these verses become historical evidence for the early prayers of the synagogue, and so, as Volz suggests, they are "a weighty document for the history of liturgy. We have here the beginnings of ecclesiastical prayer." [19]

The exilic author of this prayer was familiar with the Decalogue (Deut. 5:6-21). He addresses God as the omnipotent creator; he goes on to celebrate him as great in counsel, mighty in deeds (vs. 19), omniscient and just in retribution—the son's suffering being due to the iniquity of the fathers, as accords with the Decalogue (vs. 18). But at the same time God shows mercy to thousands. Indeed, he deals out to each his just desert (vs. 18).

At vs. 20 the suppliant enters into the sphere of history. He celebrates God as the mighty worker in Israel and in mankind, first in the great event of the Exodus from Egypt (vs. 20-21), and second in the invasion and settlement of Canaan (vss. 22-23). But God's people across the centuries have been disobedient to their Lord (cf. 7:23), and consequently the evil which Judah has experienced by exile is but its manifestation of God's judgment upon his people (vs. 23).[20] Thus speaks the hymnlike prayer, the Deuteronomic supplement to Jeremiah's own prayer.

32:17 [21] Lo, thou hast made the heavens and the earth by thy great strength and by thy outstretched arm: nothing is too difficult for thee, 18 who showest kindness to thousands and dost recompense the iniquity of the fathers into the bosom of their sons after them; the great God, the mighty Lord, 19 great in counsel and mighty in deed; by which thine eyes are opened upon all the ways of the sons of men, so thou dost give to a man in accordance with his ways and in accordance

[18] *Jeremia,* p. 300.

[19] *Ibid.*

[20] There is a clear relationship in thought between this prayer and the much more extensive prayer of Ezra in Neh. 9:6-37.

[21] The first three words of vs. 17, "Alas, Lord God," are the opening of the prayer which is introduced in 32:16 and which is continued in 32:24-25. The prayer as here given (vss. 17 ff.) begins with the fourth word of vs. 17, *hinnēh*—Lo!

with the consequences of his practices; 20 by which [counsel and deeds] thou hast given signs and wonders in the land of Egypt, even unto this day, both in Israel and among mankind, and thou hast made for thyself a reputation as obtains this day. 21 And thou didst lead out thy people Israel from the land of Egypt by signs and wonders, and with a strong hand and an outstretched arm, and with a great terror-arousing spectacle [Deut. 26:8]. 22 And thou didst give to them this land which thou didst swear to their fathers that thou wouldst give them, a land flowing with milk and honey. 23 So they entered and possessed it, but they did not listen to thy voice and did not walk in accord with thy law. Whatever thou didst command them to do they did not do, so thou didst make all this evil befall them.

4. *The Release of King Jehoiachin from Prison in Babylon* (52:31-34). Ch. 52 closes with an episode which must have been greeted with a cheer by all Judean exiles in the Diaspora in whatever part of the world they then were. The date is 561, the twenty-fifth day of Adar (February-March), the sixth day before the Chaldean New Year celebration. More than a generation has elapsed since 598, when the first company of exiles—with Jehoiachin at their head—was deported to Babylon.

Vss. 31-34 take us into the Chaldean court in Babylon where Amel Marduk, here called Evil-merodach, has just succeeded King Nebuchadrezzar on the Chaldean throne. Amel Marduk abandoned his father's policy and followed the priests. For some reason—we do not know why, although it probably had some relation to the dawning New Year— Amel Marduk released Jehoiachin from prison. Now fifty-five years of age, having been just eighteen when carried into exile, he is provided with clothing appropriate to royalty. He is given the dignity of a throne beside the Chaldean throne, a continual allowance and ration, and comradeship with the Chaldean king at the royal table. We can sense the overtones of joy in the Jewish narrator's soul as he tells the good news. How it would thrill the Diaspora! And every Judean who believed with Jeremiah in God's gracious purpose for his people must have seen in this humanitarian action of the Chaldean monarch an earnest of the "future of hope."

52:31 In the thirty-seventh year of the exile of Jehoiachin king of Judah, in the twelfth month, on the twenty-fifth day of the month, Evil-merodach king of Babylon, in the year that he began to reign, showed gracious consideration to Jehoiachin king of Judah, and released him from prison. 32 And he spoke graciously with him and set his throne above the thrones of the kings who were with him in Babylon. 33 He changed his prison garments, and he [Jehoiachin] ate bread before him continually all the days of his life. 34 His appointed portion was given him continuously by the king of Babylon, a daily ration until the day of his death.

5. *Babylon's Imminent Fall* (50:1-46). Chs. 50 and 51:1-58, while attributed to Jeremiah in the Hebrew text, in the Septuagint are not attributed to him, but are entitled simply "The Word of the Lord Which He Spoke Against Babylon." The anonymous author of these chapters lived in Jerusalem (50:5) and was in close intercourse with the Judean exiles in Babylon (51:49). He is himself dependent at various points upon Jeremiah, upon Ezekiel, and likewise upon the latest parts of the book of Isaiah (chs. 13–14; 21:1-10; chs. 34–35).[22] The historical situation portrayed in these chapters is as follows: (*a*) the people addressed are exiles (50:4-5; 51:34); (*b*) the temple has been destroyed (50:28; 51:11); (*c*) the speedy overthrow of Babylon is emphasized (50:2-3; 51:1-2); (*d*) the writer contemplates with joy the destruction of Babylon with no thought whatever that it was itself an instrument of judgment upon Judah which the Lord was wielding (50:8-10; 51:41-44); (*e*) the fall of Babylon is not seventy years distant, as in Jeremiah's thought (29:10; 27:7), but is imminent (50:8-10; 51:24).

The author is dependent, as above noted, upon Isa. 13–14, which dates from shortly after 550. Since the fall of Babylon lies for him in the future, this passage must date before 538.

The first section of this long poem has to do with the fall of Babylon— meaning by it not merely the city but the whole Babylonian (Chaldean) nation—and the emancipation of Israel from Babylonian captivity (vss. 1-7). The anonymous author receives the summons from the Lord to proclaim among the nations Babylon's imminent fall. Bel, who was originally the city god of Nippur, merged with Marduk, god of Babylon (here called Merodach),[23] when Babylon became the capital of Babylonia. Thus Bel Marduk, as here used, are two names for the one god, the state god of Babylonia. Just as Jeremiah viewed Babylon as a foe "from the north," so here "the north" is similarly viewed as the region of origin of that foe which is destined to lay Babylon itself desolate. It is likely that Persia is in the poet's mind as he speaks of that which is imminent as though it has already happened.

---

[22] So Cornill, *Jeremia,* p. 492, whose understanding of this section rests upon "the conclusive judgment" of Budde, as given in the latter's masterful study of these chapters in *Jahrbücher für deutsche Theologie* (1878), pp. 428-70, 529-62.

[23] Perles is probably correct in his surmise that the designation Merodach *(Mᵉrōdhākh)* arises from setting to the consonants of the Hebrew word Marduk, the vowels of the word for Lord *ᵉdhōnāy, Babylonische-jüd, Glossen,* p. 7.

50:1 The word of the Lord which he spoke against Babylon.[24]
2 Declare among the nations and proclaim,
    Conceal not, speak!
"Babylon has been captured, Bel has been put to shame,
    Merodach [Marduk] is dismayed.
Its idols have been disconcerted,
    Its images have been shattered."
3 For there has gone up against it a nation out of the north
    Which will put its land to desolation,
So that there will not be a single inhabitant in it,
    Whether man or beast.

When this consummation, the fall of Babylon, is accomplished, then both the exiles from the northern kingdom of Israel and those from Judah will be free to return to Palestine. "Hither" in vs. 5 suggests that it is from Jerusalem that this section comes. And they will come—for the most part the sons and daughters and grandchildren of the original exiles—headed for Jerusalem, weeping tears of penitence. They will inquire the way to Zion, bent upon the renewal and affirmation of their covenant with their Lord who has his dwelling there. It is from Zion that the author of these words writes:

50:4 In those days and at that time
    The sons of Israel, they
And the sons of Judah together,
    Shall come, going along weeping as they come,
And they shall seek the Lord their God.
5   They shall ask the way to Zion with their faces turned hither.
And they shall come and join themselves to the Lord
    With an eternal covenant which shall not be forgotten.

The Judeans had forgotten their true shepherd and their rightful resting place—the Lord. They had been a flock tended by unfaithful "shepherds," whose spiritual leaders had let them be enticed away from "the mountain," Mount Zion, their true fold, to such idolatrous worship as was performed on the "mountains" and "hills" of Canaan. Their political leaders have not shepherded but have devoured them. The prophet emphasizes, in a manner akin to the very sharpness of Jeremiah himself, the guilt not of the nations such as Assyria and the Chaldeans, who here are represented even as washing their hands of responsibility (vs. 7a), but of the Lord's people themselves, who have forgotten the God in whom their fathers had hoped. The Lord speaks:

[24] This is the title as given in the Septuagint and is manifestly the more accurate.

50:6 An erring flock have my people been;
　　Their shepherds have let them wander about upon the mountains,
　　They have enticed them away from the mountain: [25]
　　　They have resorted to the hills; [26]
　　　They have forgotten their resting-place.[27]
　7 All who have led them have devoured them,
　　And their enemies say, "We do not count ourselves guilty."
　　Rather they have sinned against the Lord,
　　In whom dwells righteousness, the hope of their fathers."

The prophet now calls upon the exiles to take the initiative and flee
from the land of their captivity. Just as male goats of the herd push their
way through the gate ahead of the flock, so let the exiles take vigorous
initiative. For against Babylon a whole troop of peoples is even now
mustering its forces, among them bowmen, famed for their unfailing marks-
manship, and soon the whole land of the Chaldeans will be but booty
for every plunderer. Thus the prophet cries:

50:8 Flee from the midst of Babylon!
　　Go forth from the land of the Chaldeans!
　　And be like goats
　　　At the head of the flock.
　9 For see, I am about to rouse up against Babylon
　　A troop of nations
　　From the land of the north, and they will draw up in battle line against it.
　　From there [i.e., the north] it will be captured.
　　Their arrows are as those of a skilled warrior;
　　They do not come back without result.
　10 And the Chaldean land will become a spoil of war;
　　Everyone who plunders it will be satiated.

Although the plundering Chaldean nation is in high spirits, like leaping
calves in spring and neighing stallions, their "mother," the land of Babylonia, is ashamed of its Chaldean occupants, for it is due to their lust for
conquest that the fair land of the Tigris and Euphrates is bound to be reduced ultimately to a deserted, uninhabitable waste such as will awaken
horror in the soul of the passer-by. Cries the prophet:

[25] As Davidson notes, *Hebrew Syntax*, p. 20, the article is omitted in *mēhar* because *har*
(mountain) refers to the temple mount, the true place of worship, in contrast to the
illicit cults "on the high hills" and "on the mountains" in the open country (Jer. 17:2-3).

[26] I construe *gibh'āh* as a collective noun for the "high hills" of the illicit cults.

[27] The sheep's resting place, the fold, figuratively for the worship of the temple.

50:11 Although you rejoice, although you triumph,
    You who plunder my property,
    Although you leap about like calves in spring,
    And neigh like stallions,
12 Your mother [i.e., Babylonia] is very much ashamed;
    She who bore you is embarrassed.
    See, this is the ultimate issue of the heathen—
    Wilderness, desert, and steppe.
13 Because of the wrath of the Lord it shall never be inhabited;
    But it shall be a waste, all of it.
    Everyone who passes by Babylon will be appalled;
    And will hiss because of all its scourgings.

The prophet now calls upon the attacking nations to draw up in battle line to assault Babylon, again singling out for special mention the famed bowmen. Let the attacking forces shout a war cry against it on all sides. At length in imagination he sees the Chaldeans, their buttresses fallen, their walls breached, "give the hand," a signal of surrender. The prophet feels in this consummation the divine retribution upon this plunderer of nations and such poetic justice as brings back what Babylon has dealt to others upon its own head. The prophet calls upon the attackers to exterminate both sowers and reapers so that Babylon can have no harvest. Let everyone flee to his own land and so escape the exterminating sword of the Lord.

50:14 Draw up in battle array against Babylon round about,
    All who bend the bow.
  Shoot at it, spare no arrow,
15   Lift the battle cry against it on every side.
  It has given its hand, its buttresses have fallen,
    Its walls have been broken down.
  For this is the vengeance of the Lord; he has avenged himself through it.
    Just as it has done, do to it.
16 Cut off the sower from Babylon,
    And the wielder of the sickle in harvest time,
  From before the sword of the oppressor.
    Let each turn to his own people,
    And let each flee to his own land.

The Lord is concerned for his scattered flock. A later prose insertion, vss. 17b-18,[28] is an explanatory comment on vs. 17a. It infers that Israel

---

[28] The later commentator explains:

50:17b "The first to devour him was the king of Assyria and this, the last to gnaw his bones, is Nebuchadrezzar. 18 Therefore thus says the Lord of hosts, God of Israel, See, I am about to punish the king of Babylon and his land, just as I punished the king of Assyria.

was "devoured" by the Assyrian Tiglath-pileser in 734, when he carried the people of Gilead, Galilee, and Naphtali into captivity in Assyria (II Kings 15:29). And it tells that Nebuchadrezzar had most recently "gnawed the bones" of Judah by carrying off the exiles of 598 and 587, when thousands of Judean captives had been taken to Babylon (II Kings 24–25). The king of Assyria had already been punished when mighty Nineveh fell in 612. And the Lord is now at the very point of punishing the king of Babylon. This will be but preliminary to the Lord's return of his exiled people Israel to its most fruitful and beloved regions—Carmel and Mount Ephraim to the west, and Bashan and Mount Gilead to the east, of the Jordan. The territories mentioned are all located in what was the northern kingdom of Israel. Thus not only the Judean but likewise the Israelite exiles are to return to their homeland, brought back by the Lord himself. And Israel's iniquity and Judah's sin will be graciously pardoned. Says this prophet:

> 50:17 A scattered flock is Israel;
> Lions have thrust him out.

He continues:

> 19 But I will bring Israel back to his pasture,
> And he shall graze on Carmel and Bashan;
> And on Mount Ephraim and Mount Gilead
> His appetite shall be sated.
> 20 In those days and at that time
> The iniquity of Israel will be sought for in vain;
> And the sin of Judah, but it will not be found;
> For I will pardon those whom I will spare.

In vss. 21-28 the prophet speaks, in sure anticipation, a message of good news to Zion, the tidings that Babylon has fallen. The Lord is represented as commanding the enemies of the Chaldeans to go up against Merathaim, the region of the delta of the Tigris-Euphrates rivers, called *nar marratu* in Assyrian documents, and against the inhabitants of *P'qodh* (Pekod), the name of a tribe in eastern Babylon (*Puqudu*) and of a canal (*Piqudu*) which branched off from the Euphrates to one of the southern suburbs of old Babylon. These two areas, however, here stand for the entire country of Babylonia, and the terms are chosen because of their respective prophetic connotation, "double rebellion" and "punishment." Babylonia is to be exterminated.

The sensitive ear of the prophet hears in imagination the crashing blows by which "the forge hammer of all the earth" is itself hewn down in utter humiliation and disgrace (vss. 22-23). The one who had trapped the nations is himself overwhelmed by the forces sent against him from the armory of the Lord (vss. 24-25). The harvest of all Babylon's cruel sowings is to be devoted to the ban (vs. 26). The forces bent on Babylon's destruction are commanded to slaughter her "steers," i.e., her princes and warriors. The time when Babylon is to be punished has at long last arrived (vs. 27). Imaginatively the prophet pictures fugitives and refugees from Babylonia declaring in Zion the vengeance which the Lord has wrought upon that nation (vs. 28).

> 50:21 Go up to the land of Merathaim, go up against it,
>   And to the inhabitants of Pekod.
> Attack and exterminate them, says the Lord,
>   And do in accordance with all that I have commanded you.
> 22 Hark! a battle in the land;
>   And a great crashing,
> 23 How hath the forge hammer of all the earth
>   Been hewn down and broken!
> How hath Babylon become
>   A butt of horror among the nations!
> 24 Thou hast laid the snares and yet thou wast captured,
>   And thou didst not know!
> Thou wert found, yes, even caught;
>   For against the Lord thou didst engage in strife.
> 25 The Lord opened his armory,
>   And sent forth the weapons of his indignation.
> For a work has the Lord God
>   In the land of the Chaldeans.
> 26 The time of harvest has come to it;
>   Open ye its granaries.
> Pile her up as those binding sheaves, and exterminate her;
>   Let there be nothing left of her.
> 27 Attack all her steers [i.e., princes and warriors];
>   Let them be prostrated for slaughter.
> Woe upon them for their day hath come,
>   The time of their punishment.
> 28 Hark! fugitives and refugees from the land of Babylonia,
>   To declare in Zion the vengeance of the Lord [our] God.

The keynote of the next section, vss. 29-32, is the presumption of Babylon. Babylon has presumed upon the indulgence of God. One senses in vs. 29 that the author is familiar with the prophet Isaiah's interpretation of the presumption of Assyria in Isa. 10:5-11. It is because of the arrogance of Babylon that the archers are summoned to surround him so that he cannot escape. His time of punishment has come. Two pictures are painted by the prophet in vss. 31-32: proud Babylon (called "Presumption") will stumble and fall; and mighty Babylon will be consumed as in a forest fire.

> 50:29 Summon archers against Babylon,
>   All benders of the bow.
> Encamp against her round about,
>   Let there be for her no escape.
> Reward her according to her conduct,
>   According to all she has done.
> For against the Lord has she acted presumptuously,
>   Against the Holy One of Israel.
> 30 Therefore her young men shall fall in her squares, and all her men of war shall be destroyed on that day, says the Lord.

> 31 See, you are presumptuous,
>   Says the Lord God of hosts,
> But your day has come,
>   Your time of punishment.
> 32 And Presumption shall stumble and fall
>   With no one to raise him up,
> And I will kindle a fire in his forest,
>   And it shall consume all that is around him.

The theme of vss. 33-40 is the release of Israel from captivity. Up until now the captured of Israel and Judah were kept in bondage by their captors. But here they are summoned to confidence. Their mighty champion, the Lord himself, will conduct their case, bringing peace to the earth, but distress to their oppressors.

> 50:33 Thus says the Lord of hosts:
>   Oppressed were the sons of Israel,
>   Together with the sons of Judah,
>   All their captors kept hold of them;
>   They refused to let them go free.
> 34 But their Champion is strong;
>   The Lord of hosts is his name.
> He will surely plead their case,
>   So as to give the earth rest,
> But cause disquiet to the inhabitants of Babylon.

Five times in immediate succession the prophet cries out, "A sword!"— the destroying sword of the Lord, poised over the Chaldean whose destruction is imminent. Babylon's inhabitants, its false prophets, its warriors, the mixture of foreign breeds which are in its army, its treasures, its canals that distribute the fertilizing water over its soil, will all be destroyed. The idols and images for which Babylon is famed, and upon whose help that idolatrous nation depends, are powerless to protect her.

> 50:35 A sword over the Chaldeans,
> And upon the inhabitants of Babylon,
> And upon its princes and its wise men!
> 36 A sword upon its false prophets, aye, let them show themselves fools;
> A sword upon its warriors, that they may be shattered;
> 37 A sword upon the mixed company who are in its midst, that they may become like women.
> A sword upon its treasures, that they may be looted as spoil,
> 38   A sword upon its waters, that they may dry up.
> For it [Babylonia] is a land of images,
> And in idols they make their boast.

The destruction of Babylonia will be so thoroughgoing that from generation to generation no human being will live there. The coastlands will be inhabited only by jackals and ostriches.

> 50:39 Therefore jackals shall inhabit the coastlands,
> And ostriches shall live in them;
> But no human being shall ever again live there,
> Nor shall it be inhabited from generation to generation.
> 40 As when God overturned Sodom
> And Gomorrah, and its inhabitants,
> No one shall dwell there;
> And no human being shall stay there.

The foe from the north is now pictured as on the march against Babylon. Allied with him are powerful kings from distant regions. Together they compose a ruthless army of warriors riding upon horses. Armed with bow and arrow, and with javelins and roaring bloodcurdling cries, they draw up the battle line against Babylon. When the report of their imminent attack reaches the king of Babylon, he is impotent and is hurled into distress comparable to the labor pangs of a woman in travail.

> 50:41 Lo, a people is coming from the north;
> And a great nation.
> And powerful kings are being roused up,
> From the extremities of the earth.

42 Bows and javelins they carry;
    They are cruel and have no compassion.
Their voice roars like the sea;
   And they ride upon horses.
They are drawn up like a man of war,
    Against you, daughter of Babylon.
43 The king of Babylon heard report of them,
    And his hands drop.
Distress lays hold on him,
    Writhing as of a woman in travail.

Vividly the prophet pictures what the Lord is about to do with the Chaldeans. He is represented as a lion coming up out of the Jordan thicket to a sheepfold, startling the whole flock and robbing it of the best of its rams. There is no shepherd powerful enough to challenge the Lord or restrain him in what he is doing. For it is his design not to stop with taking off the best of the Chaldeans, but his destruction of their nation will be complete and appalling, even to the Chaldeans themselves, accustomed as these destroyers are to leave desolate their captured areas (vss. 44-45). The whole earth will tremble at the news of Babylon's fall, and its distress cry will be heard by the nations (vs. 46).

50:44 See, as a lion goes up
    From the thicket of the Jordan to a sheepfold,
So I will startle the sheep of its flock,
    And seek out the best of its rams.
For who is like me and who can summon me?
    And who is the shepherd who could stand before me?
45 Therefore listen to the design of the Lord,
    Which he has determined upon as regards Babylon;
And his plans which he has devised
    For the land of the Chaldeans.
Surely even the most inferior of the flock shall be dragged off;
    Surely their own meadow shall be appalled at them.
46 At the report, "Babylon has fallen," the earth is made to shake,
    And its cry of distress is heard among the nations.

6. *Babylon's Complete Destruction* (51:1-58). Ch. 51 opens with an oracle from the Lord, who is at the point of stirring up in foreigners a spirit bent on the destruction of Babylon. The warriors are not to relax, but must utterly destroy the Chaldean army, sparing none. The Chaldean dead and wounded will fall in their own streets because of their guilt in the eyes of

the Lord, but Israel and Judah will live on, with the Lord as the husband and responsible protector of his people.

51:1   Thus says the Lord:
        See, I am about to stir up against the Chaldean inhabitants
          The spirit of a destroyer.
   2   And I will send foreigners to Babylon and they will scatter it,
          And empty out its land.
        For they will encamp against it from round about
          In its evil day.
   3   Let not the wielder of his bow relax;
          And let him not grow weary of putting on his armor.
        And spare not her young men;
          Exterminate her whole army.
   4   Then the slain will fall in the land of the Chaldeans,
          And the wounded in her own streets.
  5b   For their land is full of guilt
          Before the Holy One of Israel.
  5a   But Israel and Judah are not widowed
          By their God, by the Lord of hosts.

So the prophet cries to his own captive Judean people to flee from Babylon's midst, for the Lord's time of vengeance is at hand. The whole world has been intoxicated by the culture of Babylon—famed Babylon's "cup of gold"—so that the nations have been carried away by its brilliancy. But now Babylon's luster has faded and its fall is near. Indeed, Babylon is like one sick unto death. The healing skill of all the world with its medicines and physicians would have been available to Babylon, but Babylon would not be healed—such is the divine charge. And since the divine judgment cannot be checked, Babylon must be abandoned to destruction. The judgment God will mete out to it is immeasurably great. Cries the prophet:

51:6   Flee from the midst of Babylon:
          Be not destroyed by its iniquity.
        For the time of vengeance—it belongs to the Lord;
          That dealt out [by her] he will pay back to her.
   7   Babylon is a cup of gold,
          Which makes all the earth drunken.
        Of its wine nations have drunk,
          Therefore they are like madmen.
   8   Suddenly it shall fall and be broken.
        Wail over it!
        Take balsam for its pain;
          Perhaps it can be healed.

9 We would have healed Babylon, but it would not be healed;
    Abandon it and let each go to his own land.
For judgment upon it reaches to the heavens;
    Yes, it lifts itself even unto the clouds.[20]

The destroyers of Babylon are summoned to prepare for immediate on-slaught. Let them get their weapons ready to attack the walls of the city, for what the Lord through his prophets has said he would do, he is now about to do to Babylon. As for that city, famous for its irrigation system and its untold riches in treasure, it will plunder no more. The Lord has sworn that warriors in numbers comparable to a locust plague will attack it, at the same time hurling their war cries against the now-doomed city.

51:11a,b Polish the arrows!
        Fill the quivers!
12   Toward the walls of Babylon lift up a standard;
        Strengthen the guard!
    Station sentinels!
        Set up the ambush!
    For the Lord has both purposed and done
        What he said concerning the inhabitants of Babylon.
13   You who dwell beside many waters,
        Abounding in treasures,
    Your end has come,
        The limit to your plunder.
14   The Lord of hosts has sworn by himself:
        "Surely I will make you as full of men as locusts,
        And they shall chant war cries against you."

The prophet who penned the words of vss. 15-19 took them from 10:12-16, where an editor has contrasted pagan idols with the Lord. They fit in exceedingly well at this point as they give the reason why the Lord's pur-pose to destroy Babylon will not fail. Already these verses had become part of the book of Jeremiah when the prophet who wrote Chs. 50–51 makes use of them. They emphasize the Lord, the supreme "possession of Jacob," as the living and powerful Creator, in contrast to the created gods of Babylon and those artisans who manufacture idols.

51:15 He who creates the earth by this strength,
    Who establishes the world by his wisdom,
    And by his understanding spreads out the heavens—

[20] A later editor, thinking of Israel as having been vindicated by the Lord's overthrow of Babylon, added vs. 10.
    The Lord has brought our righteousness to light
    Come and let us rehearse in Zion the work of the Lord our God.

16 At his voice there pours forth a roar of waters in the heavens,
  And he causes the vapors to ascend from the end of the earth.
  Flashes of lightning he makes for the rain,
  And he sends forth wind from his storehouses.
17 Every man is stupid, without knowledge;
  Every goldsmith is ashamed of [his] idols,
  For his molten images are a fraud, with no breath in them;
18   They are nonentities, products of sham,
    At the time when they are punished, they shall perish.
19 Not like them is the possession of Jacob,
  For a fashioner of all things is he,
  And Israel is the tribe he possesses;
  The Lord of hosts is his name.

In vss. 20-26 the prophet interprets how God has used Babylon as his
own weapon of war to "shatter" nations and destroy kingdoms. Babylon has
"shattered" political leaders, military leaders, cavalry and charioteers, both
men and women, both young men and young women, shepherds and flocks,
plowmen and oxen. All this Zion has itself experienced in large measure at
Chaldeans hands. But the day of retribution has arrived. The Chaldean
nation, that mountain of destruction, will itself become a heap of ruins.
Its glorious splendor will be destroyed as in a burning oven. From its awful
ruins future generations will not find one single stone fit for use as a corner-
stone or as a foundation stone. The once glorious city will become an eternal
ruins. Thus the Lord speaks to Babylon:

51:20 A war club you are to me, a weapon of war,
      And with you I shatter nations;
      And with you I destroy kingdoms;
  23c   With you I shatter governors and prefects,
  21 And with you I shatter horses and their riders,
      With you I shatter chariots and their charioteers,
  22 And with you I shatter men and women;
      With you I shatter youths and virgins;
  23 And with you I shatter the shepherd and his flock,
      With you I shatter the plowman and his span;
  24 And I will pay back to Babylon and all the inhabitants of Chaldea
      All their evil which they have perpetrated upon Zion,
      Before your eyes, says the Lord.
  25 Lo, I am against you—
      O mountain of destruction,
      Says the Lord,

> I will stretch out my hand against you,
> And I will turn you into a heap of stones;
> And I will deliver you up to a burning oven.
> 26 They will not take from you a cornerstone,
> Or a foundation stone,
> But an eternal desolation shall be your fate.

In vss. 27-33 an imaginative, moving picture of Babylon's collapse as it is conceived in the mind of the prophet unrolls before us. He summons the nations and kingdoms to prepare to attack Babylon. A marshal is appointed to mount his horse and get into action (vs. 27). The earth quakes as the attacking forces proceed to convert haughty Babylon into an uninhabited waste (vs. 29). The terrified Babylonian soldiers cease fire and cower in their strongholds, their courage gone, their dwellings in flame, and the bars of their city gate broken (vs. 20). As though in a relay race, one messenger runs to proclaim it to another, and the last, at length, to the king of Babylon, that the city has been captured, the fords of the Euphrates seized, and that the soldiers' resistance has utterly collapsed (vss. 31-32). Babylon is like a threshing floor when the treaders are in process of treading out the grain. In a very short time the harvest of the dead will lie upon it (vs. 33).

> 51:27 Lift up a standard in the earth,
> Blow a trumpet among the nations;
> Consecrate nations against her,
> Summon kingdoms against her.[30]
> 29 Then the earth quaked and writhed,
> For a plan of the Lord is fulfilled against Babylon,
> To turn the land of Babylon
> Into a waste, without inhabitant.
> 30 The soldiers of Babylon cease to fight,
> They sit in the strongholds;
> Their valor fails,
> They have become women;
> Its dwellings have been set on fire,
> Its bars have been broken.
> 31 One runner runs to call out to another,
> And one declaring, proclaims to another,

[30] Delete Ararat, Minni, and Ashkenaz, as being contrary to the purpose of the prophet, who gives no names of the nations but is content with the general phrase "a nation out of the north"; so Rudolph, *Jeremia*, p. 226. Delete also vs. 28, which is a gloss to make vs. 27 more specific:

> Consecrate nations against her;
> The king of the Medes, his governors and all his prefects,
> And all the land of their dominion.

To declare to the king of Babylon
That his city on all sides has been captured,
32 And the fords have been seized,
And the swamp reed . . .
They have burned with fire,
And the men of war have been driven out of their senses.
33 For thus says the Lord of hosts, God of Israel:
The daughter of Babylon is like a threshing floor at the time when the
treader treads it;
Yet a little while, and the harvest will come to it.

In vss. 34-40 the theme is the retribution which the Lord is bringing upon
the Chaldeans. Jerusalem is represented as lamenting over the destruction
which the Chaldeans had wrought upon her. Vigorous figures of speech
are used by the prophet. Judah has been "devoured," "thrown into confusion," "emptied out," "swallowed up," "thrust out" (vs. 34). "May the
Lord hold Babylon and the Chaldeans responsible," prays the prophet in
Zion's behalf (vs. 35). Jerusalem cries:

51:34 "Devoured me, thrown me into confusion, has the king of Babylon!
He has made me like an empty vessel,
He has swallowed me up like the dragon;
He has filled his stomach with my dainties, he has thrust me out!
35 May the wrong done me and my destruction be held against Babylon,"
Say the inhabitants of Zion,
"And may my blood be upon the inhabitants of Chaldea,"
Says Jerusalem.

To this the Lord answers: Let not Jerusalem be anxious, for its cause
is in his hands, and God is his people's champion. Retribution is his affair.
The great Euphrates River, Chaldea's fountain of life, will be dried up, so
mighty, brilliant Babylon will be reduced to an uninhabitable ruin heap,
and become the butt of derisive scorn.

36 Therefore, thus says the Lord:
See, I am conducting your case,
And I will avenge myself on your behalf.
And I will dry up its river,[31]
And I will make dry its fountain.
37 And Babylon shall become heaps of ruins,
A haunt of jackals,

[31] Lit., "its sea"; but *yam* here refers to the Euphrates River; cf. the Nile, as intended in Isa. 18:2; 19:5.

A cause of horror and an object of derisive hissing,
Without inhabitant.

Having told what he will do to the Chaldean land, the Lord now declares through the prophet what he will do to its people. Just as the keeper responds to the lion's roar for food and the growl of the whelps for drink, so the Lord will give the Chaldeans to drink, but such a potion as will lay them prostrate (i.e., the people and their leaders) like lambs, rams, and he-goats prepared for sacrifice, in a sleep from which they will never awaken.

51:38 As young lions roar all together,
As they growl like lions' whelps,
39a When they are in heat, I will give them drink,
And will make them drunk, so that they will swoon away,
40 I will lay them prostrate like lambs for slaughter,
Like rams and he-goats.
39b So they will sleep an endless sleep,
Never to awaken, says the Lord.

A song of satire is now sung over Babylon. The city whose fame once was world wide has become an uninhabitable waste.

51:41 How hath Babylon [32] been captured and seized,
The renown of all the earth!
How she hath become a thing of horror,
Babylon among the nations!
42 Against Babylon hath the sea risen up;
By its mass of waves she is overwhelmed.
43 Her cities are doomed to be a waste,
A land desert and dry.
No one can dwell in them,
And no human being can pass through them.

The two things of greatest fame in Babylon were its god Bel and its massive wall. Bel was the tyrant deity of the ancient world, and ever since the Chaldeans had come to world domination the prestige of Bel was inestimably great. Likewise the massive wall, as archaeologists describe it, must have awakened the admiration and wonder of the world. But now the god Bel, who had "swallowed" the booty of the nations, is at the point of vomiting it out of his boastful mouth. And the majestic city wall is at the

[32] By atbash, wherein the last letter of the Hebrew alphabet is substituted for the first, next last for second, etc., so *sh sh k becomes b b l* ; *Shēshākh* is a disguise for Babel.

point of utter destruction. It is Israel's God who speaks through the prophet,
who cries to his own exiled people, "Go forth from Babylon." The Lord's
burning anger is at the point of stern retribution. Let no Israelite or Judean
stay to share Babylon's fate.

> 51:44 And I will punish Bel in Babylon,
>   And I will bring out from his mouth what he has swallowed.
>   And there shall not stream to him
>   Nations any more;
>   The wall of Babylon has fallen.
>   45 Go forth from its midst, my people!
>   And escape, each with his life,
>   From the burning anger of the Lord!

Vs. 46 is in prose and represents a later and quite different point of view
from the rest of chs. 50–51, taken as a whole. Instead of viewing the destruction of Babylon as imminent, it reckons with stormy years to be experienced
before that catastrophe comes to pass, during which there will break out
revolutions in Babylon and contests for the throne. Accordingly, vs. 46
does not have to do with historical happenings, but is eschatological and
messianic in nature. It deals with the convulsions caused by alarming news
and with turbulent events which will precede the time of the end. The Jews
are not to be thrown into anxiety by these convulsions and alarms, but are
to view them as the necessary preliminaries to the breaking in of the time
of salvation. This verse shows clearly, as Rudolph has convincingly demonstrated, that chs. 50–51 were thus later interpreted eschatologically, wherein
Babylon was viewed as "the embodiment of powers which were, generally
speaking, hostile to God." [33]

51:46 Lest your heart grow timid, so that you are afraid of the rumor that is
heard in the land, when there comes a rumor in one year and after it a rumor
in another year, and one tyrant after another deals out violence [34] in the land.

In vss. 47-48 the prophet predicts the near-at-hand fall of the Babylonians
to the foes hailing from the north. The Babylonian idols will be helpless
to protect their worshipers, who will fall in the midst of their capital, to the
cries of rejoicing proceeding from heaven and earth. Says the prophet:

[33] *Jeremia*, p. 257, see also pp. 272-73.
[34] Cf. Pedersen, *Israel* I-II, 419: "Violence is the same as falsehood, because both denote
that which deviates from the straight and just, i.e., the abnormal, which does not spring
from a healthy soul, and therefore has no root in reality."

51:47 Therefore, see, days are coming when I will punish the idols of Babylon and all her land shall be ashamed, and all her slain shall fall in her midst. 48 And heaven and earth and all that is in them shall give a ringing cry, because from the north will come her devastators, says the Lord.

Vss. 49-57 deal with the irrevocable divine resolution that Babylon is appointed of the Lord to fall, as a retribution for those of Israel (including Judah) who have been slain by her imperial ruthlessness. To these exiles who have escaped the cruel sword of the Chaldeans the prophet cries, calling upon his people, far away from their Palestinian homeland, to keep Jerusalem in their minds and hearts. Though they have suffered and still are suffering humiliation—such as they experienced when the pagan Chaldeans entered with ruthless tread into the temple area of Jerusalem—let them have confidence of their vindication in the future. However exalted and secure Babylon may seem to be, from the very presence of God devastators will be sent against her. In imagination the prophet already hears the crash of shattering blows and the cries of distress from Babylonians as the Lord is at the point of devastating their capital. Babylon's roars of haughty domination and destruction will no longer be heard. Behind the destroyer that will come against Babylon is the Lord, a God of just retribution and reward. It is the power of the Lord that will make Babylon powerless, for her leaders, drinking his cup and submitting perforce to his punishment, will sleep the sleep of death from which they will never awake.

51:49 Even Babylon is appointed to fall for the slain of Israel, just as to Babylon have fallen the slain of all the earth. 50 You who have escaped from her sword, come, do not stand still: remember the Lord from afar and let Jerusalem come into your mind. 51 "We are ashamed for we have heard scorn. Disgrace covered our face for foreigners have come in forcibly into the holy places of the temple of the Lord."
52 Therefore, lo, days are coming, says the Lord, when I will punish her idols, and in her whole land fatally wounded will groan. 53 Although Babylon should ascend to the heavens and so fortify its stronghold in the height, from my very presence devastators would come in to her. 54 Hark! A cry of distress from Babylon, and a great shattering from the land of the Chaldeans! 55 For the Lord is about to devastate Babylon, and will banish from it the great uproar, although its waves rage like mighty waters and their din gives forth a roar. 56 For a destroyer has come against Babylon and her warriors will be captured, their bows shattered; for a God of recompense is the Lord; he will surely repay. 57 And I will make her princes and her sages, her governors, prefects, and warriors drunk, and they shall sleep an eternal sleep never to wake up, says the King, the Lord of hosts is his name.

Once again (vs. 58) the prophet thinks of the majestic wall of Babylon, with its famous gates, of which the great Ishtar Gate, still in part remarkably preserved, is the most important. To men generally the destruction of that wall was unthinkable; but not to the prophet. For to him that grandeur spelled out blood money, bled by the Chaldeans from subject peoples, whose own national energies were sapped by such magnificence. Thus Babylon's tribute-paying nations were exhausting themselves to no worthy end. For that proud structure, reared at such sacrifice on the part of these nations, was doomed to go up in flames.

> 51:58 Thus says the Lord of hosts:
> The thick wall of Babylon
>   Will be utterly laid waste,
> And her lofty gates
>   Will be burned in the fire.
> And nations are wearing themselves out for nought,
>   And peoples are exhausting themselves but for fire.[35]

MESSAGES OF JUDGMENT TO JEWS OF THE DIASPORA

1. *Destruction and Dispersion Due to Idolatry* (9:12-16). This section comes from the Deuteronomic editor, who answers the question, Why has the land of Judah been reduced to an uninhabitable ruin? The Lord's answer is that the Judeans abandoned the law of the Lord, and ceasing to live by his will, followed their own inclination and worshiped the Baals as they were revered in the popular religion. Consequently they must experience the bitterness of exile, dispersion, and consumption by the sword.

> 9:12 Who is the wise man who understands this?
>   What the mouth of the Lord says to him, let him declare.
> Why has the land perished?
>   [Why] has it been desolated like the wilderness with no one traversing it?

13 And the Lord said: Because they have abandoned my law which I put before them, and have not listened to my voice and have not lived by it. 14 But they have lived by the stubbornness of their heart and by the Baals, which their fathers taught them.

15 Therefore thus says the Lord of hosts, God of Israel: Lo, I am about to make them eat wormwood and give them poisonous water to drink. 16 And I shall disperse them among the nations whom they and their fathers have not known, and I will send after them the sword until I shall have consumed them by it.

[35] The sentence is satirical, i.e., only to feed the flames of Babylon's destruction.

2. *A Warning to Jews of the Diaspora Against Idolatry* (10:1-16). It is implied here that those who are warned are living in a pagan environment. The section has to do with the worship of idols and it has much in common with the exilic prophetic teaching of Deutero-Isaiah and with postexilic psalms.[36] Presumably the redactor of the book of Jeremiah chose this place for its insertion in order to offset Jeremiah's strong emphasis upon the utter worthlessness of circumcision—a passage painful to Judaism—by warning against being impressed by the worship of idols which they see being carried on around them.

Thus although it does not come from Jeremiah, it gives us vivid glimpses into the popular appeal of the idolatry which before long Judeans were to see in various areas of the Diaspora.

It opens with an editorial introduction, an appeal to the people of Israel to listen to the Lord's word (vs. 1), then warns against the "way" of the pagan nations, that is, their manner of worship and life. The religion of these pagans makes them stand in dread before strange omens in the heavens. But that god—"Terror" is its name [37]—which strikes terror into the heart of pagans is in reality powerless. It is no more than what one sees— mere wood—part of a tree hewn down in the forest. But it is impressive, for it is overlaid with silver mined in the Phoenician colony of Tarshish in southern Spain, and with gold from Ophir in southwestern Arabia. We sense the irony in the writer's spirit as he pictures a mere craftsman making a god, then dressing it in variegated garments, and setting it up securely, fixing it firmly. There they stand, not one idol but many, motionless as scarecrows in a cucumber patch! And when they move they have to be carried. They can do neither good nor harm. It is utter folly to expect discipline, counsel, or instruction from such nonentities.

10:1 Hear the word which the Lord speaks to you, house of Israel,
  2 Thus says the Lord:
    You shall not learn the custom of the nations,
      Nor be dismayed at signs of the heavens,
      Although the nations are dismayed at them.
  3 For the Terror of the nations has no reality,
      But is mere wood which one cuts from the forest with an ax,
      The handiwork of a craftsman
  4*a*   He overlays it with silver and gold,

[36] Cf. Isa. 40:19; 41:6-7; 44:9-20; 46:5-7; Pss. 115:4-8; 135:15-18.

[37] Cf. "Fear of Isaac" (Gen. 31:42): "Terror of God" (Gen. 35:5); see Leslie, *Old Testament Religion*, pp. 67-71.

9   With silver beaten out
> Brought from Tarshish,
> > And with gold from Ophir.
> They are all the product of skilled labor;
> > Their garments are of violet and purple.
4b   He must make them firm with hammer and nails;
> > He must set them up so they will not totter.
5   They are like a scarecrow [lit., like a post] in a field of cucumbers,
> > And they cannot speak;
> Indeed, they have to be carried,
> > For they cannot take a step.
> Be not afraid of them, for they can do no injury;
> > Moreover, it is not in their power to do good.
8   But they are at once both stupid and dumb.
> > [As for] discipline from such futilities [i.e., idols] it is nonsense! [38]

In contrast to these pagan idols, nonentities, stands the Lord—alive, eternal, the ruler of the whole earth, before whose wrath no evil people can maintain itself. He is the creator, controller of rain, of the ascending mists, and of the winds. Before him at the testing time every idol maker who has believed in the power of his products, when their impotence is demonstrated, must stand in dumb disillusionment and humiliation.

10:10   But the Lord is the true God;
> > He is the living God and an everlasting King,
> At his wrath the earth quakes,
> > And the nations cannot endure his indignation.
12   It is he who created the earth by his strength,
> > Who established the world by his wisdom,
> > > And by his understanding spread out the heavens.
13   At his voice there pours forth a roar of waters in the heavens,
> > And he causes vapors to ascend from the end of the earth.
> Flashes of lightning he makes for the rain,
> > And he sends forth winds from his storehouses,
14   Every man is stupid, without knowledge;
> > Every goldsmith is ashamed of [his] idol.
> For his molten images are a fraud with no breath in them;
15   They are nonentities, products of sham;
> > At the time when they are punished they shall perish.

In how great contrast is Israel's God—the "Possession of Jacob" he is poetically designated. Finally the poet, ceasing to speak about God, speaks in awesome recognition directly to him:

[38] I am indebted to Rudolph, *Jeremia,* pp. 60-61, for his brilliant reconstruction of this difficult passage.

10:16 Not like them is the Possession of Jacob,
But the fashioner of all things is he,
And Israel is the tribe he possesses;
The Lord of hosts is his name.
6 None is like thee, O Lord;
Great art thou,
And great in might is thy name.
7 Who should not fear thee,
[Thou] King of the nations?
For reverence is due to thee,
Yes, among all the wise of the nations,
And among all their kings,
None is like thee.

The closing vs. 11 of this section is in Aramaic. It is in prose and is a marginal comment of a reader which was taken up into the text by the editor. It is his conclusion regarding the fate of idols.

10:11 Thus shall you say concerning them: "The gods who did not create the heavens and the earth shall perish from the earth and from under the heavens."

3. *The Disgrace of Judah in the Eyes of the World* (15:4). To Jeremiah's vivid realistic picture of the fate that awaits Judah (15:1-3), the Deuteronomic editor, who views the sins of King Manasseh's reign (II Kings 21) as the effective cause of the fall of the Judean nation adds:

15:4 And I will make them [the Judeans] an object of horror to all kingdoms of the earth, on account of Manasseh son of Hezekiah, king of Judah, because of what he did in Jerusalem.

4. *Forsakers of the Temple and of God* (17:12-13). Although this section contains expressions characteristic of Jeremiah, such as "thy glorious throne" (14:21), "the hope of Israel" (14:8), and "the fountain of living waters" (2:13), the emphasis on the Lord as the God of the temple is contrary to Jeremiah's basic thought, for he was by no means a cultic prophet. It comes from the exilic or postexilic times, and as Rudolph says, "We see here how the exilic and post-exilic congregation knew how to combine prophetic faith and cultic thinking." [39] Vs. 12 reminds us of Isaiah's vision of the Lord "sitting upon a throne, high and uplifted, with the skirts of his robe filling the temple" (Isa. 6:1). The verse glorifies the temple in Jerusalem. And vs. 13 reflects the spirit of revolt and retrogression of the temple community

[39] *Op. cit.,* p. 100.

about the middle of the fifth century, as is apparent in Trito-Isaiah (chs. 56–66). It centers attention upon those who are forsaking the Lord in the spirit of apostasy and revolt, thus abandoning their fountain of living water.

We feel the earnestness of this later prophet's concern for the second temple as he cries out and prays:

17:12 **A glorious throne set on high at the beginning,**
    Is the place of our sanctuary.
13 **O Lord, the hope of Israel,**
    All who are forsaking thee shall be ashamed,
    And those who have revolted [from thee] in the land shall be thrown into
      confusion,
    For they have abandoned the fountain of living water.

5. *Keep the Sabbath Holy* (17:19-27). This comes before us in the Masoretic Text as an autobiographical account of the prophet, "Thus the Lord spoke to me." Since the word "to me" (*ēlay*) does not appear in the Septuagint, we cannot say with certainty that an autobiographical narrative underlies it. In its present form its prolixity, its Deuteronomic style, and its repeated expressions indicate that it belongs to the third source which underlies the book of Jeremiah, the addresses of Jeremiah in Deuteronomic redaction. While thus not directly from Jeremiah, Rudolph is right in his judgment that

there underlies this passage an authentic word of Jeremiah who saw in the self-seeking desecration of the Sabbath a symptom of Judean disobedience and hard-heartedness. The redactor intended that the warning of the prophet should sharpen the consciousness that the catastrophe of 587 was deserved. When these verses were written down the nation had already met the decision here laid before it, the threat of vs. 27 had become reality, and vss. 25-26 remained a wishful dream which could to be sure become actuality if now the warning of the prophet were heeded.[40]

The prophet is commanded to stand in the Benjamin Gate of Jerusalem, where the kings enter and leave the city, and to repeat what he does there in all the other gates through which the rank and file of the nation's city dwellers and peasants alike go in and out. By delivering the Lord's message he is to call the people back with renewed emphasis to the ancient law of sabbath observance (Exod. 20:8, 10), which in Jeremiah's early ministry had been reissued in the Deuteronomic Code (Deut. 5:14). The situation

[40] *Op. cit.*, p. 102.

to which he addressed himself was as follows: the peasants were accustomed to bring in their wares from the countryside, and they were sold in the Jerusalem market on the sabbath (vs. 28). The later picture from Nehemiah's reforms (445 B.C.) helps us to see the developing situation where, as he tells us, he "saw in Judah men . . . bringing in heaps of grain and loading them on asses; and also wine, grapes, figs, and all kinds of burdens, which they brought into Jerusalem on the sabbath day" (Neh. 13:15). And the city dwellers carried wares out of their houses on the sabbath, bound for the market (vs. 22). The Deuteronomic writer sees the observing of the sabbath as something of extreme importance. It was a law which Judah had ceased to observe, but upon its faithful observance the fate of land and people depends. If kings and commoners alike observe it, there will be prosperity. Through its gates will then steadily pass a prosperous commerce between the city of Jerusalem and the entire land of Judah. The prophet first pictures his country in political terminology, mentioning the cities of Judah, the area contiguous to Jerusalem, and the intimately related tribal area of Benjamin. Then he pictures it in terms of the varied topography of Judah—the low-hung hills of the Shephelah, the Judean highlands, and the Negeb, the south country, Hebron and beyond. From all these regions there will pour into Jerusalem—conceived as then firmly re-established, with its own monarchs in honorable control—the people of Judah bringing all the products of the land that are essential to a well-regulated and richly furnished cultic worship in the temple. But if the law of sabbath observance is not kept, Jerusalem shall be consumed by fire kindled by the assailing enemy, as had actually happened (in 587), after which this Deuteronomic editor wrote.

The editor from whom vss. 19-27 come well knew how the warnings of Jeremiah had gone unheeded. But through his method of bringing Jeremiah's teaching to those now in exile, he suggests that the great prophet is yet speaking. His thoughts are still crucial.

The law is now achieving heightened importance, and the cult upon which Judaism was destined to rally—Ezek. 40–48 points the way—is gaining steadily increasing significance for the Jewish people. To be sure, he set Jeremiah's thoughts out of focus to some extent, but with remarkable effectiveness he brought them a new focus pertinent to the needs of a later day.

17:19 **Thus said the Lord to me: Go and stand in the Gate of Benjamin, through which the kings of Judah go out and in, and in all the gates of Jerusalem, 20 and say to them: "Listen to the word of the Lord, kings of Judah, and all Judah, and** all who live in Jerusalem, who come in through these gates. 21 Thus says the Lord: Take care at peril of your lives that you carry no loads on the sabbath day, 22 and that you do not carry out any loads from your houses on the sabbath day, and that you do no work, but that you keep the sabbath day holy, just as I commanded your fathers." 23 But they did not listen nor did they incline their ears, but they stiffened their necks so as not to hear, and so as not to accept correction. 24 But if you listen earnestly to me, says the Lord, so as not to carry a load through the gates of the city on the sabbath day, but so as to keep the sabbath day holy, not doing any work in it, 25 there will come through the gates of this city kings sitting upon the throne of David, riding in chariots and on horses, they, their princes, the men of Judah and those dwelling in Jerusalem, and this city shall abide forever. 26 And there shall come from the cities of Judah, and from the environs of Jerusalem, and from the land of Benjamin, aye from the Shephelah and from the hill country and from the south, those bringing burnt offerings and sacrifices, meal offerings and incense, and those bringing thank offerings to the house of the Lord. 27 But if you do not listen to me as regards keeping the sabbath day holy, by not carrying a load or coming with it through the gates of Jerusalem on the sabbath day, I will kindle a fire in its gates, and it shall consume the palaces of Jerusalem and shall not be extinguished.

6. *Child Sacrifice the Cause of Jerusalem's Destruction* (19:2b-9, 11b-13). This later supplement to the original account by Baruch comes from the hand of the Deuteronomic editor who had Baruch's narrative before him (19:1-2a, 10-11a, 14-15) as he wrote. This is clear because his choice of the unusual words in vs. 7, "and I will spill out," [41] i.e., "make void," the sagacity of Judah, can be understood only when there was intended by him a play on words with "a flask of pottery" [42] in vss. 1, 10. Also in vs. 12a, "so I will do" presupposes the procedure with the flask as described in vs. 10, "you shall break the flask of pottery."

This Deuteronomic supplement of Baruch's original account is concerned with what was to the Deuteronomic editor a detestable and abominable cultic rite which had swept back into Judah under King Manasseh, and now flared into new life—child sacrifice. Canaanite in its ultimate origin, it was a phase of the Canaanite fertility cult and was early practiced in Israel. Calling attention to the sacrifice of the first-born male as required in the Covenant Code (Exod. 22:29) George Harford explains: "It represents the survival of a primitive belief that life is sacred, and that the first, fresh products of fertilizing power are specially fit for sacramental use." [43] As Volz says, this cult, as practiced with great intensity in this era, gives evi-

[41] Reading *úbaqqōthí* from *bāqaq*.
[42] Reading *baqbúq*.
[43] In Peake, *Commentary on the Bible*, p. 189.

dence of "the hopeless distance between the prophet Jeremiah on the one hand, and the Judean nation on the other, in which at that time this sacrifice was still practiced: it proves at the same time how foreign influence had distorted the original, noble character of the people of the Lord and its worship." [44] Truly as Jeremiah put it, the "choice vine" had become "a rank vine" (2:21).

The Deuteronomic editor to whom we owe this supplement inserts his contribution at this point mainly because the entrance to the Potter's Gate, where the episode of ch. 19 is set, lay close to the entrance to the valley of Ben-hinnom, where the rite of child sacrifice was performed. In the judgment of the Deuteronomic editor it was the awful horror of child sacrifice which was bringing about the downfall of the Judean state in terrible catastrophe. For him it was the sin of sins in Judah. He was convinced that the valley of Ben-hinnom, now viewed as a holy place, would be shown up for what it actually was—a valley of murder. His thought goes further, as he extends the judgment upon the high place of Topheth to Jerusalem as a whole. The entire city will become a Topheth filled with the slain bodies of those whom the Lord will give over into the hands of Judah's enemies. Vs. 9, although oriented toward the future, is filled with the stark realism of the siege Jerusalem experienced in 587, and shows that this whole supplement dates from exilic times. Thus runs the supplement as inserted by the Deuteronomic editor:

19:2*b* To the valley of Ben-hinnom, which lies at the entrance of the Potsherd Gate, and proclaim there the words which I will speak to you, 3 and say, Hear the word of the Lord, you kings of Judah, and you who live in Jerusalem. Thus says the Lord of hosts, the God of Israel, See I am about to bring evil upon this place [i.e., Topheth] so that the ears of everyone who hears it will tingle. 4 Because hey have forsaken me and have profaned this place and have sacrificed in it to other gods, whom they and their fathers had not known, and because the kings of Judah filled up this place [Topheth] with innocent blood, 5 because they built the high place of Baal [cf. 7:31] to burn their sons in the fire as burnt offerings to Baal, which I did not command or direct and which did not come into my mind. 6 Therefore, lo, days will come, says the Lord, when they will no longer call this place Topheth or the valley of Ben-hinnom, but the valley of murder. 7 And I will spill [i.e., empty out, make void] the sagacity of Judah and Jerusalem on account of this place [Topheth] and I will let them fall by the sword before their enemies and at the hand of those who seek their lives, and will give their corpses as food to the birds of the heavens and to the wild beasts of the earth. 8 And I will make this city a fright and a hissing. Everyone who passes by it will be

[44] *Jeremia*, p. 201.

appalled and astounded over all its scourgings, 9 and I will give them to eat of the flesh of their sons and of their daughters, and one will eat the flesh of the other in the siege and stress into which their enemies and those who seek their life shall bring them. 11b And in Topheth they shall bury because there is no other place to bury. 12 So will I do to this place, says the Lord, in order to make this city like Topheth. 13 And the houses of Jerusalem and the houses of the kings of Judah will be defiled like the place of Topheth—all the houses upon the roofs of which they burned incense to all the host of heaven and poured out drink offerings to other gods.

7. *The Warning of Jerusalem's Destruction to the Jews of the Diaspora* (22:8-9). These verses are clearly not from Jeremiah but are an addition from a Deuteronomic editor from postexilic times. They are influenced in detail by Deut. 29:22 ff. especially vss. 24-26 (but they refer to the city of Jerusalem instead of the land of Judah) and by I Kings 9:8-9 (but they refer to the city instead of, as there, the temple). They reflect the destruction of Jerusalem and were intended by the Deuteronomic editor as a pedagogical supplement serving as a warning to the Jews of the Diaspora.

22:8 And many nations shall pass by this city and shall say, each to his neighbor, "Why did the Lord do like this to this great city?" 9 And they will say, "Because they forsook the covenant of the Lord their God and worshiped other gods and served them."

8. *When Legalism Reigned in the Congregation* (23:34-40). This is not from Jeremiah. Volz maintains that it comes from one to whom for himself and his contemporaries piety had been reduced to external things, and literal worship of the law. This Talmudic devotee of the law says that anyone, prophet or priest or a member of the laity, who keeps in use the term "burden" when he means the "oracle" or "revelation" or "answer" of the Lord, will be punished by God—both himself and his family. The Lord's word is for every person "burden" enough. The question put to the prophet when one seeks the Lord's revelation should be simply, "What has the Lord answered?" or "What says the Lord?" If they even once use the term "burden of the Lord" in the sense of revelation they will be borne off— they and their city—by the Lord and abandoned to unforgettable disgrace and humiliation. It is an indescribable relief to be quite sure that such literal, legalistic thoughts as are given in vss. 34-40 do not come from the great soul of Jeremiah. These harsh verses come from late postexilic Judaism, when legalism and literalism reigned in the congregation. Volz is

probably right in viewing this section as one of the latest passages of the Old Testament canon,[45] possibly dating *ca.* 200.

23:34 But as for the prophet or the priest or the people who continue to say, "The burden of the Lord," I will punish that man and his household. 35 Thus [rather] shall you say, each to his neighbor or each to his brother, "What has the Lord answered?" or "What has the Lord said?" 36 But "the burden of the Lord" you must not keep in use any longer, for should not his word be for each the burden? But you have diverted the words of the living God, the Lord of hosts, our God, from their right meaning. 37 Thus shall you say to the prophet, "What has the Lord answered you?" or "What says the Lord?" 38 But if you should say, "The burden of the Lord," therefore thus has the Lord said, Because you use this expression, "The burden of the Lord," even though I sent to you saying that you are not to say, "The burden of the Lord," 39 therefore lo, I will certainly carry you off, and I will abandon you and the city which I gave to you and your fathers from my sight. 40 And I will place upon you perpetual disgrace and unending humiliation which will not be forgotten.

9. *The Contrast Between the Exiles and Those Left in Judah* (29:16-20). This comes from the hand of the Deuteronomic editor. The verses are not an original part of Jeremiah's letter to the exiles, but intrusive in it. They are concerned not primarily with the exiles but with Zedekiah and those who are still living in Jerusalem. They clearly imply (vs. 17) Jeremiah's experience of the vision of the two baskets of figs as given in ch. 24, but that chapter is most likely later than ch. 29, and at any rate was unknown to the readers of Jeremiah's letter. But 29:10-14, an authentic part of Jeremiah's letter, clearly corresponds to 24:5-7, which interprets the meaning of "the good figs." So the Deuteronomic editor felt the need of adding as a supplement 29:16-20, corresponding to 24:8-10, which interprets the meaning of "the bad figs," in order to accentuate the contrast between the exiles and those in Jerusalem.[46]

Thus the Deuteronomic editor supplements Jeremiah's words:

29:16 For thus says the Lord concerning the king who is sitting upon the throne of David, and concerning all the people who dwell in this city—your brethren who did not go out with you with the company of exiles, 17 Thus says the Lord of hosts: Lo, I am about to send among them sword, famine, pestilence, and I will make them like the disgusting figs which cannot be eaten because they are so bad. 18 And I will pursue them with the sword, with the famine, and with

[45] Volz, *op. cit.*, p. 242, and for the date of the prophetic canon cf. Pfeiffer, *Introduction to the Old Testament*, p. 61.

[46] I am indebted to the careful analysis of this passage and its comparison with ch. 24 given by Rudolph, *Jeremia*, p. 156.

the pestilence, and I will make them a cause of terror to all the kingdoms of the earth, an object of curse, an occasion of horror, a butt of derisive hissing, and a target of disgrace among all the nations among whom I have banished them, 19 because they would not listen to my words, says the Lord, which I sent by my servants the prophets, early and often, but they would not listen. 20 But as for you, listen to the word of the Lord, all the company of exiles which I sent from Jerusalem to Babylon.

10. *The Moral Accountability of the Individual* (31:29-30). This appears to anticipate the pioneering teaching of Ezek. 18:1-20 on the question of God's retribution upon the individual. The early days of the Exile, when seemingly undeserved suffering was widespread, and when the exiles felt they were under the interdict of their fathers' sins, are herein presupposed. Most likely, however, the verses are later than Jeremiah and dependent upon the penetrating concept of the direct responsibility of the individual to God which we owe to Ezekiel, Jeremiah's younger contemporary. The editor who inserts these words views the fulfillment of Ezekiel's hope as still in the future.

> 31:29 In those days they shall not say any more:
> The fathers have eaten sour grapes
> And the children's teeth are set on edge,

30 But each one shall die because of his own iniquity. As for every man who eats the sour grapes—his teeth shall be set on edge.

11. *The Lord's Judgment of the World Beginning at Jerusalem* (25:18 [in part], 20, 22, 24). These verses, which reach us through the hand of the Deuteronomic editor, presuppose the final fall and destruction of Jerusalem (vs. 8) and have in the prospect of the author a universal judgment upon the nations which, beginning at Jerusalem, will come upon all inhabitants of the earth. The cup in this section is viewed as coming to all nations.

25:18 Jerusalem and the cities of Judah, and its kings and its princes so as to make them a desolation, an occasion of horror, a butt of derision and an object of a curse as is the case at this day, 20 and all the kings of the land of Uz, and all the kings of the land of the Philistines, 22 and all the kings of Tyre, and all the kings of Sidon, and the kings of the coastland which is beyond the sea, 24 and all the kings of Arabia, 25 and all the kings of Zimki [47] [i.e., Elam], and all the

[47] So read instead of Zimri with F. Perles by "Atbash," wherein one writes the Hebrew alphabet in two rows, one from the first letter (Aleph) to the last letter (Tau) and the other from the last letter (Tau) to the first letter (Aleph), and substitutes one for the other, whereby Zimki becomes Elam, so omit "and all the kings of Elam" which follows Zimki, as a gloss.

kings of Media, 26 and all the kings of the north, near and far in relation to one another, and all the kingdoms which are upon the surface of the earth, and the king of Babylon shall drink after them.

In vss. 27-31, 33, the late editor has in prospect the inescapable judgment of the Lord upon all the inhabitants of the world. All nations are to drink. The Lord's judgment begins at Jerusalem. The Lord is at the point of calling for his sword against the earth's inhabitants for his controversy is with all humanity. The roar of the Lord from his sanctuary in Jerusalem is heard in all nations. And the bodies of those slain by his sword will lie ungathered, as dung upon the ground.

25:27 And you shall speak to them: Thus says the Lord of hosts, God of Israel, "Drink and get drunk and vomit and fall down not to rise, from before the sword which I am about to send among you." 28 And it shall be that if they refuse to take the cup from your hand to drink, you shall say to them: "Thus says the Lord of hosts, you shall surely drink. 29 For lo, in this city which bears my name, I am about to begin to do evil, and as for you—will you be at all exempt from punishment? You will not be exempt, for I am about to call the sword against all the inhabitants of the earth, says the Lord of hosts. 30 So you shall preach to them all these words and say to them:

'The Lord will roar from the heights,
And from his sanctuary he will utter his voice;
He will roar loudly against his abode,
With a shout as of treaders of grapes,
31 To all the inhabitants of the earth,
Comes his battle roar,
To the end of the earth.
For the Lord has a dispute with the nations;
A controversy has he with all flesh.
The wicked I have given over [see Vulgate] to the sword,'
33 And there will be those slain by the Lord in that day from one end of the earth to the other. They will not be lamented or removed or buried. They will be like dung upon the surface of the ground."

MESSAGES OF SALVATION TO JEWS OF THE DIASPORA

1. *The Future Assembling of Exiled Judeans at Jerusalem* (3:17-18). Here (in vs. 17 beginning, "And they shall assemble") the Deuteronomic editor of the book of Jeremiah, writing in the time of the Diaspora, looks forward to the assemblage of Judeans at Jerusalem, all those now dispersed through all the nations.

3:17 And they shall assemble to it from all the nations, and they shall no longer follow the stubbornness of their evil heart. 18 In those days the house of Judah,

along with the house of Israel, will come together from the northland to the
land which I gave as a possession to their fathers.

2. *Wrath upon the Destroyers of Judah* (10:25). This verse, which appears in Ps. 79:6-7, is inconsistent in thought with Jeremiah's basic conviction (which he shared with Isaiah) that the pagan nations are instruments for the mediation of the Lord's punishment of Judah. Accordingly,
the verse is an addition from a Jewish scribe who, in a spirit quite contrary
to that of Jeremiah, prays:

> 10:25 Pour out thy wrath upon the nations
> Which do not know thee;
> Yes, upon the kingdoms
> Which do not call upon thy name.
> For they have devoured Jacob,
> And have devastated his abode.

3. *Restoration to Palestine from the Entire Diaspora* (16:14-15). In 16:10-
13 the Deuteronomic editor, writing from the days of the Babylonian exile,
answered the inevitable and pressing question of those now in exile, "What
have we done that we are thus suffering?"

But in 16:14-15, which reappear in 23:7-8, where they are in their original
context, a yet later redactor, in the light of deeper insight into the nature
and purpose of God to which Jeremiah himself had so richly contributed,
relieves the solemnity of the Deuteronomist's judgment by the glimpse of
a brighter time of salvation. In the meantime, Deutero-Isaiah (chs. 40–55)
has taught the world-wide reach and omnipotent purpose of the one God
in all the world. So our later redactor lays emphasis upon this mighty
God's power and purpose for his people. The time will come that in the
solemn moments when any Israelite takes an oath in the Lord's name, he
will invoke the God who is able to restore his people not only from the
north country of Babylonia and the other northern areas to which the
exiles of Israel and of Judah had been taken from 734 to 582, but from
every country to which they shall have been dispersed. Says this hopeful
prophetic spirit:

16:14 Therefore, see, days are coming, says the Lord, when it shall not be said
any more, "As the Lord lives who brought up the Israelites from the land of Egypt,"
15 but "As the Lord lives who brought the Israelites from the land of the north
and from the lands to which he drove them out, and will bring them back to
their land which I gave their fathers."

4. *The Conversion of Pagan Peoples to the Lord* (16:19-21).

The Deuteronomic editor here expresses his confidence in the conversion of pagan peoples to the Lord, which will follow this great achievement of a universal return of the Judean people to the homeland (16:14-15). In the editor's thought it is this return of all Judeans that will convince the pagan peoples of the superiority of the Lord's power and of the impotence of their own gods, and it will lead them to turn to the Lord. The phrase "in this moment" (vs. 21) presupposes that the hope of the acknowledgment of the Lord by the pagan peoples had already arisen but had been disappointed. It was Deutero-Isaiah (chs. 40–55) who had awakened that hope. The author of these verses believes that this hope—not realized through the return of the Babylonian exiles—will be realized "in this moment" when all the banished Judeans from all parts of the world will be returned by the power of the Lord to their homeland.

These three great verses here open with the address of a prayer to the Lord, the prophet's strength, protection, and refuge. To this active God of power, defense, and shelter come pagans from the distant inhabited areas of the earth. They come in recognition of the Lord's superiority to the gods— "nothing but deception" the prophet calls them—possessed and worshiped by their forebears, but now recognized by the pagans of the world for what they are—as insubstantial as "breath" and utterly powerless to help (vs. 19). For the deities that these pagan nations have worshiped hitherto are merely man-made idols (vs. 20). But "in this moment," when the Judean exiles from all over the world are returned by the Lord's power, the uncertainty and questionings on the part of the various pagan nations will be convincingly answered, and they will be brought to the knowledge of the Lord's name and nature (vs. 21).

The prophet prays on his own behalf, and likewise voices the confession of the nations who come to the Lord from all parts of the world:

> 16:19 O Lord, my strength and my protection,
> My refuge in the day of distress,
> To thee nations shall come
> From the ends of the earth, and say:
> "Nothing but deceptions have our fathers possessed,
> Worthlessness, with no benefit in them.
> 20 Can a man make gods for himself?
> But they are not gods!"

And the Lord answers them convincingly "in this moment" of the universal return of his people:

16:21 Therefore, lo, I am about to bring them to knowledge.
In this moment I will give them to know
My power and my might,
And they shall perceive that my name is the Lord.

5. *The Restoration of the Dispersed of Israel* (23:7-8). These verses also come from the time of the Diaspora, when the Jews had been dispersed into "all the lands to which I [the Lord] scattered them." The Exodus of Israel from Egypt represented so great a work of God that it was used as an oath asseverating the Lord as a mighty God of great power and great solicitude for his people. But the time is coming when the power of the Lord will restore the descendants of the exiles from the land of the Chaldeans in the north, and from all the other countries to which the Jews have been dispersed, to their homeland. Then men will swear by the God who will have made this new and greater exodus possbile. These verses also appear in 16:14-15, but they are here in their proper place. Writes the annotator:

23:7 Therefore, lo, days are coming, says the Lord, when they will not say any more, "As the Lord lives who brought up the Israelites out of the land of Egypt," 8 but "As the Lord lives who brought up all the descendants of Israel from the land of the north, and from all the lands to which I scattered them and returned them to their territory."

6. *Judah Will Have a Future in Palestine* (31:23-26). We rightly consider vss. 23-26 as an addition to the authentic words of Jeremiah, written by a Judean who, reading the noble promise to Ephraim given in 30:1-24; 31:2-22, hopes for something comparable to this for his beloved Judah, which is now suffering under the drastic blows which in 587 had brought the political state of Judah to a tragic end. The address to the whole land of Judah as "the holy mountain," as Cornill [48] maintains, would be strange in Jeremiah's mouth. Here in a prosperous abode Judeans will dwell comfortably in cities and towns, enjoying adequate pasturage for their herds and flocks, with the Lord caring for the weary and the hungry.

31:23 Thus says the Lord of hosts, the God of Israel: Yet again will they say this word in the land of Judah and in its cities when I shall have turned their fortunes:

"May the Lord bless you, prosperous habitation, the holy mountain."

24 And Judah and all its cities together will dwell in it, farmers and those who tend the flock. 25 For I will give drink to the weary soul and will satisfy every hungry soul.

[48] *Jeremia*, p. 342.

Vs. 26 is a marginal comment of a reader who, having read to the end this prophecy of felicity, and having lived in it with his very soul, comes back from the imaginative world of prophetic hope to face the stern reality of the problems of the postexilic era in which he lives, yet renewed and encouraged like one who awakes from a refreshing sleep. Upon the margin he writes his comment:

31:26 Upon this I awoke and looked up, and my sleep was sweet to me.

7. *The Lord Has a Future of Prosperity for Israel and Judah* (31:27-28). These two verses are editorial, their purpose being simply to connect together the prophecies concerning Ephraim (31:2 ff.) with the later message of salvation for Judah (31:23-36). Vs. 28 refers back to 1:12, wherein the vision of the almond twig teaches that God is "watching over his word." It also refers back to 1:10, but instead of Jeremiah's being the performer of the destructive and constructive action, it is here attributed directly to God. It would seem, as Volz[49] maintains, that these two verses are a gloss from a later editor who notes that the prophecy concerning Ephraim is a confirming example of that particular message in Jeremiah's call.

31:27 Lo, days are coming, says the Lord, when I will sow the house of Israel and the house of Judah with offspring of men and animals. 28 And just as I watched over them [when it was time] to uproot and to demolish, to overthrow and to destroy and to hurt, so I will watch over them [when it is time] to build and to plant.

8. *Jerusalem Will Be Rebuilt for the Lord* (31:38-40). This is a Judean addition to the prophecies of salvation for Ephraim. The section dates after the catastrophe of 587, when Jerusalem was destroyed by the Chaldeans. The Judean author takes his cue from 30:18b, "Cities shall be rebuilt upon their own tells," and from 31:4a, "Again will I build you, and you will be rebuilt." Interpreting these passages as though they had to do with Jerusalem, he attaches to Jerusalem the hope for permanence which Jeremiah had held out for North Israel in vss. 35-37. The city will be rebuilt for the Lord.

He starts with the northern boundary of the city as it was when he wrote —from the Tower of Hananel on the northeast, mentioned by Nehemiah (3:1; 12:39) and in Zechariah (14:10), to the Corner Gate, on the northwest, where some centuries before, the destruction of Jerusalem's wall by

---

[49] *Jeremia*, p. 279.

King Jehoash of Israel had halted (II Kings 14:13). The border line anticipated then continues straight out to the hill Gareb, possibly, as H. Schmidt [50]
believes likely, the hill which overlooks the valley of Hinnom (Josh. 15:8).
The line then turns round toward Goah opposite the valley of the
Rephaim,[51] where the valley of Hinnom and the valley of the Kidron meet
at right angles.[52] Included within the rebuilt city will be the entire valley
of Hinnom, filled as it now is with the carcasses of animals, and ashes of
sacrifices made to Molech. We feel with the narrator the uncleanness which
this area now has, but soon it will be sacred territory. The rebuilt city also
will include the fields over the Kidron to the corner of the Horse Gate in the
eastern part of the city. This whole area will be holy to the Lord. And the city
itself will never again be uprooted or torn down.

31:38 **Lo, days are coming, says the Lord, when the city will be rebuilt for the**
Lord, from the Tower of Hananel to the Corner Gate. 39 And the measuring line
will continue right out to the hill Gareb, and will then turn round toward Goah.
40 Opposite [53] the valley [i.e., of the Rephaim] and the place of carcasses and of
sacrifice ashes [i.e., the valley of Hinnom], all the fields over the watercourse of
Kidron to the corner of the Horse Gate in the east will be holy to the Lord. Never
again will it be uprooted or torn down.

9. *The Lord's Plan of Ultimate Salvation for The Exiles* (32:29b-41).
This section is an interpolation which grew out of the felt need to under-
gird the divine answer to Jeremiah's prayer (32:26-29a, 42-44) with later
insights that are in harmony with it. The interpolater abounds in phrases
and concepts such as characterize the Deuteronomic editor of the book, as a
comparison of vss. 29b-41 with 7:12-31 readily shows. The interpolater in
vss. 29b-41 is concerned with two questions, the guilt and the salvation of
his people. In these verses he views the Israelites, the Judeans, and the inhabitants of Jerusalem as all guilty before God, and he moves from one to
the other of these groups somewhat loosely, but his earnest concern is with
sin and guilt, specifically the sins of Jerusalem such as the worship of Baal,
and the sacrifice of children to the god Molech in the valley of Hinnom.

In vss. 36-41 the interpolater turns from the Lord's condemnation and
destruction of his people, of which surrendered Jerusalem is the symbol, to
his plan of salvation for them. We are clearly in a time later than that of

---

[50] *Jeremia*, in *Die Grossen Propheten*, p. 361.

[51] Rudolph, *Jeremia*, p. 173.

[52] Cornill, *Jeremia*, p. 356.

[53] Reading with Rudolph, *Jeremia*, p. 173, nōkhaḥ hā'emeq, and after the latter word
inserting ûm°qōm, which, due to haplography, has fallen out.

Jeremiah. God says that he is about to gather "to this place" exiles of the Diaspora "from all the lands to which I have thrust them out" (vs. 37). And this is to be not merely an outer return of God's people, but an inner restoration, as well, of heart and spirit. Echoes of Ezek. 36:26-28 show that the Lord's program of restoration is in his mind (vss. 38-39). And basic for his thought is Jeremiah's conception of the new covenant (31:31-34), which now in the interpolater's thought issues in an eternal covenant (vs. 40), a bond which will unite the redeemed people to their God forever. But in this ideal picture, where Jeremiah had emphasized the universal knowledge of God (31:34), this later writer emphasizes the fear of God (vs. 40). And it is God's eternal covenant that assures to his people permanent hold upon the land (vs. 41). Thus runs the later supplement to the brief answer of the Lord, who is the speaker.

32:29b And [they shall burn] the houses on the roofs of which they burned incense to the Baal and poured out libations to other gods, so as to provoke me to anger. 30 For the Israelites and Judeans have been doing from their youth—yes are doing—what is evil in my eyes. 31 For this city, from the day they built it even until today, so for as it concerns me, has been set toward my anger and toward my wrath, so that I must remove it from attachment to me 32 because of all the evil of the Israelites and Judeans which they have done, so as to provoke my anger—they, their kings, their nobles, their priests and their prophets, and the rank and file of Judah, and the inhabitants of Jerusalem. 33 They turned their back to me and not their face, although I taught them, speaking earnestly, and they did not listen so as to receive correction, 34 but set up their idols in the house which is named for me, thus defiling it, 35 and built high places to Baal, which are in the valley of Hinnom, to devote their sons and their daughters to Molech—which I did not command them to do, nor did their doing of this abomination ever enter my mind—so as to cause Judah to sin. 36 So now, thus says the Lord, God of Israel, concerning this city which you are saying has been given into the hands of the king of Babylon, by sword, famine, and pestilence, 37 Lo, I am about to gather them from all the lands to which I have thrust them out in my anger and my great wrath, and I will bring them back to this place, and I will make them dwell in security. 38 And they shall be my people, and I will be their God. 39 And I will give them a new heart and a spirit [54] to fear me all the days so as to secure good things for them and for their children after them. 40 And I will make with them an eternal covenant in accordance with which I will not turn away from them, and I will put the fear of me in their heart, so they will not turn away from me. 41 I will regard them so as to do them good, and I will plant them in this land in faithfulness with all my heart and with all my soul.

[54] Reading with Syriac, ḥādhāsh and wᵉrûaḥ.

10. *A Flyleaf of Encouragement for Postexilic Times* (33:14-26). This is the longest connected passage in the book of Jeremiah which is lacking in the Septuagint. If at *ca.* 200 B.C., when the Septuagint came into being, this passage was in the Hebrew text, it would certainly have been included because of its great note of hope. Rudolph,[55] calling attention to its strongly apologetic quality, its aim to defeat the pessimism which developed in the minds of those who had waited in vain for the fulfillment of the old prophecies, suggests that before it was taken up into the Hebrew text it had had an independent existence as a flyleaf of encouragement, taken indeed in large part from the prophecies of Jeremiah, and so it was later incorporated into that book and placed at the end of the prophecies of salvation.

Volz[56] is probably right in dating this section in the time of Malachi (*ca.* 500-450)), when the priesthood had become degenerate, but when the hope for a renewal of the Lord's covenant with the Levitical priesthood was very great (Mal. 2:4-9). Rudolph[57] would hold open for it the period after Ezra and Nehemiah in the time of the Chronicler, *ca.* 300.

In the first portion, vss. 14-18, the author refers implicitly to God's gracious promise to his people as expressed in Jeremiah's letter to the exiles (ch. 29). Then he takes up Jeremiah's prophecy of a Messiah in 23:5-6, but interprets it as referring not to one particular messianic king, but to a succession of kings of the lineage of David, this succession to assure permanence. And the "in his days" of 23:6 here in vs. 16 becomes "in those days." Jerusalem will then be called "The Lord is our righteousness." Moreover, to the expectation of the kingship of the Davidic line in Judah as a permanent institution, this author adds the expectation of a permanent line of legitimate priests who are charged with responsibility for supervision of the sacrifices in the temple, a thought quite foreign to Jeremiah's conception of religion, but perfectly at home in late postexilic Judaism. Thus he portrays his hope for Judah and Jerusalem:

33:14 Lo, days are coming, says the Lord, when I will carry out the good things of which I have spoken concerning the house of Israel and concerning the house of Judah. 15 In those days and in that time I will cause a righteous shoot to sprout for David, and he shall exercise justice and righteousness in the land. 16 In those days Judah shall be saved and Jerusalem shall dwell securely, and this is its name which it shall be called, "The Lord is our righteousness."

17 For thus says the Lord, There shall not be cut off from David a man to sit on the throne of the house of Israel. 18 And from the priests, the Levites, there

[55] *Op. cit.*, pp. 184-85.
[56] *Op. cit.*, p. 312.
[57] *Op. cit.*, p. 187.

shall never be cut off from my presence a man to offer whole burnt offerings and meal offerings and sacrifices.

In vss. 19-22 the writer takes up a thought which Jeremiah expressed in 31:35-37, the uniformity and dependability of nature. As surely as night follows day, there will be a perpetual succession of Davidic monarchs and of Levitical priests. And the vast increase in population destined for Israel is comparable to the stars, which by their very multitude baffle the mind of man to compute, just as do the immeasurable grains of sand on the seashore. Thus this prophet offers his hope for the stability of restored Israel.

33:19 And the word of the Lord came to Jeremiah saying, 20 Thus says the Lord: If my covenant with the day and the night should be broken, so that day and night would not come in their time, 21 only then would also my covenant with David my servant be broken, so that there would not be a son reigning on his throne or Levitical priests serving me. 22 Just as the host of the heavens cannot be counted, or the sand of the sea measured, so will I increase the descendants of David my servant and the Levites ministering to me.

In vss. 23-26 this writer meets a criticism voiced by renegade Jews who have grown cynical about any hopeful future for Judah. Once they were composed of two nations, Judah and Israel, both claiming to be the chosen of God. "But," so these apostates are saying, "look at us now. We are not even a nation" (vs. 24).

The writer answers again by an illustration from natural law. The heavens and the earth, created by God, are under his law. The provision God is making for a steady line of kings, Davidic in lineage and Hebrew in race, is as sure as that day follows night, and night follows day.

33:23 And the word of the Lord came to Jeremiah saying: 24 Have you not seen what this people are saying? "As for the two nations which the Lord chose and rejected, he has spurned his people so that they are not any more a nation before him." 25 Thus says the Lord: If I have not created day and night, if I have not established the laws of heaven and earth, 26 only then would I reject the descendants of Jacob and David my servant, so as not to take from his posterity rulers of the lineage of Abraham, Isaac, and Jacob. For I will restore their fortunes, and treat them with compassion.

Pfeiffer [58] views ch. 33 as the climax of the second act of the eschatological drama, "giving a picture of the rebuilt Jerusalem," in which "the forgiven and redeemed Jews" with "unbroken lines of Davidic kings and Levitical priests" will be feared by the nations of the earth.

[58] *Introduction to the Old Testament*, p. 510.

Abiding Values in Jeremiah

WE HAVE TRACED THE DEVELOPMENT OF JEREMIAH'S LIFE, PROPHETIC CA-
REER, AND MESSAGE SO FAR AS IT IS RECORDED IN HISTORY. WE HAVE
taken account of the transition which Judaism made from the temple-centered religion in Palestine to the synagogue-centered religion of the Diaspora,
in large part under the influence of his teachings. Moreover, we have observed that largely through the Deuteronomic redactor of the book of Jeremiah supplements to and adaptations of the prophet's words, both from
the angle of judgment and of salvation, came to Jews of the Diaspora.
The greatest centers of interest or areas of concern were Jewish communi-
ties in Egypt, Babylon, and Palestine. It remains for us to consider the
abiding values to be found in his life and work. For Jeremiah is not merely
a character in ancient history but a living voice with a message of striking
pertinency for today. Ten items summarize the contribution of Jeremiah
as a prophet and man of God.

1. *Jeremiah blazed new trails of prophetic utterance.* He was speaker,
poet, and author. Many of his utterances were aphorisms, brief pithy sayings,
concrete in imagery and packed with thought content.

> 13:23 Can the Ethiopian change his skin
> Or the leopard his spots?
> Only then could you do good
> Who are practiced in doing evil.

But he was also a master in the sustained theme where he gives a full development of particular subjects and affixes a title thereto in each case
such as "Concerning the drought" (14:1–15:3), "Concerning the Judean
royal house" (21:11–23:8), and "Concerning the prophets" (23:9-40). Here
are addresses, including in each case a considerable number of verses which
in a well-rounded way fully interpret a single theme.

It is as a lyric poet that Jeremiah is truly brilliant. The subject matter of his poetry is composed largely of the common scenes of the daily life of Judah viewed through the eyes of one who loved them. He takes us to the market place, to the open squares of Jerusalem. He takes us to the desolate desert, and to the mountaintop where we hear the shrill lament of wailing women. Imaginatively and in vivid realism he portrays war. On the battlefield the unburied dead lie prone on the ground. We note the weird silence of abandoned ruins. With him we experience the universal calamity of dearth, and we see servants returning chagrined and confounded from waterless cisterns, covering their heads in the Oriental gesture of lament.

A few vivid strokes of his brush and we see Rachel, ancestress of the northern tribes, weeping for her children, and we hear her sobbing in comfortless sorrow over her exiled sons and daughters, the descendants of the exiles of northern Israel. The prophet treasures the dear and familiar sounds of normal Palestinian life, the mirthful shouts of innocent fun in the streets of Jerusalem and in Judean cities. We hear the proud, dominating voice of the bridegroom and the gentle happy voice of the bride in response. Under his artistry we keep hearing the everywhere present sound of the grinding of the millstones in the daily routine of every village. These common sights and sounds touched something very deep in Jeremiah's nature.

Jeremiah the prophet and poet was also an author whose masterpiece (chs. 30–31) is designated as a book (*sēpher*) of salvation. It was never intended to be spoken but it was written to be read by the descendants of the exiles from northern Israel. In this little book are some of the prophet's greatest thoughts and they represent something new in prophetic technique. Moreover, he was the first of the prophets to resort to the prophetic letter, and among the most influential letters in human history is the one which he wrote from Jerusalem to those who had been taken as captive to Babylon along with youthful king Jehoiachin. It is the first employment of a prophetic technique which was to reach its finest development in the epistles of the New Testament.

2. *God is at work in contemporary history.* Beginning with his call, Jeremiah became aware that God had appointed him as a prophet to the nations. His was an age of international ferment and of swift and surprising transition. He sweeps within his survey the smaller peoples of the Palestinian area, the Phoenician city-states of Tyre and Sidon, the still largely Bedouin Ammonites and Moab and Edom. He knows their geography, their national qualities and traits, their traditions, and the things

they prize. His keen eye penetrated to these nations' essential characteristics, peoples comparable to his own Judah. But he deals also with great world powers such as Assyria, the dominant nation in the Middle East when he received his call. He was to live through and see the utter and final collapse of that supreme military machine of the ancient world. He knew the Egyptians, the strength and the weakness of their Pharaohs. He knew the Medes, just emerging into view as an ally of the newly aroused Chaldea, the nation which later at Carchemish in 605 decisively defeated Pharaoh Neco of Egypt, and by reason of which Judah exchanged the yoke of Egypt for that of Babylon.

As A. B. Davidson put it, "Carchemish was an epoch in Jeremiah's life." Going back to the time of Isaiah, when King Ahaz, against the preaching of the prophet, appealed to Tiglath-pileser III, Davidson continues:

Carchemish was to Jeremiah what the appeal of Ahaz to Tiglath-pileser was to Isaiah: like a flash of lightning in the darkness, it lighted up to him the whole line of God's purposes on to the end. He foresaw his past anticipations passing into history. The conviction seized his mind that it was the will of [the Lord] that all nations should serve the king of Babylon; to refuse his yoke, whether for Israel or another people, was to resist the decree of God.[1]

It was not by astute weighing of the military power of nations, whether great or small, or by keen penetration into the political machinations of peoples in an era of international ferment, that Jeremiah arrived at such conclusions. His presentiments were pure prophetic insights. They were revelations from God to him, no doubt often as inexplicable to himself in their origin as to others, yet bearing upon them the stamp of certainty.

3. *God is at work in the individual soul.* No prophet started from himself, his own mind, his own intimate spiritual experience, as did Jeremiah. Long before the social science of psychology had come into being his psychological insight into the workings of his own personality received his pioneering analysis and description. He had the power to stand, as it were, apart from himself and gaze into the unplumbed, abysmal depths of his own inner being, then describe in intelligible words what he saw and felt and knew. Yet to him the most significant thing in this power was not that he knew his own inner life with such objectivity and thoroughness, but that God knew him thus inwardly with perfect comprehension. Hence even when he was shamed, shocked, and humiliated by what he saw within his own heart, he found unspeakable joy in the realization that he was

---

[1] In James Hastings, ed., *A Dictionary of the Bible,* II, 571.

comprehended by God, and that he was communicating with him, receiving his word, conscious of his creative presence. Not only was God present in his soul, but transformingly present, illuminating, empowering and steadying him.

4. *The belief in a future of hope.* Jeremiah lived in a time of national collapse. He saw the fall of the Judean state, having proclaimed it for forty years before it came. There is at times a poignant pessimism in Jeremiah. With divinely illumined eyes he saw that the state of Judah was corrupt at the core. On the basis of objective moral principles he proclaimed its certain fall. He prophesied the ruin of the temple when men prized it as a fetish and crowded its courts. He knew and proclaimed that the time would come when to every Judean would be left only his own life and that "for a prey." But as George Adam Smith has said: "When the rotten surface of the national life thus broke under the prophet he fell upon the deeper levels of the individual heart, and not only found the native sinfulness of this to be the explanation of the public and social corruption but discovered also soil for the seed-bed of new truths and new hopes." [2]

In a mood of pessimism Jeremiah raised the question which the powerful grip of corrupt habits upon Judeans had caused to arise in his mind, "Can the Ethiopian change his skin or the leopard his spots?" But as Raymond Calkins has said: "Jeremiah never went to the length of believing that this defect was irradicable. He was no believer in total depravity. The ultimate truth about the human heart was not its inclination to evil, but its instinct for God." [3] One of the greatest sentences in Jeremiah is in his letter to the exiles (29:11) when he says, speaking for God:

29:11 **For I know the plans that I am forming, which have to do with you, plans for your welfare and not for [your] harm, to give you a future and a [ground for] hope.**

How that sureness of a future and a ground for hope steadied the sentiment makers among the exiles, and how it today undergirds temporary suffering, both national and personal, with faith-filled belief in a hopeful future! Here is an ultimate optimism based upon faith in God.

5. *The inner life, the heart, is the center of religion.* Among the most significant words in the teaching of Jesus is the utterance in Mark 7:21-23: "For from within, out of the heart of man, come evil thoughts, fornication, theft, murder, adultery, coveting, wickedness, deceit, licentiousness, envy,

[2] *Jeremiah*, p. 368.
[3] *Jeremiah the Prophet*, p. 358.

slander, pride, foolishness. All these evil things come from within, and they defile a man." Here is a religion of inwardness, not of outer act but of inner motive.

But centuries before these great words were uttered by Jesus, Jeremiah had blazed the trail of inwardness, when he placed the seat of religion in the heart of the individual person in words that represent the greatest single contribution from Jeremiah to religion. It is his conception of the new covenant which God will make with his people in which, according to Jeremiah, a new life with God commences. It came in the silent period of Jeremiah's ministry when he did not publicly preach but when he privately taught and profoundly thought, between the beginning of the Deuteronomic reform and the death of King Josiah. It was his noblest word in a new type of prophetic ministry to which he then resorted, wherein the written word was used instead of the—at the time impracticable— spoken word, in a message to the northern exiles. Thus the Lord speaks:

31:33*b*-34 **I will put my law in their innermost being, and upon their heart I will write it, and I will be their God and they shall be my people. 34 And they shall not teach any more—each his neighbor and each his brother, saying, "Know the Lord," but all of them shall know me, from the most insignificant of them to the most important of them, says the Lord; for I will forgive their iniquities, and their sins I will not remember any more.**

Calkins says as regards this great word of spiritual inwardness, "Nowhere does the Old Testament more nearly approximate the New than in this inspired teaching of Jeremiah." [4]

6. *The victory of conscience over inclination.* Jeremiah's whole life teaches this, not so much by word as by example. He would have escaped the compulsion to prophesy if he could. But the message of the Lord burned in his very soul. He was timid, sensitive, introspective, and full of fears. At times he longed to flee from it all, and dwell in the wilderness. To be a prophet was to him an excruciatingly painful experience. Yet he could not escape his prophetic commission. For over forty years he had to speak the Lord's word which was constantly counter to his own inclination and to that of the people to whom that prophetic word came. Throughout his life his message ever fell upon unwilling ears. Yet he went right on speaking to king, prince, or commoner the word that must be uttered for the God whose spokesman he knew himself to be.

7. *Religion in human experience is akin to instinct in the fowls of the air.*

[4] *Ibid.*

What is that element in the constitution of birds that leads them to migrate? Jeremiah saw great flocks of birds at particular times migrating to the south and at other particular times flying home again. Especially was he observant of how the storks, turtledoves, swifts, and swallows seemed thus to obey a deep-seated inner law of their being. Sensitive as he was to all aspects of nature, he saw that there was here in their obedience to this inner impulse something instructive.

Jeremiah taught that personal religion is comparable to that instinct. It is not something foisted upon a person from without. Rather is it a normal part of the constitution of man. Religion is, spiritually speaking, the soul's vital breath, its native air. It was in his own experience with God that this revelation came to him. Therefore he turned to God as naturally as a flower turns to the sun. Man's soul—every man's—is incomplete in himself and complete only in fellowship—and communion with God.

In Jeremiah we pass from "Thus saith the Lord" to "I have felt a Presence!" This consciousness of a Presence was by no means always a calm experience. Often that Other aroused a veritable storm within his soul. When one reads the prophet's own intimate reports of the struggles of his soul with God, the one impression above every other left upon him is that of reality. He is not acting a part. And eventually his storming, questioning, expostulating soul comes to repose in fellowship with God.

8. *Institutions of religion are not essential.* Jeremiah emancipated religion from all institutional trappings. There were three religious institutions that were of great historical significance in Israel, the law, the ark of the Lord, and the temple. The law, earliest of them all in its ultimate origins, went back to Moses. The beginnings of Hebrew law date from the initial revelation of God to Moses at Sinai (Exod. 24). At the basis of it are the primitive precedents which go back to his leadership and to the counsels of Jethro (Exod. 18:13-26) as "the statutes of God" and "his decisions" were made specific by Moses (Exod. 18:16) and those whom he made "heads over the people" (Exod. 18:25). The second institution was the ark of the Lord, which probably dates from the Canaanite period of Israel.[5] It was Israel's most sacred symbol of the presence of the Lord and eventually found its resting place in the holy of holies in the Temple of Solomon. The third institution was the temple itself. It grew in prestige and importance across the centuries, and in the Deuteronomic reform of 621 achieved a place of strategic importance. We have seen how the thrice-

[5] Cf. Leslie, *Old Testament Religion in the Light of Its Canaanite Background*, pp. 122 ff.

uttered mystic phrase "The temple of the Lord" gives expression to the popular sense of prestige which the temple had achieved, and the assurance of God's presence in the midst of his people which it gave.

But in that very temple Jeremiah proclaimed that the God whose dwelling it was would destroy it. Sharply he condemned the superstition that it brought security and protection to the Lord's people. Similarly he maintained that the time would come when a visible symbol of the Lord's presence, such as the ark of the Lord represented, will not be needed. It will not be missed or even remembered (3:16). And the only "law" of abiding importance will not be a legal code written upon statute books, even though it is one so great and so basic as the recently discovered code of Deuteronomy, but the "law" which the Lord will write upon the heart. For to Jeremiah the very essence of religion is not obedience to law but the direct and immediate relationship of the individual soul to God and the doing of his will from the heart.

9. *"How to the singer comes the song?"* Jeremiah gives us the clearest insight of all the prophets as regards the way in which the prophet receives the word of the Lord, and the most adequate analysis as to how to distinguish the true prophet from the false. There is remarkable progress in his thought away from the irrational and toward the rational. His intimate papers take us into the holy of holies as he receives the divine word He was definitely opposed to dreams as a means of the revelation of God's will, and to every other means of disclosure which could not stand the test of human reason. He uses two metaphors to suggest the potency of the true word when it came from God through the prophet. It is comparable to burning fire and to a hammer shattering the rock. Mystery of revelation is still here, but the dynamic place of reason and conscience in the true prophet's "Thus saith the Lord" stands out in his prophetic activity and teaching in sharp relief.

The most unanswerable indictment of the false prophets in the Old Testament is the rhetorical question raised by Jeremiah in 23:18, followed in vss. 21-22 by the divine word:

> 23:18 But who of them has stood in the council of the Lord, and has seen him
> And heard his word?
> 21 I did not send the prophets,
> Yet they ran.
> I did not speak to them,
> Still they prophesied.

22 But if they had stood in my council,
   And had caused my people to hear my words,
   They would have brought my people back
   From their evil deeds.

10. *Prayer is grappling with God.* The prayers of Jeremiah remind us forcibly of the story of the wrestle of Jacob with the angel (Gen. 32:24 ff.). Prayer before the time of Jeremiah was concerned to a large degree with external matters. Israelites and Judeans prayed that God would give them good harvests, that he would grant them victory in battles, that he would send them rain in times of drought. And they prayed for the divine forgiveness for the sins of Judah. But with Jeremiah new notes came into the prayer experience. Indeed it is a true insight of Wellhausen which led him to call Jeremiah "the father of true prayer." [6] The noblest note in his praying is that of intercession for his people, wherein identifying himself with them he cries to the Lord:

14:19 Hast thou utterly rejected Judah?
      Dost thy soul loathe Zion?
      Why hast thou struck us, since there is for us no cure?
      While we look eagerly for prosperity but nothing good comes,
      And a time of healing, but lo, dismay!

And again he appeals in the mood of lament to God:

8:22 Is there no balm in Gilead?
      Is there no physician there?
      Why then does there not come
      Healing for the daughter of my people?
9:1 O that my head were waters,
      And my eyes a fountain of tears,
      That I might weep day and night,
      Because of the slain of the daughter of my people!

In unspeakable woe of soul he cries to God:

15:18 Why is my pain persistent,
      And my wound incurable?
      Where shall I be healed?
      Alas, thou art to me
      Like deceptive waters,
      Which are not reliable.

[6] J. Wellhausen, *Israelitische und jüdische Geschichte*, 4th ed., p. 147.

His words of deep earnestness and passionate sincerity in his prayer strike us at times as almost irreverent. Here we confront the prayer of importunity, in which his soul, driven by the extremity of its need, storms the very gates of heaven as it seeks in terms of the soul's demand the divine presence. And as Harold C. Case has said: "The recording of the development of prayer as conversation with God, an intimate fellowship with the Almighty, was begun with Jeremiah." [7] Thus it is Jeremiah more than any other prophet or saint in Israel who has taught men to pray. His desperately frank and honest petitions confront God with the demand of unspeakable need. We pass from the lamenting prayers of Jeremiah to the prayers of Jesus in Gethsemane as into a familiar country.

[7] *The Prophet Jeremiah*, p. 67.

BIBLIOGRAPHY

Abel, F. M. *Geographie de la Palestine*. 2 vols. Paris: Gabolda, 1933, 1938.

Albright, W. F. *The Biblical Period*. Oxford: Blackwell, 1952.

Alt, A. *Palästina Jahrbuch*. Vols. XXI, XXIV, XXVIII.

Anderson, B. W. *Rediscovering the Bible*. New York: Association Press, 1951.

Begrich, J. *Die Chronologie der Könige von Israel und Juda und die Quellen des Rahmens der Königsbuches*. Tübingen: Mohr, 1929.

Bevan, E. R. and Singer, C. "Hellenistic Judaism," in *The Legacy of Israel*. Oxford: Oxford University Press, 1927.

Binns, L. E. *The Book of the Prophet Jeremiah*. London: Methuen & Co., 1919.

Brown, F., Driver, S. R., and Briggs, C. A. *A Hebrew and English Lexicon of the Old Testament*. Boston: Houghton Mifflin Co., 1907.

Budde, K. "Über die Kapitel 50 und 51 des Buches Jeremias," in *Jahrbücher für deutsche Theologie*, 1878, pp. 428-70, 529-62.

Calkins, Raymond. *Jeremiah the Prophet*. New York: The Macmillan Co., 1930.

Case, Harold C. *The Prophet Jeremiah*. Cincinnati: Woman's Division of Christian Service, 1953.

Charles, R. H. *The Ascension of Isaiah*. London: A. & C. Black, 1900.

Cheyne, T. K. *Jeremiah: His Life and Times*. New York: Randolph & Co., 1888.

Cooke, G. A. *Ezekiel*. New York: Charles Scribner's Sons, 1937.

Cornill, C. H. *Das Buch Jeremia Erklärt*. Leipzig: 1905.

Cowley, Arthur E., ed. *Aramaic Papyri of the Fifth Century B.C.* Oxford: Oxford University Press, 1923.

Davidson, A. B. *Hebrew Syntax*. 3rd ed. Edinburgh: T. & T. Clark, 1902.

———. "Jeremiah," in Hastings, James, ed., *A Dictionary of the Bible*. New York: Charles Scribner's Sons, 1902, II, 569-78.

Driver, G. R. "Difficult Words in the Hebrew Prophets," in H. H. Rowley, ed., *Studies in Old Testament Prophecy*. New York: Charles Scribner's Sons, 1950.

———. "Linguistic and Textual Problems: Jeremiah," *Jewish Quarterly Review*, XXVIII (1937-38), 97-129.

Driver, S. R. *Hebrew Tenses*. 3rd ed. Oxford: Clarendon Press, 1892.

———. *Book of the Prophet Jeremiah*. New York: Charles Scribner's Sons, 1906.

Duhm, Bernhard. *Das Buch Jeremia*. Tübingen: Mohr, 1901. In Marti, Karl, ed., *Kurzer Hand-Commentar zum Alten Testament*, Abteilung XI.

Ehrlich, A. B. *Randglossen zur Hebräischen Bibel*, IV, Jesaia, Jeremia. Leipzig: 1908-14.

Eissfeldt, Otto. *Einleitung in das Alten Testament*. Tübingen: Mohr, 1934.

Freedman, H. *Jeremiah*. London: Soncino, 1949.

Gadd, C. J. *The Fall of Nineveh*. London: Oxford University Press, 1923.

Gesenius-Kautzsch. *Hebrew Grammar*, tr. A. E. Cowley. 2nd ed. Oxford: Clarendon Press, 1909.

Giesebrecht, F. *Jeremia*. Nowack's *Handkommentar zum Alten Testament*, 2nd ed., III, 2 (1907).

Graham, William C. "Nahum," in *Abingdon Bible Commentary*.

Herodotus. *History*, ed., G. Rawlinson. London: 1858-60.

Hitzig, F. *Der Prophet Jeremia Erklärt*. 2nd ed. Leipzig: 1866.

Hyatt, J. Philip. "Jeremiah and Deuteronomy," *Journal of Near Eastern Studies*, I (1942), 156-73.

———. "The Original Text of Jer. 11:15-16," *Journal of Biblical Literature*, LX (1941), 57-60.

———. "The Peril from the North in Jeremiah," *ibid.*, LIX (1940), 499-513.

———. *Prophetic Religion*. New York and Nashville: Abingdon Press, 1947.

Kelso, A. P. "The Religious Consciousness of Jeremiah," *American Journal of Semitic Languages*, XLI (1925), 233-42.

Kennedy, A. R. S. "Weights, Measures, Money, and Time," in A. S. Peake, ed., *A Commentary on the Bible*. New York: Thomas Nelson & Sons, 1920.

Kittel, R. *Biblia Hebraica*. 3rd ed. by A. Alt and O. Eissfeldt. Stuttgart: Privilegierte Württembergische Bibelanstalt, 1924.

Knudson, A. C. *Beacon Lights of Prophecy*. New York: Eaton & Mains, 1914.

Leslie, Elmer A. *Old Testament Religion*. New York: Abingdon Press, 1929.

———. *The Prophets Tell Their Own Story*. New York: Abingdon Press, 1936.

———. *Intimate Papers of Jeremiah*. Boston: Boston University Press, 1953.

Lewy, J. *Forschungen zur Alten Geschichte Vorderasiens*. Leipzig: Hinrichs, 1925.

Malamad, A. "Jeremiah and the Last Two Kings of Judah," *Palestine Exploration Quarterly for 1951*, pp. 81-87.

May, H. G. "Towards an Objective Approach to the Book of Jeremiah: The Biographer," *Journal of Biblical Literature*, LXI (1942), 139-55.

Mowinckel, S. *Prophecy and Tradition*. Oslo: Dybwad, 1946.

———. *Zur Komposition des Buches Jeremia*. Oslo: Dybwad, 1914.

Nestle, E. *Das Buch Jeremia, Griechisch und Hebräisch*. Stuttgart: Privilegierte Württembergische Bibelanstalt, 1924.

Noth, Martin. *Das Buch Josua*, in Eissfeldt, *Handbuch zum Alten Testament*, 1, Reihe, 7. Tübingen: Mohr, 1938.

———. *Das System der zwölf Stämme Israels*. Stuttgart: Kohlhammer, 1930.

Nötscher, F. *Das Buch Jeremias übersetzt u. erklärt*, in *Die Heilige Schrift des Alten Testament*, VII, 2. Bonn: Hanstein, 1932.

Olmstead, A. T. *History of Assyria*. New York: Charles Scribner's Sons, 1923.

———. *History of Palestine and Syria*. New York: Charles Scribner's Sons, 1931.

Peake, A. S. *A Commentary on the Bible*. New York: Thomas Nelson & Sons, 1920.

———. *Jeremiah* (New Century Bible). New York: Oxford University Press, 1912.

Pedersen, Johannes. *Israel: Its Life and Culture*, I-IV. London: Oxford University Press, 1926, 1947.

Perles, F. *Analekten zur Textkritik des Alten Testaments*. New series. Leipzig: Engel, 1922.

Pfeiffer, Robert H. *Introduction to the Old Testament*. New York: Harper & Bros., 1941.

Pritchard, James B. *Ancient Near Eastern Texts*. Princeton: Princeton University Press, 1950.

Procksch, Otto. "König Josia," in *Festgabe für Theodor Zahn*. Leipzig: Deichert, 1928.

Robinson, Theodore H. "Baruch's Roll," in *Zeitschrift für die alttestamentliche Wissenschaft* (1924), pp. 209-21.

———. "History of the Hebrew and Jewish People," in *Abingdon Bible Commentary*, pp. 60-72.

Rowley, H. H. *Growth of the Old Testament.* New York: Longman's, Green, 1950.

———. Ed., *Studies in Old Testament Prophecy.* New York: Charles Scribner's Sons, 1950.

Rudolph. Wilhelm. *Jeremia.* Tübingen: Mohr, 1947.

Schmidt, H. *Die Grossen Propheten übersetzt und erklärt.* Göttingen: Vandenhoeck & Ruprecht, 1923.

Scott, R. B. Y. *The Relevance of the Prophets.* New York: The Macmillan Co., 1944.

Skinner, John. *Prophecy and Religion: Studies in the Life of Jeremiah.* Cambridge: Cambridge University Press, 1922.

Smith, George Adam. *Jeremiah.* London: Hodder & Stoughton, 1923.

———. *Jerusalem,* Vol II. London: Hodder & Stoughton, 1908.

———. *Historical Geography of the Holy Land.* 25th ed. London: Hodder & Stoughton, 1931.

Stanley, Arthur P. *Lectures on the History of the Jewish Church,* Vol. II. New York: Charles Scribner's Sons, 1889.

Stone, P. F. "The Temple Sermons of Jeremiah," *American Journal of Semitic Languages,* L (1933-34), 73-92.

Streane, Annesley W. *Jeremiah,* 2nd ed. Cambridge: Cambridge University Press, 1913.

Thomas, D. Winton. "The Age of Jeremiah in the Light of Recent Archaeological Discoveries," *Palestine Exploration Quarterly for 1950,* pp. 1-15.

Volz, Paul. *Der Prophet Jeremia.* Leipzig: A. Deichert, 1922.

Welch, A. C. *Jeremiah: His Time and His Work.* New York: The Macmillan Co., 1951.

Wellhausen, Julius. *Geschichte des Volkes Israels,* 4th ed. Berlin: Reimer, 1901.

Wilke, Fritz. "Kinderopfer und Kultische Preisgabe in Heiligkeitsgesetz," Festchrift der 57. Versamlung Deutscher Philologen und Schulmänner in Salzburg gewidmet. Wien: Rohrer, 1929.

Williams, A. L., ed. *Justin Martyr. The Dialogue with Trypho.* New York: The Macmillan Co., 1930.

Wilson, John A. "The Oath in Ancient Egypt," *Journal of Near Eastern Studies,* VII (1948), 129-56.

Wood, Pearl Stone. "Jeremiah's Figure of the Almond Rod," *Journal of Biblical Literature,* LXI (1942), 99-103.

Wünsche, August. *Der Babylonischen Talmud in seinen Haggadischen Bestandtheilen Wortgetreu, übersetzt und durch Noten erläutert,* Vols. I-II. Leipzig: Schulze, 1887.

Zimmern, A. *Die Keilinschriften und das Alte Testament,* 3rd ed. Berlin: Reuter & Reichard, 1902.

INDEX TO BIBLICAL REFERENCES

INDEX TO PERSONS AND SUBJECTS